Michael's Guide
California
Allan Rabinowitz

MICHAEL'S GUIDE

CALIFORNIA

By:
Allan Rabinowitz

Series Editor
Michael Shichor

INBAL
Travel Information Ltd.

Inbal Travel Information Ltd.
P.O. Box 39090 Tel Aviv Israel 61390

© 1988 edition
All rights reserved

No part of this publication may be reproduced, stored in a retrieval system, or transmitted in any form or by any means, electronic, mechanical, photocopying, recording or otherwise, without the prior written permission of the publishers.

ISBN 965-288-019-1

Graphic design: Yaron Gilad
Maps: Yaron Gilad
Cover photo: Patti MacConville (TIB)
B/W photos: Tal Glück
   San Francisco Convention & Visitors Bureau
   Allan Rabinowitz
   Amir Shefi
Typesetting: Inbal Travel Info. Ltd.
Computerized Typesetting: El-Ot Ltd.
Printing & Binding: Havatzelet Press.

UK DISTRIBUTOR
Kuperard (London) Ltd
30 Cliff Road
London NW1 9AG
tel: 01 284 0512/9
tlx: 265871 ref. AUR351

Distributors:
U.S: Hunter Publishing Inc., 300 Raritan Center Parkway, Edison, New Jersey 08818; **Argentina**: Carlos Hirsch S.R.L., Florida 1654 P. Gal. Guemes, Buenos Aires; **Australia**: Rex Publications, 413 Pacific Highway, Arparmon, N.S. Wales 2064; **Bolivia**: Los Amigos del Libro, Casilla 450, Cochabamba; **Canada**: Ulysses Books and Maps Distribution, 1208 St. Denis, Montreal, Quebec H2Y 3J5; **Denmark and Finland**: Scanvik Books aps, Store Kongensgade 59 A, DK-1264 Copenhagen K. Denmark; **Netherlands**: Nilsson & Lamm bv., Pampuslaan 212-214, 1382 JS Weesp-Nederland; **New Zealand**: Roulston Greene, Private Bag, Takapuna, Auckland 9.

CONTENTS

Preface	**10**
Using this Guide	**11**

INTRODUCTION   13

PART ONE – A First Taste of What's To Come   13
History and Population (13) Geography (19) Climate (20)
California Literature (20) Pop Architecture (21)

PART TWO – Setting Out   22
How to get there (22) Documents and Customs Regulations (22)
Insurance (23) Safety Precautions (23) When to come; National
Holidays (24) What to wear (25) How much will it cost (25)

PART THREE – Easing the Shock: Where Have We Landed   27
Transportation (27) Accommodation (35) Practical tips for getting
around (38) Food (42) Important Addresses and Phone Numbers
(43) Parks and Reserves (44)

CALIFORNIA   47

SAN DIEGO	**47**
Downtown	49
The Embarcadero	51
Balboa Park	52
Old Town	54
Coronado	55
Point Loma	55
Mission Bay	56
La Jolla	56
Toward Mexico	60

THE SOUTH COAST	**63**
Laguna Beach	65
Orange County	68
Disneyland	68

THE CALIFORNIA DESERT 73
Death Valley	76
Toward Las Vagas	79
Joshua Trees National Monument	80
Anza-Borrego Desert State Park	82
Palm Springs	83

LOS ANGELES 95
Orientation	97
Movie and Television Land	103
Downtown	104
Pasadena	110
Exposition Park	110
Hollywood	111
Griffith Park	117
Wilshire/Hancock Park	118
Beverly Hills	121
Westwood Village, UCLA	123
Around Malibu	124
Santa Monica	127
Venice	129

LONG BEACH AND PALOS VERDES 139

THE MOUNTAIN RIM 145

SANTA BARBARA 147
State Street	149
Near Santa Barbara	153
Channel Island National Park	153

SAN LUIS OBISPO 159

BIG SUR 167

MONTEREY AND CARMEL 175

SANTA CRUZ 187

SAN FRANCISCO 195
Orientation	199
San Francisco Bay	210
Financial District	211
Downtown	212
Chinatown	214
North Beach	216

Fisherman's Wharf	219
Exploratorium	226
The Mission	228
Castro Street	228
Civic Center	229
Union Street	230
Clement Street	231
Japantown	231
Haight-Ashbury	232
Golden Gate Park	234
The City's Coast	238

AROUND SAN FRANCISCO   251
The Peninsula	251
Berkeley	252
Marin County	257
Marine World	261

WINE COUNTRY   263
Napa Valley	263
Sonoma Valley	267
Russian River and Sonoma Coast	270

THE NORTH COAST   275
Mendocino Coast	275
Redwood Country	279

SAN JOAQUIN VALLEY   285
Bakersfield	287
Visalia	288
Fresno	288
Merced	289
Sacramento	290
Davis	294

GOLD COUNTRY   297
Nevada City	299
Auburn	300
Georgetown	301
Coloma	301
Placerville	302
Calaveras County	303
Southern Mother Lode	304

SIERRA NEVADA   307
Kings Canyon National Park	312
Sequoia National Park	313
Mineral King	315

Mount Whitney	315
Lake Tahoe	316
Toward Reno	322
Yosemite	323
Eastern Slope	332

SHASTA AND LASSEN 341

INDEX 341

NOTES 346

TABLE OF MAPS

CALIFORNIA	18
SAN DIEGO	48
DOWNTOWN SAN DIEGO	50
DEATH VALLEY	77
PALM SPRINGS	84
DOWNTOWN LOS ANGELES	105
DOWNTOWN SANTA BARBARA	150
SAN LUIS OBISPO	160
BIG SUR AREA	168
SAN FRANCISCO	198
DOWNTOWN SAN FRANCISCO	213
RUSSIAN RIVER	270
SACRAMENTO CITY CENTER	291
KINGS CANYON AND SEQUOIA NATIONAL PARKS	314
YOSEMITE NATIONAL PARK	324

Preface

California, the "Golden State" of America, is a legendary land of promise where anything is possible. It has attracted gold-hunters, nature lovers, loners and revolutionaries, radical reformers, refugees, waves of immigrants, and a perennial stream of tourists wanting to taste the good life.

California's extraordinary beauty and pleasant climate are no doubt part of the attraction. California was the ultimate Western frontier, and today connections extend west beyond the Pacific to the Far East. It is a land rich in resources, and the most populous state in the U.S.A., with a population of more than 23 million. Ninety-three percent of these people live in the metropolitan centers, but California also has some of the richest agricultural land in the U.S.A. and the most productive economy. The clear skies, sunny climate and wide open spaces provide ideal conditions for the aerospace industry, and "Silicon Valley" is a leading center for high technology. Hollywood, the cradle of the film industry is still Mecca for thousands of actors, scriptwriters, directors and comedians. The music industry also thrives here.

For the millions of tourists who visit California every year, the big attractions are the inspiring natural wonders of the national parks, dramatic coastlines, golden beaches, haunting desert landscapes and misty cool forests, plus the excitement of metropolitan Los Angeles and San Francisco, and the magic of Disneyland.

To compile this Guide, Allan Rabinowitz, a native Californian and a travel writer, criss-crossed the state for months, exploring national parks and historic centers, classic sites and newest happenings, discovering interesting and remote treasures off the beaten track. He observed, tasted, compared, took notes and covered California from the Pacific coast to neighboring Nevada and Arizona, from Oregon to Mexico.

We hope to introduce you to the many facets of California, and a variety of attractions in each area are presented for the traveler to make a choice, according to personal interest.

Our aim is to give you a deeper understanding of California, to help you plan an ideal trip, to lead you to the best and most exciting attractions, and to ensure that you derive maximum pleasure from your trip. We are sure that the effort invested in the compiling of this guide will be justified by your enhanced enjoyment.

Michael Shichor

Using this Guide

In order to reap maximum benefit from the information concentrated in this Guide, we advise the traveler to carefully read the following advice. The facts contained in this book are meant to help the tourist find his or her way around, and to assure that he see the most, with maximum savings of money, time and effort.

The information contained in the Introduction should be read in its entirety as it has details which will help in making the early decisions and arrangements regarding your trip. Reviewing the material thoroughly means that you will be better organized and set for your visit. Upon arrival in California you will already feel familiar and comfortable, more so than otherwise might have been the case.

The basic guideline in all "MICHAEL'S GUIDE" publications is to survey places in a primarily geographical sequence and not a thematic one. The logic behind it is that a geographical plan not only ensures the most efficient time use, but also contributes dramatically to getting to know an area and its different aspects as well as acquiring a feeling for it. Furthermore, you will be directed from a museum to a historical place, incorporating in your visit to one site several other locations which you may not have thought or heard of nor planned to visit.

Each section is accompanied by a map, especially designed to ease your way. Each has a numbered index indicating the exact location of the landmarks which have been mentioned.

Each chapter also includes a list of useful addresses and telephone numbers.

To further facilitate the use of this Guide, we have included, a very detailed index. It includes all the major locations mentioned throughout the book. Consult the index to find something by name and it will refer you to the place where it is described in greatest detail.

Because times and places do change, an important rule when traveling in general, and when visiting California in particular, should be to consult the local sources of information. We have therefore accompanied nearly every place with a phone number for last minute checks and suggest you consult the hotel concierge, the local publications and newspapers, the tourist information offices, etc. All of them can advise you of the latest updated information at the specific time of your visit.

As for updating, a guide to a place like California cannot afford to march in place, and up to the time that the Guide went to press, we attempted to confim its relevance and up-to-dateness. However, it is only natural that due to frequent changes which occur, travelers will find certain time-related facts somewhat less than precise when they arrive at their destination, and for this we apologize in advance.

To this end, cooperation and assistance is necessary and vital from those of you have enjoyed the information contained in this Guide. It ensures, first and foremost, that those who travel in your wake will also enjoy and succeed in their ventures as much as you have. For this purpose, we have included a short questionnaire at the end of this Guide and we will be most grateful to those who complete it and send it to us. A **complimentary copy** of the new edition will be forwarded to those of you who take the time, and whose contribution will appear in the updated edition.

During your visit you will see and experience many things – we have therefore left several blank pages at the back of this Guide. These are for you; to jot down those special experiences of people and places, feelings you may have had, or any other significant happenings along the way. You will always be able to look back on those words and remember.

Have a pleasant and exciting trip – Bon Voyage!

INTRODUCTION

Part One – A First Taste of What's to Come

California is a multi-faceted gem. The gleam of each facet is only partial, yet together they create a strange, enticing and unique aura. This is a land of great physical beauty and contrasts, but the physical extremes are mild compared to the social, cultural and political ones. It is a land where the freedom of life-style can verge on the hedonistic, yet where religious sects with strict codes of behaviour flourish. It is a society generally tolerant of ethnic diversity, yet is marred by a history of vicious racial outbursts. It contains the agricultural heart of the nation, just an hour away from the nerve center of the microelectronics industry. It witnessed the birth of the modern conservation movement and shows a high degree of sensitivity to the environment, yet untempered greed and rampant exploitation have been driving forces in the growth of California. The land of bean sprouts and tofu, it also sustains the most gimmicky and greasy fast-food stands. Although the cauldron of the radicalism of the 1960s, California also gave the nation Richard Nixon and Ronald Reagan, two deeply conservative presidents. It is a land that has attracted dreamers, outcasts, desperate hopefuls, fugitives, artists, rebels, ambitious achievers and more than its share of swindlers and conmen. Somehow they all managed to find a place in the cultural circus of California, as do those who arrive as casual visitors and never leave.

History and Population

For thousands of years, various Indian tribes found a foothold within every niche of California's diverse environment. In 1542, Juan Rodriguez Cabrillo, a Portuguese seaman in the service of Spain, set forth to explore the completely unknown coast north of Mexico, and to claim any lands possible for Spain. Cabrillo's expedition set out because of the Spanish empire's desire for expansion in the New World. It really was a new world, promising endless riches, but vastness and mystery as well. Only 50 years had passed since Columbus discovered America, and less than 25 since Cortes had vanquished Aztec Mexico. Cabrillo himself had marched with the famed conquistador. Mexico brimmed with rumors of vast fortunes piled in the northern hinterland. Antonio de Mendoza, Viceroy of Mexico and rival of Cortez for power, had only two years earlier dispatched Francisco Coronado to seek the fabled Seven Cities of Cibola in the region of New Mexico. Now he sent out Cabrillo, a skilled navigator, determined to break through the known limits of the earth. His quest was inspired by the legend of an island kingdom whose huge warriors carried swords of gold, as well as by hopes of discovering a secret passage to the Orient.

INTRODUCTION

Cabrillo set sail in June with two small ships from the Mexican port of Navidad, and reached San Diego Bay in late September. He pushed northward along the coast, observing the plains and mountains of the interior, toward the island of Santa Catalina. He named the landmarks he passed (most of the names have been forgotten today) and claimed each for the King of Spain. His ships hugged the coast, trailed by Indians in canoes eager to barter.

In November, Cabrillo landed in the Channel Island archipelago, probably on San Miguel Island. As he rushed to help some soldiers who were scuffling with Indians ashore, he fell and broke a leg. Infection set in, and Cabrillo's condition deteriorated over the next six weeks. Amazingly, he retained command and steered his ships north through battering storms off the coast of Big Sur.

Cabrillo sailed northward as far as present-day Fort Ross, then returned to what was probably San Miguel Island where he finally died and was buried. His grave has not been found. Under the chief pilot, the expedition continued as far north as southern Oregon before it finally returned south.

The expedition reached Navidad in April, 1543, ten months after it departed. It brought back a wealth of information about the bays, inlets, natives and rich potential of the northern coast, and made claims to California for Spain that were not challenged for almost three hundred years. However, it found no golden swords, or passage to China, and it left behind the remains of an intrepid explorer.

Cabrillo's exploration of the Pacific Coast opened California to the European world, but there was little settlement on the part of the Spanish or anyone else. In 1579 Sir Francis Drake claimed the San Francisco area for the Queen of England. Various explorers made forays along the coast, but it was only when the Russians began to move down from Alaska and establish hunting and trading outposts as far south as the Sonoma coast, that the Spanish began to initiate settlement.

The first settlement was established in 1769 in San Diego, as a joint military-religious enterprise, with Father Junipero Serra overseeing the construction of a mission intended for the conversion of the local Indians. San Diego was the first of a chain of missions which Serra built, in an effort which was continued by others after his death.

A mission often appeared first with a presidio, and only later did a pueblo – a secular civilian settlement – grow near it. This was a common pattern. The San Gabriel Mission, for example, established in 1771, provided the impetus for the construction of a small village nine miles away, called Los Angeles.

The missions were all built along the coast, about a day's journey apart. The paths and dirt roads worn between the missions were eventually spliced into a main coastal road, called El Camino Real, still marked by roadside signs today.

The padres of the far-flung Franciscan missions were immersed as much in physical labor as in spiritual. They were pioneers and settlers, as well as

*I*NTRODUCTION

Mission built in typical Spanish style

padres. It must have been an amazing time to be in California; everything was new, untouched, open, and the surrounding land so deeply beautiful.

The missions prospered. The padres tilled the fertile valleys. They planted grain crops as well as olives, figs, grape vines, and fruits and vegetables from Spain and Mexico. Their large herds of livestock grazed in the virgin grasslands. In some missions the padres built sophisticated and extensive water systems. The tracts under Franciscan ownership and tillage were immense. By the time the last mission was completed in 1823, the missions controlled one sixth of the total land in California.

But much of this physical progress rested on the backs of local Indians. Conversion was massive and rapid. Many Indians drew toward the missions and the new ways of life, while others were pressed into service. There were many forced conversions. Forced conversions brought rebellion. Rebellion brought repression and punishment. The urge to hasten the Indians' enlightenment might have been intensified if they happened to dwell upon a particularly fertile stretch of land. About 2000 Chumash Indians were removed en masse from Santa Cruz Island to the Santa Barbara mission.

Written testimony from the early 19th century details regular whippings of Indians in some missions. Even the much-praised Father Serra was reprimanded by the Spanish governor for implementing excessively heavy punishment. Moreover, the changing of age-old life patterns, and sexual molestation by local soldiers, exposed the mission Indians to epidemics. In the sixty years of Spanish control, the Indian population in those areas dropped from about 130 thousand to 83 thousand, with a much higher death rate among the mission Indians.

INTRODUCTION

Rebellion in the 1820's was anti-clerical as well as anti-Spanish. With independence won in 1833, the Mexican congress wrested the missions from Franciscan control. The missions were secularized and and stripped of their vast tracts of land. They went into decline, and some into deep decay. Various parties found ways to claim title to land parcels. Later, some of the missions were restored phsically and returned to Franciscan auspices.

The missions left a legacy for Mexican and American rule. They were the first to experiment with California's tremendous agricultural potential. They left a style of architecture harmonious with the landscape. The mission names now belong to major cities. The missions gave local Indians new skills for the new world that was fast approaching. They also reduced and deeply scarred the Indian population, but that was but a prelude to future actions.

When Mexico won her independence from Spain in 1882, the missions were secularized and efforts were made to expand and solidify settlement in California. Even then, the "Californios" felt apart from the regime to the south, and there were several attempts by the Spanish/Mexican settlers to split off from the newly independent nation. Meanwhile, an increasing number of American settlers and sailors moved into California. By the mid-1840's there was a call in the east for the annexation of California as part of the American philosophy of "Manifest Destiny"; the establishment of a republic from coast to coast. In 1846 a group of American settlers seized control of Sonoma and declared the independence of "The Bear Flag Republic", only to relinquish control to the American government after it declared war on Mexico and siezed California.

Within two years of its turnover to the United States, gold was discovered in California in the Sierra foothills of Sutter's Mill. Within a few years the population escalated by about 1000%, and California became the main attraction for American settlers who dreamed of striking it rich.

Gold-hungry immigrants used the local Indian population to work the mines. The Indians were enormously abused. California historian Josiah Royce describes how some miners used Indian villages as "targets for rifle-practice, or to destroy wholesale with fire, outrage and murder, as if they had been so many wasps' nests in our gardens at home". The 100,000 Indians in California in 1846 were reduced to 31,000 by 1852. Those left were humiliated, uprooted and exposed to epidemic diseases and alcohol. Initially herded into crowded reservations on dismal land, they found even that grabbed from them. Over 7 million acres were left to the California Indians by signed treaty in 1850, but this was whittled down to a pitiful 500,000 acres. It was only in 1963 that the California Indians were awarded $27 million by the federal government as long overdue compensation for the lands they lost.

After the Civil War, the national economy and industry boomed, and in 1869 California was linked to the east by the first trans-continental railroad.

California's history has been a record of booms and depressions; of land sales, land grabs and land frauds; of the discovery of new resources and the sudden influx of people to exploit them. The discovery of oil in Los Angeles

INTRODUCTION

and Long Beach at the end of the 19th century created an economic boom in Los Angeles.

With the creation of the movie industry in Hollywood, a new kind of wealth was created in California, and there was suddenly a large number of self-made millionaires. A glamorous "royalty" of movie stars was created, and in their wake thousands of hopefuls flocked to Los Angeles seeking glory in celluloid, but finding instead jobs as cooks, waitresses and cops.

During the Great Depression more hordes crossed the eastern hills into the valleys seeking not fame and fortune but work, bread or a little land. With this influx of "Oakies" came an ideological clash between radicalism and conservative, land-holding interests. Labor protests, which were violently supressed, burst forth everywhere.

In the 1940s fear of the Japanese replaced fear of the "Reds". In anticipation of the Japanese invasion that never came, thousands of American citizens of Japanese descent were interned in isolated camps, and much of their property was confiscated or looted.

In the 1950s post-war prosperity, the attraction of California became even stronger. The aeronautics industry drew thousands of workers and became the state's industrial and technological mainstay, which it remained until the recent surge in microelectronics took hold in the Silicon Valley (at San Jose) and revolutionized technology. A steady stream of residents still flows to California. By 1964, California had surpassed New York as the country's most populous state, and today the population exceeds 25 million.

People are attracted to the "sunbelt" of the west and southwest, including an influx of foreign immigrants. California has always attracted a variety of ethnic groups with its multitudinous economic opportunities. Today's immigrants do not come from European countries, but from the Pacific areas and Latin America.

California has been in flux from the moment of statehood. For over a hundred years, the population doubled every twenty years. Although that rate has slowed slightly, the change in the ethnic fabric of the state has accelerated. In the last 15 years the percentage of Hispanics has almost doubled and the percentage of Asians has almost tripled, while the Caucasian population has dropped considerably. Immigration is becoming one of the key issues of California's future as, in a sense, it has been for over 150 years. The number of children growing up speaking a first language other than English is rapidly growing, yet English has been voted as the single official language of the state.

Meanwhile California's breakneck development and technological advancement continues, swelling its population, taking over rich farmland and exploiting natural resources. Some demographers predict that the population could reach 35 million by the year 2000. Whatever the future holds, no doubt California will face it in its typically dynamic, experimental and completely individual way.

*I*NTRODUCTION

CALIFORNIA

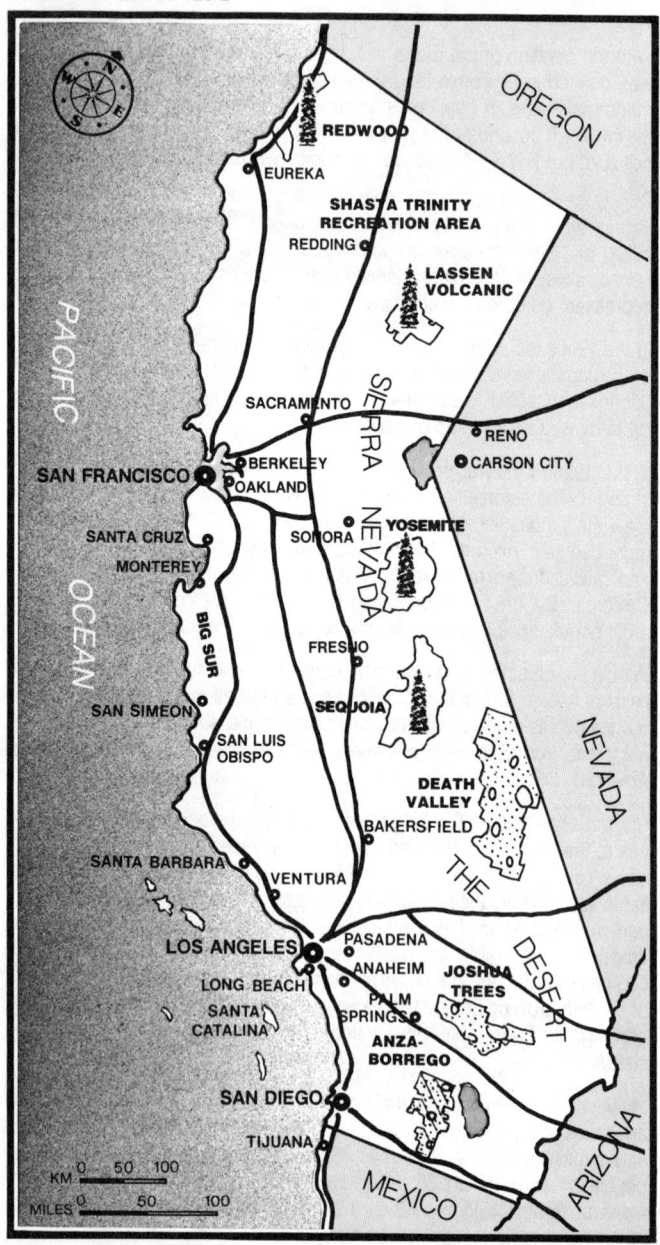

INTRODUCTION

Geography

The coast of California is about 900 miles long, from Crescent City at the Oregan border to San Diego at the Mexican border. The north coast has endless stands of tall pines and redwoods. The coast is rocky and studded with cliffs, and just beyond the beach area there are ranges of coastal mountains.

The mountain ranges stretch east, reaching towering Mt. Shasta at the southern tip of the Cascade Mountains. Beyond the Cascades, in the northeastern corner of the state, is a strange, weathered and pockmarked world of ancient lava. Below this mountainous cap, which spans the width of California, many of the state's topographical features run parallel to the coast.

Along the northern border, down past the Golden Gate and San Francisco, past Monterey Bay to the cliffs of Big Sur, the coast is stark, and the weather is foggy due to cold currents. Further south, however, near Santa Barbara, the ocean currents are warm, and the weather is gentler. The beaches are also softer. The land becomes drier and scrubbier towards the Los Angeles basin which is surrounded by mountains. South of this point the land basks in a hot, constant, semi-tropical sun.

A range of hills runs along the coast from the north almost all the way down to Mexico. They extend towards the east and in the central part of the state, reach into the rich San Joaquin Valley. This valley is a 400-mile long fertile furrow running through the heart of the state. It stretches from the foot of the Cascades in the north, (as the Sacramento Valley), past Sacramento to Bakersfield, stopping before the thin barrier of the Tehachapi range that separates it from Los Angeles. This great valley is paralled on the east by the long granite massif of the Sierra Nevada. The mountain slopes rise gently from the west, in round compact hills where the discovery of gold launched the mad rush of the 1850s. The sequioa trees, the largest living things on earth, grow higher up on the slopes of these hills.

Numerous westward flowing rivers, with the assistance of ancient glaciers, carved the cliffs, domes and cascades of the Yosemite Valley and other canyons. Yosemite National Park, Lake Tahoe, and King's Canyon/Sequoia National Parks are the main sites of the Sierras. Through the whole range runs a majestic spine of craggy and snow-covered peaks, which is superb backpacking country.

The eastern slope drops like a sheer granite wall, into a high semi arid plateau. This is the great Basin, with isolated mountain peaks, alkalai flats and ancient bristlecone pines 4000 years old. The Basin extends as far as the desert.

The desert forms the state's largest geographical entity. The desert east of the Sierras extends south towards Mexico and stretches across the border. In the east it extends to the Colorado River and into Nevada and Arizona, and in the west towards Los Angeles.

INTRODUCTION

Climate

The climate in California varies greatly according to the region. In the south, the summers are hot and dry and the sun shines most of the year. The rains usually come in winter, but interspersed with sunshine. Near the beaches especially, it may be tempered by refreshing breezes, but summer in the L.A. urban area can also bring on smog alerts, when the sky is hazy not from fog but from the brown clouds of pollution, and venturing forth in such conditions can actually be hazardous. Winter temperatures of 40 degrees Fahrenheit (4.5 degrees Centigrade) are considered cold enough here to wear minks and down jackets.

The deserts can be comfortable during most of the year but broiling in the summer. The dry heat, however, is more bearable than humidity. Desert summer nights are warm and comfortable, but temperatures can sometimes drop sharply at sunset. An occasional summer rain in the desert is a welcome relief. The clouds swirl and gleam, and the rain churns up delicious fresh smells from the desert floor. In winter the desert can be quite windy and cold.

Seasons in the California mountains are more sharply demarcated than along the coast. Summers can be hot, punctuated by rains, and summer evenings can turn breezy and cool. In the immense stands of conifers, autumn can barely be distinguished, but in some areas where deciduous trees follow stream courses, the autumnal mountains are etched with rivers of blazing gold.

The first snows can fall as early as late September, and they fall not only in soft white flutterings but in full-fledged blizzards. Snow can pile up to 20 feet or more, and last well into spring. In the mountains in late spring the many streams are turbulent and swollen with melted snow.

In the San Joaquin Valley, the summer heat is humid, and extremely unpleasant. That's when you'll want to press your foot on the accelerator and buzz along that super-highway as fast as possible.

Northern California, along the coast, is characterised by wet winters, and the rain can be very heavy. Nevertheless, there are plenty of fresh and blue-skied winter days as well. The summers can be cool, foggy and overcast, but generally not for long durations. Inland, the winters are a bit drier.

California Literature

California, as a physical reality and state of mind, has attracted both American and foreign writers since before the Gold Rush days. A number of books will give you a feel for the unique texture of California.

Raymond Chandler, mysteries: Corruption and murder in a young Los Angeles, as seen through the eyes of private eye Philip Marlowe.

Richard Henry Dana, *Two Years Before the Mast*: A vivid and detailed travelogue in the 19th-century tradition. With tremendous accuracy he describes the coast of what was then a new and wide-open world.

Joan Didion, *Slouching Towards Bethlehem*: Well-known essays on modern California life and manners.

INTRODUCTION

Allen Ginsberg, *Howl*: Ginsberg's unleashing of this powerful poem became a literary turning point in San Francisco. With Jack Kerouac he helped create a literary movement.

Dashiell Hammett, mysteries: The San Francisco bars frequented by his hard-boiled detective Sam Spade still stand today. Hammett's tough and laconic style greatly influenced many other mystery writers, particularly Raymond Chandler.

Bret Hart, *The Outcast of Poker Flat*: An American story-writer and journalist, Hart was the first to depict life in the gold-mining days.

Robinson Jeffers, poetry: Jeffers spent years on the Big Sur coast, and he uses the cliffs and waves as powerful metaphors.

Jack Kerouac, *On the Road*: This, the most popular of Kerouac's writing, preached a "spontaneous" way of life. This work helped launch the beatnik generation.

Henry Miller, *Big Sur and the Oranges of Hieronymous Bosch*: After exploring the alleys and brothels of Paris, Miller stumbled into the wild coast where he found a sense of peace and a focus for his prose.

John Muir, various writings. Elegant descriptions of nature and the wilderness.

John Steinbeck, *The Grapes of Wrath, Of Mice and Men, East of Eden, Cannery Row, Tortilla Flat, In Dubious Battle*: *The Grapes of Wrath* is Steinbeck's masterpiece about the odyssey of a migrant family to the farmlands of California. Virtually all of his best writing concerns California. No one writes of the state, and its less shining characters, with more wisdom, warmth and compassion.

Mark Twain, *Roughing It*: No one is more hilarious, or shrewdly observant in capturing the frontier and the Gold Rush.

Evelyn Waugh, *The Loved One*: A biting satire on the American undertaking industry, based around a gaudy and pretentious Los Angeles cemetery.

Pop Architecture

Weird and wonderful architectural forms are as much a part of California's heritage as the rambling Victorian buildings and stucco cottages with red tile roofs. Giant donuts, ice cream cones, owls and hearts, big hats and tractors, towering cowboys, lumberjacks and dinosaurs decorate the California landscape.

Imaginative architecture which served as advertising sprang up in the 1920s, with the advent of the automobile, a growing highway system and a newly mobile middle class. Even during the Depression years such building continued. It became the expression of hundreds of small private dreams and fantasies.

California soil seemed fertile for such imaginative advertising. Space was wide open, land was available, and already the state was becoming based

INTRODUCTION

on the automobile. There was relatively little existing architectural tradition, and the commercial and imaginative climate was right for a bit of profitable whimsy. Any commercial gimmick that might turn a buck had a fighting chance in California. You might say that scattered along the highways of southern California were the precursors of Disneyland. Igloos and castles, southern manors and quaint thatched-roof villages became landmarks. The **Tail o' the Pup**, on the 300 block of La Cienega in Los Angeles, was clever play on the word "hot dog". An L. A. institution, it has appeared in many movies including the recent *Ruthless People*. In Castroville, during a public-relations effort to get the local artichokes on the map, a 16-foot artichoke complete with spikes was planted in the ground.

The king of pop art architecture in California must be **Dinny the Dinosaur**, at the Cabazon exit off I-10 on the way to Palm Springs. It is the creation of Claude Bell, who was inspired as a boy by a giant elephant-shaped hotel in the New Jersey resort of Margate. He designed many sculptures and buildings for fairs and parks.

When he moved to California and bought a desert plot on which he opened a restaurant, his dream really evolved, in the shape of a brontosaurus three times the size of a real one! Dinny was a labor of love that took ten years to build. His belly houses a museum and small apartment, reached by a stairway through the tail. He surpasses other roadside models not only in size but through the graceful proportions and meticulous detail, down to the wrinkles and lumps in his hide. Bell was still busy working on his primeval pets into his nineties, having added a tyrannosaurus (with a viewing platform on its head and a slide down its back) to keep Dinny company. The two pre-historic reptiles are clearly visible from the highway and look poised to gobble up the trucks lined up outside the restaurant.

Part Two – Setting Out

How to get there
By air: The two major airports in California are **Los Angeles International Airport (LAX)** and the **San Francisco Airport (SFO)**. Both airports are served by major international and domestic airlines. San Diego airport also serves an increasing amount of national and international air traffic. Special offers of air tickets are worth investigating.

By land: Main train routes to California run from Seattle to San Francisco, Chicago to San Francisco and Chicago to Los Angeles. Major bus companies are *Greyhound* and *Trailways*, which both have special offers and various travel options. Car rental is probably the best way of getting around California.

Documents and Customs Regulations
Visas
Foreign visitors must enter the United States with a valid passport and visa.

*I*NTRODUCTION

Most B-2 tourist visas are valid for 6 months. A lost visa can be replaced through the embassy of the visitor's country. To apply for a visa extension, or to replace the arrival/departure form received on arrival, a foreign citizen must go to the nearest U.S. Immigration and Naturalization Service office.

If you have any problems, it is advisable to contact the nearest consulate of your country. Many countries have consular offices in Los Angeles and/or San Francisco.

A foreign visitor can bring in $100 worth of gifts to the U.S. duty-free, up to 200 cigarettes, and a liter of alcohol. There is no limit on currency. Prescription drugs should be clearly visible and labeled, accompanied by a copy of the doctor's prescription.

International Driver's License
A driver's license valid for the U.S. should be obtained in the country of origin. It will not be issued in the U.S.

Student Cards
Students with proper identification can often receive considerable discount on transportation fares, hotels rates and admission prices. Proper identification includes either a valid university identification card, or an **International Student Identity Card (ISIC)**. The latter, which costs $8, can be obtained with proof of full-time student status. This could be a university identification card, a stamped letter from the registrar, a current grade report, etc. Students enrolled at school for the previous fall semester are eligible to receive the card. In certain cities, with junior colleges, full-time registration costs are negligible, and people have been known to register for a semester just to obtain a student card.

The Council on International Educational Exchange (CIEE) sponsors a special discount plan which, for a small sum, entitles the holder to 25% savings on room rates at various lodgings. Much additional advice on travel is available. To use these services, an ISIC is required, and is obtainable from the CIEE.

Insurance
Insurance is essential. Do not play games with health or medical emergency, even though most major centers do have crisis centers or public clinics that can and will offer immediate care to the uninsured. University hospitals will often do the same. Call the local emergency number, or the crisis center mentioned in this book.

The insuring of valuable objects such as cameras is obviously a personal choice. In the big cities especially, professional thieves abound and are very smooth. This is not meant to frighten you off, but it is best to be realistic. In one moment's carelessness a camera can disappear. Insurance can sometimes be purchased through a travel organisation.

Safety Precautions
It is best to avoid bus terminals and train stations late at night, and it is not

INTRODUCTION

advisable to walk at night in deserted downtown neighborhoods. Avoid public restrooms in the cities.

It is advisable to keep some money separate from your wallet, and to keep a list of traveler's checks separate as well. Make a note of important numbers – driver's license, credit card, passport – and keep it somewhere safe.

Many travelers choose to carry money and important documents in a money belt that fits around the waist inside the shirt, or one that hangs around the neck. Some go so far as to carry a "decoy" wallet in a pocket, to draw attention away from the money belt. All this is a matter of personal choice. The most important thing is to take the steps necessary for your own peace of mind and maximum enjoyment.

When to come; National Holidays

California is a vacationland for all seasons. During every season of the year, there is at least one part of the state where the weather seems just perfect.

Most people flock to California in the summer, and in most tourist areas prices tend to rise accordingly. The exception to this is the desert resort of Palm Springs where prices actually go down in summer due to the intense heat. Winters in southern California are delightfully sunny and warm; summers in northern California are refreshingly cool. In the Sierra Nevada and the other mountain ranges, each season has its own beauty and activities. Some mountain passes are closed in winter, but the mountain ski resorts are popular.

Planning a time for your visit may be not so much a matter of weather, but rather a matter of crowds. There is no doubt that most tourist facilities are far more crowded in summer, with a commensurate rise in prices. If possible, try and avoid traveling on the following days:

Memorial Day weekend, around May 31st
Independence Day weekend, around July 4th.
Labor Day weekend, at the beginning of September.

From Memorial Day onwards, there is a great increase in the number of vacationers on the roads. After Labor Day there is a sharp decline in the number of vacationers. In fact, in terms of numbers, prices, and the accessibility of facilities, early fall is an ideal time to travel. Children are back at school and students are back at college.

The weeks surrounding Christmas and New Year's Day are also crowded with visitors. However, the rest of the winter is considered off-season, other than for ski resorts.

American public holidays include:

New Year's Day, January 1st.
President's Day, the third Monday in February.
Memorial Day, the last Monday in May.
Independence Day, July 4th (businesses close on the nearest Monday or Friday.

INTRODUCTION

Labor Day, first Monday in September.
Columbus Day, second Monday in October.
Veteran's Day, November 11th.
Thanksgiving, last Thursday in November.
Christmas, December 25th.

What to wear

Clothing to be packed depends upon the region to be visited. For southern California, be sure to pack a heavy sweater and light waterproof coat for the winter. For northern California be sure to pack a heavy sweater and light waterproof coat for the summer. Style in California tends to be casual.

Ties are usually worn by businessmen, but this is not as strictly required as it is in the east. Colors for both men's and women's fashions are brighter in California than in some other regions, and also brighter in the south than in the north. California casualness has become a fashion in its own right, blending a bright, tailored tapered look with comfort. Shoes can also be casual. A good pair of walking shoes can serve in a number of situations. There always seems to be a sale at one or another of the numerous clothing stores, so it is easy to pick up what you need. For women, slacks are acceptable in almost any situation, and are worn by many.

California is also the place for down-to-earth second-hand artistic funk. "Contemporary Salvation Army" is becoming so popular that charity and second-hand stores have begun to raise their prices, and some have turned downright chic.

If planning to enjoy California's natural wonders, be sure to include sturdy durable clothes and shoes. In southern California especially, a hat, preferably broad-brimmed, is advisable during the summer. Sandals are increasingly accepted as everyday summer footwear. Birkenstocks, though more expensive than some others, are sturdy, long-lasting, comfortable and popular. For hiking shoes, the new models made of material which is light yet water resistant, are gaining in popularity. These are suitable for California's diverse terrains.

How much will it cost

The amount of money a visitor will spend is, of course, a very subjective matter, depending on the individual's needs, tastes and style. The point to remember is that California, more than many other areas, provides enough variety in resources and alternatives for most people to relax and enjoy themselves within their means.

The main expense, besides the cost of getting to California, will naturally be **lodging**. The prices of average lodging has sky-rocketed in recent years. Even Motel 6, which made its name an advertisement of its price, would have to change its name to Motel 21.50 to be accurate today. For a standard basic motel room, expect to pay a minimum of $23-$30 per day. Most cost considerably more. For an average motel room or a room in a B&B a visitor could easily pay $50-$60 per day. Of course there are plenty of better hotels that charge up to $150 per day for their amenities; spending more is never a problem.

INTRODUCTION

Nevertheless, a person on a strict budget can definitely find cheap accommodation, and in some comfort, if he or she shows some flexibility. Hostels, for example, though not the last word in luxury or privacy, rarely cost more than $8 per day, and provide a unique traveling experience. YMCAs offer another inexpensive solution. The person determined to backpack can do so and still have access to the major cities. Car-camping is popular, and private and public campgrounds are numerous, ranging between $6-$15 per night depending on the place, facilities, etc.

Transportation costs can also vary greatly. Car-rental can range from $20-$40 per day, depending on circumstances. Insurance is added on a daily basis (see "Car Rental"). Local bus systems may cost between 50 cents and $1, usually with some sort of transfer arrangement. Transportation between major cities is private. Buses cost approximately $14 between Los Angeles and San Diego, and $25-$40 between Los Angeles and San Francisco. Private vans, airport shuttles and so forth can start at about $7 and go up to $20.

Those preferring to work on a firm transportation budget may want to base costs on monthly car rentals ($400 and up, plus insurance), or monthly bus or train passes. These can be combined with local public transportation, daily car rental or bicycle (see "Transportation").

As for **food**, there is a wide range of budgeting possibilities, especially in the two major urban areas, where the choice and variety is enormous. Cheapest of all is to buy from grocery stores, delis and fast-food stands, but a good and filling meal in certain restaurants can be had for as little as $3-$5. Good breakfasts can cost from $1.50-$3.50. Many places, especially simple Chinese restaurants, have lunch specials costing $3-$5. Mexican restaurants cost slightly more, with large meals running from $4.50-$6. Salad bars start at about $3.50 and up.

Steak or fish meals in good restaurants start at about $10, but the same meal, during an "Early Bird Special" will cost about $6.95. (There is almost no upper limit.) At the lower limit, even a really inexpensive special will cost about $5, including beverage and tip.

California, especially southern California, is a shopper's and bargain-seeker's paradise. Discount houses proliferate and large drug-store chains sell merchandise at cut-rate prices.

Entertainment – night clubs, concerts and shows – can be expensive. Many clubs include a cover charge and a one or two drink minimum. For a couple, that could reach approximately $20. First run movies cost about $5-6. Such attractions as amusement parks are especially expensive. Admission for some of these private tourist attractions is over $10 per person, with a parking fee slapped on top.

On the other hand, some of the top museums in the country are found in California, and are open to the public for nominal prices. Many museums, as mentioned throughout the book, set aside special hours or days when admission is free.

INTRODUCTION

Part Three – Easing the Shock: Where Have We Landed?

Transportation
Airports: The two major airports in California are the **Los Angeles (LAX)** and the **San Francisco (SFO)** airports. LAX is one of the busiest in the world. All major domestic and just about all major international and foreign lines serve the two airports. There is also an extremely busy commuter lane between SFO and LAX, in addition to numerous flights taking off to and from smaller airports within the same corridor.

The **San Diego** airport (SAN) also services flights along the coast and handles an increasing amount of national and international traffic.

There are several airlines that operate mainly in the west, and others that operate solely within California. It is possible to fly all around the state with small airlines such as Pacific Coast, Sky West, Mid Pacific, as well as on larger regional airlines such as PSA or Western. A number of smaller metropolitan airports handle major national carriers. This not only reduces the strain on the major airports, but allows the visitor greater flexibility. During high-season or on busy holiday weekends, it is sometimes wise to avoid a major center such as LAX and rather to land in a less frenetic local airport. The possibilities for direct air connections to the lesser-known areas of California are often much greater than visitors realize.

The following airports handle national airlines:
Arcata/Eureka: Tel.707-445-7791.
Bakersfield (Meadows Field): Tel. 805-393-7977.
Burbank-Glendale-Pasadena: Tel. 818-840-8843.
Fresno: Tel. 251-6051.
Long Beach: Tel. 213-421-8293.
Los Angeles: Tel. 213-646-5252 (also for international flights).
Monterey Peninsula: Tel. 408-373-3731.
Oakland: Tel. 415-577-4000 (also international flights).
Ontario: Tel. 714-984-1207 (also international flights).
Palm Springs: Tel. 619-323-8163.
Reno: Tel. 702-785-2575.
Sacramento: Tel. 916-929-5411.
San Francisco: Tel. 415-761-0800 (also international flights).
San Diego: Tel. 619-231-5220 (also international flights).
San Jose: Tel. 408-277-5366.
Santa Barbara: Tel. 805-967-1613 or 805-967-7111.

Since the deregulation of the airline industry a few years ago, and with new companies springing up and competition growing intense, the air traveler has been benefiting. If you shop around and are a bit flexible with your flying schedule, you can find some amazing flight deals, especially compared with what passengers paid some years back. Of course this could change. The

INTRODUCTION

airline industry, at least in America, is in great flux, but right now it is a fliers market.

When booking a flight, do not settle for the first answer you get, from either an airline or a travel agent. Try other airlines and other agents, until you have a good idea of the price range.

It might be up to you to ask the pertinent questions. Sometimes you must ferret out the details: they will not always be volunteered. Are there student fares? Stand-by fares? Midnight fares? Does a round-trip bought in advance cost less? Would the price be lower during another season? Airline officials often cannot answer all your questions because they do not know. With some special flight bargains, however, the deal comes with restrictions which will be made clear to you.

If you have purchased a round-trip ticket to the United States from abroad (some companies may require foreign residency), then you can buy a **VUSA** (Visit USA) ticket. This allows you to fly literally all over the United States for one set price – generally between $200-$400 – which is usually less than one standard cross-country flight. There are several similar types of VUSA tickets, based on a system whereby you pay a set price, and take an unlimited number of flights within a specific time limit on the airline issuing the ticket. The only restriction is that you cannot leave from or enter the same terminal more than twice.

Even if you plan to stay within one region, such as California or the West Coast, a VUSA might still be worthwhile, as it may cost the same as one standard flight from the East Coast. Furthermore, some regional airlines have arrangements which honor the VUSA ticket of certain major airlines. If, for example, you buy a VUSA from Northwest Airlines, you can use it on PSA all through California and the West with no extra charge. Check this out, because the arrangements can change periodically.

Many airlines have introduced, to the travelers' delight, a variety of **Frequent-Flyers** programs, in which the miles you fly can be used as credit toward free future flights. Businessmen who travel frequently can clock up enormous amounts of free mileage. The system is generally based on miles flown. Check these plans carefully, because with some companies you are given points only for the number of flights, regardless of of the mileage of each flight. PSA seems to have the best frequent-flyer program in the West, more advantageous than that of Western, its major competitor.

There is also the new unofficial "bumping game" that has taken over the airlines. Airlines now make a practice of overbooking certain generally crowded flights, to compensate for the number of people who make reservations and who do not turn up. If most or all passengers show up, however, then the airlines have more people than seats. Thanks to the efforts of consumer advocate Ralph Nader (after he himself was ignominiously "bumped" from an overbooked plane), government regulations require that passengers bumped involuntarily must be given cash payments, sometimes double the cost of the ticket; and they can still sue.

*I*NTRODUCTION

Financially ailing airlines, to avoid having to fork out cash, have come up with another solution. They ask for vounteers to give up their seat, and offer free tickets to various destinations, in addition to a guaranteed seat, on the next flight. This has become so commonplace that people make a sport of it. They've learned the angles and purposely book themselves on busy flights, their hands ready to shoot up the moment volunteers are requested. Businessmen have become pros. You may not be in their champion class, but if your schedule is flexible, the wrong flight may turn into the right flight, resulting in a voucher for a free trip somewhere.

Trains: Train travel is a throwback to a bygone world. The conductor rattles off the names of exotic sounding frontier towns. The train pulls into an elegant Spanish-style station or past a small smudged brick depot bordered by decrepit hotels and bars. People casually get acquainted in the lounge car. The countryside glides by at eye-level. The traveling becomes as rich an experience as the arrival.

Amtrak, the national passenger rail carrier, made a big push recently to encourage train travel by introducing extended routes, lower rates, package tour deals, streamlined equipment and so forth. All this is geared to fill their trains, which were for a while pitifully empty.

The main train routes leading into California include:
Seattle to San Francisco (The Coast Starlight).
Chicago to San Francisco (The California Zephyr).
Chicago to Los Angeles, either directly through San Antonio, or through New Orleans (The Desert Wind).

An intricate system of buses and local commuter trains connects with Amtrak rail lines, greatly extending access by train.

There are several main routes within the state. The Coast Starlight takes ten-and-a-half hours between Los Angeles and San Francisco. This route affords a slow but pleasant way to travel between the major cities without the hassles of driving. Although it does not follow the rugged Big Sur Coast, the train passes some gorgeous shoreline.

In the San Francisco area, the actual departure station is in industrial Oakland. A special Amtrak bus connects to the San Francisco station, the trans-bay terminal, at 1st and Mission.

The California section of the Zephyr follows the route of the early transcontinental railroad, with access to the Truckee-Lake Tahoe area, as well as to Reno just across the Sierra Nevada.

The San Joaquin route runs through the main cities of the Central Valley. From Bakersfield in the south, a special Amtrak bus brings passengers to the Amtrak station in the Los Angeles area. In the north, the train connects with the main east-west line and with the train going north to Seattle. At various points along this route, there are connections with local and regional bus lines. At the Merced station, a private bus runs to Yosemite Park.

At the time of writing, Amtrak has a special scheme whereby for any regular

INTRODUCTION

ticket purchase of $60 or more, the return fare is only $7. In California, even some routes with fares less than $60 qualify for the special return fare, such as the routes between Los Angeles and San Diego, and between San Francisco and Bakersfield. You need to return by the same route, and there are no stopovers. The $7 fare is good for 45 days after the original trip. There are certain peak traveling seasons when the ticket is not valid, so check this out carefully.

Amtrak also has special fares for traveling within or between various regions of the country. If you are journeying to California from the east, a $250 fare allows you to weave towards the west along whatever route you want, with three stopovers within 45 days. Coming from the mid-west the fare is $200. To zig-zag throughout the western region, from El Paso, Texas to Spokane, Washington including all of California, costs $150. As with the airlines, Amtrak's offers change often, so it is important to call for updated information.

Amtrak also offers total travel packages with hotels, tours, etc. There are such tours for Hearst Castle, the wine country, San Francisco and Disneyland. Trains have sleeping accommodation ranging from a pillow for the seat to separate bedrooms complete with bathroom. Some trains – or specific types of cars – require reservations, while others do not. If you buy your ticket on the train, when the station booth is open, you will be required to pay an additional $3. It is possible to bring bicycles aboard certain trains without dismantling them.

For general Amtrak information and reservations: Tel. 1-800-872-7245. This number will give you various local Amtrak numbers, if needed.

Buses: The two major private bus companies are *Greyhound* and *Trailways*. Both companies offer special excursion fares, summer-travel fares and so forth. As with Amtrak, these rates and schedules change often, so it is always worth double-checking. Greyhound with its *Ameripass*, and Trailways with its *Eaglepass*, both offer unlimited travel for a fixed price within a fixed number of days. Although most buses are stream-lined and comfortable, there is a limit to how long you can remain seated, especially when you push yourself because you want to get the most for your money. Compare prices with Amtrak. In some cases, surprisingly, the train's bargain pass may actually be cheaper, and they are certainly more comfortable. For those wanting to reach California cheaply, both bus companies offer a 15-day one-way fare, in which travel in one direction for up to 15 days costs about $100. Stops are permitted.

Children between 12-16 ride for half-fare, and ages 11 and under ride free. Seniors receive a 10% discount except on special fares. Bicycles can be stowed in the baggage compartment. This opens the possibility for a hop-scotch travel schedule of bus rides and bike rides.

Bus stations almost always seem to be located in the bad part of town. If possible avoid arriving late at night or having to wait around a dingy and depressing bus station in the wee hours.

INTRODUCTION

Green Tortoise buses offer alternative tours which are adventurous (slightly), eccentric and cheap. The company once had a reputation as the "freak" bus line, but now it draws a wide variety of people, from hippies to foreigners to professionals and spunky seniors seeking an unusual travel experience. The buses have bunks (bring your own sleeping bag or bedding), and two drivers to allow night-time traveling and daytime excursions and diversions. For the lone traveler with a budget one notch above hitching, Green Tortoise provides a chance to meet similar travelers, to make contacts, to pick up traveling tips and just to have some company.

Green Tortoise conducts trips to Alaska, Vancouver and cross-country tours varying in duration and routes (one tour hits the major national parks). A cross-country to California costs about $200. There is also a strong schedule within California, including $25 trips between San Francisco and Los Angeles with stops for exploring. There are also trips to Yosemite ($49-$59). Communally-cooked vegetarian meals fuel the crew and the travelers. Each bus has a stereo, and you can volunteer your own cassettes.

Green Tortoise Main office: P.O.Box 24459, San Francisco, 94124. Tel.415-821-0803. There are offices on the east coast and along the west coast, and a toll-free number, Tel. 1-800-277-4766.

Car Rental: Renting a car can be the most convenient and the most expensive means of travel in California. It is worth calling up several agencies because rates and conditions vary widely. For a day, a car could cost from $16-$30, and per month between $450-$550. The larger agencies – Hertz, Avis and National – are available at airports and major tourist centers, but do not necessarily offer the best deals. Sometimes, the small agencies boast the best prices. Most major California cities have the equivalent of "rent-a-wreck" car rentals, giving just what the name applies, at commensurate prices, along with a certain distance radius.

When renting a car, make sure to check certain points:
Must you drop off the car in the same place or same city, or can you return it to another point?
Are you prescribed by a particular radius of miles?
For extended use, can you lease the car?
Are the weekly and monthly rates cheaper than the daily rates? Does the rental contract include road service in case of breakdown?
How much free mileage is included per day? Per week? Per month?
How much do you have to pay per extra mile?

3000 miles a month – the average amount given – may seem like sufficient distance, but that breaks down to just over one hundred miles per day, which, if you are a hard-pushing traveler, is not really very much. Los Angeles commuters easily cover that distance daily.

The real hitch to renting a car can be the insurance, which may cost $6-$8 per day. You can apply your own liability insurance, but only if you are an in-state driver with a California license. Of course, in that case there is less chance you would need to rent a car: one of life's little ironies. If you are

INTRODUCTION

entering California from outside the state and want to rent a car, you almost have no choice but to take the insurance as well. Some agencies might advise you to attach yourself to the insurance of a relative, but be very wary of this as it stands on shaky legal ground. When inquiring about the insurance, find out exactly what is covered. Agents have been known to quote insurance prices, only to reveal later that the coverage is only partial, and they then try to convince you to take on "extra" protection ("Perhaps you'd like your left tires covered as well?").

The larger agencies sometimes offer special weekend rates. These can start as early as Thursday, with a package deal for rental through Sunday.

Having access to a car makes all the difference in the world, especially in Southern California. For both the business traveler on a strict schedule, and the tourist, it may be best to fly between destinations and rent cars locally. California's excellent in-state and inter-region air connections allows this to be done with flexibility and ease.

A **drive-away** company offers a slightly uncertain but inexpensive way to travel, both to California and within the state. These companies find drivers to transport cars from one destination to another. It is usually easy to find cars being transported from coast to coast. Sometimes you may need to be a bit flexible and accept a car to Bakersfield even if you want to end up in Los Angeles. The driver leaves a deposit, usually around $100, and picks it up from the company's office at the other end of the line once the car is safely delivered. The time and mileage allowed is limited, but it is sometimes possible to squeeze in a short excursion to a nearby sight. Such transport is needed within the state of California as well, but cars between Los Angeles and San Francisco are not easily found and are snapped up quickly. Major cities in the country have such offices. Check in the phonebook under car transport, auto transport or drive-away.

Roads

California has an excellent road system. Interstate and in-state freeways criss-cross the entire state. What they provide in directness, speed and convenience, however, is paid for by taking the boring route. Nothing can be more dangerously mesmerizing to a night driver than an endlessly flat and straight road with one white stripe after another passing in front of you.

The driver who tries a backroad here and there and passes through tiny towns will enrich his or her visit. Sometimes, it is good to ask a waitress or gas station attendant a question just to start them talking.

Along the interstate highways, rest stops are interspersed. These usually include rest rooms, drinking water, a patch of green, some picnic tables, and perhaps a map and additional information about the area. It is perfectly okay to park here overnight and sleep in the car, and usually safe, especially if several large trailer trucks are parked nearby. People sometimes flop their sleeping bags down on the grass. Usually they are not disturbed, but officially it is not allowed.

INTRODUCTION

Some Driving Tips
In both San Francisco and Los Angeles, parking can be a problem. Parking is not allowed alongside red or white curbs, green curbs mean limited-time parking only and even at unpainted curbs parking may not be allowed during rush hours, street-cleaning hours, etc.

Right turns are allowed at red lights, unless otherwise indicated. Drive here as you would at a stop sign. At a marked crosswalk, drivers must yield to pedestrians. This can sometimes be annoying and some pedestrians exercise their power by giving a driver little time to stop. As a pedestrian, however, you will appreciate the law.

The maximum speed limit on highways and freeways is 55 miles per hour, though there has been much grumbling about that, and on the L.A. freeways many drivers ignore the speed limit. In residential areas the speed limit is 25 mph. On main thoroughfares the speed limit may vary.

California has one of the strictest drunk-driving laws in the country, requiring the immediate arrest of anyone found to be driving under the influence of alcohol.

Auto Clubs
The **American Automobile Association** is the best known of the auto clubs. Membership fees vary from state to state, ranging from about $20-$50. Services include trip planning, maps, travelers checks (American Express) and – especially important – 24-hour emergency road service anywhere. Also worthwhile is the club's auto insurance.

In Northern California, the AAA is listed as the California State Automobile Association. In Southern California it is listed as the Automobile Club of Southern California (ACSC).

Accidents
Call the police immediately for any accident. On municipal streets, call the local police. On freeways even within cities, and on highways and roads between cities, call the **California Highway Patrol (CHP)**. On city freeways, the phones in the emergency callboxes link automatically to a CHP office. Otherwise, ask the operator for Zenith 1-2000, the CHP emergency number.

Rides and Hitchhiking
Someone seeking a passenger to share expenses and company, or someone seeking a ride, would do well to check the nearest college or university. Most such centers have some sort of "ride board". Alternative radio stations and newspapers also provide this service.

Hitchhiking has declined a bit in California, for whatever the reason. There is no doubt that gruesome incidents, with both drivers and passengers as the victims, have occurred. How much this will dominate someone's thinking or decisions is a personal matter. Obviously, the vast majority of hitchhikers and helpful drivers are unhurt.

*I*NTRODUCTION

Hiking

*I*NTRODUCTION

As either the driver or the rider, ask a few questions first before entering the situation, all the while trying to size up the person the best you can. In a region of a national park, a hitchhiker with a backpack standing in the middle of nowhere has probably just emerged from a trail and is trying to reach the nearest bank, shower and burger stand.

Hitchhiking within the city is generally less successful than between cities. It is generally easier to find the nearest bus.

Sometimes, if waiting by a restaurant or gas staion, approaching a driver will more likely get a positive response. Sometimes it will get a cold shoulder.

Backpacking

California offers a whole world to explore for the backpacker. Information about backpacking is easily accessible, and trails in parks around the state are well-maintained.

Numerous guide books on hiking and backpacking are available. Likewise, many stores sell camping equipment. Sometimes the big department stores and discount houses sell good equipment at cut-rate prices. Always check, though, that the equipment is of good quality.

Army-navy surplus stores, often found in the downtown sections of larger cities,can supply many of the smaller items. Today, camping has become a gigantic business,and new and improved equipment is produced annually. Everything but a jet-propelled backpack is on the market!

The **Sierra Club** is an excellent source of information for camping in California. Although a national conservation organization, the club originated in California. In addition to organizing hiking trips for members, the various branches will be able to provide printed guides and maps on specific regions in the state.

Accommodations

The range of accommodation in California is almost unlimited. Luxurious hotels which look like old Roman villas, quaint lodges perched above the beach, sleazy downtown rattraps, sterile stucco motels, homey inns, and trailer campgrounds resembling suburbs on wheels – they are all here.

Lodging is not particularly cheap, and real bargains in overnight accommodation are hard to find. Most decent and reliable facilities, even in a standard motel, begin around $25.

Many local Chambers of Commerce distribute lists of local accommodation, as do visitors centers. Policies vary at these agencies about listing prices or making recommendations. Those who list accommodation are all members of the local chamber.

A list of suggested accommodation is available from the **California Hotel and Motel Association**, 414 29th st., Sacramento, CA 95816. Tel.916-444-5780.

Remember when considering price, that hotels in California tag on a hotel tax. This rate differs from area to area, ranging usually from 6% to as high as 10%.

INTRODUCTION

The major hotel chains are well-represented in both the major cities and outlying areas of California. In resorts, prices tend to rise on weekends. In major cities, hotels which cater to a business population and host conventions often change things around: they offer discounts on weekends, which are sometimes very sizeable ones. This may be done on a haphazard basis by the individual hotel depending on the booking situation that weekend, or it may be part of a regular weekend special program followed in many branches of a hotel chain. This is worth checking out, for the reductions are substantial and allow for a luxurious weekend at very reasonable prices. Often these rates will only be mentioned upon request, so be sure to inquire about any weekend discount or special package. Below is a sampling of some of the available specials. The toll-free numbers listed are generally reservations and information numbers that give details about weekend specials or refer you to particular hotels. Even within a single hotel chain, the discount may vary from hotel to hotel, city to city or season to season.

Best Western International: Tel. 800-528-1234. Discounts of 20-50% off regular rates.

Hilton Hotels: Various areas have their own 800 numbers. Ask specifically about the "Rainbow Weekend".

Hyatt Hotels: Tel. 800-288-9000. Various weekend programs may include reductions of up to 50% on deluxe rooms.

Marriott Hotels: Tel. 800-2888-9290. Ask about "Super Saver" and "Escape" packages for weekenders.

Ramada Hotel Group: Tel. 800-272-6232. "R and R" weekend specials.

Sheraton Hotels: Tel. 800-325-3535. Ask about "Time of your Life" weekends.

Westin Hotels: Tel.800-228-300. Most have lower weekend rates.

Motel 6 is a safe, standard, reliable and inexpensive motel-chain. Most have pools but television is extra. There is nothing surprising here, either pleasant or unpleasant. The price, about $21, is relatively inexpensive. There are about 400 motels in the chain nation-wide, and almost 100 in California alone. For a directory, write: Motel 6, Inc., 51 Hitchcock Way, Santa Barbara, CA 93105.

The *Quest International* hotel marketing organization, for a $99 annual membership fee, arranges a 50% discount off regular rates at more than 500 hotels in the United States, British Columbia and San Juan. The half-price reduction is offered no matter how seasonal prices may fluctuate. Quest International, Chinook tower, Box 4041, Yakima, WA 98901. Tel. 509-248-7512.

Bed-Breakfast (B&B) Inns have increased in number and popularity in recent years. There are several hundred scattered throughout California, but they are found predominantly in the north. They tend to be rustic and old. Some may be refurbished farmhouses, others old family-run hotels or Victorian houses. Each one is individual, expressing its own personality and that of its owners. Many are small, family-run operations, perhaps even in a wing of a private home. The rooms vary in style and furnishings and often there is an emphasis on old-time decor. Such inns may be located in the

INTRODUCTION

center of town, in completely residential areas, or in the country side. They can offer an inside glimpse of country life that hotel guests may not otherwise see. Staying at a B&B is a little more adventurous than staying in a conventional hotel. The atmosphere is often warm and casual, it is easy to meet the other guests or the owners. The breakfasts may include such touches as freshly-squeezed juice and home-baked muffins, as opposed to the standard coffee-shop fare. Often there are complimentary afternoon beverages, or use of the library or a bicycle, or other touches that make the experience more home-like.

There was a time when B&Bs were generally less expensive than hotels. Now the prices are on a par, and sometimes they are over-priced, not to mention outrageous. Nevertheless, there are plenty around which, while costing no more than the average motel, offer an individual experience to which a motel cannot compare. Because each inn is run at the fancy of its owner, features you would expect at a motel must be double-checked in a B&B: How big is the bed? Is the room furnished? Is the bathroom private? Is there a bath or only a shower? Are there any extras? Is breakfast full or continental (beverage, juice and rolls)? Are there weekday or off-season rates?

Various organizations who represent B&Bs in different regions have appeared, making it easier for the visitor to find a special one. These organizations know the characteristics of the different inns, and can also make suggestions and sometimes handle bookings.

Besides the B&Bs, there is also the "homestay", in which guests actually rent a room in a private residence. This can be less expensive and more homey than a B&B. Information is often available through the B&B associations.

In addition to the associations noted below, smalller organizations represent the inns of specific regions.

Bed and Breakfast Innkeepers of Southern California: P.O.Box 15385, Los Angeles 90015. Tel. 805-966-0589.

Bed and Breakfast Innkeepers of Northern California: 2030 Union st., Suite 310, San Francisco 74123. Tel. 415-563-4667.

Association of Bed and Breakfast Innkeepers of San Francisco: 737 Buena Vista W., San Francisco 94117. Tel. 415-861-3008.

A brochure listing B&Bs throughout the state is published by the California Office of Tourism in Sacramento.

Youth Hostels provide another lodging alternative. A national network of Youth Hostels is operated by *American Youth Hostels* (AYH). The AYH is part of the *International Youth Hostel Federation*. Its membership card is valid for International Youth Hostel facilities. Conversely, a card from abroad is valid in the United States.

Hostel facilities are often found in schools, old hotels, and YMCAs, but sometimes they have their own buildings. Some hostels have smaller private rooms as well as dorm-like rooms and most have kitchen facilities.

Youth hostels are by no means only for youth. Many others, such as

INTRODUCTION

professionals and seniors, use hostels in order to spice up their vacation. Hostels are ideal places for the lone traveler to strike up acquaintances and pick up travel tips.

Overnight fees are usually around $5-$6 for members, and a dollar or two more for non-members. AYH offices can be found in most major cities in the country.

In California there are over 30 hostels. Information can be obtained on them from your local AYH office. Some of the California hostels in which membership is sold include:
In San Francisco: 240 Fort Mason, S.F. 94123. Tel.415-771-7277.
In Los Angeles: 1502 Palos Verdes dr., N Harbor City 90710. Tel.213-831-8109.
In San Diego: Armed Services YMCA, 500 W. Broadway, SD 92101. Tel. 619-232-1133.

The AYH operates other youth hostels as well in these metropolitan areas.

YMCAs have traditionally provided wayfarers with decent and simple lodgings, often in dormitories. Today they may range from the very inexpensive to the price of an average motel room. Usually the price includes use of some or all of the sports facilities. The lodgings may range from shabby to sleek. Reservations are often recommended. For a listing of YMCAs and general information, contact: *The Y's Way*, 356 W. 34th st., New York, NY 10001. Tel. 212-760-5856. If you want a catalogue, send a self-addressed stamped envelope.

The Young Women's Christian Association (YWCA) offers the same type of lodging and facilities, but generally for women only. Contact: *The Young Women's Christian Association*, 726 Broadway, New York, N.Y. 10003. Tel. 212-614-2700.

Practical tips for getting around
Mail
Mail can be received at hotels. It can also be sent to the General Delivery of the post office of any city or town. In a large city this is usually found in the main post office downtown. Users of American Express traveler's checks can use that company's offices to receive mail, but only if they previously request to do so.

Telephones
Telephone numbers are preceded by a 3-digit area code. There are 9 area codes within California. In some areas the boundary for area codes may fall within a populated area. Dialing from one area code to another, the prefix "1" must sometimes be added. By no means is it assured that within one area code all calls are local calls. In the Los Angeles area, with the recent splitting up of ATT, additional charges may be added to calls within the same area code. At public phones, local calls in some areas cost 20 cents. The phones take nickels (5 cents), dimes (10 cents), and quarters (25 cents). The operator is not needed to make a long-distance call from a pay phone. Just

_INTRODUCTION

Keeping in touch

dial "1", the area code and the number, and an operator or a recording will tell you how much money is needed, so keep a pile of change handy. If an additional charge is owed at the end of the call, the phone will ring when you hang up.

Long-distance rates are substantially lower between 6pm and 8am, and on weekends from 11pm Friday to 5pm Sunday. For international calls, the lowest rates are between 3pm and 9pm.

Many companies now use toll-free numbers, recognizable by the 800 prefix to the number. No area code is necessary to call this number, but sometimes a "1" must precede the 800. An 800 number which is good for in-state calls may not be operable for calls from outside the state, and some companies have both in-state and out-of-state toll-free numbers. Local Yellow Pages list a company's toll-free numbers.

Currency and Exchange
Foreign currency can be exchanged in international airports and certain banks. If possible buy travelers'checks in American dollars, at the appropriate exchange rate. Foreign currency will not be honored in the United States.

To send money to the United States it is best to give the name and address of an American bank correspondent to your bank at home. Money can be cabled, usually within 48 hours, for a charge of up to $25. A draft check, sent by mail, is a little cheaper but much slower.

Banking
Banking hours in California are from Mon.-Thurs. 10am-3pm, and 10am-5pm

INTRODUCTION

on Fridays. Some banks keep later hours, usually only until noon or 1pm. Electronic tellers are now common and widespread among all major banks.

Travelers' Checks
Travelers' checks are a must. They are available at banks or through organizations such as American Automobile Association, at a reduced price or at no charge.

American Express Travelers' checks are the most widely recognized, and the company provides a measure of assistance and reassurance to those whose checks have been lost or stolen. American Express Travel Service offices will help arrange temporary identification, cash personal checks, arrange for new travelers' checks immediately, report and cancel credit card numbers, and in general provide assistance. In addition, if arranged by mail beforehand, check holders may use the local American Express office as a mailing address.

Credit Cards
A credit card is worth taking as an emergency source of cash or to pay for large items. Recognized credit cards will allow the holder to withdraw in cash the sum remaining in his credit. Make sure you know where to report a lost or stolen credit card, and do so immediately. Major credit cards such as Visa, Masterchage and American Express are recognized throughout California. If coming from another country, check whether your credit card is affiliated with an American company. When using a credit card, always check the amount before signing, and be sure to get the receipt. In addition, ask for the black carbon and destroy it immediately. Occasionally, a business will want to keep the carbon. Refuse stubbornly and on all counts. Carbons have been used to produce counterfeit credit cards and should never leave the owner's possession. Likewise, never give your credit card number for identification purposes; use a passport or driver's license instead. Credit cards can also be used for long-distance calls in specially equipped public telephones.

Electricity, measurements, time
Electric current is 110-115 a.c. 60Hz. For those planning to buy American appliances, note that the American plugs are two flat pins which will require adapters. Foreign appliances brought to the United States generally require a transformer as well as adapters.

Measurements: The American measurement system is not a decimal one. Following are several conversion tables and "instant" tricks.
Weight
28.349 grams – 1 ounce
0.453 kilograms – 1 pound
Volume
0.473 liters – 1 pint
3.785 liters – 1 gallon
Distance
2.540 cm – 1 inch
30.480 cm – 1 foot
0.914 meter – 1 yard

INTRODUCTION

1.609 km – 1 mile
Temperature
To convert Fahrenheit degrees to Centigrade (Celsius) subtract 32 from the Fahrenheit temperature, multiply by 5 and divide the total by 9.

Time: All of California is within the Pacific Time Zone, which is GMT-8. This is one hour behind the Denver region, two hours behind Chicago and the Midwest, and three hours behind the east coast. Daylight Savings Time begins on the last Sunday in April, and ends the last Saturday in October.

Smoking, alcohol, drugs

Smoking is no longer "cool" in health-conscious California. It is prohibited by law in elevators, city buses and many public rooms, and is permitted only in restricted areas in restaurants and inter-city buses. Californians have become increasingly bold and insistent in requesting others in their proximity not to smoke.

The drinking age in California is 21. It is against the law to drive with an open container of alcohol in the car. Drunk-driving laws in California are strict and strictly enforced.

California is viewed by many as the land with a free-and-easy attitude towards drugs, especially marijuana. Possession of marijuana is no longer a felony, though one sometimes has to pay a fine. Marijuana is, frankly, very common and accepted, but it is not something to be brazen about, and foreigners should be especially careful.

Photography

If you are a photography buff, you will find ample material in California among the stunning and diverse natural scenery and among the tremendous mixture of people and lifestyles.

If wanting to buy a camera, you might wait until you reach California, where competition is fierce, and many discount houses and department stores have camera departments which undercut the prices of regular camera shops. The camera shops, however, can give expert advice, which a clerk in a discount house is unlikely to have.

In the urban areas, one-hour and one-day developing services can easily be found. The large chain drugstores will often handle developing, and periodically run specials, such as two rolls for the price of one.

Disabled Travelers

New hotels and other public buildings must, according to California law, be accessible by wheelchairs. Businesses and communities are becoming more aware of the needs of the disabled. Car rental companies can supply special cars for the disabled. Greyhound, Trailways, Amtrak and the airlines are now equipped to accommodate the disabled. Some companies give special rates to the disabled as well as to the elderly. Special parking spaces are reserved for the disabled.

For information on travel for the disabled, contact: **The Society for the**

*I*NTRODUCTION

Advancement of Travel for the Handicapped, 26 Court st., Brooklyn, N.Y. 11242. Tel. 212-858-5483.

Senior Citizens

Many seniors are taking advantage of travel discounts and programs oriented towards them. Discounts are available in theaters, museums, on public and private buses and in many other places. **The American Association of Retired Persons (AARP)** offers information on traveling for seniors, as well as considerable discounts on lodging and other travel expenses. For information contact: AARP Membership Communications, 1909 K st. NW, Washington, DC 20049. Tel. 202-872-4700.

Food

As with almost everything else in California, the world of food is rich, colorful and diverse. Eating out is a common pastime. Restaurants range from the elegant, elite and outrageously expensive to the incredibly cheap. In addition to American steak restaurants, Chinese and Mexican restaurants are extremely popular, widespread and accessible to any budget. More varieties of both Asian and Latin American food are becoming available. Italian restaurants are very common as well.

The grilling of fish and meats on mesquite coal is common in many California restaurants, especially in the north. There is an emphasis on fresh produce of excellent quality mixed together in myriad ways. In recent years, with an increased emphasis on health, vegetarian cooking has developed into an art. Vegetarian restaurants are common, and serve a surprising variety of dishes, some tremendously imaginative. In conjunction with this is the increasingly common appearance of the salad bar, available as part of a larger meal or by itself. These salad bars are creations in themselves; the old days of tomatoes and shredded lettuce are gone. An average salad bar may include an array of cheeses and dressings, several kinds of nuts, potatoes, bread, fish, noodles and fruit – in other words, a salad can be a delicious and filling meal in itself. One of the best and most reliable salad bars can be found in the *Sizzler* chain of restaurants. The emphasis in this buffet type restaurant is on steak, but the salad bar at about $4.25 is a welcome sight to those who prefer not to eat red meats.

Fast-food stands line the highways of California. They have branched out from the old simple burger stands and now include pizza, tacos, roast beef, chicken and ice cream. Prices at different branches of the same company are generally uniform. Occasionally a chain will run some sort of special and proclaim it in the media, but sometimes a typical burger-fries-milkshake meal at a fast-food stand, besides containing dubious nutritional value, can cost as much as a sit-down meal at, for example, a small Chinese lunch counter.

The 24-hour coffee shop chains form another characteristic California institution. They are far from the down-home diners of yesteryear. In each chain there are standardized designs, prices, menus, quality and employee uniforms. One can imagine that the same innocuous soft music plays simultaneously at hundreds of different coffee shops.

*I*NTRODUCTION

However there can be something comfortable about these places, especially when it is 2am and up ahead at the next highway exit the bright sign of a *Denny's, Sambo's, Norm's* or *Bob's* shines invitingly in the darkness. The soft lights, familiar booths, smiling waitresses, never-ending coffee and precisely sliced pie is somehow reliable and reassuring, even if rather bland.

Instead of tasting California's superb produce in a restaurant, it is possible to get it yourself direct from the farm. As mentioned throughout this book, many regions publish maps showing which local farms accept visitors, what the farm produces, etc. This is a good way not only to obtain fresh produce, but to break out of the tourist mold and meet the locals in an unusual setting. The produce you can sample ranges from vegetables and fruits to nuts, wines and cheeses. The regional directories can be obtained through local chamber of commerce offices, or through one central office: The Dept. of Food and Agriculture, 1220 N st., room 427, Sacramento 95814.

Important Addresses And Phone Numbers

California is a very tourist-oriented state. Material written to assist visitors is voluminous and accessible, from public and commercial sources. The **California Office of Tourism** in Sacramento, will, for the price of postage, send its booklets to those interested. This office can provide a directory of Chambers of Commerce and Visitors' Bureaus throughout the state, a map and small pocket guide, a calendar of events, and a listing of Bed & Breakfast Inns. Write to: California Office of Tourism, Publications, 1121 L st., Suite 103, Sacramento, CA 95814. Tel. 1-180-TO CALIF for toll-free information.

Some other useful addresses and numbers:
Department of Parks and Recreation: Distribution Center, P.O.Box 2390, Sacramento 95811. A guide to California's state parks is available for $2.00.
State Park Campground Reservations: Tel. 1-1800-IGO-PARK.
National Park Service Information: 450 Golden Gate ave., San Francisco, CA 94102.

California Region, U.S. Forest Service: 630 Sansome st. San Francisco, CA 94111. For national forest information. A wide range of brochures available.

Ticketron Information: Northern California, Tel. 414-393-4089 or 393-6914. Southern California, Tel. 213-642-5870.

Department of Fish and Game: 1416 9th st. Sacramento, CA 95814. For fishing and hunting information and regulations.
U.S. Bureau of Land Management: 2800 Cottage Way, Sacramento, CA 95825. For a list of BLM campgrounds.

The Sierra Club: 530 Bush st., San Francisco, CA 94108. For information on California's ecological resources, as well as the clubs organized trips.
The Nature Conservancy: Western Regional Office, 425 Bush st., San Francisco CA 94108. Information on educational trips designed to teach about the environment.

INTRODUCTION

Restaurant at State Park

The Wine Institute : 165 Post st., San Francisco, Ca 94108: A free booklet, "The Pleasure of Wine with Food" is available.

The local Chamber of Commerce of any city or small town is a resource worth exploring throughout your travels in California. These offices can tell you about small, obscure attractions that you would otherwise miss. The people in these offices are proud of their hometowns – sometimes inordinately so – and can share unusual stories. In the popular resort areas, many Chambers of Commerce carry fliers with various discount coupons for sites in the area. Most interesting of all is the opportunity to meet people. If you express curiosity and interest in someone's hometown, you may be surprised at the open response.

Parks and Reserves

National Park Service (NPS)
An extraordinary diversity of preserved land is under the juristriction of the National Park Service including Yosemite, Death Valley, the Channel Islands and Redwood.

The park service enforces strict rules about the protection of natural areas. Entrance fees are charged and camping fees are extra, starting at $4. Fees for primitive campsites are nominal, and for backcountry free, but permits are required.

INTRODUCTION

The *Golden Eagle Passport* allows unlimited entry into national parks for the holder and accompanying passengers in a single car. The pass costs $10 and can be purchased at a national park or NPS regional office.

The *Golden Age Passport* is free to seniors from age 62. It provides free lifetime entry to all park lands, and 50% discounts on various fees, such as camping. Available at most national parks, it must be obtained in person. A similar pass, the *Golden Access Passport*, is available for blind and disabled individuals. This too must be obtained in person.

National Forest Service
National Forest Service lands differ from National Parks in that they are multi-purpose. Logging and grazing, for example may be permitted under carefully controlled conditions. Few specific sites or regions are preserved for public visits, and there is not the same system of guided tours and activities as in National Parks. National forest land can, however, be stunning and certain areas have been designated as protected wilderness. There may be extensive trail networks throughout national forests. Camping is usually less expensive than in national or state parks, and in many areas it is free.

A new system allows campers to buy *camp stamps* at designated retail outlets or forest service offices, equal to the necessary camping fee. The users pays only 85% of the amount listed, thereby saving 15%. For further information contact National Forest Service headquarters in San Francisco.

State Parks
California runs a huge state park system, with some land as stunningly beautiful as that protected in the state's national parks. There are extensive camping and hiking possibilities within the park system. With its mobile and recreation-oriented population, California's state parks can often be crowded. Campsites can cost $6 or more per vehicle, 50 cents for walk-ins and bicycles. Backcountry sites are generally free but permits may be required. At most parks reservations are accepted. They may be made through any Ticketron outlet (with an extra fee tagged on) or by a new reservation system called MISTIX. Call toll-free Tel. 1-1800-I GO PARK.

BACK PACKER
Taking time to appreciate the wonders of nature.

CALIFORNIA

San Diego

San Diego spreads around San Diego Bay on the California coast just north of Mexico, almost reaching the border. Established in 1769 as a mission and presidio, it was the earliest settlement in California. In the not so distant past it had the image of a sleazy, run down sailors' town. Today, however, San Diego has been officially recognized as America's Finest City, something San Diegans were convinced of anyway. The physical setting is a stunning combination of ocean, mountain and desert. The cultural ambience is sophisticated and pleasure loving. There is always some festival being held under those endlessly bright skies, and there is a thriving theater scene and plenty of music from classical to jazz. Although it is California's second largest city, in some ways San Diego has the atmosphere of a smaller city. Thus far it has managed to keep urban sprawl and congestion in check, and most of the main attractions are easily accessible by bus. There are many places just to stroll down and watch the passing crowd, and there are others where one can enjoy the sand and ocean undisturbed. Seventy miles of beaches are punctuated by bluffs, coves and tidepools. The constant sea breezes keep the air fresh even in summer, and the winters are warm. People here love their outdoor recreation and there is plenty of it, from windsurfing to desert trekking. It is the kind of city where many visitors flock, and a good number end up staying.

Visitors can enjoy San Diego without a car. Many attractions appear in clusters: Point Loma, Balboa Park, Mission Bay, downtown and the waterfront, La Jolla and so forth. The bus system is extensive within the main urban radius. Within the main clusters of attractions, there is often plenty to explore on foot beyond the principal sites, even if only an old neighborhood or a stretch of beach and cliff. Bus routes extend everywhere within the main urban radius.

How to get there
By air: The **San Diego International Airport** at Lindbergh Field straddles the northern curve of San Diego Bay. It is close to downtown, the resort hotels of Mission Bay, the string of motels north of Old Town, and the northern beaches. The airport has an east and a west terminal with information desks, transportation stations and Traveler Aid offices in each. Both public and private transportation is at hand. Unlike the Los Angeles Airport, the San Diego airport is not overwhelming.

By land: The main traffic artery reaching San Diego from the north is I-5, which parallels and sometimes merges with the Pacific Coast Highway. The drive between Los Angeles and San Diego takes about two hours along this freeway. I-5 runs into and through downtown and continues right to the border crossing with Mexico at San Ysidro. Coming from Los Angeles, the

SAN DIEGO

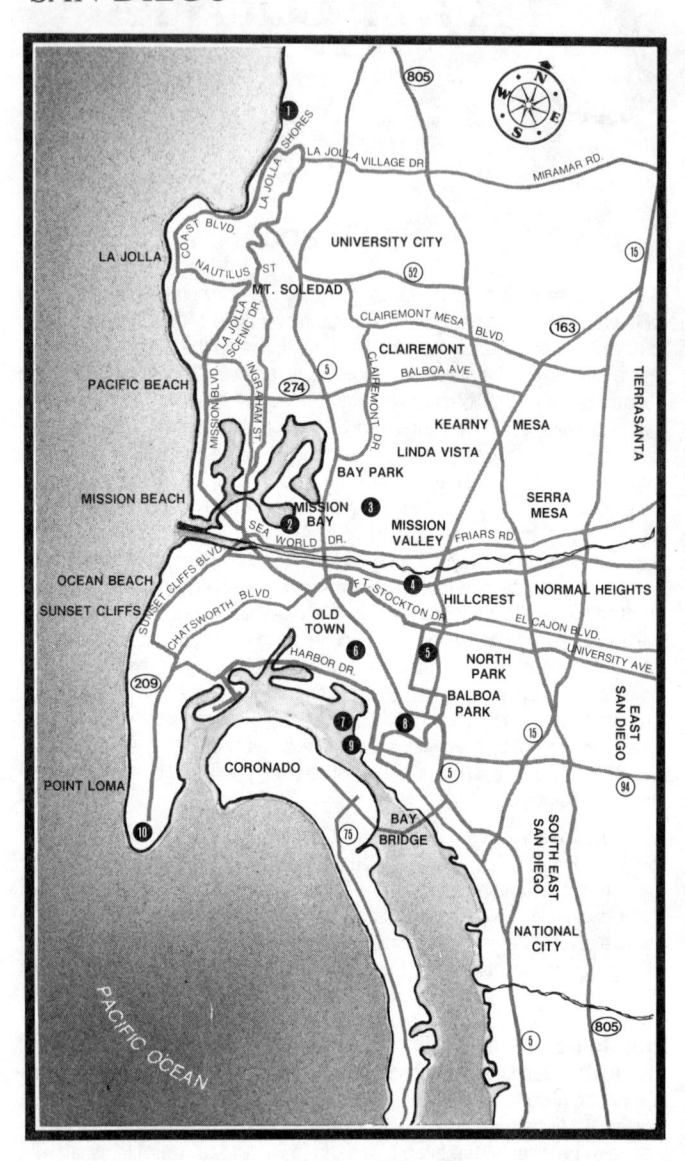

Index
1) Scripps Aquarium
2) Sea World
3) Serra Museum
4) Hotel Circle
5) San Diego Zoo
6) Airport
7) Maritime Museum
8) Downtown
9) Embarcadero
10) Cabrillo National Monument

CALIFORNIA

coastal route is more scenic, but slower. From Arizona, I-5 crosses the desert and the hothouse of the Imperial Valley toward the city.

Buses: San Diego's **Metropolitan Transit System** (MTS) is a meshing of municipal, county and regional systems. All passes and transfers are reciprocal, and the systems interlock at various points. The nerve center of the system, and the place to go with any question or confusion, is the Transit Store at Broadway and Fifth, downtown. Many bus lines converge in the immediate vicinity. The clerks there are helpful and patient, and any pass can be bought there. Ticket prices vary, depending on the system and distance. They start at 50 cents, with transfers starting at 25 cents. Exact change is required on buses. "Day Tripper" transit passes allow unlimited usage for one to three days for $3, $5 or $7. The **Regional Transit Guide,** available at the Transit Store or any public information office, details the extensive and sometimes complicated system.

The **San Diego Trolley** leaves from near the Santa Fe Depot, on C st. at Kettner, for the border crossing at San Ysidro. From 5:30am-9pm. Tickets cost $1.60, and for seniors and disabled, 60 cents. The trolley is accessible by wheelchair.

You can travel virtually everywhere by bicycle in San Diego, from the northern coast to the Mexican border, and you need not be a champion racer. An extensive network of bicycle paths overlaps with a grid of specific bus routes for buses equipped with bicycle carriers. Using these bicycle carriers at no extra charge, a cyclist can catch a bus, hop off with his bicycle and ride to another point in the system where he can catch another bus. A detailed regional cycling map shows the cycling paths and the cycle-bus routes, stops and parking lots with bike lockers. The map is free and is available from any Visitor Information Center and many bicycle stores. For information on bicycle routes, call Tel. 231-BIKE.

Public transportation is supplemented by a number of private companies operating buses and jitneys (passenger vans), many of which serve the military facilities, hotels and tourist attractions. Information for these can be found through a single clearinghouse, the **Commuter Computer**.

Downtown

Financier Alonzo Horton was convinced, in the 1860s, that San Diego would burgeon if located closer to the port. He bought a tract of neglected land at about 27 cents per acre and distributed it – gratis – to parties who promised to build there. "New Town" was born and "Old Town" was doomed. The appearance changed with the location, and adobe was replaced by the Victorian style.

Downtown centered around Fifth Avenue and from there spread north, but the district, which became known as the **Gaslamp Quarter,** fell into disrepute, and became a haven for prostitutes, criminals and rowdy visiting sailors. By the 1900s the original core of downtown was deserted; the quarter continued to decay and never recovered.

DOWNTOWN SAN DIEGO

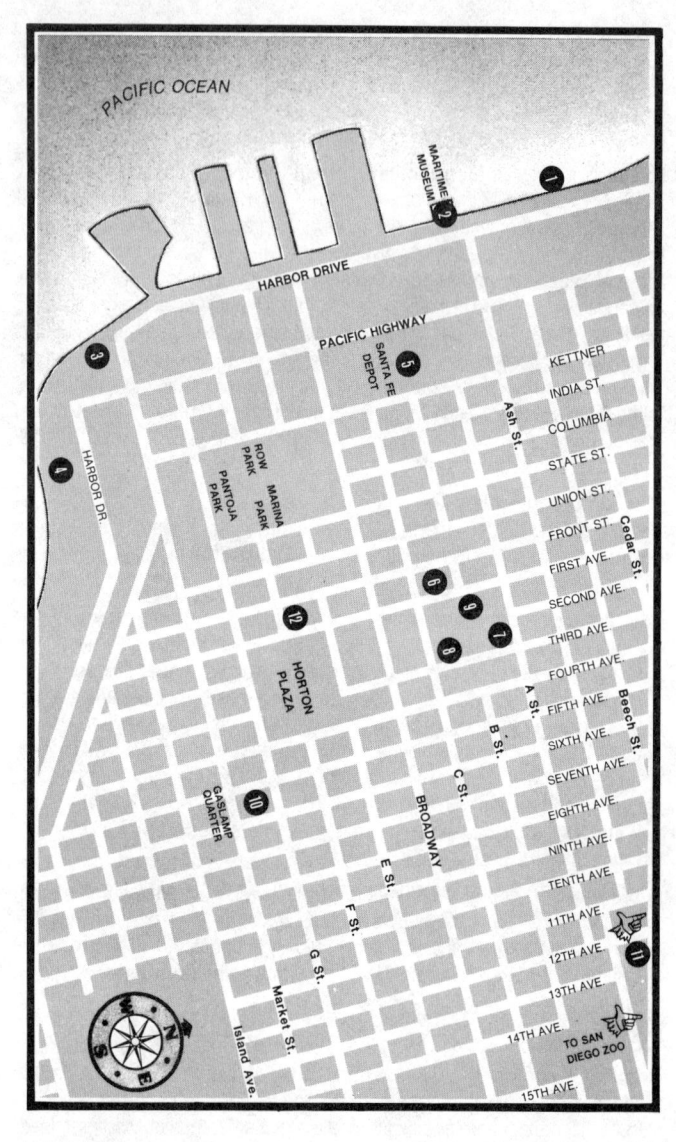

Index

1) Embarcadero
2) Maritime Museum
3) Harbor Seafood Mart
4) Seaport Village
5) Santa Fe Depot Information Center
6) Chamber of Commerce
7) Convention and Visitors' Bureau
8) Civic Theater
9) Convention and Performing Arts Center
10) Gaslamp Quarter
11) Balboa Park
12) International Visitor Information

CALIFORNIA

In recent years civic groups have worked to restore the Gaslamp Quarter. They received a boost when the neighborhood was declared a Nationally Registered Historic District. Currently it is still part antique store and polished bar, part porno theater and fleatrap hotel.

Between 4th and 6th Avenues, and L Street and Broadway, the Gaslamp area invites daytime browsing and exploration. The buildings are being refurbished with great care, their exquisite details honed and polished. Stylish restaurants, wood paneled and filled with ferns, are springing up and some of the tiny storefront diners still serve great meals. Today, murals add to the atmosphere of the quarter. One of the largest, on the south wall of the **Gollan Hotel** at Fifth and Island, depicts a turn of the century scene, but with the faces of today's Gaslamp characters.

The intimate **Gaslamp Quarter Theater** (547 4th ave. Tel. 234-9583), is housed in an old 1920s dance hall and stages professional productions. Note the box office, which is the original dance hall ticket booth. The Gaslamp Quarter Foundation, in the **William Heath Davis House,** (410 Islan ave. A $2 donation per person is requested. Tel. 233-4694). conducts tours of the quarter on Saturday at 10am and 1pm.

Just west of the Gaslamp Quarter, along Broadway, is **Horton Plaza,** the bright and crowded shopping hub of a revitalized downtown. The multistoried complex, part of which resembles a multi-colored battleship prow, features street performers and live music during the day. The **International Visitor Information Center** is located under the shopping level of the plaza, with its entrance at 1st ave. and F st.

The Embarcadero

Once teeming with steamers and sailing ships, San Diego's harbor today is dominated by fishing fleets (tuna is the main catch), pleasure crafts and naval vessels. The city is essentially a massive naval base with approximately 100,000 active sailors and marines on any given day. The **Embarcadero** area which is most often visited is concentrated between **Seaport Village Shopping Center** in the south, and the **Maritime Museum** in the north. The walk is easy and refreshing, and the views across the bay peaceful with a gleaming skyline. If you enjoy seafood, visit the **Harbor Seafood Mart** with its fresh fish markets and restaurants. Just north of the mart, at the **G Street Mole**, many of the large tuna seiners pull in. Look at the immense piled up nets. The cruise ships dock at the **Broadway Pier** and **B Street Pier** to allow passengers to board or disembark. Several companies offer excursions around the bay.

Nearby, at the Embarcadero and Harbor drive is the **San Diego Maritime Museum** (Open daily, 9am-8pm. Adults $3.50; seniors, military and age 13-17, $2.50. Tel. 234-9153). The museum is comprised of three ships: an old San Francisco ferry, an old luxury yacht and a 19th century square-rigged cargo vessel, the **Star of India**. This is the centerpiece of the museum. The oldest merchantman afloat, this ship circled the globe many times, carrying

CALIFORNIA

emigrants from England to Australia, and bearing cargoes of timber and salmon.

Balboa Park

Balboa Park extends almost as far as downtown, yet it has a sheltered and other-worldly atmosphere. The Spanish buildings are graceful and exquisite, the gardens blazing with color. It is a pleasure to wander along the quiet paths among the art studios in the re-created Spanish village. There are also a number of museums here, and the world-famous San Diego Zoo.

The Spanish buildings were built for the 1915 Panama-California Exposition, which marked the completion of the Panama Canal. San Diego was to be the first American port reached by ships cutting westward through the canal, and the city went all out for the celebration. A whole Spanish mini-city was created, and the buildings standing today are but a small remainder of those built for the celebrations.

The main concourse is **El Prado**, leading from Laurel st. to the **Plaza de Panama**. This plaza is the center of the park. Just east of the plaza is the **House of Hospitality**. The information center here (open 9:30am-4pm daily) can supply brochures and details on museums and activities in the park, as well as general city-wide information. Be sure to ask about any upcoming concerts or performances because there is always something going on in the park. Glance into the central courtyard, with its sculpture of an Aztec woman pouring water.

The array of museums concentrated in this park is mind-boggling. One could easily spend a few days here doing nothing but museum-hopping. On the first Tuesday of every month entry to the museums is free.

The **Botanical Building** offers guided tours of its tropical and semi-tropical plants. At the **Spreckels Organ Pavillion**, the largest outdoor organ in the world is played during free recitals every Sunday at 2pm. The **Museum of Art** displays masterpieces which include examples of modern American realism, in addition to the works of Henry Moore and Alexander Calder. You can also enjoy a cup of coffee in the **Sculpture Garden Cafe**. The sculptures on the entrance facade are of 17th-century Spanish painters, including El Greco. The adjacent **Timkin Art Gallery** displays work by El Greco, as well as by Rembrandt, Brueghel and others.

In the planetarium of the **Reuben H. Fleet Space Theater and Science Center** the sophisticated equipment makes you feel as if you have been seized and hurled into the galaxy. The range of shows is expansive, including music from the rock group Pink Floyd, and a stunning visual trek into the Grand Canyon. There are children's workshops, free films and ongoing, ever-changing demonstrations. Other interesting places to visit include the **Centro Cultural de la Raza**, with its exciting Chicano murals, and the **Museum of Photographic Arts**, in the **Casa De Balboa** on the Prado. This museum is a gem. Exhibits have included the black-and-white works of virtuosos such as Ansel Adams and Henri Cartier-Bresson, as well as bright and abstract

CALIFORNIA

Flamingoes at San Diego Zoo

experiments in all sorts of photographic media. The bookstore located here also makes for interesting browsing.

Other museums include the **Museum of Man**, the **Aero-Space Museum** at the end of the **Pan American Plaza,** the **Museum of San Diego History**, the **Model Railroad Museum** and the **Hall of Champions** honoring San Diego's star athletes. The **Natural History Museum** presents the regional wildlife found in the diverse surrounding ecological regions. It also sponsors whale watching trips in the winter (places must be reserved in advance). The **Old Globe Theater**, near the Plaza de Panama, resembles the original theater in London. Here, and at the adjacent **Cassius Carter Center Stage**, Shakespearean productions are staged, plus some other dramatic works. Tours of the theaters and backstage area are given on Saturday and on weekends at 11am.

Just north of the Natural History Museum, the small neat cottages of the **Spanish Village** house studios for potters, woodworkers, weavers and other craftsmen. The quality here is generally very high. Visitors are free to observe, browse and buy.

Just a bit further along is the 1910 **carousel**, where you can ride on a hand carved giraffe, dragon, ostrich or zebra. Pull the brass ring, win a free ride and impress your companion. 50 cents per ride – a bargain.

A visit to the justly famous **San Diego Zoo** deserves a full day. (Admission $6.50, under 16 $2.50, active military personnel free. Deluxe packages

CALIFORNIA

including tours are available. On Founder's Day in early October, admission is free. Open July through Labor Day, 9am-5pm; Post-Labor Day through June 9, 9am-4pm. Tel. 234-3153 or 231-1515.)

The 100 acres of exotic gardens and superb recreations of the animals' natural habitats are marvelous, and some of the world's rarest animals are found here. Because of the mild, steady climate there is no need for closed shelters.

The zoo is as concerned with preserving and breeding rare species as it is with showing them to the public. The Galapagos Turtle and Koala Bear are among the endangered species which find sanctuary here.

Old Town

Old Town San Diego State Historical Park, wedged in between I-8 and I-5, is a combination of historical sites and tourist shops. By exploring among the adobe brick buildings with their rough hewn doors and beams, it is possible to sense the atmosphere of the original village that sprang up here and which later became the city of San Diego.

Gaspar de Portola, a Spanish commander, and Padre Junipera Serra initiated settlement in San Diego and California in 1769, with the establishment of the presidio and mission on the adjacent hill. The mission later moved but the presidio remained. As retired soldiers and other settlers sought homes, the small village spread below the presidio, in a typical settlement pattern. Its growth continued after Mexico won independence and stripped the mission of its lands. Americans also arrived here, some as sailors on the Yankee merchantmen that shipped tallow and hides to the eastern seaports. When the U.S. took over San Diego after the Mexican War, American settlement naturally increased, and the town took on a more American character. Some of the settlers had witnessed all three periods of rule, as did the village itself, with its smattering of stately Spanish baronial, plebian pueblo brick, and clapboard-and-frame architecture.

In 1867 the town's fortunes plunged when financier Alonzo Horton initiated the building of a new town. The old town declined and a fire then destroyed most of it. It remained a ruin until historical renovation began.

Most of the remaining Old Town structures are included within the state park. The Park Service conducts a free one-hour walking tour everyday which leaves from the **Casa de Machado-Silvas**, near the plaza. The park information center, at the corner of San Diego and Mason, provides information for self-guided tours. The **Casa de Machado-Stewart**, mentioned in Richard Henry Dana's *Two Years Before the Mast*, suggests the simple and hardy life of an early settler. The **Casa de Bandini** emanates old-world elegance (and houses an excellent restaurant), as does the **Casa de Estudillo**, where Don Jose Antonio Estudillo managed to keep his public positions through three separate national reigns. In 1867 two partners launched a newspaper in a small general store on Twiggs st., and today that newspaper, the San Diego Union, has bought its birthplace and turned it into a small newspaper museum.

CALIFORNIA

The **Historical Museum** displays a model of Old Town in 1870. A collection of horse-drawn vehicles fills Seeley Stables. The old schoolhouse is worth looking at as well.

The Presidio is a gentle uphill walk from Old Town – there's no need to get in your car again. The **Serra Museum** sits on the site of the original mission within the bounds of the old presidio. A replica of the original mission, the museum is the headquarters for the San Diego Historical Society and features exhibits from the Indian, Spanish and Mexican periods.

Coronado

It is a beautiful drive from downtown San Diego to the peninsula of Coronado, along the **Coronado Bridge** which curves across the bay like a ribbon lifted by the breeze. The centerpiece of Coronado, which is a small separate community once reached only by ferry or a long southern detour, is the **Hotel del Coronado**. Built in 1887 as a seaside resort, this multi-turreted and gilded masterpiece has hosted royalty, dignitaries and American presidents from Benjamin Harrison to Ronald Reagan. The hotel has also been used as a location for filming. The lobby and main dining room are dazzling. Feel free to wander, especially in the Hall of History, where old newspaper clippings tell the story of a bygone age.

In the neighborhood there are several stately turn of the century mansions. **Silver Strand State Park**, south of Coronado, has some nice beaches on the bayside. The Coronado **Municipal Beach**, comprising virtually the whole shore, is a popular swimming beach.

Point Loma

At the tip of Point Loma, the **Cabrillo National Monument** juts south into the Pacific. Juan Rodriguez Cabrillo was the first to discover and enter San Diego Bay, which he described as a harbor "closed and very good", and the natives who greeted the ships were "comely and large".

In the visitor center there are exhibits on Cabrillo and the main features of the park; the Bayside Trail winding down to the eastern shore; the tidepools pounded by Pacific surf along the western shore, the 1859 lighthouse and the whale overlook. The visitor center presents a regular schedule of programs guided by rangers. (Open daily 9am-5:15pm. Tel. 293-5450.)

The monument is a prime spot to observe the annual southern migration of the Gray Whales, which occurs between late December and the end of February. The whales pass Point Loma on their way from the Arctic Ocean to the lagoons of Baja California, where the pregnant females bear their calves. From the overlook the whales are visible beyond the kelp beds. During the migrations rangers present programs on the natural history of the whales.

The rhythms of marine life can be more closely observed among the rocky tidepools on the monument's Pacific shore. Best visited during the low tides of autumn, winter and spring, the pools allow glimpses of anemones, limpets, starfish, crabs and an occasional octopus.

CALIFORNIA

On the western edge of Point Loma, north of the national monument, begin the beautifully sculpted Sunset Cliffs, paralleled by Sunset Cliffs Boulevard. The shoreline here is rippled with tidepools, and is particularly beautiful at sunset.

Ocean Beach, further north, is a favorite teenage hangout and surfing beach where surfboards can be rented. The municipal pier is well-known for its fishing, and boards can be rented here too. During the day, it seems that all the radios on the beach are tuned in to the same punk station, and at night the dark beach glitters with bonfires. Newport Avenue, the main drag for a few blocks, has some "down-home" restaurants which serve generous and reasonably priced breakfast and lunch specials. Lodging on Newport is sparse and not especially appealing.

Mission Bay

Mission Bay Park, a small resort just north of the airport, is a maze of waterways and islands. Its attractions include shoreline walks, swimming, sports fishing, boating and cycling. Some luxury hotels perch over the water. Just off I-5, along the eastern edge of Mission Bay, is a visitor information center, which is clearly marked from the highway.

Along the narrow peninsula extending north from the bay, one can take a walk either along the bay side or the ocean side. Try to plan it for sunset. A stern-wheeler plies the waters between the Bahia Hotel, near the southern end of this strip, and the Catamaran Hotel at the northern end.

Sea World is the star attraction of Mission Bay, and Shamu the killer whale is the star of Sea World. (Open 9am-dusk daily, summer season until 10pm. Adults $11.95; seniors and ages 3-11, $8.95. Special facilities for the handicapped. Tel. 226-3901; or in Los Angeles, Tel. 714-826-7213.) In addition to the elaborate animal shows there are collections of animals including sharks and a colony of penguins in a simulated arctic environment. The coral reefs and the fish among them are dazzling. Hydrofoil and other rides are available. Various touring companies serve Sea World, as do public buses. If you are arriving by car, take the exit west from I-5 on Sea World Drive.

On the ocean side of Mission Bay, **Mission Beach** and **Pacific Beach** are two more links in the chain of beautiful swimming beaches. **Ocean Front Walk** is a popular stretch for jogging and cycling.

La Jolla

Academia and entrenched wealth form a strange blend in La Jolla, a beautiful semi separate community perched on its own small promontory and beach north of the city center. The **University of California at San Diego (UCSD)** is located here. The town is famous for its small sea cave and the adjacent cove which is a favorite scuba diving spot. **Windansea** and **Tourmaline** are both popular surfing and swimming beaches. Expensive boutiques, galleries and restaurants line **Prospect Avenue** above the beaches.

*C*ALIFORNIA

Leaping dolphins

The **La Jolla Museum of Contemporary Art**, is devoted to the trends of minimal, pop, abstract, modern and post-modern art. (700 Prospect ave. Open Tues., Thurs. and Fri. 10am-5pm; Wed. 10am-9pm; Sat. and Sun. 12:30-5pm. $2 admission, $1 for seniors and students.) The **Mingei International Museum of World Folk Art** has an eclectic collection of folk arts and crafts as well as programs in folk music. Don't let the setting, a

CALIFORNIA

shopping mall, thwart you. (4405 La Jolla Village dr. Open Tues.-Sat., 11am-5pm, Sun., 2-5pm. Donations Tel. 453-5300.)

North of the bluffs, along North Torrey Pines Rd, is the **Torrey Pines Glider Port**, where hang-gliders gracefully leap into nothingness. The less adventurous can take some great photos here.

UCSD consists of four separate colleges on one campus, each college with its own theme and architecture. Attached to the University is the famous **Scripps Institution of Oceanography**, one of the finest oceanographic research centers in the world. Its aquarium and museum present a fascinating insight into the marine world, through such devices as its tidepool models. (8602 La Jolla Shores Dr. Open daily 9am-5pm. Admission free. Tel. 452-6933.)

On North Torrey Pines Rd., the strange jutting corners of concrete belong to the **Salk Institute for Biological Studies**. (Tours offered from Mon.-Fri. 10:30am-3pm.) Though research in many fields is conducted here, there is great focus upon neurological functions.

North of La Jolla on North Torrey Pines Rd, extending almost to Del Mar, is the **Torrey Pines State Reserve**. Only one other grove of the trees exists, on the Channel Island. The scraggly trees grow in strangely sculpted beds of eroded sandstone. It is pleasant hiking among the trees and along the beach. (Tel. 755-2063.)

Accommodations

Hotel Circle, on both sides of I-8 just east of the junction with I-5, is just that: a circle with about as many standard hotels, motels, and coffee shops as you'll want to see at once. You can find just about anything you want here, from a Motel 6 and several equivalents, to the mini-kingdom of the *Town and Country Hotel*, where attendants on golf carts drive you to your room.

Groupings of resort hotels are found along the coast from Coronado in the south to La Jolla in the north, with many centered around Mission Bay and Mission Beach. The star of all these is the *Hotel del Coronado*, dating from 1887. Two man-made islands, Shelter Island and Harbor Island, offer boating and marina activities, and both have stylish restaurants and hotels. Harbor Island is just south of the airport.

The downtown area has some old residential hotels as well as newly refurbished luxury hotels such as the *U.S. Grant*. Some of the old residentials may seem like bargains, but location is crucial; be wary of anything too far south of Broadway.

The neighborhood around the train station is better. East of downtown, on El Cajon blvd., toward San Diego State University, there are many inexpensive motels.

San Diego has some bed and breakfast inns, but not in the same profusion as smaller cities up north. A referral service can help you find one: *San Diego Bed & Breakfast Register*, P.O. Box 22948. San Diego 92122. Tel. 560-7322 or 453-6745.

CALIFORNIA

Hotel Churchill (B&B) 827 C St., 92101. Tel. 234-5186. Toll-free in-state Tel. 800-621-5650, then 168-802. About 100 rooms, centrally situated in downtown. A variety of rooms. $40 and up.

Hotel del Coronado, 1500 Orange ave., Coronado 92118. Tel. 135-6111. The king of hotels, the hotel of kings. Its restaurants are ranked among the best in San Diego. $100 up.

Hanalei Hotel, 2770 Hotel Circle N., Tel. 297-1101. In-state toll-free Tel. 800-542-6082; out-of-state toll-free, Tel. 1-800-854-2608. Stylish, with a conspicuous Hawaiian motif. Very popular. $65 up.

Western Shores Motel, 4345 Mission Bay dr., 92109. Tel. 273-1121. Across from Mission Bay golf course, near Sea World. Short walk to the bay. $29 up.

There are five American Youth Hostels in the area: *Imperial Beach, La Mesa, Julian* and two in San Diego. For information call the main facility, 1031 India st. Tel. 239-2644.

Camping: There is no camping in the city itself. Near State Beach camping facilities are found in South Carlsbad, San Elijo, and Silver Strand south of Coronado. Tel. 237-6770. Camping reservations are made through Tel. 1-800-446-PARK.

The County Dept. of Parks and Recreation has its own system of campgrounds, many in the mountain and desert areas. Tel. 565-3600. For camping within the Cleveland National Forest, call headquarters at Tel. 293-5050.

Food

There is no shortage of restaurants here, and there is a proliferation of fast-food stands as well. There are clusters of elegant restaurants, at Shelter Island, Mission Bay and Coronado.

There are many elegant restaurants around the resort areas in San Diego, but the city is best known for its outstanding Mexican food. It abounds with excellent Mexican restaurants, some are lavishly ornamented with *pinata* and other south-of-the-border kitsch, while others are tiny downtown storefronts with formica counters, a table or two, and mouth-sizzling, belly-filling portions.

Many elegant restaurants are concentrated in the main resort areas: Mission Beach, Mission Bay, La Jolla, Coronado, and the Gaslamp Quarter. The Embarcadero has a wide range of seafood restaurants. The restaurants in La Jolla tend to be expensive, but there are some surprises.

Chuey's Cafe, 1894 Main st., Barrio Logan. A local favorite. Don't be put off by the Quonset hut. Huge portions, excellent food and reasonable prices.

Casa de Bandini, 2654 Calhoun st., in Old Town. Festive feeling amid fountains. Fantastic food.

Anthony's Seafood Mart, 555 Harbor Lane. Quick service, fresh seafood, filling and fair.

CALIFORNIA

New Peking, 807 Broadway, downtown. A great Chinese buffet, all you can eat. $2.95 until 3pm, $3.45 after 3, but still a bargain.

Garcia's of Scottsdale, 3106 Sports Arena Blvd. in Point Loma area, in Glasshouse Square. A bright Mexican setting, interesting combinations for those unfamiliar with the food. Heavy on the guacamole and sour cream.

Important Addresses And Phone Numbers

San Diego Convention and Visitor Bureau: 1200 3rd ave., suite 824. Tel. 232-3101 or Tel. 239-9696 (recording of events).
Visitors Information Center: 2688 E. Mission Bay dr. Tel. 276-8200.
International Visitor Information Center: 1st ave. & F st. (in Horton Plaza). Tel. 236-1212.
San Diego Council American Youth Hostels: 1031 India st. Tel. 239-2644. Will supply list of hostels in other areas.
Travelers Aid: Airport. Tel. 231-7361.
Travelers Aid: 1122 4th ave, suite 201. Tel. 232-7991. 24 hour service.
Tijuana Tourism and Convention Bureau: 7860 Mission Center Court, Suite 202, 92108, San Diego. Tel. 298-4105.
Old Town and State Park Info: 2645 San Diego ave. Tel. 237-6770.
San Diego County Department of Parks & Recreation: 5201 Ruffin rd. Tel. 565-3600.
National Park Information: Tel. 237-6770.
Public Transit Information: Tel. 233-3004. 5:30am-8:25pm.
Greyhound: 120 Broadway, at 1st ave. Tel. 239-9171.
Trailways: 310 W.C st. Tel. 232-2001.
Amtrak: Santa Fe Depot, 1050 Kettner blvd. Tel. 239-9021. For schedules, Tel. 800-872-7245.
Commuter Computer: Tel. 237-POOL.
Bicycling Information: Tel. 231-BIKE.
Airporter Express: Tel. 231-1123. $5-$10 for most destinations.
Beach and Surf Conditions: Tel. 225-9492.
Weather: Tel. 289-1212.
Arts/Entertainment Hotline: Tel. 234-ARTS.
Area Code: 619.

Toward Mexico

South of the town **San Ysidro** is the entrance to Mexico, an arch extending over 16 lanes of traffic, and two miles beyond that is the city of Tijuana.

Tijuana is a major international tourist attraction. Traffic floods over the border into the teeming city center. It was once a rather sleazy tourist trap, but now is much more attractive, and even if it is not absolutely authentic, it is bustling and exciting and very different to its northern neighbor San Diego.

The main street, **Avenida Revolucion**, is for seven blocks a lively gallery of tacky, cheap and gawdy displays. The **Tijuana Tourist Information Booth** is at 4th and Revolucion. At 8th and Revolucion you can see the ornate and

CALIFORNIA

gracious **Fronton Palacio**, a city landmark and the home of the fast-moving *Jai alai* games, held Fri.-Wed., throughout the year, with *pari-mutuel* betting. On some of the side streets, and on **Constitucion**, which parallels the main street, the shops are smaller and geared more to locals than tourists.

If you search through the trinkets, some good handicrafts can be found: bright tiles, hand-tooled leather, pottery etc. With the city's status as a free port, foreign imports such as French perfumes and Belgian glass can be more easily acquired.

Tijuana has two bullrings. **El Toro**, just south of downtown, presents fights each Sunday from spring through fall. **Plaza Monumental**, five miles west of downtown toward the ocean is second in size only to one in Mexico City. Thoroughbred and greyhound racing at the **Hippodrome**, south of El Toreo, is also a major attraction.

Ensenada is famous for its sports fishing. It is about 70 miles south of Tijuana on the Baja Peninsula in a protected harbor, and is accessible from Route 1. The pace is relaxed and quiet compared to Tijuana. **Punta Banda**, at the tip of the bay's southern promontory, is famous for the sea geyser shooting up due to the power of the surf against the coast.

East of Tijuana along Mexican Route 2 is **Mexicali**, the capital of Baja, and comparable in size to Tijuana. It can also be reached by Route 80 on the California side, as the highway passes through Calexico. Without Tijuana's colorful hustle, it still has many restaurants, shops and local entertainment.

How to get there
San Diego Metropolitan Transit buses, and a light rail trolley head for the border, and from there cabs are available to Tijuana, for about $1. The trolley leaves from the Amtrak depot at Santa Fe Station. Mexicoach and Greyhound have daily service to Tijuana, and Grayline operates tours.

Border Formalities
Holders of U.S. citizenship do not require a visa for travel to Mexico. If you travel more than 75 miles, or stay in Mexico more than 72 hours, a tourist card is required. This is obtainable free from the Mexican Consulate or Mexican Government Tourist Office, for those with proper U.S. identification. Citizens of other countries will also require tourist cards, and sometimes also a visa. They should inquire at the Mexican Consulate. To re-enter the United States, foreign citizens must have valid multiple entry visas and passports, except Canadians, who need only show proof of Canadian citizenship.

Auto insurance
If driving in Mexico, auto insurance is essential; an accident can be a criminal offence. Insurance for Mexico must be handled by a Mexican agency. No American or foreign agent is licensed to sell auto insurance for Mexico. A number of Mexican firms have offices in San Diego. Some can be found on the road to San Ysidro. The Convention and Visitors' Bureau in San Diego can also suggest firms.

CALIFORNIA

Useful Addresses And Phone Numbers

Mexican Consulate: 225 Broadway, Suite 225, San Diego 92101. Tel. 619-231-8414, or 125 Paseo de la Plaza, Los Angeles 90012. Tel. 213-624-3261.

Mexican Tourist Office: 600 B st., Suite 1220 San Diego 92101. Tel. 619-236-9314, or 9701 Wilshire blvd., Beverly Hills 90212. Tel. 213-274-6315.

CALIFORNIA

The South Coast: From San Diego to Los Angeles

From the area north of the San Diego urban area, to Orange County and the lower reaches of the Los Angeles urban octopus, the coastal highway is studded with small beach towns. A string of state beaches and state parks line the shoreline, some with camping facilities. Inland rise the mountains, sometimes reaching forward to the beach, sometimes receding.

Northeast of San Diego, near Escondido and still in San Diego County, is the **Wild Animal Park**, run under the same auspices as the celebrated San Diego Zoo. (Open from late June through Labor Day, Mon.-Thurs. 9am-6pm, Fri.-Sun. 9am-8pm. After Labor Day to late June, 9am-4pm. Ticket package including monorail and all amenities is $10.70 adults, $6.20 age 3-15, free under 2. Admission without monorail available. Tel. 619-234-6541, 480-0100.) Here, however, it is the visitor who is enclosed while traversing the animals's turf. A monorail carries visitors along the five-mile tour through this 1800 acre reserve, where herds of animals from Africa, Asia and Australia roam through open environments similar to their own. During the summer there are evening trips as well.

The Animal Park can be reached from San Diego by following the I-15 north, to Via Rancho Parkway, and then following the signs. Public transportation is available from Escondido. Gray Line offers tours from San Diego which include the admission and monorail.

Oceanside is an ordinary beach town, a watering hole for the Marines stationed at adjacent Camp Pendleton. Route 76, heading northeast from town into the mountains, climbs into some beautiful, rugged country and passes some interesting sites. Five miles up the road, **Mission San Luis Rey** overlooks a lovely valley. Founded in 1789, this was at one time the largest and most populous Indian mission in both Americas. In mid-July stop in for the fiesta. (Tel. 619-757-3250.)

Further up on Route 76 is the **San Antonio de Pala Mission**, a branch of the mission down below. The rough-hewn building with the Indian paintings still extant gives one a better impression of what life must have been like here than the slicker renovations in other missions. There is a cemetery with hundreds of unmarked Indian graves.

The road dips into the Pauma Valley and winds upward toward the silver dome of the **Palomar Observatory**. (Open daily 9am-4pm. Tel. 619-742-3476.) Operated by the California Institute of Technology, it holds some of the biggest and most advanced telescopes in the world. The tour includes a museum and exhibit hall presenting celestial photographs. It is

CALIFORNIA

Mission San Juan Capistrano

advisable to bring a sweater as the dome is kept at night-time temperatures.

The **Palomar Mountain State Park** and the adjoining **Cleveland National Forest** contain low canyons and high peaks, pine forests, and several short nature trails. Camping facilities are available. Headquarters are in Escondido. (Tel. 745-2421.)

North of Camp Pendleton and San Clemente (home of Richard Nixon's "Western White House") are San Juan Capistrano and Dana Point. **Mission San Juan Capistrano**, built in 1777, is famous for its legendary swallows. The swallows return each year, from the beginning of March. The complex is set around two colorful, peaceful courtyards. The seventh mission in Father Junipero Serra's chain of missions, the mission includes the **Serra Chapel**, the oldest building in California and the only chapel in which it is known that Serra officiated. (31882 Camino Capistrano. Open 7am-5pm, $2 admission. Tel. 714-493-1424.)

The nearby old **Santa Fe depot** is used today by Amtrak. The old fixtures, railroad cars and even advertisements have been preserved, and a bar has been opened. Between the station and the mission is the *Green Burrito*, a small stand serving delicious and filling meals.

The harbor at Dana Point, is well known among fishermen. Dana Wharf also has a protected beach especially good for young children. For the first three weekends in February, the Dana Point Harbor Festival of Whales has various programs and tours to celebrate the southern migration of the grey whales.

CALIFORNIA

Laguna Beach

Laguna Beach, famous for its art colony, elegance, and stunning cliff and beach, is the main attraction on the coast between San Diego and Los Angeles. The high chaparral hills here slope down to a line of bluffs, beaches and coves.

Perched in the hills there are gorgeous homes, matched only by the those built into the bluffs above the beaches. Along the Pacific Coast Highway and its side streets are clustered galleries, shops, restaurants and hotels. Sea breezes temper the summer heat, and in winter the temperature rarely drops below 50 degrees Fahrenheit (10 degrees Centigrade).

How to get there

The coastal approach to Laguna Beach is pretty and hilly from both north and south, and is punctuated with state beaches. From the north this route can become congested as far south as Newport Beach during the afternoon rush hours. For a faster route from Los Angeles, take I-5 south (called the Santa Anna Freeway in the L.A. region) and exit west on Laguna Canyon Road, which winds through some gentle hills into town. By freeway, Laguna Beach is little more than an hour from Los Angeles, and just over half-an-hour from Disneyland. Laguna Beach is a lovely place for a relaxing evening after a full day's stimulation in the magic kingdom.

The **Laguna Beach Municipal Transit System** reaches the beaches and major points in town. Tickets are 50 cents, seniors over 65 free. During the summer festival season special tram routes connect the various parking lots with the town.

Thousands of visitors flock to the town in July and August for the Laguna Beach **Festival of Arts**. Launched during the Depression as a desperate move by local struggling artists to arouse interest in their work, the festival has since become an established local institution. The festival includes the **Pageant of the Masters**, in which local residents pose in live versions of great artistic masterpieces.

Concurrently held are the **Sawdust Festival** (which began as an alternative to the main festival and places emphasis on crafts) and **Art-a-Fair**. It seems that on every holiday there is some sort of art or crafts fair.

The whole town buzzes during the festival season and the galleries and studios do a brisk business. A large concentration of them are found on the 300 block of the North Coast Highway. On the first Saturday of every month a **Gallery Row Art Walk** is held on this block between 4-7pm, where one can meet local artists. Refreshments are usually served.

Unlike the beach cities to the north and south, Laguna Beach is not just one stretch of beach. Its beaches are separate scalloped strands, with coves, cliffs, tide pools and arches carved by the waves. The surf and breaking waves vary from beach to beach.

One of the prettiest is **Crescent Bay** near the northern boundary at the end

CALIFORNIA

"Art" in Laguna Beach

of Crescent Bay dr. (turn west at the 76 gasoline station). Steep stairs lead down to a secluded beach with tide pools at the northern end.

Further south, **Heisler Park**, has winding footpaths among beautiful flowers. The paths follow the bluffs and provide a great overlook for sunsets. Toward the end of December, it is a popular spot for watching the grey whales as they migrate south from the Arctic region.

From the center of town, where Broadway meets the coast highway, to the

CALIFORNIA

south, the shore is lined with restaurants and hotels. **Victoria Beach**, toward the southern end of town, is a secluded public beach that is often almost empty. The tall tower, that looks as if has been transplanted from a medieval castle, houses a spiral staircase for a house atop the cliff. Park on the highway by Victoria drive and follow the street to the steep stairs descending to the beach.

Accommodations

Pleasant lodgings can be found in town, but they are fairly expensive. For more standard and less expensive motels, head north or south of town, or inland toward the freeways and the more suburban areas of Orange County.

The closest beach camping is found in the south, at three state beaches in the area of Dana Point and San Clemente. These, however, tend to be crowded.

Casa Laguna Inn, 2510 S. Coast Highway, Laguna Beach 92651. Tel. 714-494-2996. Toll-free in-state, Tel. 1-800-233-0449. A small verdant maze of balconies and patios, this B&B inn at the south end of town is very classy. Each room is furnished differently. Breakfasts are home-made. There are many personal touches, such as complimentary afternoon tea and wine. It is located near secluded Victoria Beach. Starting at $85 single/double. For a weekly stay the last night is complimentary.

Hotel Laguna, 425 S. Coast Highway, Laguna Beach 92651. Tel. 714-494-1151. Toll-free in-state, Tel. 1-800-524-2927. Located in the center of town right on the beach, this old hotel is a local historic landmark. Many rooms overlook the beach. Some are a bit more plain than the exterior would suggest. The location is unbeatable. Starting at $55 single, $65 double.

Food

Laguna Beach has the atmosphere of a Mediterranean resort. There is a daily influx of beach-goers, and many elegant seaside restaurants, pizza stands and delis, plus as many brands of frozen yogurt as you'll see in one place.

The White House, 340 So. Coast Highway. Tel. 494-8088. Terrific early bird specials include baked fish, lamb, chicken teriyaki or other main courses, with all the trimmings and a glass of wine, for $6.95. Sun.-Thurs. 5-7pm and Fri.-Sat. 5-6:30pm.

Renaissance Bakery and Coffee House, 234 Forest ave. The blintzes, piroshkis, strudels and borscht create a touch of Europe in the California sun. A nice place to sip a cappuchino and watch the people go by.

Useful Addresses And Phone Numbers

Area Code: 714.
Emergency: 911.
Chamber of Commerce: 357 Glenneyre st. Tel. 494-1018. This town churns out the public relations brochures and weekly visitor papers. Check through them for discount coupons for restaurants.

CALIFORNIA

Laguna Beach Municipal Transit: Tel. 497-3311, ext. 246.
Orange County Transit District: Tel. 636-RIDE.

Orange County

The sense of remoteness in Laguna Beach is deceptive. The development of Orange County creeps steadily along. The acres of orange groves have long since been uprooted. A bastion of arch-conservative politics (the John Birch Society is well-entrenched in local politics), the area is also a center for the sprouting of instant towns. The closest thing to a downtown is the newest shopping mall. Only along the coast have the towns clung to any sense of separate identity, and these are primarily enclaves for the affluent.

Newport Beach is a few miles north of Laguna Beach, separated by a long open stretch of beach. The bay between the narrow **Balboa Peninsula** and the mainland is a beautiful harbor filled with gleaming pleasure crafts in the dark blue waters. Partway along the extremely narrow peninsula is a cluster of trendy bars, eateries and shops in a simulated old-time carnival surrounding. The streets and wharfside walks are bedecked with lights on a summer evening and filled with young people whose tans seem to shine in the dark. A vintage ferry makes the short run between the peninsula and **Balboa Island**, where a few more cafes and restaurants line the street and expensive houses are packed tightly together. Costing a mere 20 cents per standing passenger, the ride is refreshing and especially beautiful on a balmy summer night when the strings of multi-colored lights are reflected upon the water.

The Balboa Peninsula's famous **Wedge** is a section of beach that draws ten-foot waves, surfers who challenge them, and spectators who hang-ten vicariously. Walk out toward the end of the long rock breakwater extending from the end of the peninsula, and you can feel the surge and rush of the ocean around you.

Huntington Beach has been the cutting edge of California's surf scene, ever since the days of the Beach Boys. Even today brightly-painted surfboard shops line the coastal highway, and barefoot kids in bathing suits ride their bicycles clasping their boards under their arms. The beach at night still sparkles with bonfires, and the bar scene is still young and rowdy. Today the up-and-coming bands play new wave and their hair is purple.

For the more sedate, strolling to the end of **Huntington Pier** is a popular past-time. At the end is the appropriately named **End Cafe**, a nice place to sit, have a bite, sip coffee and gaze at the sunset blazing before you.

Disneyland

Besides the beaches, the main reason to linger in Orange County is a visit to Disneyland. Opened in 1955, with a 1950s vision of fantasy and the future, this amazing bubble of imagination in Orange County still draws almost 12 million visitors a year. Even with the opening of Disneyworld in Florida, the original still enchants and fascinates.

*C*ALIFORNIA

Fantasy at Disneyland

Disneyland is located at 1313 Harbor boulevard in Anaheim; you won't miss the signs, and the Matterhorn is visible from the street. Summer hours are Sun.-Fri. 9am-midnight, Sat. 9am-1am. In spring, Mon.-Fri. 10am-6pm, Sat.-Sun. 9am-7pm. For the weeks surrounding Christmas and Easter, check for special hours. In the fall and winter, closed Mon.-Tues. Admission $17, discount for children 12 and under, and for seniors on Thurs.-Fri. Tel. 714-999-4565 or Tel. 213-626-8605.

One quality that has perpetuated Disneyland's excellence is the tremendous detail with which larger visions are carried out. The fantasy is complete in every facet. In frontierland, every prop down to the garbage cans blends in with the wild west. And in the exhibits themselves the attention to detail is incredible, down to the spider webs in the Haunted House.

CALIFORNIA

Disneyland – All creatures strange and wonderful

The park is divided into seven areas: Adventureland, Bear Country, Fantasyland, Frontierland, Main Street USA, New Orleans Square, and Tomorrowland. The main gate leads into Main Street, which is the trunk from which the other theme lands branch out. Tours which take two-and- a-half hours are available to acclimate the novice to this new world. Alternately, one can go on the **Disneyland Railroad** around the park's perimeter for an overview. After the full circle you can remain on board, and then disembark where you please.

Disneyland seems to have everything, including a place to park the kids and the dog. The restaurants are very reasonably priced. They range from burger stands to an elegant full-course restaurant on a Louisiana bayou in perpetual night, complete with fireflies.

You can easily spend a full day here, and you will need more time if you want to see everything. During the summer the lines for popular attractions can easily be over an hour long. With extended hours during the summer, you might consider arriving in the late afternoon, when the heat and crowds begin to ease, and then staying late. Actually, one of the best days you can choose for Disneyland is Christmas, when you can practically walk right into any ride or show without waiting at all.

To reach Disneyland by car, exit south on Harbor boulevard from the Santa Anna Freeway, or north from the Garden Grove Freeway. Disneyland is accessible by public bus from downtown Los Angeles, Long Beach and various points in Orange County. Check with the appropriate municipal bus system for details. The Gray Line offers Disneyland tours, and Airport Service connects with Disneyland from the Los Angeles, Long Beach and John Wayne Airports.

CALIFORNIA

Knott's Berry Farm

Knott's Berry Farm, in Buena Park, is older and larger than Disneyland, but its upstart neighbor left it far behind. (8039 Beach blvd, Buena Park. In summer, Sun.-Thurs. 10am-10pm, Fri. 10am-midnight, Sat. 10am-1am. Winter hours vary, call to verify. Admission $12.95, discounts for children 3-11 and for seniors. Tel. 714-220-5200). This amusement park started as a berry farm, and even now it emphasizes the old-time rural flavor, and the tone is one of nostalgia for Americana.

There is the hold-up of the Butterfield Stagecoach, the ride down the old-time logging flume, and a recreated Fiesta Village and Roaring Twenties scenario. Some of the rides, such as the roller-coaster called Montezooma's Revenge, are real stomach turners. The park's restaurant is known for its good and reasonably priced fried chicken dinners.

COYOTE
The coyote belongs to the wolf family, but in appearance looks more like a fox, although it is bigger. Its fur is golden brown and coarse. Its habitat is the desert regions of the western U.S.A.

CALIFORNIA

The California Desert

Hemming in the packed urban areas of Los Angeles and San Diego from the east are several mountain ranges, and beyond them lies the desert. The California desert actually comprises the bulk of what we generally refer to as Southern California. The desert reaches the borders of Nevada and Arizona in the east, extends south to the Mexican border and beyond, and a narrow piece of it stretches to the northeast beyond the eastern slope of the Sierra Nevada.

There are two deserts, actually: the high **Mojave Desert** to the north, and the lower and more southern **Sonoran Desert**. There are great differences between the two in rainfall, topography and the range and complexity of ecological systems. The two California deserts are actually the western fringe of the massive desert that encompasses the entire southwestern part of the country and continues into Mexico. The California deserts, far from being one flat and uniform bloc of desolation, are punctuated by sharp, truncated mountain ranges, dry canyons, playas, plateaus, and miles of huge sand dunes that give the impression of an ocean just over the horizon. Streams are usually dry and waterholes few.

The desert is filled with numerous life forms and communities, which are variegated and specialized, each using ingenious methods to cope with the harsh environment – which is nevertheless delicately balanced and easily scarred. Time and the cycles of life redefine themselves here. Life lies patient and dormant in this parched land. After a rainfall, the desert bursts into a profusion of colors and shapes, as flowers open and plants live through their life cycles in accelerated rhythms. Animal life is hard to detect in daylight, but it fills the desert at night, and the morning sands are stitched with tracks.

Man penetrated this harsh region at least 12,000 years ago, and as early as 60,000 years ago according to some scholars. Small groups lived by the shores of ancient lakes. As the lakes dried up about 7000 years ago, the groups became semi-nomadic. In families and clans they wandered the high and low deserts. Strict rules and taboos on relationships and marriage held the groups together in the vastness of the desert. Precursors of the modern Indian tribes left behind huge drawings and petroglyphs depicting hunting scenes and creation myths.

Struggles in the desert continue today, but they are not struggles of survival fought by the Indians or by early pioneers crossing and trying to settle the desert. Today the fate of the desert itself is in question.

There are thousands who head for the desert every weekend with dune buggies and other exotic off-the-road vehicles to release their tensions ripping through the sands at Imperial Dunes and other places. For ranchers

CALIFORNIA

the desert provides a place to grow winter vegetables under irrigation. Mining companies want to mine gold, gypsum, tungsten and other minerals found in the desert. For the military, the isolation, open space and steady weather provide excellent conditions for field exercises and weapon testing. Environmentalists and scientists want to preserve as much of the delicate desert environment as possible, while archeologists rush to locate and study ancient sites before they are defaced or bulldozed. Chemical companies and other industries which have moved out from the urban area emit noxious clouds into the pristine sky, and energy companies and research firms conduct experiments using geothermal, solar and wind energy (forests of propellered towers can be seen on the way to Palm Springs). Meanwhile, developers and speculators urge the building of more suburban neighborhoods, more shopping centers and more resorts.

Suburban areas have crossed through the passes of the San Bernardino and San Gabriel Mountains into the western fringes of the Mojave desert, as the urban amoeba of Los Angeles spreads.

Most of the 25 million acres of desert is currently in federal hands and under the juristiction of the Bureau of Land Management which in 1980 formulated a giant regional planning program that designates virtually every inch of this seeming emptiness for some purpose or other. Even today the various conflicting interest groups are interpreting the results of the huge project, each of course with its own interests and belief at heart.

Even today there is something foreboding, isolated and wild about the desert. Sprinkled throughout its immensity are escapists and pioneers. Children in some towns still attend one-room school houses, and ranch hands drive a hundred miles for a hoe-down at the general store. Right-wing survivalists and left-wing revolutionaries have hidden and trained here. Cargos of Mexican marijuana are smuggled into clandestine airstrips here. Squatters and hermits, fugitives and religious cultists seek refuge in the desert.

It is still possible, however, for the average traveler to find a pocket of solitude in the desert and wilderness, and to glimpse a fascinating and primeval world. Those who camp here, either on the roadside or on wilderness trails, will find some sparsely visited yet spectacular landscapes. Even on a one-day visit, the city dweller can enjoy the silence, stillness and elongation of time which is uniquely the desert's.

The fall and the spring are great times for a desert visit. The weather is more moderate, the roads and campgrounds uncrowded. In the spring you can glimpse green hills and valleys that will be parched in a month's time.

In addition to the largest and best-known desert preserves – Death Valley National Park, Joshua Trees National Monument and Anza-Borrego Desert State Park – there are smaller parks, some quite remote, featuring some unusual land form, caverns or hot springs. Other areas are protected by various state or federal agencies, and offer opportunities for fishing, recreational boating, hiking etc. For the tourist these are likely to be of

CALIFORNIA

secondary interest. If by chance you are entering California from Arizona or Nevada, you will cross into the lower desert across the natural boundary of the Colorado River. That once raging water course which carved the Grand Canyon has at this section been tapped and channeled, largely to supply water for Los Angeles and the surrounding area. Several artificial lakes were formed by the damming of the river. The largest is **Lake Havasu** which, since its creation in 1938, has become a recreational center for both Arizona and California. Along 16 miles of its shoreline is **Lake Havasu State Park**, which offers a welcome respite for anyone traveling from the east. At **Lake Havasu City** on the Arizona side there are many motels and tourist facilities and... the famous **London Bridge**, constructed in 1831 and moved block by block to the desert resort town.

The **Providence Mountains State Recreation Area**, off I-40 about 40 miles west of the Arizona border, is a popular backpacking area, with its 4000-foot overlooks gazing upon the desert. The **Winding Stairs Cavern** and **Mitchell Caverns** discovered by prospector and homesteader Jack Mitchell in 1929, contain a subterranean garden of stalactites and stalagmites.

Some 12 million acres of public land are administered by the BLM. There are some primitive BLM campsites with water, which cost $2 per night. In addition, camping is allowed on these public lands 300 feet from any road that is not closed. The BLM lands also include scenic areas. A free recreation guide-map is available from the BLM at 1695 Spruce st., Riverside, 92507.

Some Tips for Desert Traveling

Population centers and tourist facilities can be few and far between in the desert. Sources of drinking water are limited. Temperatures may shift from 100 degrees Fahrenheit (37 degrees Centigrade) to freezing within a day. A trip to the desert may require a little thought and planning, but do not let that stop you.

The intensity of the desert sun can be deceptive. Even if you feel fine in the morning, you are losing liquid, up to a gallon a day. In the midst of a pleasant hike you may suddenly be hit by the signs of dehydration – weakness, headaches, dizziness and fatigue. By then, drinking will not help. Drink plenty of water **before** you set out on a walk or car tour, and take plenty with you to drink along the way. Coffee and alcohol do not count, as they actually dehydrate the body.

If you are driving through the desert keep extra water on hand both for drinking and for the radiator. Fill the gas tank when it reaches the halfway mark just to be safe, as the heat and general driving conditions can be a strain on the engine and burn extra fuel.

Wear a broadrimmed hat, sunglasses, protective suncream and layers of loose cotton clothing. In summer as well as winter, bring a sweater for the evenings, which are cool. The desert heat can slow a walker's pace, and makes you feel exhausted, so walk in a relaxed and unstrained rhythm.

CALIFORNIA

Serious accidents involving snakes, scorpions or spiders are rare, but caution is advisable. Place your steps where rocks or logs won't overturn. Don't go prancing around in sandals. At night sleep on a groundcloth, and close your sleeping bag tight if you are not in a tent.

There are ten species of rattlesnakes in California's deserts. Self-treatment for a snake bite should be avoided if a doctor can be reached within two hours. The coyotes that slip like shadows among campsites in the evening are not dangerous; they only want food. They should not, however, be approached.

Death Valley

Although separated by only 40 miles, Mount Whitney and Death Valley are worlds apart. Whitney, the highest point in the contiguous United States, towers at about 14,500 feet, while Death Valley, at almost 300 feet below sea level, is the lowest point in the western hemisphere.

Death Valley National Park is not all valley, and far from being dead. The valley is ringed by the Panamint Mountains on the west and the Argossa range on the east, with barely a drop of rain breaching the mountain barriers. The lowest spot can be pinpointed at Badwater, 283 feet below sea level. From Telescope peak or the other peaks exceeding 10,000 feet, the depression takes on a strange other-worldliness, as does the whole valley at times. Distances become distorted, far-off points shimmer and seem deceptively near. The absolute silence and solitude can make you almost dizzy.

Average rainfall is only 2 inches per year here, but the number means nothing when a sudden storm breaks and creates violent floods down the slopes and canyons. They are spectacular, but very dangerous. After a flood the explosion of wild flowers is immediate and fantastic, like the moment when *The Wizard of Oz* turns from black-and-white to color.

In summer average tempertures exceed 115 degrees Fahrenheit (45 degrees Centigrade). Even the cooler evenings may be in the 80s, while mountain slopes are still breezy and pleasant for hiking. A hat is essential and so is plenty of drinking water. Not surprisingly, winter is the most popular season for visitors. Temperatures may hover around 60 degrees Fahrenheit, but sometimes also drop to the 30s.

Be sure to stock up on food and essentials and to fill the gas tank. Commodities are more expensive within the park than in the outlying towns. Be especially cautious with gasoline. You'll be surprised at how fast the heat, steep roads and general conditions burn fuel, so fill the tank whenever possible. There are only three gas stations in Death Valley: at Scotty's Castle in the north, Stovepipe Wells toward the west, and at Furnace Creek near the center. Keep plenty of water on hand for drinking and the radiator. Stations for radiator water are placed along the road (and marked on many park maps), but this water is not suitable for drinking.

*C*ALIFORNIA

DEATH VALLEY

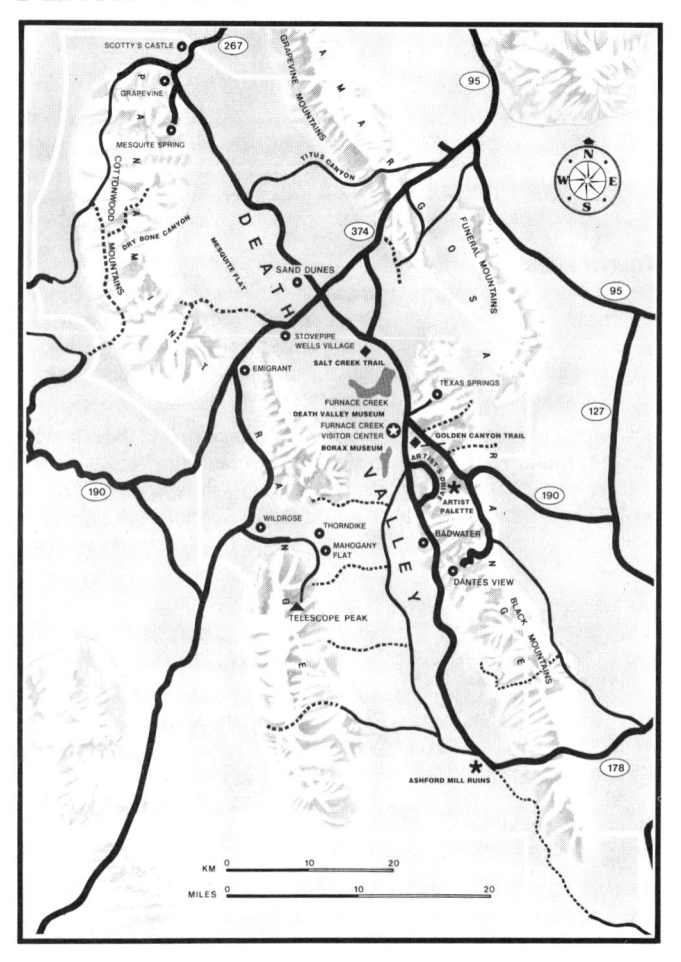

How to get there
Two main routes lead to Death Valley. From Los Angeles I-15 passes through Barstow on the way to Las Vegas, and route 127 veers north to Death Valley. Many people make a detour to the park coming to or from the gambling center. In my opinion, only rolling down a glacier into a hot spring could cause a greater shock! I-395 runs along the eastern fringe of the Sierras, and near **Lone Pine** (also the turnoff for the approach to Mt. Whitney to the west) Route 136 turns east to the desert reserve. If approaching from the east, Route 178 affords the chance to drive through the southern length of the

77

CALIFORNIA

park. For a fantastic and leisurely detour, take the winding one-way road through **Titus Canyon** from Route 374 in the northeast (across the Nevada line). Only drivers who feel confident on winding and narrow mountain roads should cross the western mountain passes to Emigrant or Wildrose. These approaches are higher than those in the east, and open up immense vistas of the scorched basin below.

Access to Death Valley without a car is extremely limited. For bus service write to: Las Vegas-Tonopah-Reno Stage Line, 922 E. Stewart ave., Las Vegas, Nevada, 89101. Amtrak and interstate buses serve Barstow and Las Vegas. Car rentals are available in both cities; reservations are advisable.

Tourist sites

Death Valley's main centers at Furnace Creek, Stovepipe Wells and Scotty's Castle can get crowded with people and trailers on holidays and long summer weekends. But there are many small roads and short, easy trails to lure you into the desert. Follow them and you'll discover hidden valleys, canyons and ancient Shoshone Indian rock carvings.

Sooner or later every visitor passes through **Furnace Creek**, the hub of the park. The **Death Valley Museum** and the **Borax Museum** feature excellent displays on the tenacity and built-in genius of desert life forms, and on the human struggle for survival here dating back thousands of years. The visitor center provides information on trails, off-road camping and desert survival in the summer.

Guided walks and auto caravans are offered in the winter. There are also regular evening programs. The park's private concession, based in Furnace Creek, also offers tours of the Park but for a very high price, starting from about $20 per person.

Easily accessible from Furnace Creek is the **Artist's Drive** loop, so-named for the broad palette of natural colors. Just north of Artist's Drive is the short **Golden Canyon** interpretive trail, an excellent place to get a feel for this low desert without venturing far from your car. Cautious driving on unpaved **West Side Road**, which parallels Route 178, will take you through some especially rugged and beautiful desert scenery.

Scotty's Castle is the best known man-made feature in the park. The elaborate home did not actually belong to "Death Valley Scotty". He persuaded a wealthy and ailing friend from the Midwest to build in Death Valley, and after the death of his friend, Scotty spent the rest of his life living in the castle.

From Emigrant Canyon Road on the west, a road leads to **Wildrose Canyon**, with its row of abandoned charcoal kilns constructed more than a century ago. Even in this barren wilderness, patterns of modern society held sway; the kilns were built by Chinese laborers and tended by Shoshone Indians. Beyond the kilns, at the Mahogany Flat Campground, is the trailhead for the hike to **Telescope Peak**, the highest spot in the park, offering a panoramic view across the sunken valley. Plan on a strenuous all-day hike to the summit. Once there, you'll find a stand of bristlecone pines. Although the

CALIFORNIA

age of these particular trees is not known, they belong to the oldest living species on earth. Examples of such trees in the White Mountains to the north are estimated to be 4000 years old.

Accommodations
The only private lodging in the park is the *Furnace Creek Inn and Ranch*. It is overpriced at about $50 per couple, and because of limited space, it is usually necessary to book in advance. The private portion of Furnace Creek is part amusement park, part shopping center, and is wholly abrasive in the midst of this wilderness.

The park has nine campgrounds. Three are open all year, the others during particular seasons. Check with rangers for details on roadside and trailside campsites. Overnight hikers must register first.

Around Death Valley
Facilities are cheaper in the little towns along the approaches to Death Valley. Most of the motels are of the usual cardboard cut-out variety. It is wise to check the room first. The *Little Lake Hotel* in Little Lake, on I-395 about 25 miles south of the 190 turnoff to Death Valley, is clean and friendly and has more character than many others. If approaching from I-15, try the *Armagosa Hotel* in Death Valley Junction (Armagosa), at the junction of Route 127 and 190, just east of the entrance to the park. For an unexpected bubble of culture, visit the **Armagosa Opera**, which has shows of dance and mime. Call the 619 operator and ask for Death Valley junction no. 8.

Toward Las Vegas
If you drive through the desert towards Las Vegas at night, it appears suddenly like a psychedelic Emerald City, and on closer approach the dazzling waves of light only appear more surrealistic. The city's strip, sometimes known as Las Vegas boulevard, never closes. People stand glued to the slot machines and computerized games. Old ladies dressed up like teenagers guard their spots jealously. The lights keep flashing and the money keeps flowing, most of it in one direction. The official euphemism for gambling is "gaming".

The biggest hotels and casinos and half of Nevada's population are found in Las Vegas. Lodging and food are incredibly cheap, which is part of the attraction, but the losses are all made up in the casinos.

Transportation
By air: McCarran Airport, at the southern end of the strip, is served by major national carriers.

By land: Las Vegas is easy to reach. Along I-15 from Los Angeles it is a five or six hour drive through the Mojave Desert. Bus tours called "Gamblers' Specials" leave L.A. frequently, usually early in the morning, returning late at night or the following day. They range from $5-$10 but on special offer may cost as little as $1. Tourist information centers, hotels and travel agents can

CALIFORNIA

provide details. Greyhound, Trailways and Amtrak all reach Las Vegas from L.A. but their prices are higher than the "Gamblers' Special".

Besides gambling and other forms of sin, the main activities in Las Vegas are wandering through the streets and gazing at the people playing the machines, eating, watching spectacular shows and trying out the downtown bars and discos.

The major hotels with casinos include the *Aladdin, Caesar's Palace, Circus Circus, The Dunes, MGM Grand Hotel*, and *Del Webb's Sahara*. They stage spectacular shows, featuring some of the biggest names in show business. Dinner and a show in these hotels can run up a hefty bill.

Accommodations

Accommodation is easy to find. The best deals may be as low as $10, both during the week and on weekends. The buffet breakfasts, lunches and dinners are famous. Off the strip, in downtown, there are many restaurants, not quite the bargains of the casino restaurants, but still excellent.

Check through the various brochures found at the local Visitors'Center (which is right off the strip) and at the casinos and hotels, to find out about special discounts, dinner specials etc. Many motels as a matter of course offer guests coupons for breakfast, gambling, complimentary drinks, etc. As long as you keep control of your wallet, Las Vegas can provide an entertaining, dazzling and inexpensive excursion, but if you do not join in the search for El Dorado, the glitter and novelty soon wear thin.

From Las Vegas, it is an easy trip to the imposing **Hoover Dam**, which created **Lake Mead** when the Colorado River was dammed. Grayline runs tours to Hoover Dam.

Important Addresses And Phone Numbers
Emergency: 911.
Area Code: 702.
Las Vegas Convention and Visitors Authority: At the Convention Center, 3150 Paradise rd. Tel. 733-2323.
Greyhound: 3000 Las Vegas blvd. (at the Stardust Hotel on the strip). Tel. 734-6961. Also 200 Main st. Tel. 382-2640. Open 24 hours.
Trailways: 217 4th st. Tel. 385-1411.
Amtrak: 1 N. Main st. Tel. 384-3540. Buses run very frequently along the strip.

Joshua Trees National Monument

California's two large deserts, the Mojave and the Sonoran, merge within **Joshua Trees National Monument**, located 50 miles east of Palm Springs. Few areas better illustrate the sharp and subtle contrasts in the vegetation, wildlife and landscape of the two distinct desert systems. Within the compact borders of this shifting desert region, the arroyos, canyons, granite monoliths and steep cliffs create a sharp mosaic, intense in its beauty and delicate in ecological complexity.

CALIFORNIA

The Joshua Trees are abundant at the higher elevations, in the western portion of the park. The tree, a giant yucca, received its common name when Mormons heading west were reminded upon seeing them of Joshua raising his arms as he led his people to the promised land. With a fiery sunset as backdrop, it feels eerie to see a landscape full of twisted, distored human-like silhouettes frozen in dance around rock domes and outcroppings.

Joshua Trees is usually entered just north of I-10, east of Palm Springs. It is far enough from Palm Springs and the other resort centers to seem wild and isolated, yet close enough for a day's excursion. For a leisurely unusual drive, approach the park from the forest-covered San Bernardino Mountains. Take Route 38 to Route 18. Follow the meandering curves into the desert below you, and then head southeast on Route 247 to the park itself. The contrast as you wind down from mountain to desert is stunning.

Like other desert parks, Joshua Trees is difficult to cover without a car. Rentals can be arranged in Palm Springs and Indio. Fill up on gas as there is no fuel in the park.

Public transportation is limited at best. *Desert Stage Lines* runs from Palm Springs to Twenty-nine Palms. From there you're on your own. Tel. 367-3581.

The **Oasis Visitor Center** at **Twenty-nine Palms** features displays that explain the natural and human history of this haunting region. Information is available and the staff are helpful. In the midst of this seeming desolation, the oasis is a haven for birds. A self-guiding nature trail starts here. Ranger-led walks, hikes and campfire talks are offered primarily in spring and fall. Information is posted on the campground bulletin boards, at the Oasis and Cottonwood visitor centers, and at the ranger stations in the park. Drinking water is available only at the facilities at the edge of the park: Cottonwood, Oasis, and Black Rock Canyon.

The main roads penetrate into the park. One axis connects the Oasis Visitor Center in the north with the Cottonwood Visitor Center in the south. Off this splits a road to the northwest, into the rugged high desert. Several dirt roads are open to passenger cars in dry weather. The paved road to **Kets View** climbs the stark Little San Bernardino Mountains, for a beautiful view over the Coachella Valley.

There are trails here for the one-hour walker and the serious desert explorer. The **Cholla Cactus Garden** offers a short loop through a compact juxtaposition of rock formations and desert vegetation. **Pinto Basin**, in the eastern section, is almost entirely wilderness, with trails for experienced and well-equipped desert trekkers. Consult a ranger before beginning a long hike.

In the northwest section of the park, south of the entrance at the town of Joshua Tree, a short nature trail goes through Hidden Valley, a crazy jumble of piled boulders which, according to legend, once sheltered cattle rustlers and stolen herds.

CALIFORNIA

Accommodations
Joshua Trees has nine campgrounds, but no other lodging. There are campsites for overnight hikers, who should first register at a ranger station. The main center for lodging out of the park is Palm Springs. There are motels in Indio, closer than Palm Springs, and in the little towns to the north: Yucca, Joshua Tree and Twenty-nine Palms. These towns have the usual array of coffee shops as well.

Anza-Borrego Desert State Park
The gigantic Anza-Borrego Desert State Park is about a three-hour drive east of San Diego. It runs almost the entire eastern length of San Diego County from the Mexican border up to Riverside County. The largest state park in the country, it encompasses over two-thirds of all lands in California's extensive state park system. Between the 6000-foot peaks and the depressions 100 feet below sea level near the Salton Sea, lies a vast territory of sculpted desert landscape: bare mountain ridges, steep-cliffed canyons, oases, and bizarre sandstone formations. If you're lucky enough to catch a brief summer downpour you'll witness torrential and transitory waterfalls.

Within this vast desert, the diversity in life is incredible. Hundreds of native plant species range from pines to palms to cactus and to the thick-trunked elephant tree, found only here, north of the Mexican border. In addition to the rare bighorn sheep for which the park is named (*borrego*, in Spanish) there are mule deer, rarely seen mountain lions, rodents, reptiles and the flocks of birds congregating around the oases.

Over a million visitors a year visit this park. Many come just to witness the explosion of wildflowers, which can begin as early as February in the lower elevations, and which last until June in the higher ones. This park is so huge and varied, however, that even in the crowded season you can find spots to avoid the crowds and can camp virtually alone.

I-8, the super-highway following the Mexican border between San Diego and the Arizona line, runs just below the park boundary. S-22, a much slower, more circuitous route along the northern section of the park, off Route 78, offers spectacular views from the western heights. This highway passes through the town of **Borrego Springs**, surrounded by the park, and nearby Borrego Palm Canyon. These two points form the center for park activity.

The cafes and restaurants in Borrego Springs are of reasonable standard but are generally not great bargains. Commodities, not surprisingly, are more expensive than outside the park. Enter the park with as full a gas tank as possible and you might want to stock up on food.

Don't try to see the whole park. Head first for the modern **visitor center**, two miles west of Borrego Springs. The vivid audiovisual presentation and other exhibits will give some perspective to the size and diversity of the park, and the maps and guidance of the rangers will help you find your bearings and choose which section you want to explore. The center sponsors, except in summer, a full schedule of guided walks, campfire programs, lectures and

CALIFORNIA

ranger-led car caravans. There are several short, self-guiding nature trails, many spectacular turn-outs and overlooks, and the staff of the visitor center know them all.

There is a very accessible nature trail at **Borrego Palm Canyon**, climbing along a rarely flowing stream into a shady paradise of over 1000 palm trees. The nearby drive to **Font's Point** leads to a view of the strangely eroded sandstone cliffs of the Borrego Badlands.

If you follow S-22 to the east you will descend down the cliffs until you reach the Salton Sea, just outside the park boundary and about 230 feet below sea level. This is an artificial and accidental lake, caused by an overflow of the Colorado river resulting from some channeling. The winter temperatures can be comfortable, between 50-80 degrees Fahrenheit (10-26 degrees Centigrade), but you'll broil in the summer.

About 600 miles of roads traverse the hills and flatlands of Anza-Borrgeo. Besides the main scenic routes are many small dirt roads that penetrate the wilderness. Some are appropriate only for four-wheel vehicles. Check with a ranger about which roads are recommended and accessible.

There are plenty of trails for day hikes and backpacking. Hikers can follow the dirt roads as well. Again, check with a ranger for conditions and specific information. Always drink plenty of water beforehand and take plenty with you. Several canyons in the Anza-Borrego Desert State Wilderness, which is in the northwest portion of the park, are very popular with backpackers. The Pacific Crest Trail skirts the northwest corner.

Accommodations

Borrego Palm Canyon and Tamarisk Grove have well equipped campgrounds. Reservations should be made through Ticketron. The others range from less-developed to non-developed and are all on a first-come-first-serve-basis. Anza-Borrego is unique in that camping is allowed anywhere along travel routes, with no payment or permit required. It is easy to find wide open, virtually empty spaces where not one set of headlights will pierce the star-filled night.

Reservations are recommended for the motels found in Borrego Springs. For a listing of local lodgings write to the Chamber of Commerce, Borrego Springs, 92004. El Center and Smaller Ocotillo, to the southeast of the pack along I-8, also have motels. El Center in the Fertile Imperial Valley has greater variety.

Palm Springs

In Palm Springs, the annual Christmas parade is made up of golf-carts and Rolls Royces. The visitor's brochures tell which starlet Howard Hughes signed into a hotel under a pseudonym, which hotel Clark Gable honeymooned in, and what kind of fur stole Joan Crawford wore to ward off the desert chill. The hotel bellhops may wear uniforms designed by Pierre Cardin. Outside air-conditioning keeps revelers cool on the veranda while

CALIFORNIA

PALM SPRINGS

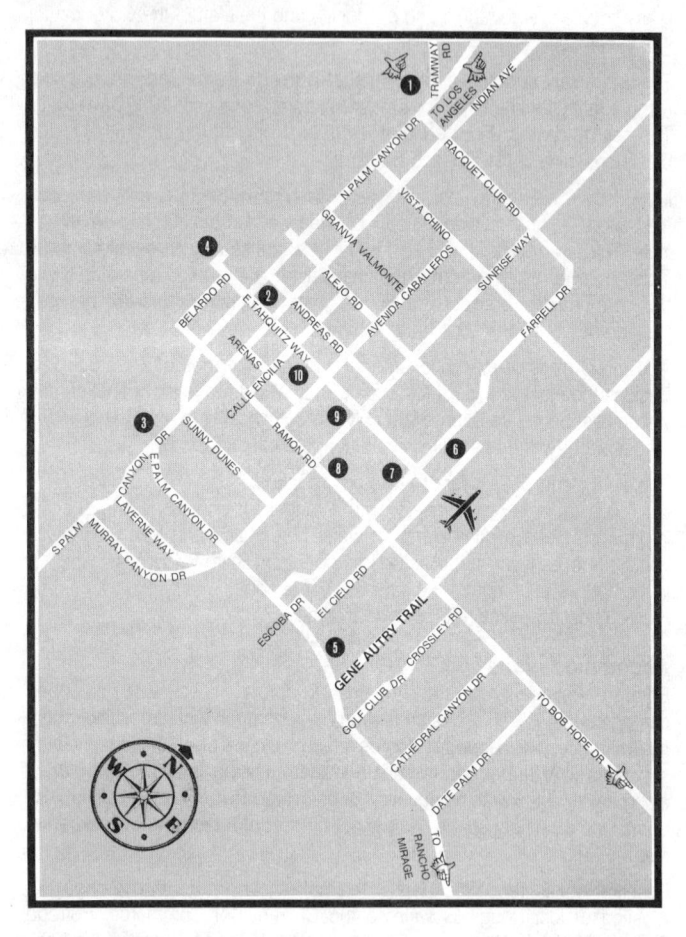

Index
1) Aerial Tramway
2) City Center
3) Desert Botanical Gardens
4) Desert Museum
5) Muncipal Golf Course
6) Palm Springs Convention & Visitors Bureau
7) Palm Springs Mall
8) Public Library
9) Palm Springs Tennis Center
10) The Courtyard

CALIFORNIA

using a mere sixty gallons of water per hour. Foreign industrialists fly in their overseas associates for one day of meetings and one night of billiards. It's the place where water is pumped across the desert not to water vegetables, as is done in other countries, but to water golf courses, 70 of them. This is the "golf course capital" of the world, so the locals say, and probably the only spot in the world where politicians and pop stars mingle.

Palm Springs, with its natural hot springs, was once a Cahuilla Indian settlement and burial ground, and then a tiny settlement with a few rail-road workers and some farmers who grew date palms. With summer temperatures reaching 120 degrees Fahrenheit (48 degrees Centigrade) and powerful winds funneling through the mountain passes in the west, a resort seemed about the last business appropriate here. However, the dryness of the heat, the nearby springs, the privacy, and the advertising campaigns of developers began first to attract movie stars, and then the people who were attracted by the movie stars. Errol Flynn, Greta Garbo, Clark Gable, Spencer Tracy and many others began to visit and then to buy homes here.

Land values soared in the once worthless desert. Following the lead of Palm Springs, the towns of the western Coachella Valley have blended into one glittery resort. Beyond the southern end of Palm Springs, Route 111 has become an endless strip of restaurants, motels and shopping centers.

With the influx of wealthy Whites, the local Indians found themselves in a struggle for survival as great as adaptation to the desert. They managed to regain legal title to their lands, but only after much of it had been built upon. Palm Springs is now laid out in a checkerboard grid of private and Indian ownership. The Cahuillas grant 99-year leases to the hotels and other establishments and collect the rents while retaining the land they need for themselves.

About a two-hour drive from Los Angeles and slightly longer from San Diego, Palm Springs spreads almost to the eastern slopes of the San Jacinto Mountains. The mountains, with their snow covered peaks, make a sharp contrast to the desert resort.

One need not be ultra wealthy to enjoy Palm Springs these days, especially during the summer. In contrast to the rest of the state, summer prices here actually drop. The summer here is not for everyone. The basin becomes one huge oven. Your nostrils sting with each breath and the perspiration pours down. You can, however, still enjoy yourself and be active because the heat is so dry. Some of the museums, restaurants and hotels are closed for vacation and repairs; the valley has a quiet, peaceful atmosphere.

How to get there
By air: The Palm Springs Municipal Airport, at the east end of town, is served by regional and California carriers (Western, Air Cal, American Eagle) as well as TWA and American Airlines, thus linking Palm Springs to the main air routes. The airport is just across the road from the Convention and Visitors Bureau.

CALIFORNIA

By land: The main route to Palm Springs from the Los Angeles region is I-10. From San Diego the most direct freeway route is like an upside-down L: I-15 north, to I-215 northeast, then to Route 60 and I-10 headed east.

Greyhound serves Palm Springs, with a terminal downtown. The nearest Amtrak connection is at Indio. From there a Greyhound can be taken to Palm Springs, but it's a tiring trip.

Desert Stage Lines provides daily bus service to Twenty-nine Palms, at the northern edge of Joshua Tree National Monument and Yucca Valley. There are weekend routes to and from L.A. and San Diego.

The Sun Bus provides local transportation. Routes extend throughout the Coachella Valley urban area. Tickets cost 50 cents, with add-ons for crossing into other zones. Operates till 6pm. Buses run downtown very often.

Well-marked bicycle trails are located throughout the city. Bicycle maps are available from the Leisure Services Dept. or from the Visitor Center.

Tourist sites

People do not visit Palm Springs for serious cultural edification. This is the kingdom where the rich play and the rest play rich. The style here is bright and casual all year round. Ties are rarely called for and orange pants are not confined to the golf course.

If you visit here in the fall or spring you'll want to get out into that open desert air for golf, tennis, jogging, hiking, all those things that healthy people do. And in the summer your main activity will be groping along the pool ledge for your beer.

The many tourist bureaus in Palm Springs and the surrounding resorts will supply you with more information about the place than you ever imagined. The **Chamber of Commerce** and the **Visitors Information Agency** are conveniently located downtown, and the **Convention & Visitors' Bureau** is very near the airport. Two periodicals – *Palm Springs Guide* and the *Desert Arts Calendar* – detail events, sites and museums. Cycling maps and lists of restaurants and accommodation with prices are available.

You do not need to stay at a five-star hotel in order to have access to athletic facilities. The Swim Center of Palm Springs is open to the public, with recreational swimming starting as early as 6am. For exact schedules, call Tel. 323-8278. The Visitor Center can provide a list of golf courses and tennis courts that are open to the public. Some private facilities open their doors to members of clubs from other areas.

Palm Canyon Drive is the center of downtown Palm Springs, paralleled by Indian Ave. Along these two streets, on either side of Tahquitz ave., are the old established shops and restaurants. They are stylish, chic and expensive. Here, as well as in the newer shopping centers, are the same stores that you find in Beverly Hills. Two early homes – the **McCallum Adobe Museum**, built in 1884, and the **Miss Cornelia White House**, 1983, are found in the Village Green, off South Palm Canyon dr., but these historical restorations are not all that interesting. The external adobe architecture is the most interesting feature here.

The nearby **Palm Springs Desert Museum** (101 Museum dr. off Tahquitz just west of Palm Canyon dr. Open Tues.-Fri. 10am-5pm. $3 adults, $1.50 seniors; students and children with adults free. Free admission the first Tuesday of every month. Closed for about a month before Labor Day. Tel. 325-71860.) This museum is a good introduction to the land, people, culture and art of the desert. The vivid natural history diaramas reveal the complexity, fragility and variety of desert ecology. The museum has a beautiful collection of Asian art left by the late actor William Holden. An extensive collection of Indian crafts from the American West includes some intricate, finely worked weavings, baskets, rugs and pottery. There are several galleries, a sculpture garden and a theatre for the performing arts. The museum provides good tours, nature walks, films, workshops and all-day ranger-guided hikes.

The most thrilling and worthwhile attraction in Palm Springs is the **Aerial Tramway**. From the foot of the San Jacinto Mountains, the 18-minute climb seems to carry you straight up above the Sonoran desert, revealing wonderful views of the valley. The granite escarpments below are sheer and almost within reach. The steel-girdered towers are anchored on tiny rock shelves with seemingly not an inch to spare. Five separate plant zones pass before your eyes. Reaching the top, at a height of 8500 feet, you suddenly stand in an alpine world of rarified air, pine forests and snow. This is a completely protected isolated area without cars or roads. This is the kind of wilderness that people drive for five hours along twisting, ice-covered roads into the Sierras to reach.

The turnoff for the tramway is on Highway 111 about a 15-minute drive from downtown Palm Springs. (The first car goes up at 10am, and 8am on weekends. From October to April the last car leaves at 7:30pm, and from May through Labor Day the last one departs at 9pm. Closed for a few weeks after Labor Day. $11.95 round-trip, $7.95 ages 3-12. Tel. 325-1391. For snow and ski conditions in winter, call Tel. 325-4227.)

The single outpost of civilization is the chalet-type bar and restaurant at the top of the tram line. The buffet dinner is moderately priced, and the desert views unmatched. The tramway's "Ride & Dine" package, costs $15.95. Open from 4pm.

Just past the chalet is a ranger station offering information, maps and regularly scheduled guided walks. Several short trails branch out from here, which lead the hiker into the mountains and still leave him time to catch the tram back down to Palm Springs. In the winter, cross-country skiers ride the tram into the mountains and follow the little-used cross-country trails, while below it may be swimming weather.

Indian Canyons, reached by toll road at the end of S. Palm Canyon dr., include several oases with large and very old stands of palms, as well as some spectacular rock formations, hiking and riding trails. Indian handiwork is sold here. The scenery has often appeared in Hollywood movies. (Open Oct-May 9am-4pm. Closed in summer. $2.50.)

CALIFORNIA

Aerial Tramway – Gateway to heaven

Desert environments are recreated on large tracts in the **Living Desert Reserve** in Palm Desert (47900 Portola ave., Palm Desert. Open Sept.-May 9am-5pm. $2.50 adults, $1.50 seniors. On Tuesday free for those under 17. Tel. 346-5694.)

There are two main walks, one short and one about five miles. Animals can sometimes be spotted pursuing their nightly activities. A special viewing platform allows one to view the desert's nocturnal creatures.

Near Palm Springs are the mineral pools of Desert Hot Springs. There are several spas, with prices ranging from $2.50-$4:
Tropical Motel Spa: 12962 Palm dr. Tel. 329-6610.
Hot Springs Spa: 10805 Palm dr. Tel. 329-6495.
Hacienda Riviera Spa: 67375 Hacienda. Tel. 329-7010.

CALIFORNIA

Also in Desert Hot Springs is **Cabot's Old India Pueblo** (67616 E. Desert View ave. Open daily except Tues. 9:30am-4:30pm. $2, seniors $1.50, ages 5-16 $1. Tel. 329-7610.)

Cabot Yerxa was a genuine desert character, who walked into the valley in 1913 with a quart of water and food in a paper bag, and remained there until his death in 1965. He built a rambling house which was inspired by the pueblos of the Southwest Indians, but became the product of his own imagination. When he started his pueblo he was an isolated settler who walked miles for water and supplies. He scavenged many of the materials. He pieced together his maze with cement, scrap lumber, and broken glass fashioned into windows, and filled it with Indian and Eskimo artifacts.

The highway from Los Angeles to Palm Springs passes the small city of

CALIFORNIA

Beauty treatment at Glen Ivy Springs

Riverside, which straddles the metropolitan area and the open, rugged desert terrain.

Downtown is the famous **Mission Inn**, a huge historic hotel built in the early California mission style, with turrets, towers and high thick-beamed ceilings. (3649 7th St. Riverside. Tel. 714-784-0300.) The place must be filled with stories and legends. Among the extensive collection of artifacts is a chair used by President Taft, illustrating how big if not great, the man was.

The almost life-sized figures on the tower clock in the courtyard revolve on the hour. Call before visiting because the hotel has been undergoing renovation.

South of Riverside are the **Glen Ivy Hot Springs**, where you can loosen your tensions as you smear yourself with red clay and look ridiculous. True believers are convinced that this mud cleanses the skin of toxins and cures everything from arthritis to acne. But in any case it feels great to let yourself bake in it until you feel like a mummy. There are pools shallow and deep, sunny and shady, some with whirlpools and some without. The spa is the favorite hide-away for a growing horde of Glen Ivy groupies. Bring your own bathing suit and towel. Pampering yourself with massages, herbal body wraps and other processes designed to transform your body are extra. Live music is performed on some summer evenings.

Glen Ivy is about an hour's drive from Los Angeles, slightly further from San Diego, and near the main route to Palm Springs. Wend your way to the section of I-15 south of the Riverside Freeway (Route 91). Just a few miles south of that junction you'll come to Temescal Canyon Road, and from there the signs will lead you to the spa, at 25000 Glen Ivy Road. Admission is a reasonable $9.75 per day, $12.75 on weekends. Tel. 714-737-4723.

CALIFORNIA

Dinny the Dinosaur

Around Palm Springs

At Indio, to the southeast, the resorts of the Coachella valley taper off and the desert farmland takes over. Here you'll see towering desert palm groves. In Indio, as they say, the fruit doesn't fall far from the tree, and the roadside stands that alternate with the groves offer every variation of a date recipe you can imagine. You can even get plain dates. The **Date Festival**, held towards the end of February is a colorful affair with an Arabian theme, and in fact the early farmers gave their towns such exotic names as Sahara. The highlight of the fair is the camel races, but the ostriches aren't bad either.

Route 74 loop brings the motorist through the same contrast of landscapes, from desert floor to snowy peaks, as seen from the aerial tram. Pick up Route 243 south from Banning on I-10, and continue south on Route 74. Or start the route at its southern end, where Route 74 heads south from Route 111, beyond Palm Springs.

At the southern end of the San Jacinto wilderness area is the small mountain resort town of **Idyllwild**, built in contemporary piney-woods. A nice place to stop for a meal or coffee. State Park and National Forest headquarters are located here. A local branch of the University of California, and the **Idyllwild School of Music and the Arts**, with its classes and regularly scheduled summer performances, help make Idyllwild idyllic. Tel. 659-2171 for performance schedules.

You know you're getting close to Palm Springs when you see the signs for **Hadley's Dates**, and then the huge green dinosaur (named Dinny) lumbering by the highway. Hadley's looks like one of those huge highway discount houses, cleared out and filled with fruits and nuts instead. A great place to browse and munch. Dinny the brontosaurus and his tyrannosaurus

CALIFORNIA

buddy are the creations of the owner of the adjacent Whell Inn. There's a museum in his belly. For both these stops take the Cabazon exit.

Accommodations

Palm Springs and the adjacent resort towns spill over with hotels and motels. The reputation for luxurious hotels is well-founded, but nearby there might be that plain old stucco, low-roofed motel with a tiny pool and plastic grass.

Winter and spring are the peak seasons here. During the roasting summer many hotels close, while many others drop their rates, often by as much as 50%. The visitor center and chamber of commerce provide full lists of accomodations.

With an abundance of vacation homes in Palm Springs, various rental agencies can arrange for rentals usually by the week or month. This can work out more economically than commercial lodging.

Lodges and cabins are more expensive than "down below", but not out of reach. For lodging information, contact Associated Idyllwild Rentals, PO Box 43, Idyllwild 92341, Tel. 659-2933. Cheaper but less interesting lodgings are found in Banning and Beaumont on I-10.

Camping can be found about an hour away from Palm Springs, in the desert of Joshua Trees National Monument to the east, or in the state park or national forest campgrounds in the San Jacinto Mountains. The national forest sites are cheaper, and some are free. Check with the forest service in Idyllwild. If you are really exhausted and/or really broke as you drive through the Palm Springs area, there are rest areas on either side of I-10 near the juncture with Route 111, with restrooms. There you will be lulled to sleep by the rumbling of passing trucks.

Palm Springs Spa, 100 N. Indian Ave., 92262. Tel. 325-1461, or 800-472-4371. An opulent and elegant Palm Springs oldie-but-goodie, this five-story hotel captured the town's hot springs. The spa is still the biggest draw. Tennis, and playing arrangements with golf courses. Prices vary with the season. Singles and Doubles start at $130 in winter, go down to $90 and up in autumn and spring; in the summer they drop to an amazing $45-$70.

Gene Autry Hotel, 4200 E. Palm Canyon dr. 92264. Tel. 328-1171, toll-free 800-4 Gene Autry in U.S. Another Palm Springs stalwart, 4.5 miles from downtown with balconies, patios and bungalows on beautiful grounds. A fine tennis resort, play arrangements with golf courses. $85 up.

For those a bit more modest in requirements or means:

Villa Royale, 1620 Indian Trail. Tel. 327-5172. A variety of rooms, each done in a different national motif: Dutch, Spanish, English, etc. $55 and up in winter, $44 and up in summer.

Pepper Tree Inn, 645 N. Indian ave. Tel. 325-9124. A popular and moderately priced B&B, but in a standard motel court setting. Some variety among the rooms. Reservations recommended even in summer. Starting at $49 in winter, $30 in summer.

CALIFORNIA

Sandstone Inn, 2395 N. Indian Ave. Tel. 325-7191. More standard, more reasonable. Some long-term residents, and budget-wise young foreigners. Starts at $30 in winter, $25 in summer. Weekly rates available.

Food

If you're looking for that cheap little two-bit hole-in-the-wall grease-coated gem of a diner in Palm Springs, forget it; it's long since been bought out. There are diverse restaurants, within a certain range – lots of steak, lobster, Italian, some high-priced delis, with a recent influx of sushi and other oriental food. South of downtown along Route 111 are many more standard cut-out coffeeshops and franchises.

Aerial Tramway, at the top of the cable ride. Tel. 325-1391. The "Ride & Dine" package, $15.95 (tram tickets alone cost $11.95) includes a nice buffet and unmatchable views.

Bono, 1700 N. Indian Ave. Tel. 322-6200. Well-known for its Italian food and the friendliness of its famous owner, Sonny Bono of the one-time star duet of Sonny & Cher. Dinners $10 up, lunches $4.75 up.

Last Casuelas, the original, 368 N. Palm Canyon dr. Tel. 325-3213. A local hangout since 1958, this family-operated Mexican restaurant has since opened two branches. The decor is cluttered and colorful, the food is fine, filling and moderate. Crowds at dinner. Lunches start at $2.95, dinners at $4.95.

Louise's Pantry, 124 S. Palm Canyon dr. 325-5124. A good-ole' American counter place, with solid filling breakfasts and meat dinners, great pies, and lines.

Useful Addresses And Phone Numbers

Area Code: 619 (in the mountains, some numbers have a 714 area code. These are shown).
Emergency: 911.
Fire and Medical Aid: Tel. 327-1441.
Chamber of Commerce: 190 W. Amadao, off Palm Canyon dr. Tel. 325-1577.
Palm Strings Convention & Visitors Bureau: 255 N. El Cielo rd. Tel. 327-8411. Opposite the airport.
Desert Resort Communities Convention & Visitors Bureau: 74-284 Hwy 111, Palm Desert. Tel. 568-1886.
Visitors Information Agency: 113 S. Indian ave. Tel. 327-7534.
Leisure Services Dept: Tel. 323-8272.
Hiking, Backpacking Information: Tel. 327-0222.
Greyhound: 311 N. Indian ave: Tel. 325-2053.
Desert Stage Lines: 367-3581.
Amtrak: In Indio. Tel. 800-872-7245.
Sun Bus: Tel. 343-3452.

Public Tennis Courts:

Ruth Hardy Park, 700 Tamarisk rd. Eight courts, six lighted, no fee.

CALIFORNIA

De Muth Park, 4375 Mesquite ave. Four lighted courts, no fee.

Idyllwild
Idyllwild Chamber of Commerce: 54274 N. Circle dr., in the Sugar Pine Shop. Tel. 714-659-3259.

Idyllwild County Park Visitor Center: Route 243 just north of Idyllwild. Tel. 714-659-3850.

U.S. Forest Service: 25925 Village Center dr. Tel. 714-659-2117. Maps, camping permits, trail info.

Mt. San Tacinto State Park and Wilderness: 25905 Route 243. Tel. 714-659-2607.

CALIFORNIA

Los Angeles

Los Angeles is a huge metropolis buzzing day and night, conventional but always offering something new, with a constant bombardment of audiovisual electronic stimuli. It is a city which typifies futuristic America – for better or worse. L.A. is the new Ellis Island, but the huddled masses arrive not in rotting freighters but by 747, and they are greeted not by the Statue of Liberty but by air like pea soup.

L.A. is a city of many faces...two-bit conmen...an old Chinese man in the snack-bar of a gigantic discount store, eating a hot dog and tortilla chips with a Sony Walkman over his Dodger's cap...a young blonde man in a three-piece suit wearing an earring.

L.A. means freeway hypnosis and palm trees silhouetted against a green sunset. Here imitation itself becomes the new culture, with false-fronted replicas of quaint fishing villages and frontier towns. Trendy new 1950's style rock'n roll diners are complete with spinning stools, Elvis posters – and a Filipino manager shouting "cheese burger, fries and strawberry shake – hold the mayo!". Tanning salons are crowded even when the sun is shining, and driveways are lined with marble pillars.

L.A., "the city you love to hate", has become the city I hate to love, but do.

Los Angeles is the name of a city, a county and the basin which embraces them. The basin is surrounded by several mountain ranges which arch from the southeast to the northwest. A long mountainous ridge north of the basin stretches toward the Pacific, and to the south, the Palos Verdes Peninsula thrusts out like a hammerhead. Between these two points lie the long, straight Los Angeles beaches. South of the city are the twin ports of Los Angeles and Long Beach.

The basin is roughly 75 miles from north to south, and 70 miles from east to west. Once rich agricultural land, almost every inch has been transformed into housing tracts, swimming pools, malls and shopping centers, freeways, parking lots and wide streets lined with fast-food joints. This urban development continues to spread, creeping over every mountain pass into the desert, and along the coast in both directions. It reaches and lends its name and culture to a territory far exceeding that of the Los Angeles basin itself.

Somewhere in the midst of this endless grid is the city of Los Angeles itself, which covers but a small section of the basin. Scan a map for the largest tangle of converging freeways: the 5, 10, 101 and 110. There you will find original downtown Los Angeles. From here, the city expanded west through Hollywood, Beverly Hills, and West Hollywood to the bluffs and beaches of Santa Monica and Malibu.

CALIFORNIA

Neon sign in Tinsel Town

Amazingly, this gargantuan urban area is still surrounded by large tracts of undeveloped land. The mountains are dotted with small towns, summer homes, ski resorts, man-made lakes, state parks, trails, and campgrounds. You can easily ski and swim on the same day in the L.A. area, if you can push through the traffic. The highest peak in the region, **Mt. Baldy** in the San Gabriel range, is over 10,000 feet high, and is visible on a clear day even from the southern edge of the basin, near Long Beach. The beaches extend from Zuma in the north, south to the beaches of Orange County; wide, flat, and almost uninterrupted.

CALIFORNIA

But pristine days are becoming rare. Even with stringent restrictions against pollution enforced in recent years, L.A. continues to be plagued by a serious smog problem, and summer "smog alert" days are all too common and are now part of the local vernacular and thinking.

The same features which make L.A. a unique and desirable region also contribute to that brown smog hovering over it all. The ocean winds, blowing east, push industrial fumes into the basin, where they are trapped by the mountains. The higher warm air currents trap the poorly ventilated layer of pollutants below. It is estimated that up to 65% of the pollution in the area is caused by automobiles, but L.A.'s love affair with and dependence on the automobile seem irreversible.

Climate

The weather is extremely mild and pleasant, day after day after day. There's hardly a breeze in the air or a cloud in the sky. For the traveler, it makes packing easy. A light jacket, heavy sweater and raincoat are usually adequate year round. When the temperature dips below 45 degrees Fahrenheit (7 degrees Centigrade), the locals take out their designer down vests. Dramatic weather changes do occur over the years – the average rainfall of 14 inches may, in reality, indicate 25 inches one year and 3 the next.

The weather varies more from place to place than by season. The temperature along the beaches can be 10-20 degrees cooler than inland, and the winds strong enough to dispel the smog. The inland San Fernando and Gabriel valleys are generally hotter in summer and colder in winter than the coast. Spring can be cool and foggy along the beaches, while inland the temperatures are fair and the skies clear. The summers can be hot, and choking with smog, though it is generally less noticeable along the coast where the sea breeze circulates. The inland communities, such as Riverside, are stuck with the brown smog blown in from the west. Do not expect the crisp autumn of New England, with its vague scent of rotting apples. There's hardly a deciduous tree to turn color. Here, fall is the season of the Santa Annas, the scorching, dry winds from the desert, similar to Mediterranean sirocco winds.

The sunny, warm weather, and the openness of L.A. society, lend themselves to a casual and bright clothing style. Jackets and ties are not often necessary at restaurants. In certain occupations it is quite acceptable to wear a sports jacket without a tie. Men's clothing tends to be brighter and lighter in color than on the east coast.

Orientation

Very few neighborhoods in Los Angeles are clearly demarcated or defined. Downtown lies within the square roughly formed by the Hollywood Freeway (101), the Santa Monica Freeway (10), the Harbor Freeway (11) and the Golden State Freeway (5). To the northeast is Pasadena, anchored at the base of the San Gabriel Mountains, and to the southwest is Exposition Park with its museums. To the northwest are Griffith Park, Hollywood and West

CALIFORNIA

Hollywood, all bordered on the north by the Santa Monica Mountains. To the west, beyond Hollywood, lies Beverly Hills, and the Westwood Village/UCLA area. Wilshire Boulevard extends due west from downtown, through a variety of neighborhoods, past the museums and tarpits of Hancock Park through Beverly Hills, into Westwood and out to Santa Monica. Santa Monica is the main beach community west of downtown. To the north lie the hills and curving coast of Malibu. To the south lies the funky ocean walk of Venice, the huge pleasure boat harbor of Marina Del Ray, the airport, and a series of beach neighborhoods leading to the jutting Palos Verdes Peninsula. To the east of the peninsula lies the port of Los Angeles, and the city of Long Beach. Orange County begins south of Long Beach.

A glance at the map will suffice to show that these areas form only a portion of the Los Angeles urban area. The remainder of that huge territory is filled with endless tracts of houses and shopping centers. There may be some tourist sights scattered among them, but most places of interest are concentrated in the areas mentioned, mainly from downtown toward the west.

The less often you need to board a bus or climb into your car, the happier your day will be. Distances between or even within neighborhoods are greater than they seem on a map. If you can plan your excursions so that you spend, for example, one day in the Venice/Santa Monica/Malibu region, you will find your visits more enjoyable. During rush hours – which seem to get longer every year – traffic can be brutal. The best way to handle the rush hour is simply to find one place to stay in and stay off the roads.

Los Angeles can overwhelm the most intrepid explorer. It is highly recommended to make a bee-line for downtown and the **Los Angeles Visitors and Convention Bureau**, at 505 S. Flower st. on the B Level of the ARCO Plaza. The staff here are patient and helpful and have seen their share of confused visitors. Help is available in a variety of languages. Brochures are abundant. *The Dateline*, published four times a year, lists special events. Many of the brochures include coupons for assorted discounts. A listing of accommodation is available and the staff will help you choose a place best suited to your needs.

There is an amazing amount to do in Los Angeles. Every type of entertainment and culture seems to prosper in the Southern Californian sun and freedom. First-run movies are shown everywhere. There are 150 local theaters. From classical to jazz, from folk, country and western to hard rock and punk, the best of every kind of music can be found. Museums and galleries are constantly presenting new exhibits. However long you stay in the area, there is enough to keep you busy day and night.

An excellent array of weekly publications keeps the visitor informed of various happenings. The *L.A. Weekly* and *The Reader* are both free and are geared towards younger audiences, with reviews of rock groups and so forth, but with plenty of general information. They also carry some local investigative articles. The two main daily papers, the *Los Angeles Times* and the *Los Angeles Examiner*, both publish Sunday editions with cultural events and

CALIFORNIA

schedules. *The Times* is generally considered one of the best papers in the country. The thick Sunday edition will hold your attention right through Sunday brunch and endless cups of coffee.

In addition, there is a flurry of small neighborhood papers which deal mostly with local matters, and which can be interesting. They can be found in restaurants, laundromats and coffee shops.

Phones

The area code for most of L.A. is 213. In the northern part, including the San Fernando Valley, a new code of 818 was recently introduced. In Orange County the number is 714. All the numbers that have been listed here are under the 213 area code unless otherwise noted. The basic price of a public phone call is 20 cents, with additional coins required when indicated by the operator.

Transportation

Los Angeles International Airport (LAX) is huge, being the third busiest airport in the world. From the adjacent freeway a wide half-circle of jetliners can be seen hovering in the haze, each awaiting its chance to land, in an endless precise succession.

Once dangerously chaotic, the airport is now well-organized after extensive renovations. It is shaped like a long, double-tiered horseshoe, the upper tier for departures and the lower for arrivals. In the central space are parking structures, and a tower with a well-reputed restaurant on top. Concrete islands for all buses, vans and other airport transportation are found outside the lower tier, in front of the luggage carousels. The horseshoe is divided into nine terminals which are connected by shuttle buses. At its curved end is the **International Terminal**, though many international airlines operate out of terminal 2 as well. Between the two, LAX handles flights to and from all over the world.

The newly streamlined airport still has a hazardous and hopelessly inadequate entrance. Basically, one road leads to the airport from the San Diego Freeway, and the lane which leads to the airport is regularly jammed with traffic. Be sure to give yourself adequate time to reach the airport. Arrival by bus or van, though it might be an extra expense, may prevent headaches.

The airport has a well-developed information network. For general information on current carriers, airline location, etc. call Tel. 646-5252.

Yellow courtesy phones are available in all terminals and connect to the airport information aides, on duty from 7am-11:30pm. There is a central visitor information number and a number just for transportation information. Each terminal offers Travelers Aid information, with an attendant or recorded information, and printed information. For the extremely rumpled, there are showers and sleeping facilities in the International Terminal, which are paid for by the hour.

The central parking structures are convenient but can get crowded, and are

CALIFORNIA

expensive for any period exceeding two hours or so. "Remote lots" are cheaper and help one to avoid the snarl of traffic at the terminals. Lots C and D at Sepulveda and 96th and lot VSP at L.A. Cienege and 111th are connected to the airport by free tram. The first two hours at these lots are free. At lot C, a special mini-van provides free service to passengers in wheelchairs.

Public buses (RTD) serve the airport but do not enter it directly. They stop at the **transfer terminal** at Vicksburg and 96th, and the RTD shuttle (3608) scurries between the transfer point and the airport terminals, from 5am-1am. From the airport the shuttle costs 50 cents, and a transfer to an RTD bus is free. Transfers for the shuttle are also free for those who come to the airport by city bus. In either direction, remember to request a transfer.

Bear in mind that city buses have little or no luggage space and no attendant to leap down and help you. Depending on the hour, the bus might be crowded and the ride drawn-out. You might have to wait for the shuttle and for the connecting city bus. Consider whether this is worthwhile after a long flight.

A more expensive but faster and infinitely more convenient alternative is provided by **Airport Service**, a private company running buses from the airport to various destinations in the basin. They run to the various hotel districts, to downtown, to Pasadena, and to the airports in Long Beach and Orange County, as well as to Disneyland. In addition, there is a wide array of vans and limousines providing direct connections from LAX to regions as far away as Santa Barbara and San Diego. Information is available at the airport.

Car rental counters are available at every terminal. Taxi fares are steep, about $25 to downtown.

Each terminal has phones connecting directly to specific hotels. The closest hotel district that does not gaze over a parking lot is at nearby Marina Del Ray, with a sheltered beach and the largest man-made pleasure-craft marina in the world. Hotels here range from upper moderate to deluxe. Most of the large chains are represented. More relaxing places to ease out your travel kinks can be found.

Airport Information
LAX, main number: Tel. 646-5252.
Visitor Information (multilingual): Tel. 488-9100.
Transportation, parking information: dial AIRPORT.
Travelers Aid: In all terminals, with live information or a recorded message, and printed material. Tel. 646-2270.
Airport Visitor Center: 380 World Way, 8:30am-9:30pm. Tel. 215-0606.
Services for the handicapped: Tel. 646-8021, or 646-6402.
Airport Security: Tel. 646-6254, 24 hours.
Lost & Found: Tel. 646-2260 (also call the airline).

*C*ALIFORNIA

Airport Service Buses:
Los Angeles: Tel. 723-4636.
Long Beach: Tel. 596-1662.
Orange County: Tel.714-776-9210.

Public Transport

Buses and trains: Greyhound, Trailways, and The Green Tortoise (the alternative inexpensive bus company with bunks in the bus) all serve Los Angeles, with connections to most major cities. The Greyhound station is in skid row; try to avoid it late at night. Trailways is located in the beautiful Union Station which is also used by Amtrak. Today only a few trains a day pass through it as part of the beautiful coastal route.

The Freeways

Mass hypnosis captures Los Angeles every morning as people, half-asleep climb into their cars, rev the motor, turn up the radio and air conditioner, and squeeze into the morning crawl of traffic on the nearest freeway. On every freeway in the complex network, cars are packed tight from horizon to horizon. It is impossible to imagine Los Angeles today without the freeway system. It is common for people to commute up to a hundred miles each way. The traffic never really lets up beyond a certain point. At five in the morning traffic already streams toward the city.

The afternoon rush hour may begin before three and continue well after six. During these peak hours the surface streets which parallel the main freeways often move faster than the freeways which were built to bypass the surface streets.

The Los Angeles freeways can disconcert the unfamiliar driver. Be cautious when entering the freeway. At some entrances, exits and entrances use the same ramp, inviting accidents.

Yield to the driver already on the freeway, but try not to stop and break the flow of traffic behind you. Ease gently into the flow. Beware of tailgating; chain-reaction pileups occur in a flash. Ignore those who get their kicks weaving between lanes. Shift lanes sparingly as long as the traffic is flowing.

The Santa Monica Freeway(10) is the main east-west axis from downtown to the western beaches. Paralleling the coastal areas, from the northern San Fernando Valley all the way south to San Diego is the San Diego Freeway 405, becoming 5 in Orange County. These two roads draw some of the heaviest congestion. From Hollywood to downtown take the Hollywood Freeway (101). Between downtown and the harbor area take the Harbor Freeway(110). These four freeways link up with almost every other one in the complex.

In-town transportation

Buses: Contrary to popular rumor, Los Angeles has an extensive public bus system. It is, however, complicated, involving interchanges and crossovers between the **Southern California Rapid Transit District (RTD)** and other

CALIFORNIA

local and regional bus lines. Buses often follow long, indirect routes through city streets, and may run well over half-an-hour apart even during peak hours. A trip including a transfer between buses may require two hours.

RTD's **customer centers** throughout the urban area, including one downtown (see below), can provide all the necessary information as well as schedules and various passes. Information is available by phone from 6am to midnight, but the wait can be excruciatingly long. A visit to the nearest customer center is preferable if possible.

When obtaining bus information, be sure to ask about express routes (following the freeway or a combination of freeway and street). Unless you specify, you might receive information concerning the stop-and-go street routes only. Express buses are much faster than the street routes.

Basic fare is 85 cents, 40 cents for handicapped and seniors. Transfers are 10 cents. Express routes cost an additional fare depending on distance. Monthly passes for unlimited use cost $32. Monthly passes for limited use are available for $15.

RTD runs three shuttles: the Westwood Village Shuttle, the downtown shuttle and the airport shuttle (each is detailed under those subtitles).

Buses run till the wee hours and some run all night. As one who waited downtown at night and received an enormous variety of propositions within an hour, I recommend avoiding the Greyhound Bus terminal (which is also the downtown hub for RTD) and environs late at night if possible.

A written request to RTD will get you enough information for a suitcase. A brochure for self-guided tours is offered, as is information for routes in specific areas, and a guide to wheelchair accessible lines. Write: RTD, Los Angeles 90001.

Some of the same destinations in the L.A. area served by RTD and other public bus companies are also served by Greyhound and/or Trailways. These lines are more expensive, but save time and are more convenient.

Transportation Information
Amtrak: Union Station, 88 N. Alameda. Tel. 624-0171.
Greyhound: 6th st. & Los Angeles. Tel. 620-1200.
Grayline Sightseeing Tours: Tel. 680-1980.
Green Tortoise: Tel. 415-285-2441.
RTD: Tel. 626-4455. Service is faster if called from an RTD customer center.

RTD Customer Centers:
ARCO Plaza: 515 S. Flower St., Level B. Mon.-Fri. 7:30am-4pm.
Hollywood: 6249 Hollywood blvd. Mon.-Sat. 10am-6pm.
Main Office: 419 S. Main. Mon.-Fri. 8am-4:30pm. The California Mart: 1016 S. Main. Mon.-Fri. 7am-7pm, Sat.-Sun. 10am-6pm.
Wilshire (temporary): 5315 Wilshire blvd., (just west of La Brea ave.) Mon.-Fri. 8am-5pm.

*C*ALIFORNIA

Reclining star

Movie and Television Land

Television studios issue tickets for the viewing of the live taping of their shows. Some are available from the Visitors Information Center in the ARCO plaza. The center will also send them to an in-state address. Out-of-state visitors can receive "guest cards" or a letter by mail which are redeemable for tickets. Inquire at the Visitors' Center.

Universal Studios has transformed tours of its back lots into a thriving business in itself. Thousands visit the studios daily. Allow four to six hours for the entire visit, which includes a 2-hour tram ride through exhibits of props and scenes followed by the staging of various shows. You will see the house from *Psycho*, stunts from the *A-Team*. You will be attacked by the shark from *Jaws* and captured by inter-galactic bad guys. But the biggest and newest star on the lot is the gigantic King Kong, who will gaze at you with curiosity as you cross the Brooklyn Bridge, and then roar with rage, so close that you can see his huge cavities and feel his hot banana breath – but don't worry, you will miraculously escape!

Universal is located just off the Hollywood Freeway, via the Barham boulevard or Lankershim boulevard exits. (Open 9am-5pm summers and holidays; 10am-3:30pm off-season weekdays, and 9:30am-3:30pm on off-season weekends. Admission is a steep $14.95 from age 12 up; $10.95 ages 3-11. Free under 3; $11.55 for seniors age 55 and over. $2 parking. Tel. 818-508-5444.)

Not far from Universal, television studios offer tours which concentrate less on gimmicks and fanfare, and show more of what the operation of a major commercial studio entails. Visitors are shown some special effects exhibits.

CALIFORNIA

You might be chosen to fly across Los Angeles as Superman, or you may meet the stars who happen to be filming that day.

Arrive early to precede the crowds, thereby improving the chances of obtaining free tickets for the live taping of a show. (3000 W. Alameda ave., Burbank, CA, 91523. Tours from 9am-4pm weekdays, 10am-4pm Sat. 10am-2pm Sun. Adults $5.50, ages 5-14 $3.25, under 5 free. Tel. 818-840-3537.) To write for tickets earlier, include the name of the show, the date and number of tickets desired and a self-addressed stamped envelope.

ABC offers tickets for show taping. Write ABC-TV, 4151 Prospect, Hollywood 90027.

For tickets to **CBS-TV** shows: CBS-TV Ticket Office, 7800 Beverly blvd. Hollywood 90036. Tel. 852-4002.

Downtown

L.A. really does have a downtown and it can be fascinating, but you must hunt out its interesting and eccentric corners. Downtown L.A. is roughly oblong, and runs approximately from Chinatown in the north to the Santa Monica freeway in the south. It is a composite of several sections: the financial district, the small ethnic communities and tourist centers (Chinatown, Little Tokyo, Olvera St.), the commercial wholesale areas, and skid row around the Greyhound Station.

The downtown minibus, called **DASH**, Connects Olvera St., Little Tokyo, Chinatown, City Hall, The World Trade Center, ARCO Plaza, and other downtown points, as far south as the Trans America Center on 12th St. It also passes produce markets on the eastern edge. The buses run every 10 minutes or so, from 7am to 6pm, but sometimes they arrive up to 20 minutes apart. Most main attractions are on this convenient line which costs only 25 cents. Tel. 800-8-SHUTTLE.

The **Arco Plaza**, at 505 S. Flower, is a logical place to begin a downtown tour. The seven acres of this underground world might be the prototype for futuristic cities; quiet with pumped in air, dim lights, pleasant music and almost hermetically sealed from obtrusive outside noises. It is gleaming, spotless and bland. Here you'll find the **L.A. Visitor Information Center** with its helpful staff and all the information you need. (Open Mon.-Fri. 10am-6pm, Sat. 11am-5pm. Tel. 628-3101.) Just around the corner, offering information schedules, is an **RTD Customer Center**. The **ARCO Center for Visual Art**, (Open Mon.-Fri.10am-6pm, Sat. 11am-5pm. Free admission. Tel. 448-0038.) sponsored by the oil giant, exhibits contemporary art in two galleries. The plaza is at the heart of the new mushrooming downtown , with the **Benaventure Hotel** (404 S. Figuerua st.) as the centerpiece. The glass, light, winding staircases, transparent elevators and reflecting pools give the structure an other-worldly feel from within. The 34th Lounge (on the 34th floor) offers drinks and a dizzying view.

The **Civic Center** area, bounded by Temple, Main, First and Spring (with a

CALIFORNIA

DOWNTOWN LOS ANGELES

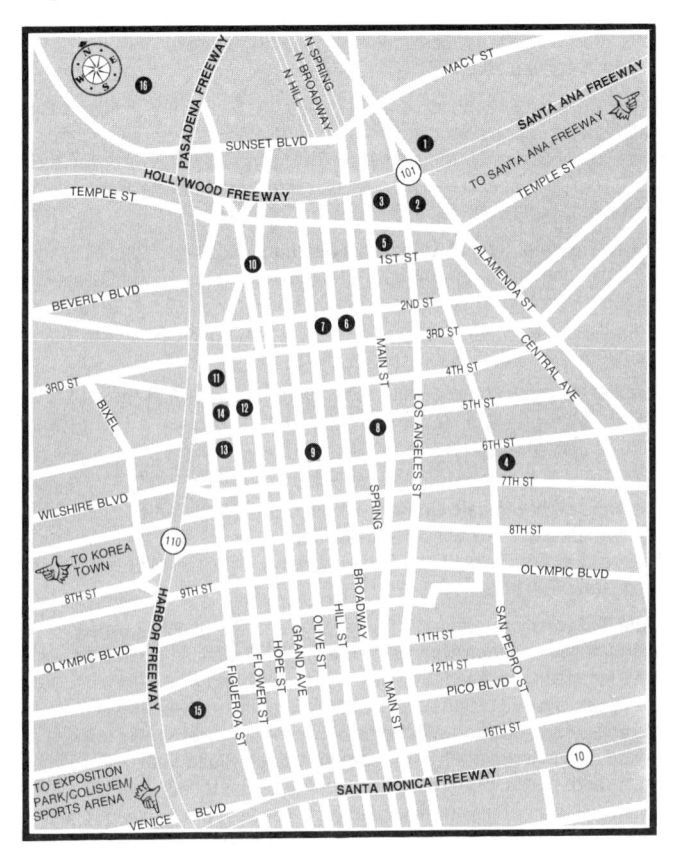

Index
1) Union Station
2) Federal Building
3) Los Angeles Mall
4) Greyhound Bus Terminal
5) City Hall
6) Bradbury Building
7) Grand Central Market
8) L.A. Theater Center
9) Pershing Square
10) Music Center
11) World Trade Center
12) YMCA
13) Arco Plaza (Visitors Information)
14) Bonadventure Shopping Gallery
15) Los Angeles Convention Center
16) Dodger Stadium

CALIFORNIA

little spillover across these boundaries) encompasses the largest concentration of government bureaucracy outside Washington D.C. As with other civic centers, the scattered presence of homeless indigents on the lawns highlights a certain irony.

There was a time when, from the observation deck on the 27th floor of **City Hall**, you could see from the San Gabriel Mountains to the sea; today, you must first check smog conditions. (200 N.Spring st. Open Mon.-Fri. 8am-5pm. Admission free. Free 45-minute tours, Mon.-Fri. 10-11am. Call two days ahead for reservations, Tel. 485-4423.)

Across the street, the **L.A.Children's Museum** encourages kids of all ages to handle and play with exhibits. (310 N. Main st. Mon.-Fri. 11:30am-5pm, Sat.-Sun. 10am-5pm. Admission $2.75. Tel. 687-8800.) It's an unusual, stimulating place, with displays on the city's ethnic communities, and a children's T.V. station.

Keeping the pulse on the bureaucratic complex is the **L.A. Times**. (202 W. 1st St., Mon.-Fri. at 3pm. Children must be 10 or over. Meet guide at entrance. Tel. 972-5000.) It is generally considered one of the top newpapers in the country. A free tour takes you behind the headlines.

Los Angeles' new **Music Center**, just west of the Civic Center, includes the Dorothy Chandler Pavilion, the Mark Taper Forum and the Ahmanson Theatre.(135 Grand ave. For a free guided tour, Tel. 972-7483. For general information, Tel. 972-7211.)

Little Tokyo is located mainly between 1st and 3rd Streets, between Main and Alameda on the minibus loop. The thriving Japanese population which was uprooted, humiliated and interned during World War II, returned with energy and vigor to create a new community for themselves. This is a quietly interesting neighborhood with tastes of Japanese culture in little pockets all around. The main center is the **Japanese Village Plaza Mall**, with its stone paths and ponds. The plaza and surrounding streets are lined with restaurants, Sushi bars and small Japanese specialty products, artwork, and books. The toy stores sell some unusual Japanese gimmicks including weird wind-up monsters and robots. Restaurant windows display bright models of the cuisine that are tantalizing works of art, and delicious enough to eat. Sushi is one such example. It has captured the west coast from Los Angeles to Seattle.It basically consists of raw fish and birds' eggs on little beds of rice at $3 for a few pieces. However unappealing this may at first sound, Sushi is, in fact, exquisite cuisine. From the precise presentation to the delicate blending and contrasts of taste, it is Japanese through and through: elegant, refined, colorful, yet with something sparse about it.

In a land where the visual presentation of food is as important as its taste and quality, the Sushi chef is both a visual and a culinary artist. He learns his profession during a long apprenticeship, starting with the most menial tasks in the restaurant. It may be a year before he handles a knife. He learns how to select fresh fish, and even the correct preparation of rice may take him years to perfect.

CALIFORNIA

Rice, far from being simply an accompaniment, is the foundation of Sushi. It is steamed and tossed in a dressing made of rice vinegar, sugar and salt, while simultaneously being fanned to cool quickly. The kernels must be just the right size and consistency to be shaped into pads.

Look for a Sushi bar where there is a Japanese clientele. Although some Sushi bars have tables, sit at the counter so you can watch and talk to the chef. He will take your order directly. Watch him perform his rituals of precise preparation. Since the fish is eaten raw, the slicing is crucial. The Japanese have developed it into a highly formalized art. Particular fish must be sliced in particular ways. Some are cut into regular rectangles, some are cubed, others sliced paper thin.

The rectangular or square pieces of sushi are set out carefully to blend with the colors. The reds, yellows, gold, translucent pink, deep green of the seaweed casings, and pure white of the fillet combine to make the plate a work of art.

If you are new to the Sushi world, ask the chef for some suggestions and advice. Although quantities are not huge, Sushi is very filling. Try some saki, tea or Japanese beer with your meal.

The **New Otani Hotel**, on Los Angeles St. between 1st and 2nd, symbolizes the growing connection between the Japanese American community and the developing economy of the Pacific nations. One of a chain, the hotel has both American and Japanese rooms. The two-room Japanese suite overlooking the garden and pool costs a mere $250 per night. If that is a bit too much, enjoy a Saki at the bar. The new **Japanese American Cultural and Community Center** offers rotating exhibitions in its gallery.

Tours of Little Tokyo, lasting about an hour and a half, are available through the **Little Tokyo Business Association** by pre-arrangement. (244 S. San Pedro St., 501. $1 for adults and 50 cents per child. Tel. 620-0570.)

At the edge of Little Tokyo is the **Museum of Neon Art**. (407 Traction Ave. Tel. 617-1580.) There are displays of the history, variations and possibilities of what almost amounts to an American folk art.

Many art galleries in downtown Los Angeles have organized under the umbrella of the **Los Angeles Visual Art** (LAVA) movement. Check with LAVA for a report of exhibits at the various member galleries.

The Chinese community of L.A. dates back to the Gold Rush days of the 1850s. The local Chinese were greatly abused, and in 1871 nineteen Chinese were killed in riots in which police participated. Deep prejudice and bigotry continued into the next century, albeit a little less violently. The present Chinatown, north of Little Tokyo, was built in the 1930s, when the Chinese community was moved from its home near Union station. The deliberate exaggeration and ornateness was part of a conscious effort to attract tourists.

At the gate to **Chinatown** is a statue of Sun Yat Sen, father of the Chinese Republic. The Chinese in Los Angeles drilled for and later took an active role

CALIFORNIA

Marilyn Monroe in Chinatown

in the revolt against the Manchu Dynasty. The Chinese markets and the restaurants are enough to whet anyone's appetite, and there are plenty of moderately priced eateries in the Food Mall.

The **El Pueblo de Los Angeles State Historical Park**, and Olvera street preserve what was the founding site of L.A., as well as a number of historical buildings surrounding it. What is today a sprawling city, started as a village of 44 in 1781, with about half of those being children, while the adults consisted largely of Indians, Blacks and Mulattos. A meagre simple village until the 1850s, it was seized by the newly independent Mexico from Spanish rule in 1822, and then seized in turn by the Americans. During the gold rush days the worst American elements – the ones who could not find a footing in the North or were kicked out by vigilantes, drifted down to L.A. and helped make this one of the wildest towns in the West where murder was a daily event and where for a while no one would pick up the sherrif's badge. The railroad connection in 1869 brought in streams of immigrants, and as a result the downtown area spread west.

Olvera Street today is a carefully ornamented Mexican stageset. For a throbbing Mexican atmosphere and much better and cheaper Mexican food, head south to the Grand Central Market.

Near Olvera st. is the city's train depot, **Union Station**, huge and graceful and beautifully decorated in Spanish style. Today the cavernous hall is empty, but when L.A. became a major shipping point for the Pacific theater during World War II, crowds of servicemen lined up at train platforms and ticket booths or waited in line for a last call to their loved ones.

The once lavish theaters on Broadway were built in the early decades of the century for the booming movie business. South Broadway is now a central avenue for the Hispanic section of downtown, as the store signs and movie marquees show. For a pulse of Mexico which you will not get on Olvera st., join the thousands of people from all over the city who flow through the **Grand Central Market** (317 S. Broadway), hunting and finding bargains. Mounds of nuts, fruits, cheeses, squid, eggs, pigs and poultry line the market. Mexican food is plentiful, delicious and authentic.

Nearby is the **Bradbury Building**. (304 S. Broadway. Tel. 489-1411.) This famous building is a Los Angeles landmark and a site used in many movies. The exterior is plain, but the inside resembles one of Max Escher's self-perpetuating illusions, flooded by light. The building was designed by George Herbert Wyman, a draftsman with no architectural experience, who accepted the commission only after he received a message from his dead brother, and found the inspiration for his design in a nineteenth-century utopian novel.

The wholesale markets in lower downtown will open views that even most locals miss; you need only wake up at or stay up till four of five in the morning. In the huge **flower market** on Wall street between 7th and 8th, fresh flowers are frenetically unloaded and haggled over. The bursts of color and scent are almost hallucinatory in the pre-dawn darkness. Trucks packed with luscious California produce from the San Joaquin and Imperial Valleys roll into the produce market's two locations, off 9th and San Pedro, and along Central avenue between 7th and 8th. Men unload the crates, as they shout in a babble of languages. All-night diners and little Mexican cafes serve the workers mounds of ham and eggs or *huevos rancheros* and cups of steaming coffee.

Toward Pasadena

Northeast of downtown, at Highland Park, the **Southwest Museum** houses some of the finest collections of Indian art and artifacts in the United States. (234 Museum Drive, access off the Pasadena Freeway. Open Tues.-Sat. 11am-5pm, Sun. 1-5pm. Admission $1.50 adults, $1 seniors and students. Tel. 221-2163.) Permanent exhibits provide vivid visual narrative of the diverse cultures of the Indians of the Great Plains, the Southwest coast and California. Also included are exhibits of Meso-American and South American pre-Columbian pottery artifacts. The museum offers a year-round schedule of lectures, films, music and theatrical events. Hispanic folk and decorative arts are on show in the adjacent **Casa de Adobe**, which was constructed by a local adobe craftsman.

CALIFORNIA

Pasadena

Pasadena is one of the older suburbs that first branched out from Los Angeles. Sitting right at the base of the San Gabriel Mountains, there is excellent access to the winding roads and hiking trails that climb the range. Pasadena is known to most of the country as home of the **Tournament of Roses** parade and the **Rose Bowl**, held each New Year's Day. So popular is the event that people camp out overnight to secure good seats.

Pasadena is the home of several excellent museums. The **Norton Simon Museum of Art** is superb. (411 W. Colorado blvd. Open Thurs.-Sun. noon-6pm. Adults $2, $3 on Sunday, students and seniors 75 cents.) The most famous artists in the world are well represented here. From Rubens and Rembrandt to Van Gogh and Picasso, all the masters are here and all the major movements represented.

Henry Huntington, early railroad mogul, built a lavish 207-acre estate and filled it with art treasures, rare books, and a stunningly landscaped and variegated botanical garden. Today, the **Huntington Library, Art Gallery** and **Botanical Gardens** are a cultural landmark. (1151 Oxford rd., San Marino, 911080. Open Tues. 1-4:30pm. Admission free. $2 parking. For tickets on Sunday, request ahead by mail, with the date requested and a self-addressed stamped envelope. Tel. 792-6141.) The art gallery is installed in what was the residence, and it places a heavy emphasis on 18th and 19th century paintings. The holdings of the library include a Gutenberg Bible. The garden is overwhelming. There are 12 acres of desert plants alone, plus Japanese and Australian gardens, and the 1060 varieties of roses of Shakespeare's garden.

Exposition Park

Exposition Park, home of several large museums and public buildings, lies south of downtown, too far to walk. Once an open-air market, the area became a haven for horse racing and saloons until an enterprising judge asserted that no more appropriate place could be chosen for a center of good uplifting culture.

You can't miss the complex of the **California Museum for Science and Industry**. (700 State Dr. Open 10am-5pm daily. Free admission. Tel. 744-7400.) Inside you'll find exhibits on subjects ranging from computer technology, to nutrition, anatomy and natural resources. This is a great place to bring children. There are buttons to push and levers to pull everywhere.

Outside the museum is the tranquil and fragrant **Exposition Rose Garden**, with almost 200 varieties. (Open daily 10am-5pm. Admission free.)

The **California Afro-American Museum** offers an excellent introduction to Black culture, with exhibitions ranging from books clandestinely published by Blacks in the ante-bellum South to contemporary sculpture. (600 State Dr. Open daily 10am-5pm. Admission free. Tel. 744-7432.)

The **County Museum of Natural History** is vast and fantastic, spanning the

CALIFORNIA

natural world and development of culture. (900 Exposition Blvd. Open Tue-Sat. 10am-5pm. Admission. Tel. 744-3411, 744-3430 for live recording.)

The huge private **University of Southern California** is famous for such modern disciplines as film and football, but some of the old buildings emanate an aura of medieval scholasticism. The **Fischer Art Gallery** houses the large Armand Hammer collection of 18th and 19th century Dutch paintings. For general campus information, Tel. 743-2388.

Northeast of USC is the Hebrew Union College and its **Skirball Museum**. (3077 University Ave. Open Tues.-Fri. 11am-4pm, Sun. 10am-5pm. Admission free. Tel. 749-3424.) It has a collection of artifacts from Biblical archeology and Judaica from ancient times to present. "A Walk Through Time" recreates a Biblical environment.

The predominantly Black Watts neighborhood boasts the **Watts Towers**, art that is a testimony of persistent imagination and innovation. (1727 E. 107th st. Open Mon.-Fri. 9:30am-2pm. Tel.569-8181.) From 1921 to 1954, working alone, Simon Rodia created towers over 100 ft. tall from bedframes, old pipes, scrap metal, and anything else he could find. He scaled the growing towers in a window washer's rig, and decorated them with bits of glass, plates, sea shells and tiles. Rodia eventually moved away, leaving his property to a neighbor. A proposal to have the sculpture demolished sparked a local rescue effort, and it is now a State Historical Park, operated by the city. The Watts Towers Arts Center leads tours inside the towers.

Hollywood and Environs

The corner of **Hollywood and Vine**, once a meeting place and buzzing center of mythic proportions, still best expresses Hollywood today. On one corner is a porno theater, and nearby a store advertising such fashions as sharply studded wristbands. One block away is a tattoo shop. Up Vine is the famous **Capitol Records** headquarters, shaped like a stack of records (one source says it was inspired by Nat King Cole). Down Vine Street is a vegetarian fast-food stand, an Ethiopian restaurant, a blues club and a wig shop with the surrealistic vision of hairdressers preparing wigs on the heads of mannikins in the front window. At night, the streets are patrolled by prostitutes of assorted genders, and preachers of various salvations, as well as punks with hairdos shaped like dinosaur spines, and an occasional wide-eyed youngster lugging his guitar.

In other words, it ain't what it used to be. Stroll down Hollywood Boulevard, but don't expect to see more than a few tawdry, slightly sad, nostalgic remnants of a world so glittery, fantastic and unreal that it could never last.

The area of Hollywood was once a camping ground for the Cahuenga Indians, who were then a small farming community, until some enterprising practitioners of the new fangled technology of motion pictures set up shop in an abandoned tavern. The area attracted more of the same, partly because laws involving the movies were hard to enforce out in these parts, and because Mexico was a hop away. By about 1915, the movie industry was already entrenched and fortunes were being made by producers and stars. Movies provided the narcotic of fantasy during the Depression and the Hollywood studios rolled out hundreds of them. Their creators and stars became fabulously wealthy and created their exclusive colonies in Beverly Hills, Belle Aire and Malibu Canyon. Gaudy neo-classical architecture sprang up in private mansions, department stores and theaters themselves.

Hollywood's dominance did not last as most of the studios moved over the hills. The huge giants were challenged by smaller independent studios. Stars grew more independent and assertive in creating their roles (and their box office percentage). Television, too, helped speed the studios' demise.

On **Hollywood Boulevard** you can still see glimpses of the glitter that pervaded. Just look at the sidewalk, in which the names of numerous stars are enshrined.

Hollywood's most famous symbol is **Graumann's Chinese Theater**, a strange collection of pagoda like entrances, dragons' faces and tails. The same Sid Graumann erected his **Egyptian Theater** (6708 Hollywood blvd.), where the usherettes were outfitted like Cleopatra.

The **Chinese Theater** (6925 Hollywood Blvd. Tel. 464-8111.) opened in 1927 with the premiere of Cecil B. De Mille's *King of Kings*. Afterwards it became famous for its shots of stars exiting from limousines and strolling into the theater past crowds of ogling and drooling fans. Graumann himself wrote and directed shows to introduce the movies, some bordering on the outrageous. He cemented the fame of his stars with imprints of various appendages in wet cement in the theater courtyard. Today, every tourist wanders around the courtyard staring at the signatures. Alas, Graumann's theater is no longer Graumann's, as it was bought up by the Mann theater chain. Movies are still shown there.

Near the Chinese Theatre are numerous tour companies offering guided tours of the stars' homes in Beverly hills. If you want to take the tour by car, you can buy a map here (they are also sometimes sold on various corners near the Beverly Hills area, but you are more assured of obtaining one on Hollywood blvd.). The tour guides on the buses, though corny and sometimes obviously bored, can at least tell some juicy stories you wouldn't get driving along a winding road, messing with a map and trying to squint through the foliage at Charlie Chaplin's house. So, as long as you're playing the gawking tourist, you might as well pay (about $10) and get your money's worth.

Hollywood on Location provides the chance to see live stars at work. (8644 Wilshire. About $20 for the service. Tel. 659-9165.) Every morning this office publishes a list of shooting locations with directions, maps, stars, the shot, etc. You'll need a car for a day to make full use of the information.

The **Capitol Records Tower** conducts free tours on Tuesdays and Thursdays. (1750 Vine. Tel. 462-6252.) **On Location**, installed in a refurbished drug store, features several scale models of old Hollywood, built with exactness and detail, and accompanied by miniature spotlights and

CALIFORNIA

Graumann's Chinese Theater

dramatic music and narration. For all the kitsch, it gives a good feel for Hollywood in its heyday. In contrast to this, the **Hollywood Wax Museum** is not worthwhile.

The decaying heart of movieland has an excellent concentration of bookstores, once haunted by the writers attracted to Hollywood by high and regular script fees. The selections are wide and varied, and are a goldmine for anyone interested in movie history. At the corner of Hollywood boulevard and Las Palmas is a long newsstand stacked with periodicals from around the country and the world. The boulevard has a number of inexpensive ethnic foodstands serving satisfying portions of Italian, Middle Eastern, Mexican and Chinese cuisine. Its costume shops will outfit you with a jewelled crown, giant sword and horrifying mask for your next soiree. Perhaps some sociological insights can be gleaned from **The International Love Boutique**, toward the west end of the boulevard's commercial strip. Ten years ago, its jokes, props and rubber gadgets would have been sold behind a door marked XXX, but today they are displayed in a chic scented setting with soft music.

The **Hollywood Bowl**, designed by Frank Lloyd Wright, is a delightful place for a concert on a summer evening. Tradition calls for a picnic beforehand. The wooden seats are hard, so its worth bringing a pillow Some seats allow a view of the huge HOLLYWOOD sign, which makes you feel – well, in Hollywood. The **Los Angeles Philharmonic** regularly plays "the bowl", as do star performers from all realms of music. Students and seniors with identification are eligible for $5 tickets to any Tuesday or Thursday L.A. Philharmonic concerts, as well as some others performed by the orchestra. These "rush" tickets are on sale the day before and on the day of a concert at the Hollywood bowl box office. The evenings can be cool, so bring a sweater. There is a mid-priced restaurant on the grounds selling pre-packaged dinners. Concerts can get crowded and parking difficult. Call for details on special park-and-ride buses to the amphitheater from various locations throughout the L.A. area. The amphitheater is accessible to the handicapped, and a brochure titled *Guide to the Hollywood Bowl for Patrons with Disabilities* is available upon request by phone. Tel. 876-8742.

The Museum on the Development of Music in Los Angeles is small but very interesting, giving a glimpse of the popularization of jazz and blues. (2301 N. Highland Ave. Take the Highland Ave. exit from the Hollywood Freeway. Tel. 876-8742.)

The famous **Hollywood Sign**, hovering over Mt. Cahuenga above the Hollywood Freeway, was originally part of an advertisement for a subdivision called Hollywoodland. Acquired by the local Chamber of Commerce, the sign was refurbished and edited into a larger than life advertisement and symbol.

The Hollywood Hills and adjacent areas boast not one but two **Forest Lawn Memorial Parks**. The one in Hollywood (6300 Forest Lawn Drive, Tel. 984-1711) houses a museum of early American history. The **original cemetery** in nearby Glendale is famous for its artistic replicas as well as its

CALIFORNIA

The Hollywood Bowl

inspiration for *The Loved One*, Evelyn Waugh's scathing satire on Southern California. (1712 S. Glendale ave. Tel. 254-3131.)

Toward the east end of Hollywood, north of downtown, Silver Lake and Echo Park give Hollywood more of a neighborhood feeling. The **Street Fair** at Sunset and Santa Monica boulevards held in August, attracts a wild mixture of characters.

The Sunset Strip
Sunset Boulevard, the traditional center of West Hollywood, was once the hub of nightlife in the city. After a hard day's work at the studio, it was natural

*C*ALIFORNIA

Hollywood...

for the star being chauffeured home to Beverly Hills, Brentwood or Malibu to stop at one of the posh clubs on Sunset. In the 1960s Sunset became the magnet for psychedelics and flower children. Then, when the flower children began to wilt, Sunset attracted more hard-core weirdos per square foot than any other street in the city or state. Today it has renewed its place as a bejeweled string of chic night spots, mostly rock clubs.

Looking south from various points along Sunset at night, the vast glimmering grid of Los Angeles is visible and overwhelming as is the array of huge handpainted billboards. Do not think that only stars make it up there. Rich hopefuls have been known to attract attention for their clients from the many producers who drive this way to their homes in the western hills. At this writing, the star of the billboard parade was a gigantic Howard the Duck, complete with a protruding bill and a cigar puffing real smoke. Several comedy clubs have appeared here, presenting famous comedians and those longing to become one. On amateur nights the admission is usually cheaper, but then you must take your chances; you might glimpse tomorrow's Woody Allen, but you might squirm in embarrassment all night long.

The Fairfax area, squeezed in near West Hollywood and Beverly Hills, has an

CALIFORNIA

ambience of its own, considerably more modest than its neighbors. The main sights are the Farmer's Market, the CBS studios and the Jewish section.

The **Farmer's Market**, at the corner of Third street and Fairfax, is a puffed up tourist rip-off. Not in every farmer's market can you buy a replica of a classical vase or a David Bowie poster. It was once a real farmer's market selling real produce at reasonable or even cheap prices. Although the produce can still be found, and though it often looks beautiful, reasonable bargains are rare. The food bars, however, sell an amazing array of cuisine and delicacies. Top off your crepe or shrimp salad with Chinese chestnuts or toffee peanuts.

Near the Farmer's Market are the **CBS Television Studios** where various game shows are broadcast before live audiences. Tickets must be arranged in advance. Tel. 852-2624.

Just two blocks up begins the concentrated **Jewish section** of Fairfax. A center for the Jewish community since World War II, Fairfax still has an Eastern European atmosphere, though many families have left. More than a pinch of the Middle East has been added now that immigrants from Israel have begun to congregate here. On the street you will hear Hebrew, some Yiddish, and a little English. Bakeries, kosher delis, Israeli restaurants and felafel stands line the street. A potato knish or two can keep you going a long while.

Several stores specialize in Jewish books and Jewish and Israeli music. A large newsstand at Fairfax and Oakwood carries international periodicals. A few semi open-air markets sell produce far more cheaply than the Farmer's Market down the street. With other small ethnic restaurants moving in – Korean and Yugoslavian, for example – the street has the atmosphere of a city neighborhood not found much in L.A. these days.

Griffith Park

In the hills northeast of Hollywood is **Griffith Park**. With 4000 acres, it is the largest municipal park in the country. A large portion was left undeveloped for hiking and riding. Maps are available at the four main park entrances. Bus 97 goes to the park, but it is hard to get around here without a car.

The **Greek Theater** is a beautiful place for an evening concert, and there are presentations of everything from classical music to Neil Diamond. (Tel. 216-666.) Nearby is the cool, shaded **bird sanctuary**, which is as much a sanctuary for people. Walking tours are given on Sunday at 1pm. (Open daily from dawn to dusk.) Children can ride the railroad and climb on trolleys, old cars, planes and ponies at **Travel Town** (200 Drive. Tel. 662-5874.) The distinguished white building with the green copper dome is the **Griffith Observatory and Planetarium**, a L.A. landmark. The Hall of Science offers basic displays with lots of button-pushing. The planetarium show is done well, and the popular Laserium will bombard you with sound and light. There is a telescope for public use on summer evenings until 10pm and in winter from Tues.-Sun. 7-10pm.

CALIFORNIA

Planetarium shows: Open daily during summer, 1:30pm, 3pm and 8pm, Sat.-Sun. also 4:30pm. In winters Tues.-Fri. at 3pm and 8pm, Sat.-Sun. 4:30pm. Admission, seniors discount. Tel. 664-1191 for recording, Tel. 664-1181 live. For Laserium schedule and programs, Tel. 997-3624.

The **Los Angeles Zoo**, though not on the level of the San Diego Zoo, is interesting, with animals grouped by continent. Many touchable creatures for children. (5333 Zoo dr. Open 10am-6pm in summer, 10 am-5pm in winter. Admission. Tel. 666-4090.)

There are over 40 miles of horse trails in the park and commercial stables on the park's edges. They take only cash and require a deposit.

A great network of hiking trails picks up from various points in the park. The bird sanctuary and observatory trails lead to the top of Mt. Hollywood from where you can see all of the L.A. basin. Several guided hikes begin at the ranger station on Crystal Spring Rd. Free trail maps are available here. Tel. 665-5188.

Wilshire/Hancock Park

During the real estate boom of the 1880s, an entrepreneur named H. Gaylord Wilshire portioned out a tract along a country lane and named it after himself. After Edward Doheny discovered oil, wells popped up all through the neighborhood and property values shot higher than the black geysers.

A line of stores built during the 1930s was dubbed the **Miracle Mile** to attract shoppers from the central city. This section has some of the finest examples of the old art deco architecture that proliferated in Los Angeles. The gem of the street, **Bullocks Wilshire** was touted as the city's first suburban store. Set up as an elegant establishment to draw the wealthy from downtown, it retains that image today, including its 5th-floor tea room.

Wilshire blvd. extends for 16 miles from downtown to the Pacific, cutting through the financial district, through neighborhoods of Asian and Latin American immigrants, through the old stylish neighborhood of Hancock Park, through Miracle Mile, and finally out to trendy Santa Monica.

The strangest sight along gleaming Wilshire is the ancient mastodon wallowing through a pond of black tar in the **La Brea Tar Pits**. You can almost hear it bellowing in fear and frustration. In 1910 the first fossil discoveries were made at the La Brea pits, which ultimately yielded the well-preserved remains of an enormous variety of animal life from the Pleistecine period, down to about 6000 BCE. Mastodons, saber-tooth tigers, ground sloths and native American horses, all roamed the area now covered by housing tracts and parking lots. Among the other remains were those of a woman.

The George C. Page Museum displays the findings from the adjacent tar pits.(5801 Wilshire blvd. Open Tue.-Sun. 10am-5pm. $1.50 adults, 75 cents for ages 6-17, seniors and students. Free on the second Tuesday of each

CALIFORNIA

Wallowing mastodon at La Brea Tar Pits

month. Admission to both the Page Museum and adjacent L.A. County Museum of Art is $2, and $1 ages 6-17, students, seniors. For a recorded message call Tel. 936-2230, for other queries call Tel. 857-6311.) Through a variety of techniques, bones have been fleshed out, thereby recreating a vivid picture of the area's natural history and the evolution of the animals. Through plate-glass windows visitors can observe paleontologists at work. This museum is imaginative and thought-provoking.

The **Los Angeles County Museum of Art**,(5905 Wilshire blvd. Open Tue.-Fri. 10am-5pm, Sat.-Sun. 10am-6pm. Same admission as the Page Museum.

CALIFORNIA

St. Elmo Village

Tel. 937-4250), immediately west of the tar pits and Page Museum, consists of three separate buildings which house some amazing collections from all regions and all historical periods of the world: ancient Near Eastern, Western European painting and sculpture, American Painting. The collection of Indian, Tibetan and Nepalese art is highly acclaimed. A sculpture garden featuring bronzes by Rodin connects the buildings. On Monday evenings in winter there are concerts of contemporary music. On weekends the museum's plaza turns bright and lively with street performers. There is a cafeteria, museum shop and art rental gallery. Guided tours of the permanent collections are available.

CALIFORNIA

The **Craft and Folk Art Museum** across Wilshire, is a small museum featuring both the traditional and contemporary in folk art. (5814 Wilshire blvd. Open Tue.-Sat. 11am-8:30pm, Sun 10am-6pm. Free admission, donation suggested. Tel. 937-5544.) The balcony of the Egg and the Eye restaurant peers out over the exhibition floor.

South of the towers and elegant stores of Wilshire, in a nondescript, predominantly Black neighborhood of small houses and bungalows, there is a surprisingly rich collection of art in the museums and galleries. **St. Elmo Village**, (4830 St. Elmo dr. Tel. 931-3409) is a non-profit community arts center, surrounded by gardens, sculptures and color – on the sidewalk, in the courtyard, on fences and garage doors there are beautiful and blazing murals.

The creation of the village began when the land was slated to be sold. Two artists who had lived there initiated what became a huge grassroots effort to buy the property and turn it into a neighborhood center. Funds were raised with snowballing support from neighbors, community groups, politicians and celebrities. Now, in a neighborhood of gangs and easy access to drugs, the village fosters creativity, community pride and constructive achievement. The artists who live in the village offer workshops to children, the elderly and anyone interested. On Sunday a small cafe is open, with photos on the wall relating the birth and history of the center. The annual **Festival of the Art of Survival** initiated as a fund-raiser, has become a jam-packed colorful celebration, often attended by prominent local leaders, such as Mayor Tom Bradley and big-name performers. The village wecomes visitors. (4830 St. Elmo dr. Tel. 931-3409.)

Further along Wilshire, art of a different sort can be found at the **Martyrs Memorial and Museum of the Holocaust**, in the Jewish Community Building, (6505 Wilshire blvd. Open Mon.-Thurs. 9am-5pm, Fri. 9am-3pm, Sun. 1-5pm. Admission free. Tel. 852-1234 ext 3200.) The museum presents a stark presentation of Hitler's "final solution." The presentations can shock, but the paintings and drawings created by people trapped in ghettos and death camps are amazing and inspiring statements.

Beverly Hills

At the turn of the century, the Beverly Hills region was open rolling farmland where shepherds grazed their flocks. Some oil speculators, hoping to cash in on the region's oil boom, purchased the property, but the wells turned no profit: The investors, to recover their losses, sub-divided the property for an exclusive subdivision, near but separate from the growing city of Los Angeles. By 1914, the wealthy had bought tracts and were moving in. Douglas Fairbanks started the migration of movie stars to the area. He bought land and developed it into Picfair, his private residence at 1143 Summit dv., where he lived with Mary Pickford. Separate municipal status allowed the stars and wealthy to develop their enclave as they wished, which meant no annoying industry and strict regulations on parking, signs and preservation of trees.

CALIFORNIA

The main shopping area is formed by the triangle of Wilshire blvd., Little Santa Monica blvd. (a smaller street just to the south of and parallel to Santa Monica blvd.), and **Rodeo Drive**. Rodeo drive is famous for its exclusive stores: Gucci, Ralph Lauren, Yves St. Tropez, and many more. The **Beverly Wilshire Hotel**, considered one of the most prestigious in the world, is an enormous spread out structure with cobblestones and marble arches. The oasis of accessibility within this opulence is the Foodshow.

At the southwest corner of Beverly Hills is **Century City**, a complex of condos and an even more expensive shopping area extending over a three-block long strip between Santa Monica blvd. and Pico along the Avenue of the Stars. This was the 20th Centry-Fox back lot until the studio found it more economical to shoot on location. The **ABC Entertainment Center** is found here (see "Movie and Television Land"). Also in the complex is **The Hollywood Experience**, a multi-screen one-hour show on the history of tinseltown. (Tel. 553-0626.)

Some of the city's most famous, elaborate and expensive restaurants are found on La Cienega blvd. between San Vincente and Wilshire, known as **Restaurant Row**. Famous among the famous is *Lawry's Prime Rib*.

In stark contrast to the ornamentation of Century City, is the adjacent **Simon Weisenthal Center**, the comprehensive museum and archives on the Holocaust and related contemporary human rights issues. (9760 W. Pico blvd. Open Mon.-Thurs. 10:30am-4:30pm, Fri. 10:30am-2:30pm, Sun. 11am-4pm. Admission free. Tel. 553-9036.) The museum includes original memorabilia and publications. The center offers a steady schedule of lectures, films and educational programs on the Holocaust

The most amazing homes in Beverly Hills are, predictably, in the hills. Some can barely be seen from the road. Buy yourself a star-gazing map if you wish from the vendors along Sunset blvd. or from the souvenir shops along Hollywood blvd. Guided tours are also available.

The **Beverly Hills Hotel**, near the corner of Sunset and Benedict Canyon Rd., is a four-story luxurious example of mission architecture, set back amid 12 acres of lush grounds. It was built in 1912, with many subsequent replacements and additions. Film stars often relax at the hotel's **Polo Lounge**.

Greystone Park was built by Edward L. Doheny, years after he had, as a laborer, discovered oil with his shovel and was smart enough to exploit his finding. His baronial mansion overlooking Los Angeles symbolizes an amazing story of one man's rise to wealth and power. The stables, tennis courts, kennels and lake paved over for parking, and the 55-room mansion are all testament to the vastness of his wealth. The main building is closed to the public, but the grounds are open and summer concerts are held here. Call for ticket information and tour reservations. (905 Loma Vista Dr. Open 10am-6pm. Admission free. Tel. 550-4864.)

CALIFORNIA

Westwood Village, UCLA

Westwood Village was a small Mediterranean style shopping center until the **University of California at Los Angeles (UCLA)** opened to the north of it. Westwood now serves a huge student body. The nice thing about this area is that there is much to do in an area small enough to walk through – no car is needed. There are campus museums, beautiful buildings and gardens, and a steady schedule of activities.

Westwood is filled with restaurants and theaters. First-run movies are shown at a hefty $6 per ticket. The shops and galleries are bizarre, exotic and chic. On weekend nights the scene is manic, as youths, punks, performers, and tourists join the trim, tan students who pour out of the campus area.

The main street, **Westwood Boulevard**, runs south from the campus to Wilshire. The intersection is insanely busy. Some of the more interesting shops and restaurants are on the side streets. The smaller and more unusual bookstores are clustered on Westwood blvd. south of Wilshire. Car traffic through campus is limited, and parking is tough. Buses 20, 21 or 308 run along Wilshire to Westwood. From the parking lot 32 on Weyburn St. there is a free shuttle to campus. You can sometimes find parking spots south of Wilshire or on the hilly streets south of campus where the fraternities are. It may be better to accept fate, drive into one of the university parking lots and pay $3 for the day. The RTD Westwood shuttle runs from 6:30pm to 1am on Friday, and 11am-1:30am on Saturday. Route maps are available at various spots in Westwood or in a RTD customer service center. The shuttle runs to the Federal Building at Veteran and Ashton, just south of Wilshire, where there is free parking.

UCLA is rated one of the top universities in the country. The school is well-known for its graduate programs, perhaps its medical school especially. The campus is beautifully landscaped and it is easy and tempting to get lost here. **The Quadrangle** near the center of the campus was featured in the film *The Graduate* as the campus of Berkeley (other scenes were shot in Berkeley). The visitor center is in **Dodd Hall**, east of the Quad. Tours and maps are available here. (Open Mon.-Fri. 8am-5pm. Tel. 825-4338.)

Ackerman Union is the student center. Many films are offered on campus but rules forbid their announcement off-campus. At the Union (as well as bulletin boards around campus) you can catch up on everything. This is the buzzing central hive of all student activity. Downstairs there is travel information, a ride board, a bowling alley, cafeteria, and smaller eateries reasonably priced for student budgets. (Tel. 825-0611.)

The **Murphy Sculpture Garden** exhibits pieces by Rodin, Lipschitz and Moore, among others. The **Museum of Cultural History**, at the southern part of the campus has exhibits of folk and primitive art. The observation deck of the **Ralph Bunche Social Work Building** affords a view of the campus, hills, coast and ocean on a clear day. Near the Quad is **Royce Hall**, named for noted Californian historian Josiah Royce. Recently refurbished, its auditorium hosts top performers. For ticket information, call Tel. 825-2953.

*C*ALIFORNIA

Waiting for the big one at Malibu

The **Mathias Botanical Garden**, in the corner of the campus, is a shaded area of redwoods and palms, a beautiful place for a picnic or just to rest in a peaceful and shady spot.

Around Malibu

From L.A. County's northern border with Ventura County, its coast is dotted with state beaches and parks. The beaches may be narrow and rocky, or broad and smooth. Some are backed by cliffs, while others slope gently.

On a hot summer's day it seems that half the basin's population flocks to the

CALIFORNIA

L.A. beaches, but despite crowded roads, parking problems and crowds, there is always room on the beach. Even on a crowded beach you are spared that east-coast phenomenon of picking your way over oil-covered bodies and spreading your blanket as if staking a gold claim.

Leo Carillo State Beach, in the north, is a favorite for windsurfers. Across the road is the outlet for a network of trails penetrating into the valleys, canyons and chaparral-covered hills. (Tel. 818-706-1310.) Several beaches to the south is **Zuma Beach**, which is county-owned. It is comparatively large, with concessions, restrooms and crowds. To the south juts **Duma Point**, and on the other side of it is a beautiful crescent shaped beach, hidden by tall bluffs. This is a hot spot for surfers and their groupies. Duma Point gives a view of the coast in both directions, and clearly shows where the beach was washed away in the giant storms of 1983. Guns were positioned here during World War II against the Japanese invasion that never came. Be careful parking; local authorities regularly hunt down illegally parked cars and slap on hefty fines.

The stretch of beach at Malibu was once owned by the Rindge family, who did their best to keep it private and intact. When the husband died his widow fought the authorities with everything from lawsuits to dynamite, but public transportation and private developers won out. Jutting far west beyond Los Angeles, **Malibu** has its own special atmosphere, and stunning beaches where the scrubby mountains slope down to the sea. It rapidly became a haunt for Hollywood stars. Rock stars from the Beach Boys to Joni Mitchell have immortalized Malibu, and Bob Dylan built a house there. Malibu is where the beauties come, where the muscles flex, where beaches are private and where the sheriff wears bright green shorts and matching T-shirt. Along this stretch of beach are intermittent public beaches, some with facilities. Roadside stands are interspersed with expensive seafood restaurants perched above the waves. Just east of town are several popular beaches. Parking is expensive. Cars park on the PCH while there's room.

The **Paul J. Getty Museum**, off the Pacific Coast highway in Malibu, offers a taste of culture that seems incongruous with the sun worshippers just across the street. An enormous recreation of a Roman country house, the museum displays a magnificent private collection of Western art. It is mind-boggling to see how much great art one man could acquire. Getty devoted himself to preserving these treasures for posterity and public appreciation. He lived most of his life in Europe and, ironically, never saw the museum he created.

The Getty collection emphasizes five major areas: Greek and Roman antiquities, 18th century decorative art (clocks, chairs, carpets, etc.), Western European paintings from the 13th to the 19th century, drawings of the old masters, and illuminated medieval and Renaissance manuscripts. The museum also runs a library, mostly for the work of researchers and scholars. All galleries and most gardens are accessible by wheelchair. Lectures on art are held every Thursday evening. The museum also has a tea room and bookstore.

CALIFORNIA

Malibu – Paradise on earth

Parking facilities are limited, and advance parking reservations are required, preferably at least a week in advance. Visitors without a car, or who are unable to make parking reservations, may enter the museum grounds by bicycle, motorcycle, taxi or RTD bus 434 (request a museum pass from the bus driver). Located at 17985 Pacific Coast Highway, one mile southeast of Topanga Canyon rd. (Open Tue.-Sun 10am-5pm. Gate closes at 4:30pm. Parking, admission and lectures are free. For parking reservations and lecture reservations, Tel. 459-2003 or 459-8402.)

From the Pacific Coast Highway, a turn onto **Topanga Canyon blvd.** leads into the rugged Santa Monica Mountains. This island of wilderness is right in the middle of the metropolis, squeezed between the San Fernando Valley suburbs on the north, Santa Monica and the rest of L.A. on the south, the Ventura Freeway on the east and the ocean on the west. Within these boundaries is a maze of winding roads with hairpin turns. Wend your way with a map north and west to **Malibu Canyon rd.** for spectacular views of the hill, canyon, coastline and ocean. Alternately, you can follow Mulholland dr. and Mulholland Highway along the crest of the mountains.

Topanga Canyon once sheltered opium dealers, smugglers, rum-runners and a brothel. Ensconsced here today are the hippest of the rich and richest of the hip. This is commune, ashram and religious-retreat country. The town of Topanga Canyon, with its organic restaurants and cafes, preceded, and outlasted the hippie movement.

The Santa Monica Mountains provide beautiful hiking trails ranging from easy to rugged. **Malibu Creek State Park**, accessible either by Malibu Canyon rd. from the Pacific Coast Highway, or from the south on Las Virgenes from the Ventura Freeway, is a secluded park with a creek, a lake and 15 miles of trails. Bicyling and riding available, no camping. (28754 Mulholland dr. Tel. (818) 706-1310.)

The larger Topanga State Park also has beautiful trails for hikers and riders. From Topanga Canyon rd., turn west on Entrada rd. Tel. (818) 706-1310.

Santa Monica

South of the hilly peninsula jutting into the ocean at Malibu, nestles Santa Monica and Santa Monica Bay. About 15 miles west of downtown and connected by the Santa Monica Freeway, Santa Monica was once a resort village for city residents. Today, its beaches and bluffs are popular and its pier with its amusements has become a landmark. But Santa Monica still clings to a certain apartness. Incorporated as its own city, it is a center for liberal and socialist activism. Liberal forces have gained substantial representation (Tom Hayden, one of the radical student leaders of the 1960s, and husband to Jane Fonda, is the state assemblyman from Santa Monica). Interests urging greater development have met stiff organized resistance from groups urging strict controls on growth. The rent control laws protecting tenants (often viewed as radical, leftist or progressive legislation) are extremely stringent here.

The deceptively pretty bay actually hides a serious problem. For more than 20 years, industries discharged huge amounts of DDT and other toxins into the ocean off Santa Monica. The kelp beds, mussels, fish and invertebrates that thrived in these waters have declined and some have disappeared.

Despite recent steps to prevent further dumping and to clean up the bay, the concentrations of DDT found in fish in Santa Monica Bay are reportedly among the highest in the world.

It is easy to understand why the city is popular with young professionals and singles, and the artists who managed to slip in before rents leaped. One

CALIFORNIA

Carnival time

could stay in Santa Monica and have all major needs satisfied. The beach and pier, the trendy shops, the downtown shopping center and the bluff park are in close proximity. The bluff park is filled with joggers, walkers, chess-players, and some homeless types who stretch their sleeping bags beneath the wind-sculpted trees. The beaches below are wide, roomy even on a crowded weekend. The famous **Santa Monica Pier**, battered and partly washed out during heavy 1983 storms, is still a popular place to stroll. Hints of yesterday are found in the old boardwalk, the painted signs and hand-carved horses on the carousel, which was seen in the movie *The Sting*.

The Pacific Coast Highway comes down from the north and turns inland at Santa Monica. From the east, the Santa Monica Freeway provides the easiest access. Streets and the beach to the south run into Venice. Parking near the beach area is difficult. But there is cheap and sufficient municipal parking a few blocks inland off Santa Monica blvd. For a couple of bucks you park almost all day.

Santa Monica runs its own bus company. The express bus 10 runs to downtown Los Angeles. If you want to reach downtown Los Angeles, parking your car in the Santa Monica municipal lot and riding the 10 express bus is

CALIFORNIA

highly recommended. It takes about 45 minutes (the route along city streets can take twice that). Two buses also run to Venice.

Bicycling is a convenient and popular way to travel along the stretch of beach. A bicycle path starts at Santa Monica and heads south through Venice to Marina Del Ray. To the north, cyclists follow the Pacific Coast Highway.

Touring and bus information is available at the **Visitors Assistance Stand** (Ocean ave. near Arizona st. Open daily 10am-4pm in summer; Tues.-Sun. 11am-3pm in winter. Tel. 393-7593.)

Santa Monica's older, outside shopping mall, along 2nd and 4th sts. between Broadway and Colorado, has some small and interesting shops and no traffic. But this has been appended to the modern **Santa Monica Place**, a slick and trendy version of other indoor malls.

Further south, on Main st. between Ocean Park and Pico, are two blocks of restaurants, boutiques, galleries, antique and specialty shops. Most are geared toward the young upwardly mobile or already-arrived. Here you'll find some small bars where the locals hang out.

Santa Monica, with its hip population and concentration of neighborhoods with small houses, is excellent turf for a favorite Southern Californian pasttime: yard-saling. People cruise around the neighborhood in their cars on a weekend, following the cardboard signs tacked to telephone poles that will lead them to the numerous yard-sales and, hopefully, fantastic bargains. With a little hunting they can be found.

Venice

The Hare Krishna are out dancing, chanting and jingling tambourines. The one-man electric band on roller skates weaves among the muscled strutters, the gawking tourists, the punks, joggers, jugglers and black kids dancing. The outdoor cafes are packed. Middle Eastern music blares from a booth selling cassettes. A greying man stands on a bench attacking Reaganomics while from another bench a preacher in a green irridescent suit proffers God with the slick rhythm of a huckster selling miracle serum... It's a typical summer Sunday on **Venice Beach.**

The American version of Venice was founded in 1904 by tobacco magnate Abbot Kinney, who came west hoping to help the Indians, but succumbed instead to a fantastic vision. Kinney became determined to single-handedly create a mecca for high culture in America, and to recreate an imitation of Venice, Italy. He dug 30 miles of canals, complete with gondolas and imported gondoliers, and he created replicas of Italian palazzos and arcades. For a while, the rich of Los Angeles flocked to the pleasures and posh clubs of Venice, but gradually the place deteriorated physically, and then socially. Venice became a tawdry, seedy carnival which attracted hustlers and eccentrics, as well as artists, outcasts and radicals. By 1930 the area had been absorbed by the city and all but a few miles of the canals had been filled.

CALIFORNIA

Venice – Cardboard cults

CALIFORNIA

Wow!

The old run-down buildings offered comparatively cheap rents, attracting artists and social rebels, outcasts and hard-timers. During the 1950s Venice became L.A.'s outpost for the Beatniks, during the 1960s for the hippies, and during the 1970s for casualties and survivors of both previous epochs.

Almost invisible beneath the glittering eccentricity of Venice lives another group of survivors, the old Eastern European Jews. Once ten-thousand strong, with thriving cultural and social centers, this community has steadily diminished through the pressures of urban development that pushed them out and the natural ravages of time. Some sit on benches, facing the ocean or the parade of humanity. They play backgammon or chess, and read the Yiddish papers. Some, old radicals from another world, pass out political pamphlets to young people.

Venice is easily accessible from Santa Monica by bus, automobile or bicycle or on foot. Pacific Ocean Park, marking the northern end of the beach walk, has a sizable parking lot. Parking along the streets near the beach, especially during the summer, can be an exercise in masochism, but parking can be found some blocks to the east.

A tour of Venice simply involves walking and taking in the crowds. At

CALIFORNIA

Winwood and Pacific, a few blocks in from the beach, are the last vestiges of the colonnaded arcade which was part of Kinney's creation. Winwood and Main, where the streets form a traffic circle, was once a circular canal that formed the hub of the system. The post office on the west side contains a mural illustrating the history of Venice. Between Venice and Washington blvds., just east of the ocean front walk, lies one of the last segments of the canal, filled with ducks, lined with little bungalows and crossed by arched bridges. Watch for the beautiful murals along the boardwalk area. There are several huge and detailed depictions of Venice, such as Venice under a blanket of snow. At the southern end of Ocean Walk, at Washington, is the pier with its bars and restaurants, and beyond that begins opulent Marina Del Ray. Some of the ocean side cafes and restaurants stay open late, but in general the area empties quickly and closes down with sundown. Street people fill the doorways, only to be moved along by the cops. This can be a dangerous area at night.

Accommodations

Most of the hotels and motels in the Los Angeles area are modern structures, some ultra modern sky-scrapers. The major chains, both of motels and hotels, are well represented in most major tourist areas. They are spread throughout the city, but the main areas are Marina Del Ray, Beverly Hills, West Los Angeles and Santa Monica. These areas are generally more expensive.

The downtown area may be less expensive, as it is not yet very fashionable although it has been largely renovated. West of Broadway there are many hotels and motels to choose from. Here there are some older and more moderately priced hotels, as well as luxurious ones. The major information centers are found in this area.

Downtown Accommodation

New Otani Hotel & Garden: 120 S. Los Angeles st., L.A. 90012. Tel. 629-1200. U.S. toll-free 800-421-8795, toll-free CA 800-252-0197. A world class, luxurious hotel. Some rooms are centered around the Japanese garden, as are the bar and several restaurants. Located in Little Tokyo. Airport service. $98 up single, $113 up double.

Biltmore Hotel: 515 S. Olive st., L.A. 90013. Tel. 624-1011 or 800-252-0175. A refurbished red-brick downtown hotel, with a Spanish lobby of marble and intricately hand painted ceilings. Its bar is popular, its coffee shop reasonable and its French restaurant, *Bernard's*, an expensive L.A. classic.

Figueroa Hotel: 939 S. Figueroa st., L.A. 90015. Tel. 627-8971. Toll-free U.S. 800-421-9092 or toll-free CA 800-331-5151. Spanish style, comfortable rooms, old fashioned bathrooms. Near the Convention Center. Airport service and other amenities. $48-$58 single, $58-$64 double.

Rainbow Hotel: 536 S. Hope st. L.A. 90071. Tel. 627-9941. Toll-free 800-435-9153. In the heart of downtown, recently renovated, a popular and recommended moderately priced hotel. $44 up single, $50 up double. Near airport bus.

CALIFORNIA

Hotel Carver: 460 E. 4th st. L.A. 90013. Tel. 972-9228. A clean, friendly inexpensive little hotel in Little Tokyo. Many Japanese guests. $15-20 single, $30-$36 double.

Mitchell Hotel: 1072 W. 6th st. L.A. 90017. Tel. 481-2477. Basic low budget hotel with small rooms, but safe and reliable with good downtown access. $16 single, $21 double.

There are several American Youth Hostel facilities in the metropolitan L.A. area. None are right downtown, but most have access to public transportation and the staff know the bus routes. Most cost $6-$8 for members, and slightly more for non-members.

Hollywood Hostel: 1553 N. Hudson ave. Tel. 467-4161. Often crowded. Located in the *Hollywood YMCA*, which also offers rooms and is also crowded. Tel. 467-4161.

Bill Baker International Youth Hostel: Westchester YMCA, 8015 S. Sepulveda blvd. Tel. 776-0922. Near the airport.

Los Angeles International Youth Hostel: 1502 Palos Verdes dr. N., Harbor City. Tel. 831-8109. Near the Palos Verdes Peninsula and Long Beach.

Huntington Beach Colonial Inn Hostel: 421 8th st., Huntington Beach. Tel. 536-3315. One of the most pleasant in the area, near the beach, in an old house.

Food
Downtown
The Far East Cafe: 347 E. 1st st. A great Chinese restaurant found at the edge of Little Tokyo. With its original wooden booths and deep interior, this is the place you'd come to for a secret assignation. The detective film *Farewell My Lovely* included scenes shot here. The lunches are good and filling, under $5.

The Biltmore Bar: 515 S. Olive st. In the beautifully renovated red-brick hotel, a relaxing and popular place to wet the whistle. The *Biltmore Coffee Shop* offers the standard fare at reasonable prices.

The Grand Central Public Market: 317 S. Broadway. This bazaar is a sight in itself (see "Downtown").

Vickman's: 1228 E. 8th. Opening at 3am, this is one of the best-known restaurants catering to the early morning produce workers. Fresh bakery.

The Pantry Cafe: 877 S. Figueroa st. Open 24 hours, and busy for most of those, serving steak, sourdough and hashbrowns for the same way since 1924.

Cafe Pasquini: 701 W. 7th. Antipasto, pasta, expresso, sunlight and European ambience. Breakfast and lunch.

Clifton's Cafetaria: 648 S. Broadway. An original cafeteria, from 1912. No waiting, great variety, great prices, great show on the walls and maybe at the next table. Kitsch raised to an art.

CALIFORNIA

Hollywood

Along Hollywood boulevard, and in the surrounding area, you can find classic Hollywood restaurants, reasonable ethnic restaurants and fast food stands.

Musso and Frank Grill: 6667 Hollywood blvd. Tel. 467-7788. An overpriced but classic Hollywood establishment dating back to 1919.

C.C. Brown's: 7007 Hollywood blvd. The decor of this ice-cream parlor is from the 1920s, the prices from the 1980s. They claim to have invented the hot fudge sundae, and they do indeed serve a great fudge.

Addis Ababa: 6263 Leland Way. Tel. 463-9788. Ethiopian cuisine presented in a converted house near the corner of Vine. Very warm and homey, with small rooms available. A delicious vegetarian dinner served on *injira* (Ethiopian bread) starts at $4.95.

Orean: The Health Express: 1320 N. Vine. Tel. 462-9945. Simply fantastic for anyone wanting the service and price of a fast-food stand but concerned about health. All their food is vegetarian, including soy burgers and bran pancakes. Tables are of polished wood, and ferns decorate the interior. There is a great menu which contains information about famous vegetarians and vegetarianism, plus a quote from George Bernard Shaw: "Animals are my friends...and I don't eat my friends."

Seafood Bay: 3916 blvd. Tel. 664-3902. Crowded and extremely popular. The food is delicious and reasonably priced.

Cantor's Fairfax Restaurant Delicatessen and Bakery: 419 N. Fairfax ave. Tel. 651-2030. Open 24 hours a day, often frequented by Hollywood stars. Tremendous variety on the menu.

Tex Mex Cafe: 1108 N. Flores st. West Hollywood. Chic, cool and pleasant with a shaded patio. Serves huge portions of delicious non-greasy Mexican food. A deep dish tostada is big enough for two.

The Tail of the Pup: 311 N. La Cienaga, across from the Beverly Center. The ultimate hot-dog stand. It has been featured in several films.

The Egg and the Eye: 5814 Wilshire blvd., on the balcony of the Craft and Folk Museum. In keeping with the surrounding motif, you can create your own omelette.

Beverly Hills

Lawry's: 55 N. La Cienaga. Tel. 652-2827. Serving moderately priced ribs, ribs and more ribs. People wait in line to get in.

ddl Foodshow: 244 Beverly dr. Tel. 859-2700. A DeLorean production, done with panache. Exotic delectables everywhere, from seafood to chocolates to cheeses and coffee. A store and a restaurant.

Santa Monica

Pioneer Boulangerie: 2102 Main st. A bakery, cafetaria and restaurant, and a popular local spot.

Cafe Casino: Arizona and Ocean Park. A Mediterranean style outdoor cafe

CALIFORNIA

with cafeteria prices. Refreshing breeze from the sea across the street, and foreign languages spoken all round.

Todai: Arizona and 2nd: All you can eat for $10, and delicious too.

Charmer's Market: 180 Pier ave. A combined delicatessen and restaurant, specializing in imported and exotic delicacies for the gourmet.

Entertainment

An endless variety of entertainment keeps Los Angeles alive and vibrant all the time. Concerts range from classical to punk. There are night clubs, dinner clubs, dancing clubs and comedy clubs. Everyone who wants to make it in the entertainment world tries their luck out here. Consequently, there is an enormous variety and range in the quality of the entertainment. The local papers and weekly guides keep up to date with current performances.

If you want to catch a uniquely Los Angeles aspect of entertainment, check out some of the comedy clubs. Los Angeles is obviously a major center for aspiring comics. In the last few years, the number of clubs concentrating solely on comedians has grown. Most of these have some sort of amateur night, in which unknown aspiring artists have a chance to show their talent. Occasionally some famous "graduates" of a particular comedy club return to check out the hopefuls or to polish their own acts. These amateur or showcase nights offer a glimpse of the inner workings of show business, and some of the performers are incredible.

Comedy Store: 8433 Sunset blvd., W. Hollywood. Tel. 656-6225. One of the earliest of the comedy clubs here, it has grown to a three-room operation, each with a different focus.

The Improvisation: 8162 Melrose ave., W. Hollywood. Tel. 651-2583. Another comedy institution, presenting both stand-up comics and improvisational theater.

The Laugh Factory: 8001 Sunset blvd., Sunset blvd., W. Hollywood. Small, more recent and more intimate than the others. The level of talent may be more variable.

Other Clubs

The Troubador: 9081 Santa Monica blvd., W. Hollywood. Tel. 276-6168. Famous as the launching pad for a number of rock stars, such as Elton John, James Taylor, and Linda Ronstadt. During the week acts range from country-rock to post new wave, and weekends feature bigger talent, with occasional famous drop-ins such as Bob Dylan.

Mischa's: 7561 Sunset blvd, Hollywood. Tel. 874-3467. A gaudy, colorful, tent-covered Russian style cabaret, kitschy and fun, featuring many famous Russian immigrant entertainers.

Important Addresses And Phone Numbers

Greater Los Angeles Visitors and Convention Bureau: 505 S. Flower st. 90071 (in ARCA plaza). Tel. 239-0204. (see "Orientation".)

CALIFORNIA

Welcome to Los Angeles: Tel. 628-5857. 24-hour recording on current and special events.
Beverly Hills Visitor Bureau: 239 S. Beverly dr., 90212. Tel. 271-8174.
Burbank (Greater) Visitor and Convention Bureau: 425-A S. Victory blvd., Burbank 91502. Tel. 818-845-4266. Information on some of the studios that moved out this way.
Marina del Rey Chamber: 4629 A Admiralty Way 90290. Tel. 821-0555. Details on the marina's many hotels.
Summer Festival: Tel. 876-8742. Details on an annual festival filled with music celebrities.
Immigration Office: Federal Building, 300, N. Los Angeles st. For extension of a tourist visa.
National Park Service: 22900 Ventura blvd., Woodland Hills, 818-888-3400. For information on the Park Service lands in the Santa Monica Mountains.
Mexican Government Tourism Office: 10100 Santa Monica blvd. suite 224, LA 90067. Tel. 203-8151. General information and brochures for visits to Mexico.
Beach and Surf Reports: Tel 451-8761.
Highway Conditions: Tel. 626-7231.
Weather: Tel. 554-1212.
Ticketron: 6060 W. Manchester ave. Tel. 216-666.

Emergency:
Emergency: Tel. 911.
Rape Crisis Hotline: Tel 392-8381.
Suicide Prevention: Tel. 381-5111.
Legal Aid Hotlines: Tel 487-3320.

CALIFORNIA SEA LION
This sea lion is an excellent swimmer and has a remarkable ability to stay underwater for long periods of time – ten minutes or more. The male can grow to more than two and a half meters in length. Its color is grey-brown, but when wet looks almost black. Its habitat is the Pacific coastline of California and Mexico.

USA RENT A CAR SYSTEM

DON KOTT EXTRA·CAR
Rent-a-car/truck/leasing

AMERICA'S FASTING GROWING CAR RENTAL
4354 EAST WILLOW ST.
LONG BEACH
CA 90815
TEL. (213) 498-7816
AND 70 OTHER CITIES ACROSS THE U.S.
GUARANTEED LOW RATES
TOLL FREE 1-800-USA-CARS
AT THE LONG BEACH AIRPORT

Official Car Rental Agent
for the
LONG BEACH CONVENTION & ENTERTAINMENT CENTER

CALIFORNIA

Long Beach and Palos Verdes

The rocky **Palos Verdes Peninsula** forms an almost right-angled buttress separating Santa Monica Bay from the south-facing harbors of San Pedro and Long Beach. The **Palos Verdes drive** follows the contours of this outcropping and is lined with exclusive homes. Much of the beach is private. The public beaches are not easily accessible, but for those willing to scramble down to them, they can offer a solitude rarely found along L.A.'s coast.

The **Long Beach Airport** serves major national carriers and is accessible from most major cities. Like LAX, it operates commuter flights to San Francisco, yet is spared the jams and delays endemic to LAX. It is a small, single-terminal airport, and passengers can be in or out in fifteen minutes. Nearby are hotels, public transportation and car rentals. Within fifteen minutes you can reach a motel near a quiet beach. Forty-five minutes by freeway brings you into downtown L.A., about the same time or less than it would take after waiting for luggage and fighting crowds and traffic around LAX. Forty-five minutes south and you are cruising through little beach towns.

The **Wayfarer's Chapel**, was built by Lloyd Wright, son of Frank Lloyd Wright. (5755 Palos Verdes dr. S., Rancho Palos Verdes. Open 11am-4pm. Tel. 377-1650.) It is a stunning glass church surrounded by redwoods. Built to honor Emanuel Swedenborg, the philospher/theologian, it is much used for weddings today.

The lush 87 acres of the **South Coast Botanic Gardens** are a popular local site. (26300 Crenshaw blvd., Rancho Palos Verdes. Open daily 9am-5pm. $1.50. 75 cents for seniors, students, ages 5-17. Tel. 377-0468.)

Marineland is part-aquarium, part-amusement park, with trained dolphins and killer whales that perform tricks and splash the audience on command. (6600 Palos Verdes dr. S., Palos Verdes. Open Wed.-Sun. 10am-7pm. Adults $9.95, ages 3-11 $6.95, seniors $5. During winter, check to confirm hours. Tel. 541-5663.) For an extra fee, visitors can swim in a tank with the fish.

The **Port of Los Angeles** is located at San Pedro, squeezed in between the Palos Verdes Peninsula and Long Beach Harbor. The Long Beach and Los Angeles ports together handle an enormous amount of shipping. The **Los Angeles Maritime Museum** is located in the harbor itself, next to Ports of Call Village which is a shopping village. (At the foot of 6th st., Berth 84, San

CALIFORNIA

Pedro. Open Tues.-Sun. 9:30am-5pm. Daily tours. Tel. 548-7618.) The museum gives a few glimpses of the American nautical past as well as the daily panorama of a huge bustling port.

Long Beach, at the southern end of Los Angeles County was for years seen only as an appendage to Los Angeles. It was a navy town, and facing Ocean Boulevard downtown were grease joints, corn dog stands, porno movie theaters, sleazy clubs, and pawn shops. Near the water stood a rickety old amusement park. For about the past 15 years, Long Beach has steadily been transforming itself. Down came the sleazy bars and the amusement park along with the ornate turn-of-the-century architecture, and in their stead rose a wall of steel-and-glass towers.

Long Beach is one of the major ports on the West Coast and a rapidly growing shipping and oil center. The Queen Mary and the Spruce Goose (the biggest airplane in the world) have become centerpieces of a large tourist development scheme for the port and downtown area, which now has a large convention center and new hotels, and will soon have a new international trade center. For the business traveler, Long Beach offers the services, facilities and ambience of an urban center without the crowds and hassles of Los Angeles. Beyond the Queen Mary and Spruce Goose, there is little to keep the casual visitor enthralled. The beach area near Belmont Shore is a pleasant and convenient base for traveling to other points.

The Queen Mary comes from the age of pre-airline trans-Atlantic luxury travel, with care and class down to the doorknobs and marbled pillars. She was huge, longer than three American football fields laid end to end, but at the same time, the fastest ocean liner of her time. First, second the third-class passengers were clearly separated, with separate entrances, and third-class passengers were squeezed into the bow, which is the narrowest and most unstable part of the ship. When converted for wartime use as a troop carrier, over fifteen thousand soldiers were packed onto her decks, and Hitler offered a special reward for her sinking. She carried many famous and glamorous people, most notably Winston Churchill. Acquired by the city of Long Beach, she made her last voyage in 1967, docked in Long Beach Harbor, and is now a hotel and tourist attraction. Steeped in history, the Queen Mary developed its own folklore and mythology. During refurbishing, and when the hotel was first opened, stories of eerie incidents spread among workers and guards, such as reports of the lingering smell of cigar smoke near Winston Churchill's favorite lounge. Visitors can walk the length of the ship from bow to stern. A self-guided tour includes the enormous engine room and a slide show of the ship's history. Inquiring about a hotel room is worthwhile, if only to catch a glimpse of the beautiful polished lobby.

In the same complex as the Queen Mary, in a huge aluminum dome, sits the **Spruce Goose**, the world's largest airplane. The plane was intended to be a prototype for giant "flying boats" which would transport troops and equipment to Europe during World War II by air so as to avoid encounters with German U-boats. Howard Hughes, aviation engineer and pioneer, movie-maker, and flamboyant millionaire, backed the project. Against harsh

CALIFORNIA

Strolling the Queen Mary's deck

criticism, Hughes determined to complete it, even when government enthusiasm waned. The plane was finally test-flown in Long Beach Harbor after the war by Hughes himself, who lifted it off the water for one mile. It was then returned to a hangar and kept hidden for thirty years.

Visitors can walk through the plane, and can also see exhibits about Hughes and the history of aviation. The most recent addition is the Time Voyager, which uses film, gravity, vibrations, visual effects, and goony dressed-up creatures to create the impression that you have penetrated time and galaxies.

Not far from the Spruce Goose is the **London Towne Village**, which is typical of Southern California in that it is completely incongruous. (Open all week, 10am-6pm in winter (box office closes at 4pm), and 9am-9pm between July 4th and Labor Day (box office closes at 8pm). Admission to the entire complex is quite steep: $13.95 for adults, $9.95 ages 13-17, $7.95 6-12. Discount for seniors. Tel. 435-3511.) In spite of its attractions it is still a bit difficult to imagine Oliver Twist and Fagin dodging among the olde tourist shoppes.

CALIFORNIA

The hub of Long Beach's refurbished downtown is a new but standard mall. One venerable institution remains, however. This is **Acres of Books**, on the east side of Long Beach blvd. between Broadway and 3rd, in a warehouse-sized used-book store that will lure and engulf book lovers. Pack a lunch.

Some fine temporary exhibits by modern regional artists pass through the *Long Beach Art Museum*, a small red brick building overlooking the sea by Bluff Park. (2300 Ocean blvd. Tel. 439-2119.)

Further east, follow Second St. to the **Belmont Shore** area, Long Beach's small beach town, with boutiques, coffeeshops, restaurants, and hip bars. A few blocks south is the beach and the Olympic-sized indoor swimming pool, which is open to the public. At the end of Belmont shore is a small library overlooking the Los Alomitos Bay, offering the perfect place to sit and browse through *Moby Dick*. Across the bay is **Naples**, a network of canals. The houses have big bay windows, a boat or two docked in front, and a car or two parked behind.

Catalina Island, 22 miles off the Long Beach shore, provides a taste of exotic escape close to the mainland. **Avalon** is the only town on the island, and the remaining territory has been left in its natural state. Cars are rarely found – which in itself is a pleasant change of pace.

Passenger ferries, operated by Catalina Cruises, leave from both San Pedro and Long Beach. A round-trip costs $21.90 and allows about four hours on the island. Reservations are advisable. Tel. 775-6111, or 832-4521.

The **Visitor's Information and Service Center**, at the pier (Tel. 510-2500), and the **Chamber of Commerce** (Tel. 510-1520), on Crescent Avenue on the Pleasure Pier, can both provide information about island activities. The Chamber can also handle hotel bookings. Camping information and reservations can be made through the **Catalina Cove and Camp Agency** (Tel. 510-0303.)

Catalina is the place to give yourself totally to play. Bicycles, snorkels, scuba gear, kayaks and inner tubes can all be rented in Avalon. Cycling is an easy and beautiful way to explore the island. The town has two pretty sand beaches. The glass-bottom boat, gliding passengers across the undersea gardens filled with colorful fish and deep stands of seaweed, is a favorite and a highlight. If staying overnight in summer, take a night cruise in search of flying fish. The boat's searchlight disturbs the fish, and they leap past and sometimes over the boat.

Back in Avalon itself, stroll along Crescent ave. Fresh seafood is plentiful. The conspicuous art-deco building is the **Catalina Casino**, a movie theatre capped by a ballroom which once swung – and still does occasionally – to the big-band sound.

Accommodations
Hotel Queen Mary: Pier J, P.O.Box 8, 90801. Tel. 435-3511. The lobby has preserved the ship's luxury, as do some of the rooms, with porthole windows

CALIFORNIA

and original handles, faucets and so forth. Entrance to Queen Mary/Spruce Goose tours included. $64 up singles, $79 up doubles.

Breakers Hotel: 210 E. Ocean blvd., 90802. Tel. 432-8781; toll-free US Tel. 800-221-5053; toll-free CA Tel. 800-221-8941. Downtown, overlooking the beaches and port, next to the Convention Center. An old ornate brick building, even more conspicious because all its old neighbors have been torn down. $70 up singles/doubles.

City Center Motel: 255 Atlantic ave. 90802. Tel. 435-2483. Downtown, near the Convention Center, reasonably priced for the area, with a pool. $38 singles, $46 doubles.

Food

Ly's Garden: Broadway and Long Beach blvd. An all-you-can-eat Chinese lunch buffet for $3.25.

Wongs: 1506 E. Broadway. Serving delicious and filling cheap lunches, this is a popular local spot, along a mildy hip gay strip.

Mardi Gras: Shoreline Village: Wear your sunglasses here against the glare of the waiter's costumes and wall hangings. Overlooking the water, a popular spot with a bar/danceroom that hops. Huge portions of delicious food. Very reasonable.

Hamburger Henry's: 4700 E. 2nd st. In Belmont shore, an easy walk to the beach, this 24-hour local landmark has had a facelift bringing it back to the boppin' 50s. Hamburgers are delicious but not cheap.

Jolly Rogers: 130 Marina dr., Seaport Village. Located very near the Pacific Coast Highway, this would be your standard coffee shop but for two things; a pretty, relaxing view over Alamitos Bay, and a great $1.50 happy hour with hors d'oeuvres.

Trader Joe's: Marina Pacifica Mall, 2nd st. at Pacific coast Highway. A cut-rate gourmet deli and a great place to stock up for a picnic. There's always something interesting on sale here, whether it be cashew nuts, fancy mustard, protein powder or rum.

Important Addresses And Phone Numbers

Long Beach Convention and Visitors Council: 180 E. Ocean Boulevard., Suite 150. Tel. 436-3645.
24-hour Events Line: Tel.432-2233.
Greyhound: 133 Long Beach blvd. Tel. 603-0141.
Trailways: 245 W. 3rd st. Tel. 436-3231.
Long Beach Transit: Tel. 591-2301. Efficient and modernized.
RDT Information: Tel.639-6800. There is an express bus between downtown Long Beach and downtown L.A.
Long Beach Airport: 4100 Donald Douglas drive. Tel. 421-8293. Can give information on carriers, schedules and ground transportation.
Airport Service: Tel. 596-16662. Private bus service extending to John Wayne Airport and Disneyland in Orange County, and LAX.

BIGHORN SHEEP
This wild sheep is excellent at jumping and skipping over mountain slopes. It is stocky and light brown in color. Its habitat is the southern area of central and western U.S.A.

CALIFORNIA

The Mountain Rim

The Los Angeles Basin is rimmed on the north and east by the **San Gabriel** and **San Bernardino Mountains**, respectively. A little further to the southeast are the **San Jacintos** (see "Palm Springs"). The first two ranges, especialy the San Gabriels, literally loom at the edge of the urban area. These ranges not only create the barrier which divides the dry basin from the true desert, but also constitute an alpine world in themselves. The lower ranges may be closed in summer due to fire hazard. This immediate proximity of true wilderness is partly what makes the L.A. region so appealing, and what makes the immense city of Los Angeles so different from other major urban centers such as New York or Chicago. Both these mountains ranges boast peaks thrusting up over 10,000 feet.

There is space to ride and hike, fish and hunt, and find solitude and undisturbed nature at the very edge of the city. Both the San Gabriel and San Bernardino ranges have become popular ski resorts in winter, even while people are surfing down below. Lift tickets often sell out. They can be bought in advance from Ticketron, which adds on a charge. Night skiing can often be a little cheaper. For ski resort information, contact the Big Bear Chamber of Commerce (see below).

The San Gabriels sit right behind Pasadena and other northern communities of the L.A. Basin. The high country contains pine forests, waterfalls, rugged hiking trails and ski resorts. Much of the region is included in the **Angeles National Forest**. Trails in the front range are easily accessible from the cities below. An exceptionally rugged portion has been preserved as the **San Gabriel Wilderness Area**, with steep slopes and canyons and trails to challenge experienced hikers.

For more information on the National Forest area write to: The Angeles National Forest, N. Lake ave., Pasadena 91104.

For the best view of these mountains you can get without hiking far, follow the Angeles Crest Highway, Highway 2, from La Canada.

San Bernardino is higher than San Gabriel. **Mt. San Gorgonio** reaches over 11,500 feet. San Bernardinos is popular and developed and is crowded during both summer vacations and winter ski season. There are many ski-areas here. **Lake Arrowhead** and **Big Bear Lake** are artificially created lakes which are surrounded by little resort towns and camping areas. The Rim of the World Drive, Highway 18, follows the ridges past some

CALIFORNIA

Pony trail in the great outdoors – Mt. San Jacinto

spectacular views. It ends with a loop around Big Bear Lake. Alternately, one can continue along Route 18 and wind one's way into the desert.

The Big Bear Chamber of Commmerce and the Big Bear Lake Tourist and Visitor Bureau can provide information on hiking, skiing, camping, etc. The Chamber of Commerce will also provide hotel or chalet information and can arrange reservations.

Big Bear Chamber of Commerce: P.O. Box 2860, Big Bear Lake, 92315. Tel. 714-866-4601.
Big Bear Lake Tourist and Visitor Bureau: P.O. Box 3050G, Big Bear Lake 92315. Tel. 714-866-5878.

CALIFORNIA

Santa Barbara

Santa Barbara is situated on the gentle slopes between the Santa Inez Mountains and a westwardly arching coast. The southern orientation of its beaches and harbor and the Channel Islands temper the Pacific squalls. The deep channel supports a rich marine life, and the mountains make up a rugged, preserved wilderness area in startlingly close proximity to the city. The light here has a strange, vibrating brightness, and when the morning fog lifts, the greenery, the horizon, and the golden ridges against the blue sky stand out in sharp and brilliant relief.

Santa Barbara in some ways typifies the very best that Southern California offers. While buffered from the urban sprawl of Los Angeles by the town of Ventura and the intervening mountains, it is by no means isolated. Santa Barbara has flash, style and urban sophistication. The University of California, at adjoining Isla Vista, adds to the cultural vibrancy and the obsession with health and recreation. Yet the tone here is casual, relaxed, friendly, and community-oriented. Santa Barbarans are deeply proud of their home and convinced that they dwell in the closest thing to earthly paradise.

The town began as a resort for the rich, something which has not changed. When a 1925 earthquake destroyed much of the city, residents had the vision and resources to rebuild it as a planned community, preserving the old Spanish influence. The restoration was meticulous and the character of the central district has been preserved to this day. The commercial center around State Street has been reshaped into one unified adobe aisle with tiled edgings and plazas with fountains. Nothing is out of place or abrasive here. The vegetation is lush, but pruned and trimmed. There are strict controls on such intrusions as billboards. Local residents fought persistently and successfully to keep Route 101 a regular thoroughfare rather than to build an obtrusive freeway (resulting today, ironically, in congested traffic).

Wealth and urbanity still flow here from Los Angeles. Young successful professionals live here and commute to the metropolis 90 minutes away. Personalities from the art and movie worlds take refuge here, as does Ronald Reagan.

Cynics refer to the place as Santa Boutique, but it is true that the gem has another facet. You can glimpse it on the manicured lawns of the majestic Spanish buildings, where the homeless catch some sleep. On a summer's evening large groups of these people from all walks of life, congregate around the railroad tracks, or in one of the public buildings or churches which is to be used that night as shelter.

There is much in Santa Barbara to keep the visitor busy and fascinated. Many sites and attractions are free or nominal in cost. Restaurants are wide in

CALIFORNIA

variety and price and can fit anyone's budget. Lodgings tend to be a little over-priced, but here too there is great variety.

How to get there

By air: Santa Barbara has its own airport, about eight miles from downtown, at which several state and regional carriers land, in addition to American Airlines and United Airlines. There is also direct bus service from the Los Angeles Airport.

By land: The drive to Santa Barbara from Los Angeles is easy using the 101 freeway, but the traffic can snag in Santa Barbara itself. The Pacific Coast Highway is slower, but passes through some small, scenic beach towns. From the north, the main approach is again the 101 freeway. From Las Cruces in the north to Santa Barbara, Routes 1 and 101 have merged into one freeway.

Buses: Amtrak, Greyhound and the Green Tortoise (the alternative bus company) serve the city.

In-town transportation

The **Santa Barbara Metropolitan Transit District** provides excellent bus service. A convenient map and riding guide, with major tourist sites is available from the Chamber of Commerce. The **Transit Center**, on Chapala st. at the Greybound terminal, also distributes the guide. It is also the transfer point for many bus routes. Fares 50 cents, transfers free, exact change. On weekdays during morning and evening rush hours as well as lunchtime, free shuttlebuses run downtown along several routes at ten minute intervals. Details are available at the transit center or by phone.

The **Santa Barbara Trolley Company**, a private service, runs on regular scheduled routes between major hotels, tourist areas and downtown. Fare is $1, and schedules are available from the Chamber of Commerce or company offices.

Cycling is easy along the flat areas or gentle hills. Many streets have special bike lanes, and drivers are aware of cyclists.

Tourist sites

Santa Barbara sustains a lively and diverse cultural and entertainment world. Galleries, clubs, theaters and museums are abundant and thrive here.

The Weekly and the *Visitor Press* are two free papers which list weekly cultural events. They can be found in stores and restaurants throughout the city. The Chamber of Commerce also publishes updated information on what's happening.

The Arts and Lectures program of the University of California sponsors student productions, as well as visiting performers. For information on events call Tel. 961-3535.

Isla Vista, the student neighborhood near the university, offers rowdy bars with live music.

CALIFORNIA

If you visit in early August you will have the good fortune to be in time for the **Old Spanish Days Fiesta**. Modeled after the old Spanish harvest festivals, this is not a trivial county fair with *tortillas* replacing burgers. For a week the town goes crazy for everything Spanish. Office workers are released early and the bars are packed day and night. There are free events in the plazas, dancing in the courthouse courtyard, parades with fancy floats and street performers everywhere. The festival draws world-renowned performers such as guitar virtuoso Carlos Montoya. Some events cost money, but you can be easily and endlessly entertained without spending a dime. Just bring your camera, appetite and dancing shoes. Make your room reservations well in advance. The schedule of events is available from the Chamber of Commerce.

State Street

State Street, between De La Guerra and Anapamu, is the heart of the renovated commercial district and has a concentration of beautiful public buildings. The adobe fronts, red tile roofs, wrought-iron filligree and semi-tropical gardens are everywhere. You can pick up a map at the Chamber of Commerce for a self-guiding tour.

At the heart of State st. is the **Santa Barbara Museum of Art**, a real treasure house. (1130 State st. Tues.-Sat. 11am-5pm, Thurs. 11am-9pm, Sun. noon-5pm. Tel. 963-4364.) Though a small museum, it attracts some of the finest exhibits touring the country. Its own collection includes classical antiquities and the works of the Renaissance painters, the French Impressionists and American moderns. Photography receives a strong emphasis. There is a concert every Sunday at 2:30pm. lectures every Thursday at 7:30pm, and a regular schedule of special events.

The museum is connected by a grassy plaza to the **public library**, which fits into the Spanish motif and makes a soothing spot to escape the eternally bright sun and rest your weary feet.

Also near the museum is **El Padeo**, a shopping arcade with stone sidewalks, Spanish tiles and a fountain. Across the street, at the Plaza De La Guerra, is the site where the first city council met in 1850.

The **Arlington Theater** is an old 1930s movie palace. (1317 State st. Tel. 966-4566.) It is ornate, lavish and conspicuous and features a continuously changing program ranging from drama to rock, and classical music to classic films. The murals above the entrance depict scenes from old Mexican California and are worth viewing even if you do not see the show.

The County Courthouse is a dazzling architectural puzzle not to be missed. The winding staircases, Tunisian tile patterns, turrets, towers, and off-center arches – all somehow fit to create a harmonious assymetry.

Do not miss the historical murals inside. An elevator will take you up to **El Mirador**, the 70-foot observation and clock tower from which you can see Santa Barbara spread out beneath you. (1100 Anacapa st. Open 8am-5pm

CALIFORNIA

DOWNTOWN SANTA BARBARA

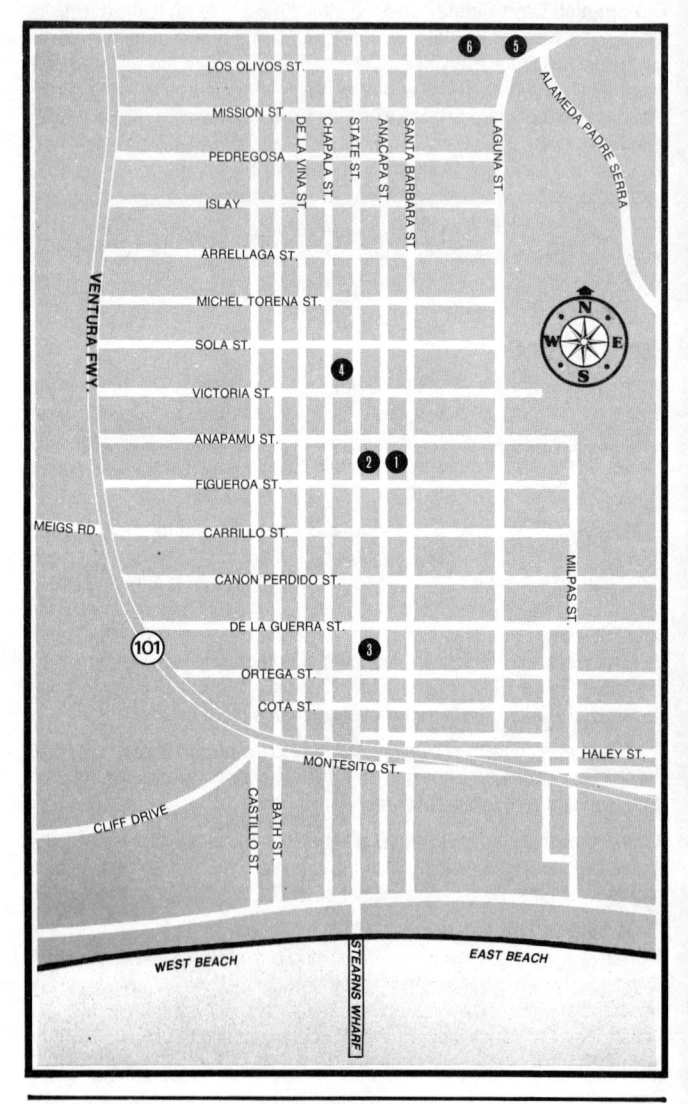

Index
1) Court Museum
2) Art Museum
3) City Hall
4) Arlington Theater
5) The Mission
6) National History Museum

CALIFORNIA

weekdays, 9am-5pm weekends and holidays. Free guided tours each Friday at 10:30am. Tel. 962-6464.)

Beyond State Street

The Santa Barbara Mission, completed in 1786, was the 10th in a chain of Franciscan missions in California. Referred to today as the "Queen of the missions", it is a massive and imposing white adobe building with two towers, offset by lush greenery both outside and within its courtyard.

An elaborate aqueduct, built by the local converted Indians, channeled water from mountain creeks to the mission's extensive landholdings, which grew grains, vegetables, olive trees and grape vines. The **Mission Museum** reconstructs the padres' workshops, kitchens and sleeping quarters, vividly depicting the rustic and simple mission life. (Laguna st. near Mission st. Open daily 9am-5pm. The museum costs 50 cents, children free. Tel. 682-4713.)

The site of the dam built by Indians for mission lands is part of the **Santa Barbara Botanical Gardens**, just north of the mission. (1212 Mission Canyon rd. Open daily 8am-sunset. Guided tour on Thurs. at 10:30am and Sun. at 11am. Admission free. Tel. 682-4726.) Three miles of nature trails weave through stands of cacti, wildflowers and other native plants, that are arranged by ecological zone.

The Santa Barbara Museum of Natural History displays the rich environmental and biological diversity of the Pacific coast, in a graceful Spanish building. (Puesta del Sol rd. two blocks north of the mission. Open Mon.-Sat. 9am-5pm, Sun. and holidays 10am-5pm.)

The museum also organizes trips, including expeditions to the Channel Islands.

The **Santa Barbara Historical Museum** is housed in an adobe building. (136 East de la Guerra st. Open Tues.-Fri. noon-5pm, Sat.- Sun. 1-5pm. Tel. 966-1601.) The museum covers the major periods in local development, and the emphasis is on Mexican and Spanish history.

Santa Barbara is a haven for antique collectors or browsers. There are almost a hundred shops in the area, with a sizable cluster along **Brinkerhoff Ave.**, off Haley between Chapala and De La Vina sts., not far from downtown.

Santa Barbara's harbor has, like many others, found tourism increasingly profitable, while the traditional activity of commercial fishing struggles along. There are as many pleasure boats in the channel as there are fishing vessels, but at twilight you can still watch the fishing boats haul in catches of shark, halibut, sole and shrimp. Tourist shops and seafood restaurants line **Stearns Wharf**. Steamed lobster or crab can be bought and eaten on the spot. The wharf is lined with anglers and no license is required to join them. The **Stearns Wharf Winery**, with its open deck, is a fine place to indulge in a little wine-tasting. Amid the more commercial storefronts is the **Santa Cruz Island Project** visitor center of the non-profit **Nature Conservancy**, with video and photographic exhibits and information on the Channel Islands. (Open 11am-2pm daily.)

CALIFORNIA

Where it all began – Mission at Santa Barbara

A refreshing shoreline route for walking, jogging or cycling runs from Leadbetter Beach, just west of The Breakwater, past West Beach near Stearns Wharf, to East Beach near the Andree Clark Bird Refuge. If you still have some excess energy, the **Cabrillo Bathhouse Pavilion** on East Beach has a new weight room and beach volley ball courts. (1118 E Cabrillo Blvd. Open 8am-7pm. Tel. 965-0509.) Open to the public, the weight room, lockers and showers cost $1.50 per day.

Parking at Stearns Wharf can get crowded (1$ per hr, free if validated with a $3 purchase). At the foot of the wharf or in the harbor lot, parking is 50 cents per hour. On Cabrillo there is free 90-minute and all-day parking.

The Santa Barbara Harbor is the place for water sports: boating, diving, fishing, surfing, windsurfing, bodysurfing and body-watching. Rentals and lessons for windsurfing, scuba diving and sailing are available from various outfits on Stearns Wharf and the Breakwater.

At the end of East Beach are the **Santa Barbara Zoological Gardens** and the adjoining **Andree Clark Bird Refuge**. (Open 10am-5pm daily. The zoo costs $2.50, discounts for children, teenagers and seniors. Tel. 962-6310.)

CALIFORNIA

The zoo is small but a lot of fun for kids. The bird refuge, set around a lagoon, has paths for walking and cycling and is delightful. You can pick up a pamphlet on birds at the Natural History Museum to bring with you here.

Craftsmen and artisans from the region spread their wares out along Palm Park in a weekly bazaar every Sunday from 10am-sunset.

On Chapala st. near the foot of State st., the immense **Moreton Bay Fig Tree**, a Santa Barbara feature by now, casts shade upon locals and wanderers. Transplanted in 1877 from Australia, the tree became a local cause celebre when it was threatened with destruction to make room for a gas station.

Near Santa Barbara

Northwest of Santa Barbara, Route 1 splits off from Highway 101 and become a small country road leading towards the coast. It might be preferable to take the faster inland route here. Little of the shoreline is easily accessible in this area, and a more interesting detour is found to the east.

If heading north from Santa Barbara, follow Route 154 rather than Route 101. This will link up with 101 again at Beullton. But first the road winds into the rugged, scrubby Santa Inez Mountains, and over the San Marcos Pass, from which you can see the Channel Islands. There is rugged hiking in the **San Rafael Wilderness** (part of the Los Padres National Forest) and this road provides the closest access. Further along, Lake Cachuma – a popular recreation area – spreads to the right. The public campgrounds here fill up fast.

A little further along Route 154 is the junction with Route 246 which heads west, to the town of **Solvang**. Settled in 1911 by Danish-Americans, the town was small and obscure until after World War II. Now it has been rediscovered, restored and sugar-coated, and its original quaintness has been lost – but there is no doubt about the scrumptiousness of the pastries.

Nearby **Mission on Santa Ines**, built in 1804 as 19th in the mission chain, was largely destroyed over time. The chapel appears as it did in the early days, but the tour-by-loudspeaker leaves a bit to be desired.

The Santa Inez Valley has seen a resurgence of the wine industry. The Solvang Chamber of Commerce can supply details on wineries which offer wine tastings.

Follow 254 back to the 101 highway, at Beullton, and at the junction you'll find *Anderson's*, justly famous for its pea soup.

Channel Islands National Park

Five of the eight islands in the Channel Island chain, off the Santa Barbara coast, comprise the **Channel Islands National Park**. Isolation from the mainland, the mingling of warm and cold water currents in the deep channel, and exposure to the harsh Pacific elements, have created unique and delicately balanced ecological zones here. They differ as sharply from each other as they do from the mainland ecology. Many organisms and

CALIFORNIA

Pigeon hole at mission

communities, highly specialized, belong to both land and sea, and any change in either environment has far-reaching effects.

Seafaring Chumash Indians lived on these islands for thousands of years. When explorer Juan Rodriguez Cabrillo explored the coast on behalf of Spain, he found about 2000 Indians living on one island alone. Cabrillo himself, credited with the first exploration of the California coast, died here after a fall, probably on San Miguel Island. He is thought to be buried there but his grave remains undiscovered. By the end of the 18th century, hunters, settlers and ranchers had reached the islands, and in the following decades the Indians were removed to the mainland mission at Santa Barbara. Seals and sea otters were hunted almost to extinction. Grazing animals and foreign plant species upset the fragile ecological balance and threatened or totally erased some rare and singular species. Only relatively recently were some of the islands preserved, and the immediate marine region around them was declared a National Marine Sanctuary. The rules controlling the visits and effects of humans are strict and rigourously enforced, with the intent of restoring the previous natural balance.

Four of the islands can be visited. **Santa Cruz Island**, the largest, is currently in private hands. Only specific sections can be visited, in organized trips arranged by the private concessionaires, Island Packers, or the non-profit Nature Conservancy. **Anacapa Island**, the smallest, is actually a chain of three small islands. Near the small National Park Visitors Center on the eastern island begins a self-guiding nature trail 1.5 miles long. Guided walks and evening programs are available.

Santa Barbara Island, the southernmost in the chain, is an excellent spot for observing sea lions and elephant seals, especially during the winter when they breed on the island. On San Miguel, the westernmost and most exposed, the Pacific forces have sculpted a harsh and starkly beautiful landscape. A 15-mile round trip trail for the hardy follows the length of the island.

Anacapa and Santa Barbara Islands have primitive campgrounds, each for about 30 people. For those who enjoyed the adventures of Robinson Crusoe, obtain a permit in advance from park headquarters and and bring everything you need with you; no supplies are available.

The mainland **National Park Visitor Center** in Ventura (1901 Spinnaker Drive, Tel.664-8262), offers a 25-minute film on the park, as well as displays of tidepools, native plants and Chumash artifacts. Pick up brochures, maps and camping permits here.

Immediately next door, in the parking lot, is the office of **Island Packers**,the main concessionaire operating Channel Island expeditions. The full spring and summer schedule is curtailed after August. Reservations are advisable. Rates start, depending on the trip, from about $25 per person. (1867 Spinnaker Dr., Ventura,. Tel. 642-1393.)

The **Santa Barbara Museum of Natural History** leads trips to Santa Cruz and San Miguel Islands. Tel. 962-9111.

Accommodations

Santa Barbara started as a resort town and still has some elegant and exclusive resorts. But now the area is accessible to almost everyone, and on a summer weekend it seems that almost everyone is there. Reservations are required at many lodgings and are recommended all year round to avoid problems. Some establishments lower their prices in winter by as much as 30%.

Groups of standard motels and hotels can be found along Cabrillo near the beaches, and on State st. inland from the commercial center. B&B inns tend

CALIFORNIA

to be scattered around, some right in downtown, some in sedate residential neighbourhoods. They run in the same range as many standard motels. Most standard motel rooms, with the exception of Motel 6, start at $30-$35 a night. The cheaper old residential hotels are in the bad part of town.

There are several centralized clearinghouses for vacation lodgings, at no cost to the visitor. They will give you a wide range of detailed information.

Accommodations in Santa Barbara: 1216 State st., SB 93101, Tel. 963-9518. Centralized reservations service, for hotels, motels, B&B. No charge.

D.B. Tourist Co.: Tel 687-8605. Reservations clearinghouse. No charge.

Executive Houses of Santa Barbara: 205 E. Carrillo, SB 93101, Tel. 963-9350. Reservation service for weekend, weekly and monthly rentals in condos and houses.

Brinkerhoff Inn: 523 Brinkerhoff ave., SB 93101, Tel. 963-7844; toll-free in state, 800-BEST-BNB. An old Victorian home in a district marked by Victorian landmarks and antique stores. Small and homely, continental breakfast. $65-$90 in summer, $45-$75 winter weekdays.

Villa Motel:3885 State st., SB 93105, Tel. 687-3217. Away from downtown. $35-$45 summer, $25-$35 winter.

Motel 6: 440 Corona del Mar, Tel. 965-0300. Near the beach. Or, 3505 State st., Tel 687-5400. Beyond downtown. Reservations at both highly recommended. About $21.

Camping

Camping sites are plentiful in the general Santa Barbara vicinity, but there are few immediately adjacent to the city. The coastal state park campsites are right off the highway and become Winnebago City at night. They all require reservations except Gaviota State Park, which is 32 miles northwest of Santa Barbara and a little bit off the highway.

Santa Barbara County also operates several campgrounds, in the Lake Cachuma region and along the beach. The Jalame Beach campground, about 40 miles northwest of the city, is on a secluded stretch of coast near Point Conception, well off the beaten track. Follow Route 101 north to Route 1, take Route 1 to Jalama Rd., towards Point Conception, and follow this road to the beach. First-come first-serve, $6 per night. Tel. 734-1446.

Along the winding Route 154 which goes toward San Marcos Pass, there are a number of campgrounds in Los Padres National Forest. Some lie within access of the San Rafael Wilderness area. Fees vary with facilities, ranging from free to $5 per night. All campsites are allocated on first arrival. Check with the local Forest Service office for details (see below).

Food

Restaurants ranging from Mexican to Thai to good old burgers, as diverse in price as in menu, are concentrated downtown. There is a place for every taste, whim and budget. Very near downtown, a wide selection of ethnic restaurants line De La Vina st. between Calle Laurelles and Alamar. There are some fine bargains along here, especially for lunch.

The harbor area features some elaborate seafood restaurants, while Isla Vista obviously caters to students with many reasonable pizza and felafel stands, and lunch specials.

Joe's of Santa Barbara, (534 State st., Tel. 966-4638), is a local landmark and favorite watering hole, boasting and indeed serving the biggest drinks in town, and full hearty meals.

Lotus Thai, (2706 De La Vina, Tel. 687-0958). What that woman creates in the tiny kitchen is remarkable. Great luncheon specials, 11am-3pm, $3 up. Dinner 5pm-10pm. A real find.

Skandi Buffet, (2911 De La Vina, Tel. 682-3141). After you have jogged, swum and windsurfed for the day, come here. All you can eat from a terrific selection of Scandinavian food. Lunch from $3.75, 11am-4pm. Dinner from $5.50, from 4pm-8:30pm.

Useful Addresses And Phone Numbers
Santa Barbara Chamber of Commerce: 1330 State st. Tel. 965-3021.
Solvang Chamber of Commerce: 1623 Mission dr. Tel. 688-3317.
Airport: 515 Marxmiller rd., Goleta. Tel. 967-5608.
Airport Express: Tel. 965-1611. Service to and from Santa Barbara Airport.
Santa Barbara Airbus: Tel. 964-7374. To and from L.A. Airport.
Santa Barbara Metropolitan Transit District: Carrillo and Chapala sts. Tel 683-3702.
Santa Barbara Trolley Co.: 125 Harbor Way. Tel.962-0209.
Amtrak: 209 State st. Tel. 687-6848.
Greyhound: Carrillo and Chapala. Tel. 966-3962.
Green Tortoise: Tel. 569-1884.
U.S. Forest Service: 6144 Calle Real, Goleta. Tel. 683-6711.
Crisis Hotline: Tel. 964-6713.
Area code: 805.

WESTERN JACK RABBIT
The natural habitat of the western jack rabbit is the western U.S.A. It is a charming creature but nevertheless does enormous damage to agricultural crops. Its light brown color, which blends well with the vegetation, and its great running speed provide defense.

*C*ALIFORNIA

San Luis Obispo

San Luis Obispo nestles in a small valley between the Santa Lucia mountains and some gorgeous beaches. By no means a metropolis, it is nevertheless the largest center in the region, and the center for this cattle and dairy region. To the north, the inland valleys embrace rich wine country. Along the coast to the northwest, small towns are sparsely strung. There is something very elusive about the beauty of these coastal hills.

Downtown San Luis Obispo invites a stroll. It still has a friendly small-town atmosphere. You will find J.C. Penny's and French bakeries, junk shops and outdoor cafes, galleries showing the work of local craftsmen, and ornate, well preserved Victorian architecture.

How to get there
From San Luis Obispo south, Routes 101 and 1 converge; heading north, they split, to join again near Monterey. To the north, 101 follows the inland valleys through dairyland and the Pas Robles wine country. Route 1 continues along the cliffs of Big Sur.

SLO lies on the coastal Amtrak route. The ride by train is slower and slightly more expensive than by bus, but is relaxing and has beautiful views as it skirts the coastline. The buses run inland.

Four basic bus routes serve the town and its outskirts. The City Hall at Osos and Palm is the transfer for all buses, which operate on a half-hourly basis. Although there are marked bus stops, you can, in true small-town spirit, flag down a bus at any corner. Buses stop running at 7pm. Tickets 50 cents, transfers free. A monthly pass costs $16, and only $2.50 for seniors. Special service for the handicapped. SLOCAT (SLO County Area Transit) buses serve the coastal towns up to San Simeon. It runs a full weekday schedule, with curtailed service on Saturday and none on Sunday. Tickets from 25 cents to $1.

Tourist sites
The visitor center in downtown SLO provides a brochure for a self-guided tour of downtown, highlighting the old Victorian architecture. More interesting, however, than an old gabled Victorian building is the ceiling of the **Fremont Theater** on Santa Rosa st. near Monterey st. This art deco gem features sea nymphs riding stallions across the ceiling.

Near the visitors center is **Mission Plaza**. (Chorro st. Open in summer 9am-5pm, winter 10am-4pm. Donation requested. Tel. 543-8562.)

The adjacent mission was the first building in the area, founded by Junipero Serra in 1772 as the fifth mission in his chain. As in many cases, the town

CALIFORNIA

SAN LUIS OBISPO

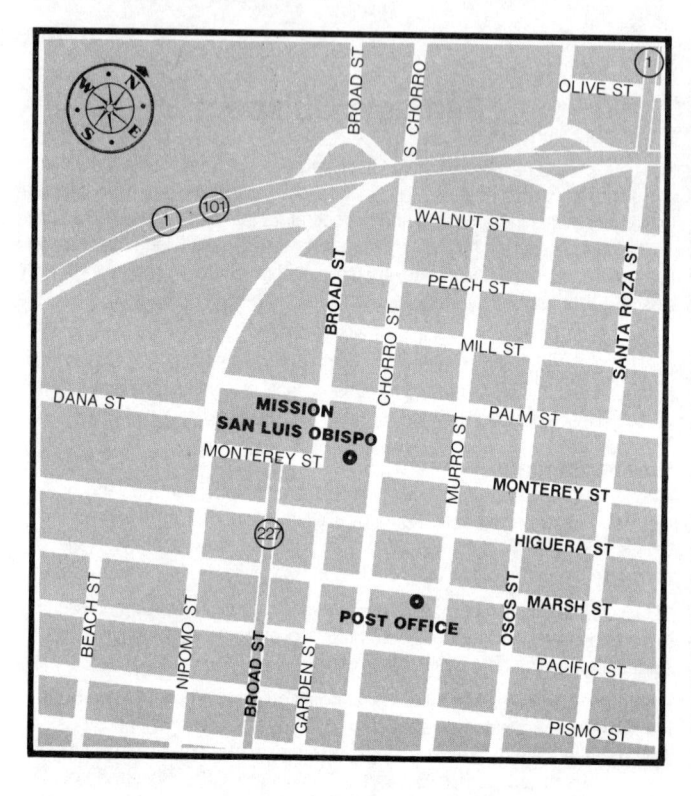

developed around the mission. This mission was the first to construct the famous red-tile roof, but the purpose was not aesthetic; it provided defense against firebrands shot by Indians on to the roofs. The mission, still used today, houses a museum with some relics, photos and prints of its history.

The plaza is the center of downtown. San Luis Creek, which supplied the early mission with water, runs past, edged with thick vegetation and an occasional cafe. It's a nice place to absorb the sun, the colors and the street music. The plaza is the focus for most festivals, both formal and spontaneous. In February there is a Mardi Gras, in spring a Spanish Fiesta, in August a well-known Mozart Festival, and in September a wine-tasting festival.

The **City Historical Museum**, (696 Monterey st. Open Wed.-Sun. 10am-4pm. Admission free. Tel. 543-0638) across from the mission, has a small collection of artifacts, including the sombrero of Pio Pico, the last

CALIFORNIA

Spanish governor of California. The employees are proud of their town and seem to know all the interesting excursions and side roads.

Two downtown mini-malls are housed in old buildings. **The Network**, on Higuera st., was an early department store, and **The Creamery**, on Nipomo, was in fact a creamery. The **SLO Art Center** on Monterey st. near the plaza highlights some beautiful work by local artists. (Open Tues.-Sun. noon-5pm.)

California Polytechnic Institute (Cal Poly in local jargon), located just north of downtown, maintains a huge working farm and extensive research facilities in agricultural subjects. The school brings an influx of young people and money to town. It also holds an amazing annual rodeo as part of the **Poly Royal** fair in late April. Tours of the farm and facilities are available, and the achievements of the school may well renew one's faith in the green revolution. Parking permits at the administration building. (Information desk. Tel. 546-0111.)

The famous **Madonna Inn**, just south of town on Highway 101, reaches new heights of fantastical architecture, decor and the plugged-in gingerbread effect. Even Alice and the Cheshire Cat would be baffled here. (For lodging details see below.)

Wineries and vineyards are clustered around the Paso Robles-Templeton area along Route 101. York Mountain Road offers a winding scenic trip across the mountains between the two main highways. There are several excellent wineries along this road, including the **York Mountain Winery**, oldest in the region. (Open daily for tasting 10am-5pm.) It dates back to 1882, with its ivy covered tasting room and rock walls dug into the hillside. A list of regional wineries is available at the SLO visitor center or the Paso Robles Chamber of Commerce.

Mission San Miguel, near 101 about eight miles north of Paso Robles, is one of the most authentic of the missions. It has not been excessively spruced up and the buildings are stark.

The frescoes inside are bright, and there must be some fascinating untold dramas behind them, for they were executed by unknown Indian painters under mission direction. Take the mission exit in San Miguel. (Open during daylight hours, tours from 10am-5pm. Tel. 467-3256.)

The beach towns to the south of SLO – Avila, Shell Beach and Pismo – tend to be overcrowded. Avila has been overrun by waves of teenagers, and the southern part of the Pismo sands have been invaded by dune buggies. However, seven miles south of Los Osos is the quiet secluded **Montana de Oro State Park**, with abundant wildlife, great beachcombing at Spooner's Cove beach, and good camping (see below).

Northwest of SLO on Route 1 is the resort and fishing village of **Morro Bay**, which took its name from **Morro Rock**, a huge rock rising 600 feet from the water. One of a chain of nine extinct volcanic cones, the rock was named by the explorer Juan Cabrillo in 1542 because it resembles the turbans worn by

CALIFORNIA

Wine country – San Luis Obispo

the Spanish Moors. It can be reached by a causeway from the beach area north of town.

South of the town, Morro Bay State Park contains one of the outstanding marine life zones on the central coast, with the habitats of a lagoon and natural bay. There are great spots for surf fishing, clamming or just exploring among the rocks and driftwood. The **Clam Taxi**, which operates year round, runs from the Morro Bay Marino at 4th st. to the park.

The **Natural History Museum**, (Open daily 10am-5pm. Tel. 772-2560) facing across the bay, covers Chumash Indian life, local geology and oceanography. There are nature walks and ranger programs.

Various types of fish, as well as abalone and oysters, comprise the local hauls and can be bought fresh at the fish markets found along the embarcadero. Otherwise, try them at one of the seafood restaurants which prepare early bird specials.

If you want to go fishing yourself, you can do it without a license at the public T-pier. There are several sportfishing outfits along the embarcadero that run cruises ranging from half-day to two days. They cost about $20 for a full day.

CALIFORNIA

Pole and tackle are extra. The **Morro Bay Marina** (699 Embarcadero. Open daily 9am-4:30pm. Tel. 772-8085) rents small motorboats for forays into the bay, at $10 per hour.

North of Morro Bay and Cayuco on Route 1 is the town of **Harmony** with population of about 20, depending on the day. Everyone in this transformed dairy town is some kind of artist or craftsman. On summer Sunday afternoons from 2pm-5pm you can catch an outdoor concert that may be jazz, ragtime or bluegrass.

Cambria, north of Harmony, is another town with many artisans, especially along Burton Drive in the East Village. Moonstone Beach Drive winds along the coast past galleries, restaurants, and the sea otter refuge at **Leffingwell's Landing**.

The Hearst San Simeon State Historical Monument – or Hearst's Castle – is undoubtedly the outstanding tourist site along the coast south of Big Sur. It is a overwhelming, flamboyant baronial twentieth-century dreamland, known by its owner as "the ranch".

The land was indeed first acquired as a ranch, by George Hearst. William Randolf, his only son, built a newspaper empire based on inflammatory "yellow journalism", which helped ignite the Spanish-American War in 1898. Before the outbreak of the war he is reported to have said to his illustrator in Cuba: "*You provide the pictures and I'll provide the war*".

When the family ranch fell to him, he spared no expense in indulging his whims and fantasies. The main building, on a hilltop in the Santa Lucias with views along the coast, boasts over a hundred rooms. Steel, cement, top soil, plants, as well as the dismantled furnishings, walls, and rooms of European estates, were shipped by steamer to the San Simeon port and hauled up the winding road. The grounds and other buildings present a dizzying clash and blend of styles ranging from Roman to Gothic to Moorish.

Medieval hangings, Chinese ceramics and other priceless antiques were flown in from around the world. The library holds the world's largest private collection of Greek vases. And yet, puzzlingly, the mansion holds a large number of cheap plaster copies as well.

Hearst's lavishness extended to the surrounding countryside, which he filled with herds of zebra, white deer and other exotic species. His private zoo held monkeys, cheetahs and lions.

The impetus for much of this frenetic construction was the creation of a hideway for his Hollywood movie queen, Marion Davies. Movie stars came up for Hearst's feasts, and other guests included Winston Churchill and President Calvin Coolidge.

There was, however, something strange and lonely in all this extravagance, a feeling best captured by Orson Welles' cinematic masterpiece, *Citizen Kane*, which is worth seeing, if possible, before a visit to the estate.

The area deeded to the state is but a small portion of the land holdings which

CALIFORNIA

San Luis Obispo

still belong to the Hearst family and which encompass most of the town and beachfront below.

Visits to the castle are by guided tour only. There are three different tours which operate throughout the year, and a fourth from April to Oct. Each tour involves a fair amount of walking and climbing and costs $8, $4 for ages 6-12. Each lasts almost two hours. The different tours can all be done on one day, or taken on separate days. The ticket office is open from 8am-4pm daily. Tours leave at least once every hour, from 8:20am-3pm in winter, and more often during holidays and the summer.

Tickets may be bought upon entry, but reservations are recommended particularly during the summer. For reservations made from within the state, Tel. 800-446-PARK, or make them through any local Ticketron outlet. For information within the state, Tel. 800-952-5580. From out-of-state call Tel. 619-452-1950 for reservations and information. For visitors confined to wheelchairs, special arrangements can be made by calling the castle directly at Tel. 927-4622.

The first tour, an overview, can accommodate about 50 people. The others

CALIFORNIA

are much smaller. Tours 2 and 3 explore the upper levels of the castle itself, while the 4th surveys the grounds and architecture.

Accommodations

If budget is your main consideration, then the most appropriate lodging will be found inland, near San Luis Obispo, rather than in the coastal towns. There are numerous motels and hotels to choose from along the coast, ranging from about $34 and up. The strip of motels and hotels in San Simeon along Castillo dr., bordering the highway, tends to be a bit more expensive than those further south, as this is the last stop for those heading north, south of Big Sur.

As with many regions some of the B&Bs are in the same price range as motels. On this coast expecially, some of the houses are very charming.

Pismo Landmark B&B Inn: 701 Price st., Pismo Beach. Suites with views and an enclosed sunroof. $50-$75. For 3 days during the week, $45 per night. Tel. 773-5566.

Madonna Inn: 100 Madonna rd., San Luis Obispo. Each room a bizarre, separate world. Go for the room in bubble gum pink. It is worth the stop just to look around. $57 single, $62 up double. Tel. 543-3000.

Blue Bell Motel: 3053 S. Higuera st. Standard, clean and cheap. $21-26 single, $24-$32 double (slightly more on weekends and holidays). Tel. 543-6807.

Silver Surf Motel: 9390 Castillo dr., San Simeon. Near the ocean. Jacuzzi and pool. $45-$75. The "Hearst Castle Special" includes 3 days/2 nights, two Tour 1 tickets, one dinner and one breakfast for two. $55 per person. Tel. 927-4661.

Heritage Inn B&B: 978 Olive st. $44-$73. Low winter mid-week rates. A small restored Victorian building, with home-made breakfasts. Tel. 544-7440.

Megan's Friends B&B referrals: 1776 Royal Way, San Luis Obispo 93401. Tel. 544-4406. Listings available by phone or mail.

Camping facilities are available at most of the state parks from Pismo Beach to San Simeon. Some are filled with trailers and dune buggies. **Montana De Oro State Park** is outstanding, situated in a deep and quiet valley, with 50 primitive sites plus some well developed sites too. 7 miles south of Los Osos on Pecho rd. (Tel. 772-2560.)

Food

Chuckwagon Restaurant: Route 1 and Moonstone Beach dr., Cambria. All you can eat of fine meat entrees and salad bar. $3.99 lunch, $5.89 dinner.

Apple Farm Restaurant: 2015 Monterey. Home-made soups and pies. Good salad bar, homey atmosphere. Moderate.

The Bakery Cafe: 1040 Broad st. Croissants and expresso alongside the creek in the heart of town.

CALIFORNIA

Budget Cafe: 1216 Archer st. It's friendly and serves filling and inexpensive dishes for $5 or less.

Cafe Roma: 1819 Osos st. Behind an old storefront, serving home-made pasta which is made fresh each day, and delicious fish. Friendly and moderately priced.

Useful Addresses And Phone Numbers

Visitor Information: 1039 Chorro st., at Higuera. Daily 8am-5pm. Tel. 543-1328.
Greyhound: 150 South st. Open 5:45am-9:15pm. Tel. 543-2121.
Amtrak: Railroad Ave and Santa Rosa. Reservations 9:30am-5:30pm. Tel. 541-0505.
State Park Info: Tel. 549-3312.
SLO Transit: 541, BUSS. Service for handicapped: Tel. 541-2544.
SLO County Area Transit: Tel. 528-7434.
Paso Robles Chamber of Commerce: 1113 Spring, Tel. 238-0506.
Area Code: 805.
Emergency: 911.
Area Code: 805.
Chamber of Commerce: 1039 Chorro st. San Luis Obispo, 93401. Tel. 543-1328.
Greyhound: 150 south st. Tel. 543-2121.
Amtrak: Railroad ave. and Santa Rosa. Tel. 541-0505.
State Park Info: Tel. 549-3312.

CALIFORNIA

Big Sur

On rising I would go to the cabin door and, casting my eyes over the velvety, rolling hills, such a feeling of contentment, such a feeling of gratitude was mine that instinctively my hand went up in benediction.

Henry Miller:
Big Sur and the Oranges
of Hieronymus Bosch.

Big Sur's mountains are not the highest, nor its forests the richest, nor its canyons the deepest, but there is something inexpressibly wild and beautiful in the rugged, ragged coastline between Carmel and San Simeon, shrouded in fog, engulfed by the sound of the crashing waves. Each promontory jutting into the Pacific foam is breathtaking.

Big Sur lies in the middle of the central coast of California, an area roughly defined as extending from the San Louis Obispo region in the south to the Monterey Bay and Santa Cruz in the north. Big Sur looms in the middle as a border between the two.

From the days of the earliest settlers, Big Sur has held a strange attraction for people. Some came to cut down the redwoods or to build a navigable port; others drifted in to find a simple basic life in nature. They lived as small farmers, carpenters and the like. A few artists discovered the area and moved in. The American poet Robinson Jeffers worked as a stonecutter in these hills while steeping himself in images of "the lean redges" and "the prehuman dignity of night".

With the building of Highway 1 (much of it by convict labor) along what was once a rutted wagon trail, Big Sur was opened up to the rest of California and the world, with the predictable encroachments, developments and eager plans for profit-making resorts. Today, bits of the cliff are dotted with expensive homes. The area became a center for people who during and after the 1960s sought quieter, simpler lives based on crafts and independent physical labor. It has attracted, as well, those who are involved in various alternative lifestyles, therapies, cults, etc.

Today there are even fewer people living in the area – between 700 and 800 in all – than there were in the beginning of the century when there were greater efforts to exploit the local resources. The "urban" area runs through the valley paralleling the Big Sur River, set back a mile or so from the coast. It extends from the Jules Pfeiffer State Park and the Big Sur Lodge, to the north for about six miles. There are a few lodges, hotels and restaurants in the area, plus an occasional gift shop, and a few mailboxes and no-trespassing signs on some dirt roads.

BIG SUR AREA

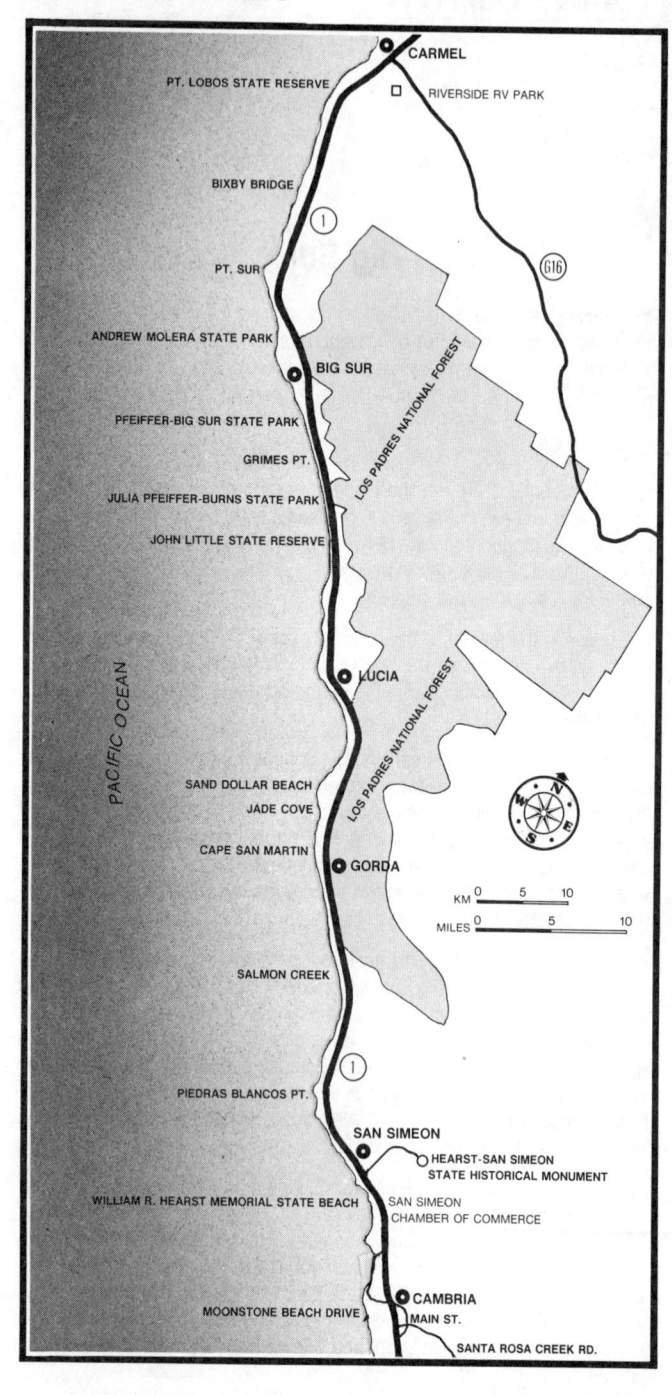

CALIFORNIA

How to get there

By car: The drive between San Francisco and Los Angeles along the gorgeous coast highway takes about 12 hours or less. At both ends of this stretch – at San Louis Obispo in the south and Monterey in the north – you can pick up Highway 101 which will bring you more rapidly to the cities. It is very difficult to reach Big Sur other than by car, organized tour, or bicycle (hitching not recommended).

By bus: The Monterey Peninsula Transit system (Tel. 372-4494) makes two round trips daily from Carmel to the Nepenthe parking lot, daily during the summer, and weekends only during the winter. As of this writing, however, the possibility was raised that this service would be curtailed or stopped for budgetary reasons, so check first. From the south, the nearest public bus that runs to Big Sur is the San Louis Obispo system bus between San Simeon and Morrow Bay.

In spring, the hills are covered with flowers all the way down to the ocean. Autumn has a burnished beauty all its own. The winter brings damp, chilly mists and heavy rainfall, but rarely snow, and the greyness is often broken by gleaming, polished blue skies. The fog bank seldom crosses the coastal ridge into the interior hills and valleys, so hikers in the interior hills and valleys may find it broiling hot while the coast is cool. Avoid the Labor Day and July 4th weekends.

Facilities vary between the very elegant and expensive cliffside or hilltop restaurants and inns, to off-trail campsites. There is little in between. Everything from gasoline to beer to a cup of coffee could cost up to double the price here, so fill up the tank, cooler, and thermos. Camp out if you can, and try, whenever possible, to park your car and go hiking. There are pull-offs along the road, as well as extensive trails in the parks. Groves of redwood trees fill the deep ravines that go right down to the cliffs, and make for beautiful walks. Some paths lead down to the beach, others along the edges of sheer cliffs. (The sign that warns of danger means business.) In Big Sur you can escape the hordes of motorists the moment you pull off the highway into a hiking area.

Public Parks and Campgrounds

Big Sur has an excellent system of parks, enabling visitors – from the casual stroller and photographer to the serious hiker – to taste the varied beauty of the area. There are enough campgrounds and enough variety to serve every kind of camper. Cyclists can stay in any state parkground for 50 cents and cannot, by law, be turned away. The different parks are listed here in geographical order from north to south.

At the northern end of Big Sur, south of the *Rocky Point Restaurant* and a few miles north of the **Point Sur Lighthouse**, Paolo Colorado Road turns to the east, toward **Botcher Campground** (Forest Service) in the hills. There is also an unnamed Forest Service campground off a dirt spur to the left, through a gate which is not always open. A drive through the lower part of the

Big Sur Coast

canyon is itself beautiful, with quaint little houses nestled between the trees, like a redwood hobbitland.

Situated near the mouth of the Big Sur River, the entrance to **Andrew Molera State Park** is on the west side of the highway, but vehicles cannot pass beyond the unpaved parking lot. From there a quarter-mile long path leads to the campsites (about 50) in an open meadow. The path continues through a pretty wood, and then to the floodplain formed by the river. The park faces both the shallow river and the rough ocean. It is pleasant to be away from all the trailers and highway noise. There are ten miles of hiking trails. Campsites cost 50 cents and have a three-night limit. For information: **Pfeiffer Big Sur State Park**, Tel. 667-2315. Adjacent to the park, **Big Sur Trail Rides** offers short guided horse rides as well as pack trips into the Ventana wilderness area. Tel. 667-2666.

The **Pfeiffer Big Sur State Park** (not to be confused with the Julia Pfeiffer Burns State Park further south) is a highly developed park, with a lodge, cabins, a store, a restaurant and campfire programs and nature walks in summer. It is a great park for hiking, as there are many short, interlocking trails that make easy loops. There is a very short nature trail, as well as longer,

CALIFORNIA

tougher trails throughout the park and trails leading into the Ventana Wilderness. Within this one park there are redwood forests, waterfalls, oak forest, high chaparral, and stunning views of the mountains and the rocky coast stretching in both directions. There is a beautiful hike to **Pfeiffer Falls** through a fern-lined canyon. The park has both campsites and trailer slots available by reservation, with a 7-day limit. For reservations write to: Department of Parks and Recreation. P.O.Box 2390, Sacramento, 95811. Contact any Ticketron office Local phone: 667-2315.

Just south of the Big Sur State Park entrance is the National Forest Service information booth. The **Ventana Wilderness**, which is part of the Los Padres National Forest, covers a large area of forest and chaparral behind the Big Sur State Park. This area is isolated, and filled with wildlife. Wilderness permits (free) are required, and are available from 8am to 4:30pm at the station or in advance by calling or writing: P.O. Box 64, Big Sur, Ca 93920. Tel. 667-2423. Maps of Ventana Wilderness trails are available at the station.

Also administered by the Forest Service is **Pfeiffer Beach**. Turn west onto **Sycamore Canyon Road**, just a hundred yards or so south of the forest service information station, down a steep short incline that leads about one-and-a-half miles to a parking lot. From there you walk. The first thing that you will notice is the large monolithic rock looming from the water like the prow of a huge ship. The beach is unusually flat and wide for the Big Sur coast, and uncrowded as well. The beach which is for day use only has spur-like cliffs at either end, and at the north it merges with the beach and hills of Andrew Molera State Park, thus providing quite a large area for beach-combing and exploration.

A little less than ten miles further south is the **Julia Pfeiffer Burns State Park**, a shady and peaceful day-use area situated right off the road. There's a charge for entering by car, but there is space to park outside by the road, and lots of people do this. Trails lead up through a narrow, dark and peaceful redwood grove, or under the highway to a waterfall that drops right into the ocean. Although camping is not officially allowed, there seems to be an understanding that in a certain area camping is permitted. Just outside the park entrance, only 30 yards or so to the south, is a gate on the ocean side of the road. Beyond this gate, a path curves around the cove from which the waterfall plunges. The path goes down through an open field and doubles back into a shaded grove just above a rocky promontory where the waves surge and blast as if through a tunnel. In this peaceful grove there is enough space for four or five tents, and it seems to be a locally known spot. But don't press your luck and start a fire. The rocky shore is a haunt for sea otters, and the area is, in fact, an underwater refuge as well. Threatened with extinction not long ago, the otters now survive among the thick offshore kelp beds.

Further to the south are two forest service campgrounds, the **Kirk Creek Campground** (Tel. 805 927-4211), at the Mill Creek picnic area, and the **Plasket Creek Campground** (Tel. 805 927-4556) near **Sand Dollar Beach** and **Jade Cove**. It is sometimes possible to find jade which has been

CALIFORNIA

washed up at **Jade Beach**, which is also a nude sun-bathing spot.

Several other sites are of interest: the **Esalen Institute**, named after the local Indians, has crystallized into an institute from all the various disciplines and forms of the "human potential movement" which is as uniquely Californian as the redwoods. As if selecting from a menu, you can choose courses in self-realization, meditation, yoga, centering, gestalt therapy, massage, holistic healing, Reichian work, etc, or, you can just come from between 1-5am to relax in the natural baths for $5. Except for these bathing hours, entry is by appointment and pre-arrangement only. The gate guards can be strict and unspiritually obnoxious. It is situated a few miles south of Julia Pfeiffer Burns State Park. Look for the wooden sign on the west side of the road and park in the lot at the top. Tel. 667-2335.

The writer Henry Miller lived in these hills for seventeen years, and wrote lovingly both of the landscape and his neighbors. One of his closest friends was Emile White, a bohemian wanderer from Europe, who Miller encouraged to paint. After Miller's death, White turned his home into the **Henry Miller Memorial Library**, crammed with White's paintings and Miller memorabilia, as well as copies of all sorts of obscure and private publications of Miller. (Across the road from Nepenthe. Open every day, with flexible hours. Tel. 667-2574.) Sales of books and posters help keep the non-profit foundation going.

Accommodations and Food

Lodging in the Big Sur area is generally outrageously overpriced, but this is something one must not allow to deter one from enjoying a vacation in a special place.

Fernwood: Lodge, campground and motel units. Restaurant. More reasonable than others. Tel. 667-2422.

Big Sur Lodge: In Pfeiffer Big Sur State Park. Swimming pool, sauna. Guests have park privileges. Fireplace, kitchen, additional. Starting from $60 for a double. Tel. 667-2171.

The Ventana Inn and Restaurant: Just south of Pfeiffer Big Sur State Park. The epitome of Big Sur luxury and Big Sur inflation. The cottages are quaint, the views stupendous. The Ventana is raved about for everything from its latticework to its chocolate torte. Rooms start at $125 for a double. Lunch entrees start at $6, dinner from about $16. Reservations for dinner only. Private campground. Tel. 667-2331.

Gorda: Towards the southern end of the Big Sur region. The restaurant above the gas station serves dinners that are good, filling, and extremely reasonable, especially for the area. Seafood specials, vegetable quiche, and fine ocean views. $5 and up.

The Nepenther: A well-known local spot with a spectacular view, supposedly where the artists hang out. Entrees from $7 and up. There's dancing around the fire pit in the summer. Open year round, until midnight in summer. Tel. 667-2345.

CALIFORNIA

Important Addresses And Phone Numbers
Area Code: 408 (north) 805 (south).
Emergency: 911.
Big Sur Emergency Road Service: Tel 667-2518.
Gas Stations: River Inn; Ripplewood; Fernwood; Loma Vista; Lucia Lodge; Pacific Valley; Gorda; Ragged Point. (Hours vary. Advisable to keep your tank full).

CALIFORNIA

Monterey and Carmel

North of Big Sur, the Monterey Peninsula juts forth into the ocean. From the northern end of the peninsula, Monterey Bay curves inland towards Santa Cruz and the mountains. The bay is studded with small fishing towns and state beaches, and inland toward the coastal mountains there are small farm towns. The towns of Carmel, Monterey and Pacific Grove are located on the peninsula. The weather is fair, sunny and breezy, with rain in winter and beautiful coastal fog which drifts in and condenses on trees and shrubbery.

The beauty and charm of this area attract over six million visitors each year. There are old hotels, quaint countryside inns, excellent seafood restaurants, numerous golf courses and tennis courts, as well as places to walk, wade and watch crabs and seals. Those interested in history, art or science can find plenty to see, and one can always sit drinking a cup of coffee, watching the crashing surf.

How to get there
By air: Monterey Airport is served by United Airlines, as well as by regional and in-state carriers.

By land: The Monterey Peninsula is located just off the Pacific Coast Highway. Just north of Monterey, this highway is connected to Route 101, which is the fast route to Monterey. Route 1 is more scenic. **Greyhound** also serves Monterey, with a depot near Fisherman's Wharf. The coastal **Amtrak** route stops in Salinas, with free bus links to Monterey. For those traveling to or from Santa Cruz, the transfer point between the Santa Cruz and Monterey bus systems is at the Watsonvillle terminal. Hopping from one local system to the next is generally a cheap but time-consuming way to travel. Greyhound is more expensive but much faster.

The **Monterey-Salinas Transit** (MST) system is convenient, and the schedule, available at the visitors center, clearly shows the layout of the routes. There are three main terminals; at Monterey, Salinas, and Watsonville. The terminal in Monterey is really just a small plaza right in the middle of downtown, where Munras, Pearl, Folk, Alvarado and Tyler converge. From here the bus lines radiate, including those to Carmel. Buses 4 and 5 run to the center of Carmel, and 1 and 2 to Pacific Grove. The main loading point in Carmel is near Ocean and Mission. During the summer, two buses a day serve the Pt. Lobos State Reserve and Big Sur, reaching as far as Nepenthe. The cost is $1.50 to Pt. Lobos and $3.00 to Big Sur. After Labor Day this service is rescheduled.

CALIFORNIA

Carmel

Carmel is a combination of a quaint country village, an artists' colony and a well guarded enclave of wealth. There are strict controls on everything including street signs, billboards, cutting trees (it's forbidden), house numbers (there aren't any), and the selling of ice cream cones. Yet, with all these stringent controls aimed at keeping the gingerbread facade from crumbling, the villagers gladly accept tourist money. The restaurants and lodgings tend to be more expensive than in Monterey, although some good eating deals can be found. Numerous galleries sell the usual luminous crashing waves, but there are many good artists in the area too, as well as further down the coast toward Big Sur.

The protective attitude on development changed last year when Clint Eastwood became the new mayor. He promised to loosen the noose around building codes and ice cream vending, and in the process has himself become a local attraction. Where else in America do gawking tourists gather outside the town hall waiting for local council meetings to adjourn? All over town his steely glare shoots forth from tee shirts, posters and paintings.

Since the late 1920s, Carmel has been a center for the art of photography. Edward Weston, who experimented with the limits of photography and influenced a whole generation of photographers, lived in Carmel for about 30 years, and came to know the area intimately. Some of his last photographs were of the Pt. Lobos coast. Carmel has many fine photographers carrying on the Weston tradition. Examples of local photographic art can be seen at the **Friends of Photography Gallery** (Sunset Center, San Carlos at 9th. Open daily 1-5pm. Tel. 624-6330), and at the **Weston Gallery** (6th and Dolores, Tues.-Fri. 11am-5pm, Sat. 10am-5pm.)

Just south of the town's center, off Route 1, is the Mission San Carlos Borromeo del Rio Carmelo – the **Carmel Mission** for short. The mission and its three museums are worth a visit. (3080 Rio rd. Self-guided tours Mon.-Sat. 9:30am-4:30pm, Sun. 10:30am-4:30pm. Donation requested. Tel. 624-1271.)

Built in 1771, this mission succeeded the one built in Monterey a year earlier. The graceful structure is one of the finest surviving examples of California mission architecture. Father Junipero Serra, the founder of the chain of California missions, is buried inside. In the cemetery some 2000 local Indians are buried, and some of the graves are marked by abalone shells.

The Carmel Mission is also the site for the highlight concert in the **Carmel Bach Festival**. This renowned and popular festival is held in July. For tickets and details contact: The Carmel Bach Festival, P.O. Box 575, Carmel, 93921. Tel. 624-1521.

Ocean ave. heads to the ocean at Carmel City Beach. From here the gorgeous beaches of central California stretch southwards. Parking can be

CALIFORNIA

a problem on weekends, but heading south just a few blocks on Scenic will bring you to easier parking and a beach with fewer people. Still further south, reachable by foot or by car along Scenic dr., is River Beach. Around Carmel Point is the **Carmel River State Park**, a great place (and legal) for a driftwood fire.

At the corner of Ocean View dr. and Scenic stands **Tor House**, which the poet Robinson Jeffers built himself using boulders from the beach. Tours Fri.-Sat. from 10am-3pm. Reservations required, admission $5. No children under 12, Tel. 624-1813.

About three miles south of Carmel, the smaller peninsula of **Pt. Lobos State Reserve** juts out into the Pacific. This mosaic of rugged headlands, coves, meadows, tidepools and rocky promontories is strictly protected and has retained its pristine character. Here you can find natural stands of Monterey pine and gnarled Monterey cypresses. The reserve has a network of easy trails heading from several parking lots, making the stunning views available to virtually anyone. Here at close view one can observe sea lions, sea otters, seals, elephant seals, grey whales and an occasional killer whale off the coast during the migration season. Deer graze in the meadows.

The adjoining tide area and the submerged rocks of Carmel Bay, just to the north of the Pt. Lobos headlands, comprise the **Carmel Bay Ecological Reserve**, and include the underwater canyon 1000 ft. deep just beyond Monterey Beach. The surf here is dangerous; children must be carefully watched, and the water approached with caution.

Pt. Lobos can be crowded on weekends, even during the winter. The main ranger station is off route 1. No camping is allowed. (Open 7am-11pm in summer, but the parking lot closes at sunset. During the rest of the year, open 7am-5pm.) On a crowded weekend, the parking lot can be full by noon. Divers interested in exploring the underwater reserve must show proof of certification and must register at the ranger station. Guided walks are led by rangers or docents, as staffing permits, usually every day in the summer, and on weekends during the off-season. Tel. 624-4909.

Monterey and Carmel are separated by the **Del Monte Forest**, a beautiful 5600 acre area turned into a barony. Entry to the famous **Seventeen Mile Drive** is $5. There are numerous turnoffs with each stunning view surpassing the previous one. If you stop to photograph the lone cypress, you won't be the only one. The forest includes a game preserve, where deer are allowed to nibble at the gardens. Behind the walls stand some modest mansions built between the world wars. There are four famous golf courses, including the one at Pebble Beach. The beautiful Lodge at Pebble Beach has sea views, several restaurants and free hors d'oeuvres at happy hour. Nevertheless, it seems unnecessary to pay good money to visit a rich man's estate when incomparable Pt. Lobos and Big Sur are just down the road. There is no charge for cyclists between 8-11am, and no charge for pedestrians at any time.

Pacific Grove is a small quiet town which is virtually contiguous with

CALIFORNIA

Monterey, and separated from Carmel by the Del Monte Forest. Tide pools are scooped out of its rocky shore. Old Victorian buildings and small cottages are common. John Steinbeck did much of his early writing in a cottage here. Waves of monarch butterflies arrive here every October and the town welcomes them with a festival. On their delicate wings the monarchs migrate thousands of miles from the autumn chills of the north. They literally hang around for months on foliage, except when warm weather allows them to seek food. When spring comes they fly north again.

The **Pacific Grove Museum of Natural History** houses displays on the Monarch butterflies as well as on sea birds and sea mammals. A relief map depicts the deep oceanic canyon off the peninsula and explains how the nutrient-rich cold water allows such great diversity of marine life. (Forest ave. and Central ave. Open Tues.-Sat. 10am-5pm.)

At **Lovers Point** there is a small rocky beach, and glass-bottomed boats are available in summer. Further on, the **Point Pinos Lighthouse**, built in 1855 and the oldest on the west coast, overlooks both ocean and golf course. There is a small U.S. Coast Guard Maritime Museum upstairs. (Seventeen-Mile drive. Tel. 373-3304. Open on summer weekends, 1-4pm. Admission free.)

Monterey

Monterey played an important role in early California history. Discovered by Juan Rodriguez Cabrillo in 1542, it was only in the 1770s that Spanish settlers, soldiers and priests began to settle in the area. Eventually, it became the capital of Spanish and later Mexican California. From the 1820s onward, a trickle of American sailors, whalers, trappers and traders based themselves in Monterey. A sea trading line was established between Monterey and Boston. After the Mexican War in 1846, with California in American hands, Monterey became the capital of the new American territory, and when California became a state, the constitution was drawn up in Monterey. However, with the discovery of gold in the Sierra foothills in 1849, the focus of business and trade shifted to the new port of San Francisco and the inland nodal center of Sacramento. The graceful capital of Old California became something of a backwater.

Monterey today has the greatest concentration of tourist attractions on the peninsula, the main ones being **Fisherman's Wharf**, **Cannery Row** and historic **Old Monterey**. It has some excellent seafood restaurants – many with great early bird specials – and a wide variety of others as well. Monterey also sustains an extremely active and lively cultural life. Literature from the visitors center or free papers found around town can keep the visitor informed of what's happening. The **Monterey Jazz Festival** in September is perhaps the biggest event in Monterey, and is also one of the biggest in jazz. Centered at the fairgrounds, it features some of the greatest

CALIFORNIA

Monterey – Patterns of light and water

names in jazz. Tickets should be purchased months in advance, and by the time the festival begins, the hotels and motels are packed.

For information, write to the Festival box office at 444 st., Monterey, or call (408) 373-3366.

Old Monterey

Over 40 original adobe buildings in Old Monterey survive from the pre-1850 era, and about 13 are open to the public, today housing museums, restaurants and a theater. Monterey's "Path of History", a self-guided tour of about two miles through Old Monterey, is available at the visitors' center. A fee of $1 per adult provides entry to all the state historical buildings for one day. Some of these are more interesting than others, and some are not interesting at all, but the stroll through the area is easy and pleasant. The transit plaza provides a convenient place to begin. Nearby Alvarado st. has plenty of reasonable eating spots. Some of the buildings on the tour are:

The Custom House: (1 Custom House Plaza, 115 Alvarado st.) The first U.S. government building on the Pacific Coast, restored and filled with piles of cargo from the era: casks of liquor, cases of coffee, and an old harpoon gun.

Pacific House: (8 Custom House Plaza.) Used as a tavern, newspaper office, court, church and ballroom over the years, and now a museum featuring the life and artifacts of the local Indians, the Spanish explorers and the early American settlers.

CALIFORNIA

Colton Hall: (Dutra and King streets.) The first constitutional Congress of the new State of California convened here in 1849. A "Path of History" map is obtainable here.

Larkin House: (Jefferson st. and Calle Principal. 35-minute tours from 10am-4pm.) Built by Thomas Larkin, the first, last and only U.S. consul to Mexico in California. The grand house could have been transferred from New England. The little house in the garden housed William Tecumseh Sherman years before he marched through Georgia. A small museum portrays the roles of the two men in local history.

Stevenson House: (530 Houston st. Hourly tours, 10am-4pm.) Robert Louis Stevenson lived in a rooming-house here in 1879, having come to visit the woman he later married. Much of *Treasure Island*'s vivid Pacific scenery was inspired by the Monterey landscape. There is a collection of Stevenson memorabilia here.

Fisherman's Wharf

You know you're near Fisherman's Wharf when you hear the hoarse yelping of sea lions begging food from tourists. The wharf is crowded and touristy. It is lined with tourist seaside restaurants and stands selling little seafood cocktails. Some of the restaurants offer early bird specials of fresh seafood. The general atmosphere of the wharf, however, is gaudy and circus like. Sport fishing and sightseeing cruises are available from the wharf, as are whale-watching tours during the winter months. Check out several offices to compare prices. A free shuttle bus runs every 15 minutes from 9am-10pm daily, from Memorial Day to Labor Day, and on weekends only after Labor Day. There is all day parking at the East Customs House garage for $3. Between the wharf and Cannery Row is a small stretch of beach and a breakwater where the more sedate sea lions bask on rocks. The adjacent strand of beach is popular for snorkeling and scuba diving.

Cannery Row

The canneries rumble and rattle and squeak until the last fish is cleaned and cut and cooked and canned and then the whistles scream again and the dripping, smelly, tired Wops and Chinamen and Polaks, men and women, straggle out and droop their ways up the hill into the town and Cannery Row becomes itself again – quiet and magical.

John Steinbeck, *Cannery Row*

Cannery Row began about the turn of the century with the building of one packing plant for the local sardines, used then as bait by salmon fishermen. With the introduction of larger, more efficient nets and seines, and modern parking systems, new canneries opened. Cannery Row became a center for the sardine industry. Small businesses sprang up to serve fishermen and cannery workers, and cheap rooming houses opened up on the blocks behind the canneries. In the middle of all this industry, a biologist, Ed "Doc" Ricketts opened a laboratory at the ocean's edge. He supplied sea

CALIFORNIA

Scuba diving

specimens for larger research facilities and conducted his own experiments. His study of marine life along this central coast was innovative, for he identified plants, animals, invertebrates and micro-organisms according to the habitat in which they lived rather than by genus or species. He noted that several distinct habitats existed along the coastline, each dependent on the others. Into this teeming, smelly, rough and tumble row wandered a local writer, John Steinbeck, who was raised just over the hills in the farm country of the Salinas Valley, and who was developing, in his own way, a penchant for writing about the little guy, the lowlife, the down-and-outers.

What was there, really, that made this row of canneries, redolent with the smell of fish, so romantic? Everywhere, neighborhoods centered around a central plant or industry, each with its own raw drama, but this one, perched on the edge of a beautiful natural realm managed to find its poet laureate, and Steinbeck captured vividly the rhythm and atmosphere of this jumble of canneries, warehouses, whorehouses, flophouses and tiny stores.

Over 250,000 tons of sardines were hauled in each year and processed through the two dozen plants along this row. Ricketts, Steinbeck's close friend, was one of the naysayers who warned that overfishing might destroy the industry. The yearly haul did indeed shrink, and disappeared completely by 1951. Workers and fishermen left, stores closed, and Cannery Row became a corrugated ghost town. In the 1960s and 70s, a few seafood restaurants opened, and suddenly developers and various commissions have become aware of the tourist potential of the area. The row of rusted canneries and rotted flophouses has become prime real estate for tourist oriented development. There are proposals for hotels to accompany the cute stores, the malls and the wax museum. The row has its protectors too, fighting to keep its historical ambience.

Walk a block behind the strip of tourist traps to catch a taste of the old world. A few tiny clapboard and shingled houses, and old flophouses and dormitories still stand. The railroad tracks are neglected and overgrown with weeds. A few of the stores on the row date back to earlier days. *Kasila's*, at 851 Cannery Row, is a funky old bar and sandwich shop. The *Old General Store* at 835 Cannery Row was once a Chinese grocery store – on which Steinbeck modeled Lee Chong's store in his book. At the back is a room of Steinbeck memorabilia. Across the street, Doc Rickett's old laboratory has been converted into a dance club, bordered by restaurants with great views, serving fresh seafood, at early bird prices of $6-8.

Opened in 1984, the **Monterey Aquarium** in the old Hovden Cannery at the end of Cannery Row, displays some of the marine life from the teeming oceanic environment in the North Bay area. (886 Cannery Row. Open daily 10am-6pm. $7 for adults, $5 for students and seniors, $3 for children aged 3-12. Tel. 375-3333.)

The deep reefs, the sandy sea floor, the shale reefs, the open sea and the wharf each support their own community of plants and animals. The kelp forest exhibit towers over the viewers' heads and shows how big these plants are, which usually we see only on the surface. During the summer, the aquarium conducts a number of half-day field trips and field courses on the marine environment and the marine biology of the Monterey Bay area.

The **Monterey Peninsula Museum of Art** focuses on Western and local art, and the Charlie Russel bronze statues will make the West leap out at you. (559 Pacific ave. Tues.-Sat. 10am-4pm, Sun. 1-4pm. Admission free. Tel. 372-5477.)

Further east, on El Estero dr. is the **Dennis the Menace Playground**, a collection of imaginative playground equipment on which the parent may want to join the child.

CALIFORNIA

Around Monterey

Due east of Monterey, at the junction of Route 68 and the 101 highway, lies the farm country of the Salinas Valley, a world away from the smells and sights of Monterey. This area, and the town of **Salinas** itself, was immortalized in the works of John Steinbeck. The Nobel Prize-winning writer was born in Salinas in 1902, in a house that still stands at 132 Central ave. (now a restaurant). He lived most of his life elsewhere, but he is buried here, and his modest grave can be seen at the Garden of Memories at the outskirts of town, at 768 Abbott st. The **Steinbeck Festival** is held in August in Salinas. The **John Steinbeck Library** has various displays on the writer's life, including original manuscripts. (110 West San Luis st., Salinas. Tel. 408-758-7311.)

Salinas is also the place to catch the **California Rodeo** in July. It's the closest this farm town comes to the Mardi Gras, kicked off by a big western dance on Saturday night. The competition draws the country's top cowboys and about 50,000 spectators. It's hot and dusty, so wear your ten-gallon hat. (Tel. 757-2951.)

South of Salinas on Route 101 and just east of Soledad, the spires and jagged teeth of **Pinnacles National Monument** jut out from the surrounding gentle hills. The pinnacles are the partial remains of a volcano, the other part of which lies far to the southeast. It was the San Andreas Fault, which runs right past this area, that split up the formation and left these jagged shapes. The terrain offers rugged hiking trails and the sheer walls challenge rock climbers. Although the roads approach the monument from both east and west, they do not connect.

This site, on the west side of the San Andreas fault, has shifted 195 miles north over the last 23 million years or so. The volcanic remains have been polished and eroded by the elements to form sharp spires thrusting up from the surrounding rounded hills. There are caves and canyons in the area. Spring is the best time to visit the park, when the trees are green and the slopes are covered by a multi-colored carpet of wildflowers. There is one campground in the monument, at Chaparral, and one private campground outside the eastern boundary. The western Ranger Station at Chaparral and the Bear Gulch Visitor Center at the eastern entrance provide information and exhibits. There are evening programs at both the east and west campgrounds. For information contact Park Headquarters, Pinnacles National Monument, Paicines, 95043. Tel. 408-389-4578.

Located in the Salinas Valley just west of Soledad, the **Paraiso hot springs** bubble up with hot, healing mineral waters. It is about an hour's drive from Monterey. The setting is tranquil and strict rules help keep the area in its natural state. There are outdoor and indoor pools in which to relax, and a library, recreation room, and free cookies and coffee. Take the 101 to Soledad, then follow the Arroyo Seco Road west to Paraiso Springs Road, and take that all the way to the springs. There are hook ups for trailers, at $19 per night, and tent cabins for $35 per night. Day rates are $8. Tel. 408-678-2882.

CALIFORNIA

Architecture of yesteryear

Just north of Monterey on Route 1 is Castroville, a small farmtown at the mouth of the Salinas Valley which would be indistinguishable from similar towns, but for its claim to be the artichoke capital of the world, and home of the annual Artichoke Festival in September. At the end of the main street of town is the Giant Artichoke, housing a gift shop and restaurant. The speciality of the house is french-fried artichoke. Incidentally, in the campaign to promote artichokes in 1947 the first California Artichoke Queen was crowned, an aspiring young actress named Marilyn Monroe.

To the north of Castroville, on Route 1, is the tiny fishing village of Moss Landing. It's just opposite the gigantic power station. Cross the tiny bridge that spans the tiny estuary to the town itself. This is a real fishing village. Near the fishing boats is a row of small dilapidated bait shops, garages and bars. Here the fishermen haul in catches of salmon, albacore and other fish, and get down to business without catering to tourists.

Accommodations
Lodgings on the Monterey Peninsula fill up very quickly and reservations are recommended year-round. During the summer, especially around the time of the Monterey Jazz Festival, reservations are essential. Fremont ave., towards the fairgrounds, is Monterey's approximation of a motel and hotel row. Here a wide range of accommodation can be found, mostly along conventional hotel and motel lines.

The Chamber of Commerce will supply a list of local lodgings. For last-minute help in finding a room, call Tel. 800-822-822 for Monterey and Pacific Grove; Tel. 624-1711 for Carmel.

CALIFORNIA

Asilomar Conference Center : Asilomar State Beach, Pacific Grove. Tel. 372-8016. A unique place to stay. Rooms are offered to travelers when not filled by pre-arranged groups. Pine lodges are scattered in a forest. Reservations can be made up to two months in advance. Lodges range from $30-$50, depending on the room and number of people.

Monterey Peninsula Bed & Breakfast Association: 598 Laine st., Monterey 93940. Tel. 375-8284. Can make suggestions for local inns. Free brochures available.

Food

Along Cannery Row are a number of seafood restaurants, each with an early bird special and each serving good seafood.

Bullwacker's : 653 Cannery Row. Tel. 373-1353. Here the specials are only $3.50, with a choice of several house specialities that include red snapper and calamari.

Captain's Cove: 643 Cannery Row. Tel. 372-4000. The early bird specials include salad or soup, pasta or fries, fresh vegetables, beverage and a seafood entree, with sparkling wine for 50 cents extra. $6.95.

Steinbeck Lobster Grotto: 720 Cannery Row. Tel. 373-1884. A fine location over the water, and a wide variety of seafood entrees. $6.95 for early bird specials.

Rosine's: 80 Bonifacio on Alvarado st. near Old Monterey. Tel. 375-1400. An elegant but relaxed setting and a wide range of entrees, with trimmings, starting at about $7.

Sancho Panza Restaurant : 590 Calle Principal. Tel. 375-0095. Set in the Casa Gutierrez, an adobe which dates back to 1841 and is part of old Monterey. The interior is dark and cosy, and the patio is beautiful. The Mexican food is good, the prices reasonable and the service friendly.

Restaurant Hotline: Tel. 372-DINE. A free service which makes recommendations and reservations for restaurants in the Monterey area.

Adobe Inn: Dolores and 8th st., Carmel. Tel. 625-1750. Excellent early bird dinner specials which include prime ribs, the day's fish catch, freshly baked bread and salad bar, for $6.95, between 5-6pm.

Hogs Breath Inn: San Carlos st. and 5th ave. A local hang-out, with a delightful courtyard and Clint Eastwood as owner.

The Whole Enchilada: At Route 1 near the turnoff for Moss Landing. An unbeatable combination of fine Mexican food and fine jazz (every Saturday and Sunday night).

Useful Addresses And Phone Numbers

Monterey Peninsula Chamber of Commerce and Visitor and Convention Bureau: 350 Alvarado st., Monterey. Tel. 649-3200. Mailing address: P.O.

CALIFORNIA

Box 1770, Monterey, 93940.
Pacific Grove Chamber of Commerce: Box 157, Pacific Grove, 93950. Tel. 373-3304.
Carmel Business Association: P.O. Box 444, Carmel, 93921. Tel. 624-2522.
Amtrak: 40 Railroad ave., Salinas. Tel. 422-7458.
Greyhound: 351 Del Monte ave., near Fisherman's Wharf. Tel. 373-4735. (They run a tour to Hearst Castle that includes entry fee.)
Gray Line: Tel. 373-4989. Tours of area, including Hearst Castle.
Monterey-Salinas Transit (MST): Tel. 899-2555. Main stop is Transit Plaza in downtown Monterey.
Sierra Club, Ventana Chapter: Box 5667, Carmel 93921. Tel. 624-8032. An ongoing schedule of trips available, to members and non-members. Brochures on trips available.

CALIFORNIA

Santa Cruz

Santa Cruz is situated at the northern end of Monterey Bay, where ocean, forested mountains and fields combine to create absolutely gorgeous scenery. The sandy beaches are sheltered by the northern promontory of land, and the water is fairly warm and the surf comparatively gentle. The northern promontory also protects Santa Cruz from the fog that saturates most of the central coast.

Like many Californian coastal towns, Santa Cruz began as a Spanish mission. Later it developed because of the availability of local resources: lumber, fishing and agriculture. Today it is a commercial center for farmers, flower growers and the region's many wineries. By the turn of the century, resort hotels had opened along the beach, and with the completion of a narrow gauge railroad link with Los Gatos, Santa Cruz became a fully fledged vacation town, which it has remained.

Perhaps because of the influence of the highly innovative University of California at Santa Cruz (UCSC), and because of its semi isolated location, Santa Cruz is a trendy rural center. Artisans here live in the hills, smoke marijuana and eat vegetarian food. There is a vibrant cultural life, a strong environmental movement and a variety of cults.

In contrast, the beach, boardwalk and old ornate amusement park are crowded with cruisers – everybody from punks to gays to staid well-dressed couples sharing a sentimental cotton-candy cone.

How to get there
From the San Francisco Bay area, the Route 17 freeway crosses over the Santa Cruz mountains from the suburban Santa Clara Valley. On a busy weekend, the traffic can crawl along bumper to bumper. Route 9 is even slower, winding through deeply shaded redwood canopies and small towns that seem a thousand miles away from an urban area. Highway 1, the Pacific Coast Highway, extends from the spreading suburbs to a peaceful coastline of state parks, beaches and small towns. From Monterey in the south, Route 1 is alternately freeway and small road. Even if traveling along the faster Route 101, you must cut over toward Route 1 from either Marina or Gilroy.

Although it is possible to travel by local transit systems to Santa Cruz, this is very time consuming. **Greyhound** is much faster, and serves both Santa Cruz and Watsonville. Santa Cruz's public bus system is efficient and extensive. It reaches all corners of this relatively spread out county. The new **transit terminal**, off the **Pacific Garden Mall** at Walnut and Pacific,

CALIFORNIA

Fun in the sun

presents schedules clearly, and also shows art from local schools. There are two other transit centers at Capitola and Watsonville. The rider's guide, called *Headways*, details the routes and schedules. Basic fare is 50 cents, $1 for an unlimited day-use pass, and $20 for one month's unlimited use. There is a half-price reduction on fares and passes for seniors and the handicapped. From Memorial Day to Labor Day, a summer shuttle runs every 15-20 minutes, connecting the **County Government Center**, the metropolitan center and the wharf area.

Santa Cruz has been a paradise for both recreational and racing cyclists for many years, and it hosts many races. Extensive cycling lanes on roads and separate bike paths criss-cross the city and reach the rural hills and flatlands. The Bikecentennial Pacific coastal route from Oregon to Baja runs through Santa Cruz. The **Santa Cruz Cycling Club** offers weekly rides that visitors can join (Tel. 425-8688). The club also distributes an excellent map of local routes, available in local cycling shops. Another map of local routes is supplied by the **Santa Cruz Transportation Commission**, 701 Ocean st., Santa Cruz, 95060. Tel. 425-2951.

One can get much information on the Santa Cruz area at the local **Convention and Visitors Center** and the **Chamber of Commerce**. The

CALIFORNIA

local free weekly paper, *Good Times*, has full listings of Santa Cruz's lively nightlife. A dozen or so local bars and clubs showcase music. Santa Cruz is close enough to the currents wafting downtown from San Francisco to foster a rich and varied music scene. The university hosts various exhibits, films, concerts, lectures and drama. For cultural events at the university call: The **UCSC Barn Theater**, Tel. 423-4734 and The **Performing Arts Theater**, Tel. 429-4168.

The **Pacific Garden Mall**, lined with flowers, trees and benches, has a relaxing small-town atmosphere, yet is also distinctly Santa Cruzian with its would-be singers crooning stoned-out versions of Dylan songs, and a store sponsored by Greenpeace, the activist ocean oriented environmental group whose boats have hurled themselves before whalers and nuclear ships. Much of the old western architecture is preserved. The shops are unusual, the restaurants varied and surprisingly reasonable, the book stores eclectic, and the cafes hip and intellectual. The mall's stores have a special atmosphere. They extend along the side streets to Front st. Both Pacific and Front extend beyond the commercial section to the beach area.

The **Octagon**, set in a beautiful old building, is a small historical museum featuring local exhibits, such as the recent exhibit of masks. (118 Cooper, Mon.-Sat. noon-5pm. Tel. 425-2540.) The **Art Museum of Santa Cruz County** presents nationally circulated exhibits. (224 Church, Tues.-Sun. noon-5pm, Thurs. 6-9pm. Admission charge except on Sunday. Tel. 429-3420.)

The **Artisans Cooperative**, on the mall, is a multi-media cooperative gallery with some pleasant surprises. (1364 Pacific Garden Mall, Mon.-Sat. 10am-4pm. Tel. 423-8183.)

The Santa Cruz **Boardwalk**, built in 1907, is the last of the elegant old amusement parks extant on the West Coast. (400 Beach st. Admission free. Individual rides cost 75 cents for adults, 50 cents for kids, with various ticket plans available. Open daily from Memorial Day to Labor Day, and weekends the remainder of the year. Tel. 426-RIDE.)

Shooting galleries, organ music, teenage boys trying to win kewpie dolls for their girls – all the grand old amusement park scenes are here. The people parading along the boardwalk range from the sedate to the ultra-hip, while the architecture and props belong to another era. The oldest ride is the 1911 **carousel**, with a pipe organ and seventy hand-carved horses, some of which are more valuable today than live ones. The Giant Dipper roller coaster is wild, rated as one of the world's top ten. Yet even at an old time amusement park time marches on, and the vintage arcade games are being elbowed out by Pac-Man and Dragon-Slayer. The **Coconut Grove Ballroom**, built in 1907, hosted most of the major big bands during the 1940's swing era, and still showcases that same sound in regular concerts today.

Beachfront Santa Cruz throbs with action. Across from the Boardwalk are the cheap beach joints with big gaudy signs that you would expect to find

CALIFORNIA

at Coney Island. Young kids zoom up and down in revved up wheels. It is only appropriate that this is the spot for the annual vintage 1950's and 60's car contest when all those gleaming '56 Chevys roll out. The **Clam Chowder Cook-off and Festival** in February draws thousands of contestants and even more volunteer tasters, but it is hard to imagine anything surpassing the **Brussel Sprouts Festival**, held every October. These festivals are held at the beach area.

At the adjacent **municipal wharf**, commercial fishermen operate and there are a number of small restaurants, bait shops and small bars. During August, skydivers land on the boardwalk every Friday at 11am, 4pm and 9pm.

It's a nice bike ride and an exhilirating walk to **Lighthouse Point** from the wharf area. Seals and surfers hang out here. The **Santa Cruz Surf Museum** recently opened in the lighthouse, and depicts Santa Cruz as a long-time surfing center, and surfing as a consuming passion. (Open daily. Hours vary. Admission free. Tel. 429-3429.)

Take West Cliff drive to the abuttment of land that marks the end of Monterey Bay until you reach the **Natural Bridges State Park**. Here the surf has pounded holes through the jutting walls of cliff. Located just west of the park, on Delaware st., is the **Long Marine Laboratory**, maintained by **UCSC**. (Open Tues.-Sun. 1-4pm. Tel. 429-4087.) East of the Boardwalk across the San Lorenzo River is the **Santa Cruz City Museum**. Just look for the stone whale. (1305 E. Cliff dr. Tues.-Sat. 10am-5pm, Sun. noon-5pm. Tel. 429-3773.) Inside, the displays focus on local tidepools, mammals, geological history and Indian culture.

At **UCSC**, hills covered in redwoods slope gently down to the ocean. Besides having a beautiful campus, UCSC is unique in the UC system, and one of the most innovative schools in the country. It is really a cluster of interdependent small colleges. Each college is a small, self-contained, architecturally distinct community. Each has its own classrooms, resident halls, library, etc., but there are various connections between the colleges through courses and various activities. The emphasis here is on theses, not on letter grades. The visitors center in Kresge Hall provides information and guided tours. (Tel. 429-0111.)

Along the coast and in the valleys to the east, apples, figs, corn, berries and other seasonal fruits and vegetables are grown, and this is also a wine region. A visit to these farms gives one a glimpse of the countryside and also a chance to pick and purchase fresh produce, sometimes at bargain prices, and a chance to meet the local people. Many farms encourage and welcome visitors, but it is best to call ahead. A self-guiding tour map is available, with a detailed listing of local farms, ranches and their produce. The Chamber of Commerce and Convention and Visitor Bureau distribute these maps. Also available is a list of regional wineries which dot the countryside.

The coast, the hills and the canyons around Santa Cruz encompass many

CALIFORNIA

state parks. **Henry Cowell Redwoods State Park**, along Route 9, is a short ride north of Santa Cruz and includes 4000 acres of magnificent redwood forest. There are 15 miles of hiking and riding trails, as well as camping. The popular trail looping through Redwood Grove begins and ends at an exhibit shelter. The largest part of the park is accessible only on foot or on horseback. **Fall Creek State Park**, a part of Henry Cowell State Park, is a hikers' park, with no roads. It is heavily forested, with deep canyons. Campfire programs and guided hikes are conducted in the summer. (Park headquarters Tel. 335-4598.)

Adjacent to the Henry Cowell State Park is **Roaring Camp and Big Trees**, where old-fashioned steam-powered trains chug along a winding narrow gauge rail line. This is a faithful recreation of the lines that carried giant redwood logs from forest to sawmill. Every Memorial Day weekend there is a three-day re-enactment of the Civil War period, including battles staged with infantry, cavalry and artillery battle tactics. Take Route 9 to Felton, turn southeast on to Graham Hill rd., and continue half a mile. (Admission $8.75, and for ages 3-16, $5.75. Trains start at 11am or noon, on a varying schedule. Tel. 335-4400.) The covered wooden bridge in Felton is not the awesome sight lauded by the local brochures, but it is a quaint photo spot.

Further to the north is the 16,000 acre **Big Basin State Park**, an immense primeval redwood forest preserve on the ocean-facing slopes of the Santa Cruz Mountains. There are 60 miles of trail in this park. From the park headquarters just opposite the campground is the popular Skyline-to-Sea trail. This is a much visited park, but since most visitors come for a picnic or short stroll through the most accessible redwood groves, it is easy to find uncrowded trails and pockets of solitude in shaded canyons or beside misty waterfalls. Guided hikes and evening campfire programs are held from mid-June to Labor Day. Pick up a trail map at the visitor center for 75 cents. The park has four major campgrounds and backcountry camping is allowed. Permits are required. To reach Big Basin, drive north on Route 9 to Boulder Creek and turn northwest on Route 236 to the park. (Tel. 338-6132.)

Accommodations

Bed & Breakfast Inns abound in Santa Cruz County. Some are in old Victorian buildings a few blocks from the boardwalk, others are in country farmhouses.

A Place to Stay: Tel. 662-3400, or Tel. 800-621-0854, ext. 622. Free referrals.

Innkeepers of Santa Cruz: P.O. Box 464, Santa Cruz, 95061. Tel. 425-8212. Free referrals.

The Tyrolean Inn: 9600 Highway 9, Ben Lomond 95005. Tel. 336-5188. A little bit of the Austrian Alps in the midst of redwood country. Cozy cabins and friendly atmosphere. Accessible by bus from downtown Santa Cruz. $34-$40.

St. George Hotel: 1520 Pacific Garden Mall. Tel. 423-8181. An old, safe, cheap residential type of hotel. Starts at about $15 without bath.

UCSC: Tel. 429-2611. Rooms available in summer.

Youth Hostels
The **AYH** operates a hostel in Santa Cruz each summer, at a temporary location. Call the hostel office. Tel. 423-8304.

Two interesting hostels run by AYH are located on the coast north of Santa Cruz: *Pigeon Point Lighthouse*, Tel. 879-0633; *Montara Lighthouse Hostel*, Tel. 728-7177. (These are described under San Francisco accommodation.)

Camping options are plentiful, and there are many state parks in the immediate Santa Cruz area so it is generally possible to find camping spots even on crowded weekends. Camping facilities range from trailer lots to walk-in primitive and isolated sites for hikers and cyclists. It is best to make reservations. For information call the *State Parks Dept.* Tel. 688-3241 or Tel. 335-5858.

Some stunning camping areas for vehicles and hikers can be found in *Big Basin State Park*. Tel. 338-6132.

Food
El Palomar: 1344 Pacific Garden Mall. Tel. 425-7575. In the old Paloma Inn. Very unusual and delicious Mexican food, from Michoacan in the south. Reasonable prices, but you might get a stiff neck while gazing at the beautifully decorated high ceiling. Live music on Friday and Saturday nights.

Sweet William's: 538 Seabright ave. Tel. 429-1077. Soup, corn bread and live jazz.

Common Ground Coffee House: 2015 N. Pacific ave. Tel. 425-8469. A popular place to sip coffee and ponder existence.

Cafe De Palma: 415 Seabright ave. Tel. 426-5558. For solid and inexpensive breakfasts.

Saturn Cafe: 1230 Mission st. Tel. 429-8505. A good way to ease into organic Santa Cruz.

Zoccoli's Delicatessen: 1534 Pacific Garden Mall, Tel. 423-2267. When you have tired of sprouts on crackers, taste the lasagna lunch special here.

Useful Addresses And Phone Numbers
Area Code: Tel. 408.
Emergency: Tel. 911.
Santa Cruz County Convention & Visitors Bureau: PO Box 1476, Santa Cruz 95061, Tel. 423-6927. Office is upstairs in the small mall at Center and Church, but call for exact directions. Much material available.

CALIFORNIA

Public Transit Information: Tel. 425-8600, or Tel. 688-8600.
Greyhound Peerless Stages: Tel. 423-1800 or Tel. 722-4457.
Green Tortoise: Tel. 462-6437.
Amtrak: Tel. 800-872-7245.
Santa Cruz Airporter: Tel. 423-1234. To San Jose Airport and San Francisco Airport.
Mental Health Crisis Counselling: Tel. 425-2237.
Crisis Line: Tel. 429-1478.
Suicide Prevention: Tel. 426-2342.
California State Parks Dept.: Tel. 688-3241 or Tel. 335-5858.

GREY WHALE
This mammal has become adapted to living in salty water. It reaches a length of 14–17 meters. The grey whale requires enormous quantities of food, mainly small fish and other tiny life forms. Its habitat is the Pacific Ocean from California to the Arctic Ocean. This whale, like many of its species, is much hunted and now faces extinction.

CALIFORNIA

San Francisco

Every year, San Francisco unleashes a "City Fair" in September, the urban equivalent of a good 'ole country fair, held until now at the old brick Fort Mason near the marina. Contests for the best apple pie are replaced by contests for the best quiche. Garbage can painting replaces quilting, and instead of bronco-riding and cattle-punching, street-wise kids laden down with earrings and medallions perform amazing stunts on skateboards and small bicycles to driving inner-city breakdance rhythms. In addition to the usual burgers and fries, there are booths selling chow mein and egg roll, sushi, enchiladas, felafel, curry, souvlaki, piroshkis, Thai broiled fish, Salvadoran rice, Ethiopian injira, and New York kosher pastrami-on-rye with a pickle on the side. At the entrance to the fair, various municipal and civic organizations dispense literature and urge support for various projects, from recycling bottles and newspapers to supporting mobile libraries for the elderly. Among the displays there is a heavy emphasis on spiritual readings.

San Francisco has the richness and diversity and the crowded neighborhoods of a major urban center, but without the hectic pressure of a big city, although it is among the largest cities in the state, and on a workday it seems that the entire bay area pours into its downtown canyons. The financial district with its glass and concrete towers, its crowds in dark business suits, and its leather-padded hide-aways could be Wall Street, yet one bus ride away there are neighborhoods of small houses and fenced-in yards, that might be found in any small town. Toward the east end of the city the streets and alleys of Chinatown are packed with crowds, noise and delicious smells, but backed by the tree-covered slopes at the western edge of the city, stroked by fog and soothed by the rhythm of surf and foghorn, you can hardly believe there's a city behind you at all.

San Francisco is a city that conjures many different images. It is the bastion of old-world, cosmopolitan urbanity, with a rich ethnic fabric. It is the epitome of wealthy, cultured and self-absorbed hedonism, a place where the leisure-loving, young and upwardly mobile love to make their money and spend it on expensive toys. Here homosexuality is open, widespread and almost fashionable, and there are enough self-liberating, consciousness-raising, spiritually awakened groups, cults and movements to form their own yellow pages. Here experimental art and theater proliferate, new ideas spring from the cultural soil, and every second clerk or waitress claims to be a painter, writer or musician.

There is, obviously, a more serious side to the city as well. San Francisco is a rapidly changing city. It was at one time the end of the American West,

San Francisco Moonscape

but now the west is extending so far west that it becomes the far east. The strong ties between San Francisco and the Far East come from several sources. Chinese and other Asian groups have median incomes exceeding those of Whites. They are hard-working, persistent, family-oriented. A higher percentage of their children attend college, often in the most technical and advanced sciences. Chinatown and the surrounding area, one of the most densely populated areas in the country, burst its seams a while ago and spilled over not only into the neighboring Italian neighborhood, but into suburban neighborhoods far away. The decrepit Tenderloin area suddenly had an influx of Cambodians and Indonesians. There is a steady influx of immigrants from Asian countries in political turmoil – Laos, Vietnam, Cambodia, Thailand and especially the Philippines

Moreover, trade with Asia has soared. Cities in the Pacific are growing rapidly. With one exception, the eight largest banks in the world are from the Pacific nations, and Pacific investors are buying San Francisco property.

Added to this ethnic mix there is a great influx of people from unstable Latin American countries (El Salvador, Nicaragua and Peru) and an increasing Mexican population. Numbers are elusive and misleading, because many of the immigrants are not legally registered.

A casual survey of Latino neighborhoods reveals a great increase in numbers and national diversity. What the influence of these groups will be in the future is anybody's guess. The Latinos have not integrated into

CALIFORNIA

SAN FRANCISCO

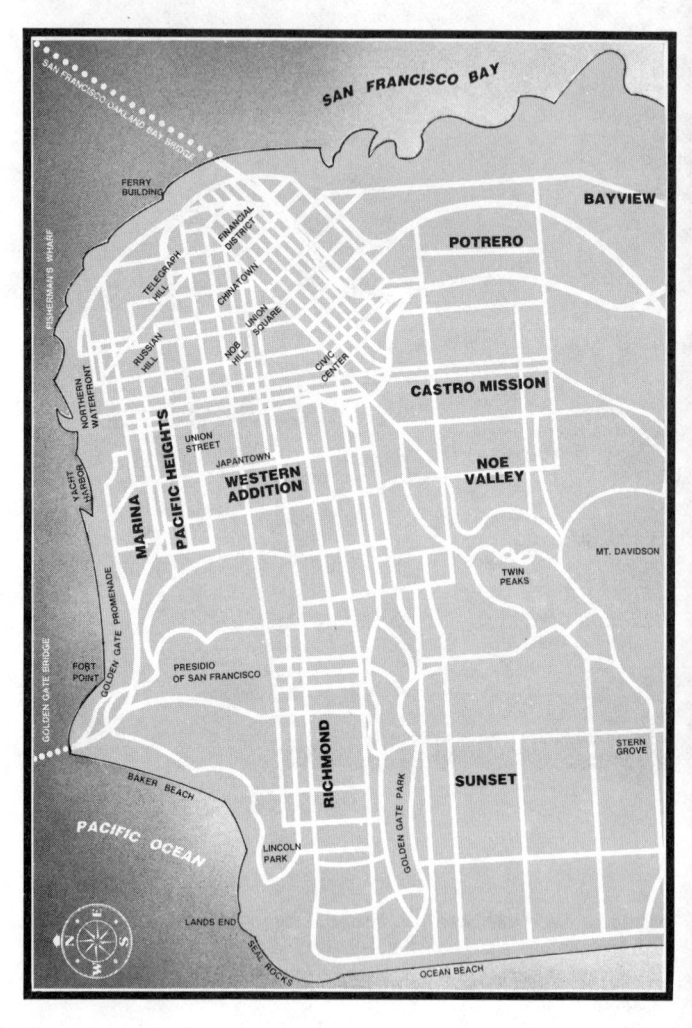

society as rapidly as the Asians, but they bring rich cultures and often a powerful sense of political radicalism. The San Francisco images of career-conscious single yuppies, prosperous gay entrepreneurs, Victorian houses and bohemian poets are partial at best. The city is changing, from its foundations upwards.

CALIFORNIA

The term "Pacific Rim" is making the rounds in California, and will in the next decade be as commonly and widely understood as "Third World", "Middle East" or "Old World". It hints at a new global orientation, towards the Pacific and the coasts edging its huge expanse. San Francisco, in the city's finest tradition, is on the cutting edge of great change.

But, back in the present, San Francisco is a traveler's city, food-lover's city, a walker's city, a music-lover's city. Eat in a burnished, padded grillroom, or survive on burritos. Have the valet park your car, or hop through the city by bus, subway and cable car. Hear the biggest names in classical or rock music, or catch a violinist in a doorway on a windy night.

Orientation

San Francisco is located at the tip of a peninsula extending north from the San Mateo hills. The peninsula separates the San Francisco Bay from the Pacific ocean. The Golden Gate, the sole entrance from the Pacific to the bay, is narrow enough to have been overlooked for over two hundred years after the first explorations of the coast.

Across this narrow strait to the north lies the peninsula of Marin. To the east, across the bay, lie Oakland and Berkeley and a series of suburban communities.

The first European settlement, built by the Spanish in 1776, included a presidio at the western tip of the peninsula, and a mission. The settlement that grew up around these two points remained small for years. At the time of the discovery of gold, the settlement had only several hundred inhabitants, and was of secondary importance to Monterey and other towns.

The sparks of the gold rush ignited an explosion of growth. The port developed at the northeast bend of the peninsula. Early photographs show a veritable forest of masts. The city expanded in a ragged progression of tents, shacks and muddy streets up the hills. From the very beginning, San Francisco was an ethnic patchwork. Gold-hungry immigrants streamed in from all over the world. Europeans, Americans, Mexicans, Central Americans and Chinese were thrown together into the maelstrom that was young San Francisco.

The core of old San Francisco was in the hilly northeast corner, and fanned out from there. The original area included the wharves of the Embarcadero, the Barbery Coast (whose dance halls and brothels were eventually replaced by the towers of the Financial District), Union Square vicinity, Chinatown, North Beach and Fisherman's Wharf.

Telegraph Hill, between the Embarcadero and North Beach, eventually became a neighborhood for Italian workers and fishermen, and is easily recognized today by Coit Tower at its peak. West of downtown rise Nob Hill and Russian Hill. On Nob Hill the industrial and financial overlords of the rapidly growing city built their mansions.

From the Embarcadero, the main thoroughfare, Market street, slants to the

CALIFORNIA

Coit Tower

southwest. The area south of Market st., SOMA, was until recently a rundown collection of warehouses and lots, but artists, dance clubs and trendy restaurants are now moving in. Further along the axis of Market st. is the expansive layout of public buildings around the Civic Center. Neither of the neighborhoods bordering the Civic Center – the Tenderloin area to the northeast, and the Western Addition to the west – is especially attractive or safe. A small Japantown clings to the northern edge of the

CALIFORNIA

Western Addition. Further along Market st., and just to its south, is the predominantly Mexican and Latino Mission District. Market street leads up to the gay Castro st. neighborhood, and to Twin Peaks Park.

Twin Peaks and the adjacent Mt. Davidson, the highest point in the city at some 1000 ft., provide breathtaking panoramas of the entire city spreading below in every direction. From here it is easy to see how the southern reaches of the city blend into the suburbs of Daly City (reputedly the inspiration for Malvina Reynolds' famous song about suburbia, *Little Boxes*).

West of the restaurants and multi-tiered malls of Fisherman's Wharf, along the city's northern shore, rises the promontory of Fort Mason, which houses the National Park Service and a youth hostel. The old red-brick military buildings on the docks have been converted into studios, museums and workspace for various grassroots organizations. Beyond Fort Mason lies the Marina, used for pleasure crafts. To the south of the Marina rises Pacific Heights, a pretty neighborhood of old houses squeezed side by side. On the way up is Union street with its refurbished Victorian buildings and its renowned singles scene.

Further west lies the residential Richmond neighborhood, with its excellent restaurants along Clement st. To the south stretches the green belt of Golden Gate Park, with Haight-Ashbury at its eastern end and the ocean to the west. Public beaches stretch in both directions from here. To the north they rise into high and rugged bluffs fringed by forest and hiking trails. The bulk of this point is part of the large army base, the Presidio. Most of the shoreline includes a recreational strip. At the northernmost point, above Fort Point, the Golden Gate Bridge stretches north toward Marin. Grass and walking paths follow the rocky shore east back to the Marina.

San Francisco's famous fogs, cold and heavy, can obscure the Golden Gate Bridge and block the sun from the western neighborhoods, while the sun still shines on the inland districts buffered by the hills. Sometimes the fog rolls over the whole city, bringing with it dampness and chill. Mark Twain said that the coldest winter he ever experienced was a summer in San Francisco. A heavy sweater can be necessary even in summer. The weather can change sharply not only between neighborhoods but within the day. Summer temperatures are generally moderate and comfortable. Cold days of damp fog or heavy rain may be interspersed with warm clear days.

Such a variety of neighborhoods, each with its own centers and identity, packed so tightly together, makes exploring this city a joy. Most popular sites are concentrated in the old northeastern section of the city. These neighborhoods can easily be explored on foot (though the hills undoubtedly pose a challenge).

The public transportation grid is extensive but takes a little time to understand. It is fairly easy to get from one area to another and tour each area on foot, and this can be a lot more convenient than going by car.

Golden Gate Bridge

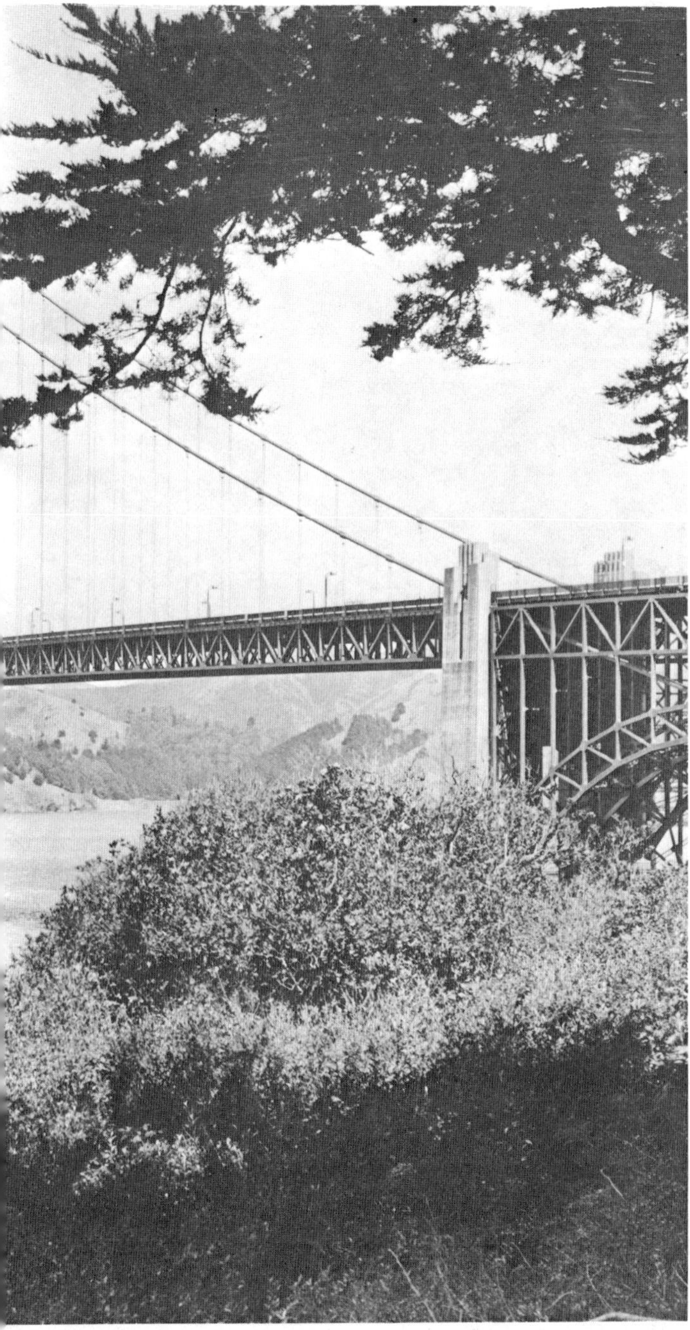

CALIFORNIA

Bridge under construction

How to get there

By air: San Francisco International Airport (SFO), serves airlines and flights from around the world, but it does not have the overwhelming bustle and chaos of a major airport. It is located south of the city on a small peninsula stretching into the bay.

There are three terminals: North, Central and South, with various airlines divided between them. The upper tier is for departures, the lower one is for

CALIFORNIA

arrivals. Traffic moves smoothly at the arrival level and Airport Information can handle all enquiries about transportation, hotels, etc.

San Francisco proves that it is an individual city even at the airport. Instead of passing the time with a cheap novel, you can visit the airport's museum, with its art exhibits, or take a tour and get a glimpse of airport operation.

The airport is easily and quickly reached by car via the Route 101 freeway. During rush hours the highway may be congested in the city itself, but once outside the downtown tangle of freeways, the traffic generally flows fairly fast. Barring a major traffic jam, it takes half an hour to reach the airport from the central city.

Public and private transportation from the airport to downtown San Francisco is convenient and inexpensive, compared to Los Angeles. If you require public transportation, make sure to ask about it specifically when seeking information, otherwise you may only receive information about private **Airporter** buses. **San Mateo County Transit** *(Samtrans)* runs buses between downtown and SFO about every half hour, from early morning to about 1:30am. These include the 7 and 7B. From the airport these buses arrive at the Transbay terminal a few blocks south of Market. From there, local public transportation pulls right up to the entrance. The neighborhood itself is not the greatest, nor are there many facilities in the immediate vicinity: something to consider if arriving at a late hour.

If traveling to the east bay area – Oakland, Berkeley – the ride downtown is unnecessary because *Samtrans* also runs a bus to the Daly City terminal of the **Bay Area Rapid Transit (BART)** system. The sleek futuristic train will whoosh you under the city and bay.

The **Airporter** bus runs a shuttle between airport terminals, and also to its downtown terminal. Buses run frequently, from 5:30-1:50am. Fare is approximately $4.

Smaller shuttle and van services go from door to door for a few extra dollars. Inquire from information services at the airport. Direct private transportation can also be obtained for outlying destinations, such as Napa. Inquire at the airport. Representatives of the major car rental firms are located in the terminals.

Major airports in Oakland and San Jose also provide full flight schedules for major national as well as regional carriers.

San Francisco International Airport (SFO) Information: Tel. 761-0800 or Tel. 876-2811.

Airporter Bus: Downtown Tel. 673-2434; airport Tel. 877-0345.

By land: The two major bus companies, **Greyhound** and **Trailways**, both serve San Francisco. The stations of both companies are open 24 hours and located on the south side of Market st. – the wrong side if it happens to be late at night. Trailways is located in the Transbay Terminal several blocks south of Market st. Greyhound is located just south of Market, and

CALIFORNIA

Route 1 – Linking L.A. and San Francisco

is a little more accessible to more transportation lines and decent, safe lodgings.

Behind the Transbay terminal is Green Tortoise, the bus line with bunks in the buses, which offers trips which are somewhat adventurous and unconventional to destinations around the state and country. There are frequent and cheap ($25) trips to Los Angeles, up the coast, to Yosemite, or across the country.

Amtrak stops (or starts) in the dregs of Oakland. A free shuttle bus connects the Amtrak station and the Transbay Terminal in San Francisco. The shuttle trip takes about half an hour.

Trains pull into Oakland from Reno and the east, from Los Angeles and Seattle.

The fastest way to get from Los Angeles to San Francisco by **car** is to take the I-5 along the western edge of the San Joaquin Valley, and then to go west along I-580 to the bay area. Route 101 is not as spectacular as the Pacific Coast Highway or as fast as I-5, but it's more interesting than the valley route. The coastal route along Route 1 through Big Sur is a breathtaking drive. From the Monterey and Santa Cruz areas, several routes approach the bay area. Route 101 swings east into the Santa Clara Valley, enters San Jose, and approaches the east bay. Route 1 becomes a freeway south of Santa Cruz, and connects with Highway 17, which crosses over the Santa Cruz mountains to the network of freeways running on both sides the bay. Route 1 continues up the coast as a small road, passing state beaches, gentle hills and several small towns before it

CALIFORNIA

pierces the lower reaches of suburbia. Another alternative route runs along Route 9 from Santa Cruz, and passes under a canopy of towering redwoods.

From the north, whether driving along Route 1 or Route 101, the two roads merge and Route 101 takes over, as the highway crosses the Golden Gate Bridge. From Sacramento, Tahoe, Reno and points east, the transcontinental I-80 leads directly to the Oakland Bay Bridge.

Local Transportation

In 1873, the cable car was invented in San Francisco, to replace horse-drawn carriages which had difficulty in climbing the steep hills. In 1912, the city launched a municipal railway street car system, the first publicly owned municipal transportation system in the country. With a tradition like that, and with its physical compactness, it is no wonder that San Francisco has a superb public transportation system today, both within the city limits and connecting its satellite communities. There is such an array of overlapping and interconnecting systems – cable cars and trolleys, buses and municipal subway, BART, AC Transit, Samtran, Caltrain and Golden Gate Transport, plus shuttles between the various systems – that it can be baffling to a visitor, especially if he must travel out of the city itself. There are also a variety of tickets, designed to save money for the regular traveler and encourage the use of public transportation.

MUNI is the principal municipal transportation system, with several components: trolley cars, cable cars, buses and the fairly new metro (subway) system. Trolleys are the cars attached to overhead wires (that spark occasionally), and cable cars are the squat multi-colored open cars that run up and down the hills near the central city. The fare is 75 cents for all systems except the cable cars, which cost $1.50 (seniors 15 cents). Free transfers are good in any direction for 90 minutes. Exact change is required. A MUNI Fast Pass costing $23 allows unlimited travel for one calendar month on MUNI (including the cable cars) and BART (Bay Area Rapid Transit – see below) within the city limits. They are available at MUNI ticket outlets, and if you are planning an extended stay in the city they are well worth considering. In addition, an all-day pass, good for the entire MUNI system, is available at automatic ticket machines located along the cable car lines.

The **cable cars** have no motors: a big motor at the cable car station pulls a steel cable, guided by an intricate network of pulleys, through a trench beneath the tracks. The cable is held and released by a grip on the car that works like a pair of pliers. The brakes are mechanical. This system was widespread in other cities as well as San Francisco, until it was supplanted by the trolley on all but the steepest routes. The trolleys draw electricity from an overhead wire to the car's motors, which propel them along the tracks. After the 1906 earthquake, they replaced the cable cars on most routes. The cable car system, overhauled in 1984, is an official National Historic Landmark that still is operational.

CALIFORNIA

The cable cars operate along three routes today. The *Powell-Hyde* line begins at Powell and Market Streets and ends at Victorian Park near the Maritime Museum and Aquatic Park. The *Powell-Mason* line also begins at Powell and Market but terminates at Bay Street, just three blocks from Fisherman's Wharf. The *California Street* line runs from the foot of Market Street to Van Ness Avenue. Cable car riders should, if possible, purchase tickets before boarding from the self-service ticket machines at all terminals and major stops.

Hop off any Powell Street line, at Washington and Mason, for a visit to the **Cable Car Museum**, the humming center of the cable car operation. (Open 10am-6pm daily. Admission free. Tel. 474-1887.) The building was restored on the original foundation in 1984 and presents a wide display of historical exhibits and memorabilia on the cable car, including the original prototype car. A 16-minute film is shown continuously.

The five-line **Metro** train system, operating both above and below ground, is the newest addition to the general MUNI system. Downtown, between the Embarcadero and the Civic Center, it follows the BART route. It then branches off to the west and southwest, reaching Castro Street, the Twin Peaks area, and the San Francisco Zoo near the beach. Another line heads for the beach, just south of Golden Gate Park. It operates from 5am-12:30am weekdays.

BART is the sleek futuristic system that shoots from Daly City in the south, through downtown, and beneath the floor of the bay to Oakland, Berkeley and other East Bay cities and suburbs. The tube under the Bay, over three and a half miles long, is one of the longest underwater crossings in the world. Within the San Francisco area (from Balboa Park to the Embarcadero stations) a MUNI pass is also valid for BART. Take time to study the charts and the system before you use it. Everything, from the ticket purchase to entry through the gate, is automatic. Fares start at 80 cents and are pro-rated according to distance, up to $3.00. There are various longer-term, regular-use tickets available, and arrangements with the other transit companies on ticket use. Should the automatic ticket system baffle you, there is an attendant at every station. If you walk out from a BART station into San Francisco, a two-part transfer at the station for 75 cents, will allow you to ride on MUNI (not the cable car) to your destination and back to the BART station. One can also take a bicycle aboard BART lines. If traveling all day through a pneumatic tube thrills you, you can buy the BART excursion ticket for $2.60, which allows you to tour all the BART stations; but the catch is that you can only leave from the station you entered, and an exit anywhere else into the sunlight will nullify the excursion ticket.

The **Trans-Bay Transit Terminal**, at 1st and Market, is the San Francisco center for three bay area bus lines. AC Transit (Tel. 839-2882) operates between San Francisco and the East Bay, and between the East Bay communities themselves. The terminal also houses Samtrans (Tel. 761-7000), connecting to the airport and to peninsula cities as far south as Palo Alto.

CALIFORNIA

California Street cable car

Golden Gate Transit connects Marin County to the city via the Golden Gate Bridge, as well as serving the cities within Marin County. The connections within Marin can sometimes be sporadic, but the 76 can bring you from downtown San Francisco right to the wild edge of the Pacific in the Marin Headlands Reserve.

Caltrain, with a terminal at 4th and Townsend, operates commuter trains between San Francisco and San Jose, and links with the Santa Clara County Transit System. Weekday shuttle buses run between the terminal and the financial district at the peak commuting hours. Also located here is the San Francisco station for Amtrak, with shuttle buses stopping along 4th st. for connections with Amtrak trains at the Oakland train station.

San Francisco Bay

San Francisco Bay is not actually a bay, but an estuary, the transition zone between fresh and salty water. The 50-mile long estuary is made up of delicate ecosystems that weave together to form a unique biological and ecological community which includes grey whales that migrate along its coast (every year one or two stray into the bay), marine organisms that are born here and migrate out to sea, and crustaceans and plankton in the inland marshes. Rivers fed by fresh water in the Sierras and the Cascades flow into the Great Central Valley, and then out into the San Francisco Bay.

Unfortunately the bay has been somewhat spoilt by landfill and dumping of wastes. Parts of the bay were filled to create additional land for residential and industrial development. Once the bay was edged by 300 square miles of delicate, biologically rich marshland, but today three quarters of this area has been filled. Untreated waste water was poured steadily into the bay right up to the 1960s.

While wastes increased, the natural flushing action that pushed them into the bay decreased. Most of the fresh water from the feeding rivers is diverted for Central Valley agriculture. This plays havoc with the delicately balanced ecosystems of the estuary.

In the mid-sixties, a citizen's organization, spearheaded by a group of Berkeley women, set out to oppose the developers and federal planners who had diverted water from and filled in the bay. The fight against many local cities and huge corporations seemed futile and quixotic at first, but a groundswell of support arose from local residents, and after tough political battles a state commission was assigned to study and control future bay development.

This fight helped to stir up environmental battles and protests across the country over projects that in an earlier era would have been implemented without forethought. The commission has even helped the bay start to reclaim a little of its lost territory, by assuring that if an area is filled, a previously filled area will be broken open to the water.

But the struggle for control of the fate of the beautiful San Francisco Bay is ongoing and endless. There are increased controls on landfill and dumping, and a vast increase in the amount of land set aside for parks and reserves, but freshwater, the lifeblood of the bay's ecosystems, is still siphoned off upriver.

There are several organizations, some educational and non-profit, others private, that provide "ecological" cruises. These examine and explain various ecological communities in the huge and variegated bay area. Some are seasonal, following the migration of the grey whales:

The Oceanic Society: Building 240, Fort Mason, San Francisco, 94123. Tel. 441-5970. Field trips in the marine environment, trips to the Farallon Islands, guided cruises to bay islands.

Nature Expeditions International: 599 College ave., Palo Alto, 94306. Tel. 328-6572. Whale-watching expeditions to Monterey Bay (January); all-day Farallon Islands trips, each weekend from mid-April through May; one-day nature cruises highlighting the natural history of the bay area.

Canoe Trips West: 217 Redwood Highway, Greenbrae, 94906. Tel. 461-1750. Canoe trips with naturalists around the marshland, several times a year. Self-guided tours of the estuaries and lagoons, all year round.

Marine Ecological Institute: 811 Harbor blvd., Redwood City, 94063. Tel. 364-2760. A four-hour "discovery voyage" in the southern bay. Also, "Bay Discovery Day".

Golden Gate Audubon Society: 2718 Telegraph ave. 206, Berkeley, 94705. Tel. 843-2222. Bay shoreline field trips, bird trips throughout northern California, spring birding cruises to the Farallons. Trips from Monterey for bird-watching and whale-watching.

The Financial District

"Licentiousness, debauchery, pollution, loathsome diseases, insanity from dissipation, misery, poverty, wealth, profanity, blasphemy and death are there. And Hell, yawning to receive the putrid mass, is there also".

Benjamin Estelle Lloyd, historian:
Lights and Shades of San Francisco

It sounds like Dante's Inferno, but the words describe the infamous Barbary Coast of San Francisco, the sleek and deep-canyoned financial district. Perhaps there is some poetic connection in that. In any case, the theme of this area is, predictably, money, money, money. Down here in this glass-and-steel grotto, you can see how it is made, where it goes and how it is spent.

At the **Federal Reserve Bank of San Francisco** (101 Market st., Tel. 974-3252), you can see "The World of Economics", a large, fascinating display that fills the lobby with computer games, video tapes and murals. A computer game gives you the opportunity to become chairman of the Federal Reserve Board for 48 months. You can fire everybody or turn the country into a kibbutz, but in the end the computer will can you, and you'll be back at your old routine.

The **Museum of Money of the American West**, in the Bank of California (400 California St. Tel. 765-2188), will give you an idea of the fever and explosion that the discovery of gold in California really caused. Continue

CALIFORNIA

your tour at the **Old Mint Museum** for still more dreams of gold. (5th and Mission. 10am-4pm. Admission free. Tel. 974-0788.)

The **Wells Fargo History Room** at the Wells Fargo Bank (420 Montgomery st. Tel. 396-0123), gives a history of the bank. An interesting stop.

The **Pacific Heritage Museum**, (608 Commercial st. at Montgomery. Mon.-Thurs. 1-4pm. Admission free. Tel. 362-4100), in the Bank of Canton Building, exhibits displays about the history of artistic, cultural, economic and other interchanges between people on both sides of the Pacific Basin. The museum emphasizes the role of various groups from the Asia-Pacific region in the development of California.

Enter the old **Monadnock Building**, at Third st. and Market to glimpse the new wall and ceiling murals that look as if they might have come from a Renaissance Piazza.

The tall sleek **Transamerican Pyramid** at Montgomery between Clay and Washington stands out among the other towers and has become a San Francisco landmark. Next to the pyramid is Redwood Park, a small peaceful haven of green, where lunch time concerts are performed throughout the summer. On the eastern edge of the financial district, the Embarcadero is currently being renovated, but the best facelift of all would be to remove the ugly freeway that cuts off the entire view of the east bay. More than one renegade town planner has suggested that. At the foot of Sacramento street stands the three-level **Embarcadero Center** (Tel. 772-0585). Attached to this complex of expensive stores is the *Hyatt Regency*, which has a high, translucent atrium and a famous revolving bar, the *Equinox Lounge*, at the top. Dress well here. You can nurse your drink for the 45-minute spin.

Also at the Embarcadero Center, the **Levi Strauss History Room** relates how an immigrant tailor and his company transformed workpants into international fashion. (Mon.-Fri. 10am-4pm. Admission free.)

Downtown

Downtown and the financial district can be spoken of separately or together. They are fused together with Market st. as their common southern boundary. The plaza where **Powell and Mason st.** (coming in from the seedy Tenderloin district to the west) meet Market is a small downtown hub of sorts. This is where the Powell st. cable car turntable is situated, for the cable car heading to Ghiradelli Square. During the summer there is always a line of tourists here, waiting for the cable car.

Downstairs, to the side of the plaza is the main visitor center for the city. The BART and MUNI metro station here can supply information on all the municipal systems – rail, trolley, bus, and cable.

A few blocks up Powell Street is **Union Square**, which fills with office workers and street performers during weekday lunch hours. The street has

CALIFORNIA

DOWNTOWN SAN FRANCISCO

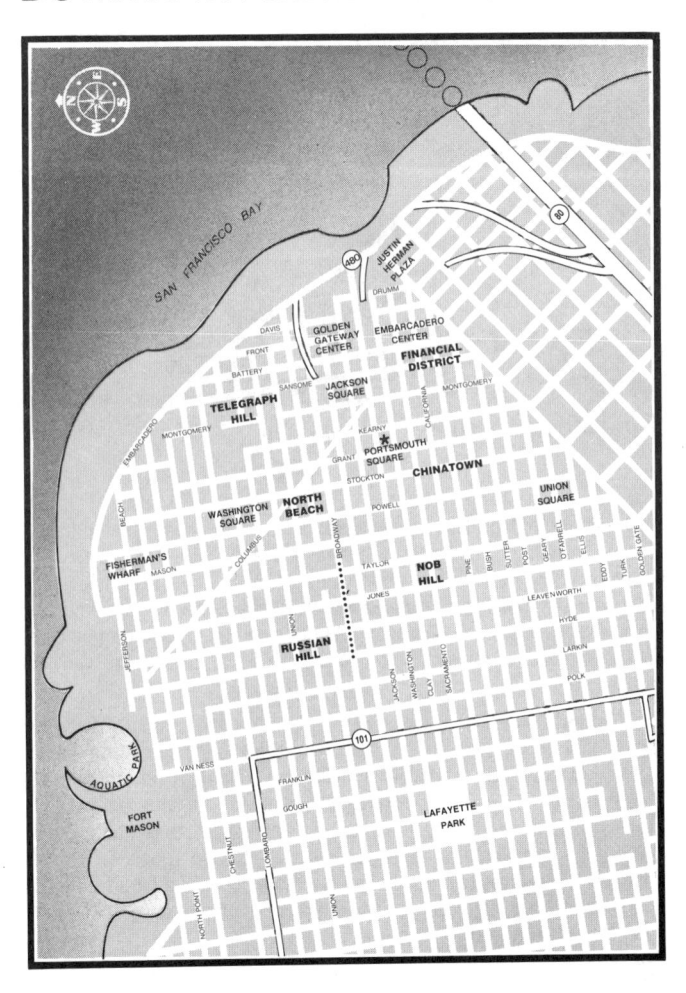

a lively atmosphere, and flower stalls on the street corners do a brisk business with the executives. Around Union Square are the big department stores, Macy's and Magnin's. On the east end of Union Square is a Bass ticket office and booking service selling tickets for a wide variety of theater events throughout the city.

On the west side of Powell st., opposite the square, is the dignified, *St. Francis Hotel*. Up the hill, west of Union Square is the wealthy

CALIFORNIA

East meets West – McDonald's in Chinatown

neighborhood of **Nob Hill**, known locally as Snob Hill. In addition to the *St. Francis*, there are other classic, established and opulent San Francisco hotels on Powell st. and on the slopes of Nob Hill. These include the *Fairmont Hotel* (950 Mason), the *Sir Francis Drake* (Sutter at Powell) and the *Mark Hopkins* (California at Mason). All of these hotels have elegant bars, cocktail lounges, or restaurants on their higher floors, offering fine views of the city.

The **Tenderloin** district, just west of the downtown area around Powell and Market, is a decrepit area of drunks, pushers, addicts, peep shows, porno movies, depressing residential hotels and boarded up shops. Yet something new is stirring here. Immigrants from Vietnam and Cambodia are moving in, and there are a number of very good, reasonably priced restaurants springing up. As threatening as it may appear, it is safe (relatively) to walk around during the day. So if you feel a bit adventurous about discovering interesting eateries, this is the place to go.

Chinatown

The old Chinatown, squeezed in roughly between Powell and Kearney, Bush and Broadway, is crammed with crowds, shops, colorful Chinese signs, and the delectable smells of Chinese food. Two cable car lines skirt Chinatown. Two blocks up the hill to the west run the two Powell st. lines. The California st. line, running between the Embarcadero and Van Ness, crosses Grant st. just where it turns into the crowded, brightly-lit and touristy main boulevard of Chinatown. Grant, lined with innumerable shops, runs north into Broadway and the Italian section of North Beach. This stretch and the surrounding streets are easily walkable. On Stockton, a

*C*ALIFORNIA

Grant Avenue – Heart of Chinatown

block up from Grant, and on some of the sidestreets, the signs and restaurant menus may be only in Chinese. The main activity in Chinatown is simply to stroll around, browse in the Chinese spice shops, examine all the strange little gadgets and trinkets being sold, stare at the meats hanging in the butcher shop windows, photograph the old men playing various games in Portsmouth Square, watch the rush of people, and breathe in the enticing aromas which beckon you from one restaurant to the next.

It is amazing how many good restaurants there are along the Chinatown streets. Each seems to have its clientele, and many have newspaper

CALIFORNIA

Famous North Beach landmark

clippings taped to the window proclaiming that particular place as positively the best Chinese restaurant in the city. Avoid the ones with gaudy, contrived settings and customers who are primarily tourists. You may make some fine discoveries of your own if you seek out that special hole-in-the-wall with bare walls, chipped linoleum tables, Chinese menus and crowds of Chinese customers.

The number of specific sites to see in Chinatown is limited. There is the large, ornate Chinese gate at Grant and Bush. The **Chinese Culture Center**, in addition to serving as a community center, houses a museum for the appreciation of Chinese arts and culture, with regularly changing exhibits. (750 Kearny st., 3rd floor of Holiday Inn. Tues.-Sat. 10am-4pm. Admission free. Tel. 986-1822.)

The museum of the **Chinese Historical Society of America** is concerned mainly with the role of the Chinese in the California gold rush, and the rapid development of the West that followed. (17 Adler Place, off 1140 Grant ave., near Pacific. Tues.-Sat. 1-5pm. Donation requested. Tel. 391-1188.)

North Beach

North Beach abuts Chinatown at Broadway, and extends north along **Columbus ave.** toward Fisherman's Wharf, and east up the steep slope of

CALIFORNIA

Broadway and Columbus – licensed licentiousness

Telegraph Hill. An old Italian neighborhood, lined with small delis, bakeries, restaurants and cafes, it became a magnet for the emerging "Beat" movement in the early 50s.

"I saw the best minds of my generation destroyed by madness, starving hysterical naked..." – with that line from the poem *Howl*, delivered in a semi-chant in a small North Beach forum, Allen Ginsberg helped to bring to the public the new Beat poetry and literature scene that had been developing in San Francisco in the post-war years, spearheaded by Ginsberg and Jack Kerouac, Lawrence Ferlinghetti and others. They headed to San Francisco for a freer atmosphere and congregated in North Beach because of the cheap rents and the village-type surroundings.

Ferlenghetti's City Lights Bookstore at Columbus and Broadway showcased the works of the Beat poets even when they were banned, and became a focal point for a new era of artistic, intellectual and social rebels.

In the clubs on **Broadway**, post-war free-form jazz bloomed, and comedians such as Lenny Bruce and Mort Sahl honed a comedy edged with piercing political and social criticism. A few years later the clubs presented the folk and protest music which emerged as a powerful influence in the early 60s.

The glitter from those lively scenes began to fade. All the old clubs became

CALIFORNIA

Washington Square

strip joints and new ones opened. Their flashing signs lined the street and dazzled the eyes. Glib "barkers" at the entrances lured in tourists with "free peeks". Finally, however, the glamour of that world dimmed too. The big signs were turned off and they still hang above boarded-up doors. Only strip joints remain. Often the girls themselves try to lure in patrons.

Broadway deteriorated and became the center of San Francisco's sleazy side, purveyor of pornography, bastion of punk music, the cruising hang-out for kids from the suburbs hunting down a little big-city action. The street witnessed a rise in crime (it is safe to walk the brightly lit street, but it is not recommended to veer into one of the small side-streets at a late hour). Grassroots groups and city planners are considering the problem of the Broadway strip, and may try to transform it into a district of small theaters.

Concurrently, there is a very marked increase in the numbers of Chinese signs which have crossed the old border of Broadway. Many of the old, reliable, family-owned Italian stores have closed. On the sidestreets at old and new cafes people park themselves at tables with notebooks and sketchpads. A few survivors from the old days hang out at *Vesuvio's*, near *City Lights*. *City Lights* itself is still open; its basement provides a peaceful

CALIFORNIA

respite from the bright rush on Broadway. On Columbus just north of Broadway are clusters of cafes and restaurants from which one can watch the passing parade. All kinds of people pass by: old Chinese, punks, open-eyed tourists, and hip young professionals.

Washington Square, near Columbus, is a nice place to enjoy a bit of greenery. All sorts of characters float by here. It is the perfect place for a picnic, with several good delis and bakeries on the edges. The slope of **Telegraph Hill** begins to the east of Washington Square. It is a steep walk, through some beautiful staired streets that are quiet even though they are right in the heart of the city. The 39 bus reaches the famous **Coit Tower** at the top of Telegraph.

The tower was erected in 1933 during the Depression by famous philanthropist Lillie Coit. (The climb or elevator ride to the top costs $1.50, $1 for seniors. Open daily 10am-6pm.) The view from the base, a smidgeon lower, is just as encompassing and free. The murals in the circular hall surrounding the lobby are impressive. They are terrific examples of the populist frescoes which emerged from the school of modern industrial realism in American art. At the time they caused such a stir because of their clear political implication about the role and destiny of workers that they had to be touched up a bit.

For a visual feast continue down the east side of the hill, towards **Filbert Street**. Along with a few old wooden houses pre-dating the 1906 earthquake, a pocket-sized Eden clings to the slope. The lovely overflowing garden was the creation of Grace Marchant who moved here in 1949 at the age of 63. She began by hauling away the bedsprings, tires and other garbage. By the time of her death at the age of 96, Marchant had transformed the neglected hillside into a lush and wild corner that attracted birds, wildlife and people.

The 39 bus runs between Coit Tower and Fisherman's Wharf. A popular route for a day's excursion could include the cable car ride up Powell st. to Ghiradelli Square, a stroll along the docks and colorful tourist traps of the wharf area, the 39 bus ride to Coit Tower, the ride or walk back to Washington Square and North Beach, continuing by foot across Broadway into Chinatown, and a walk, bus or cable car (Powell is two steep blocks west of Chinatown) back downtown or wherever you need to go. This route invites detours and diversions. One popular place that every tourist must experience once is "the crookedest street in the world", **Lombard Street** between Hyde and Leavenworth, in the northwest corner of North Beach.

Fisherman's Wharf

Fisherman's Wharf is an overpriced, gaudy, tourist trap, but it is worth strolling around, simply for the scenes flashing past, the bright and colorful crowds, and the bay shining in the sun. The old established seafood restaurants, such as *Castagnola's* and *Alioto's* have beautiful views, with their tables set beside wide picture windows over the bay, but they are

CALIFORNIA

Hairpin bend on Lombard Street.

overpriced, as are the sidewalk crab stands. There are several shopping complexes here, in gutted old brick warehouses. At the foot of Polk Street is **Ghiradelli Square** named after the chocolate manufacturer. The shops are situated in several floors around an open square. The restaurants are lavish and expensive, but it is worth indulging in Ghiradelli chocolate. Although the prices are high and lines can be long, the chocolate is outstanding.

CALIFORNIA

At the foot of Polk st., just beyond Ghiradelli Square, is the **San Francisco Maritime Museum**, part of the small **Aquatic Park** near Fisherman's Wharf. (Open daily 10am-6pm, but shorter hours in winter, closed Monday. Tours daily. Admission free. Tel. 556-2904.) The museum houses a wide range of sailing ship models, old photographs and artifacts. The photographs illustrate the phenomenal growth of the San Francisco port from a collection of tents to a sprawling city. Connected to the museum are several historic sailing ships berthed at nearby **Hyde Street Pier**. They include an old car ferry, steam schooner and tugboat. Beyond them, along the Embarcadero and the ferry to Alcatraz are two more historic ships: The **Pampanito**, a World War II submarine (Admission free. Tel. 673-0700) and the **Balclutha** (Admission free. Tel. 982-1886), a Cape Horn sailing ship. Adjacent Hyde Street Pier has the same hours, and offers guided tours, self-guided tours, films and demonstrations. (Admission free. Tel. 556-6435.)

On Hyde st., just opposite the cable car landing, is the *Buena Vista*, another venerable institution, claiming to be the first place to serve Irish coffee. It's still good after all these years, and this is one of the few wharfside spots patronized by a number of San Franciscans, often of the young sleek-suited variety.

At **The Cannery**, east of Ghiradelli, the shops are a shade lower in price but just as touristy. Amid the boutiques and cute card stores are a few art galleries with some high-quality art. There are often performers in the square. Further along Jefferson, are the Wax Museum, Ripley's Believe It or Not and other similar establishments. Fisherman's Wharf itself is a real wharf with real fishermen. If you come about five in the morning you can see them unloading their haul while the seagulls hover above. At more civilized hours, you can charter a boat from here. There are signs advertising boats for charter, or cruising, starting from about $10 per head per hour.

The history and process of wine making are displayed at the **Wine Museum**. (635 Beach st. Tues-Sat. 11am-5pm. Tours 2-4pm. Admission free. Tel. 673-6990.)

The wharf area attracts a wide variety of street performers. Some, having earned their stripes here, move on to play in places with roofs, while others fade into the sunset. One well-known attraction is the jukebox man, who will pop out of his little box on the insertion of a coin and play a tune on his trumpet; the fellow in the Captain Kidd get-up with the parrot on his shoulder wants money just for being photographed, even though the bird does all the work. Then there is the couple who combine mime and modern dance in an intricate, fantastic act set to breakdance music. You never know what you'll see.

The **Anchorage** is yet another mall. **Pier 39** is the newest, extending out over the water. **Only in San Francisco**, at the entrance of the pier, offers free information and maps, but on little else other than the pier itself. One worthwhile spot here is the old *Eagle Cafe*, which was moved from the

Fisherman's Wharf

Embarcadero and was one of the old fishermen's and longshoremen's cafes during the port's heyday.

Near **Pier 41**, just west of Pier 39, is the docking point for the **Red and**

White Fleet, which operates ferries to Angel Island, Sausalito, and Tiburon. Eat at one of several restaurants in Tiburon and save $2 on the ferry ticket. Red & White also supplies free maps. (Tel. 546-2896. In-state, Tel. 1-800-445-8880.)

CALIFORNIA

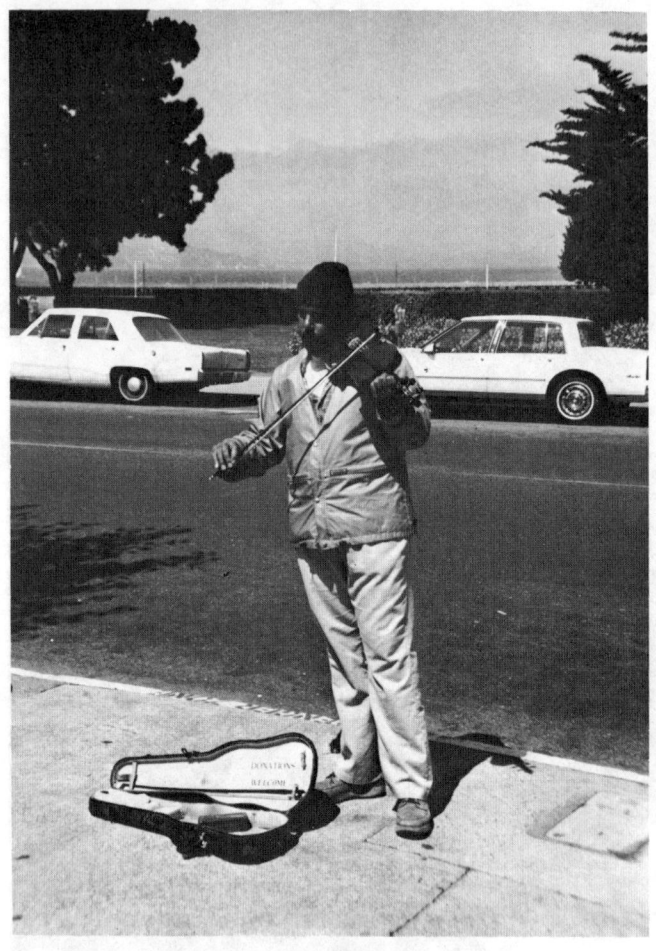

Performance near Fisherman's Wharf

The **Blue and Gold Fleet** runs loop tours between the Golden Gate and East Bay bridges. (One-and-a-half-hour tours for $10, $5, ages 5-18, free under five. Tel. 781-7877.)

In the middle of the entrance of San Francisco Bay, with an enticing view of the sunset beyond the bridge, the silvery towers of the city and the green mountains to the north, sits **Alcatraz**, "the rock". Alcatraz, not the typical national park, is worth a visit. A complete visit lasts about two hours. Wear

CALIFORNIA

View of Alcatraz

good walking shoes and bring some warm clothes even in summer. (Boats leave every 45 minutes from Pier 41 at Fisherman's Wharf, from 8:45am to 2:45pm in winter and to 5pm in summer. Tickets are available at the pier or through Ticketron. $4.25 adults, $3 to 12, 75 cents under five. Tel. 556-0560 for information Tel. 495-4089 for reservations. Advance purchase is recommended in the summer.)

A tour of Alcatraz makes it easier to understand how, surrounded by tantalizing beauty, some of the hardened criminals in this maximum security federal prison must have reached the depths of hopelessness. On Alcatraz, rehabilitation was an unknown word. Guards were plentiful, discipline harsh, the routine rigid, endless and boring. The most notorious gangsters – Al Capone, Machinegun Kelly and Doc Barker – were incarcerated here. It is hard not to admire the desperate determination of the 39 men who tried to escape across the expanse of freezing cold water with its strong currents. Ten died, most were recaptured and five disappeared.

Six years after it was abandoned as a prison, Alcatraz had a brief renewal of life when 85 Indians seized it and declared it an Indian cultural center, in an "occupation" that lasted one-and-a-half years.

Fort Mason
Situated on the promontory between San Francisco's Marina and Aquatic Park/Fisherman's Wharf, Fort Mason has two main functions. The upper part houses the headquarters of the National Park Service, which is the central information source for all the scattered portions of the Golden Gate

National Recreation Area, in San Francisco and Marin County. An AYH youth hostel is also located here.

The lower part of Fort Mason, among the old docks and brick military buildings, serves as a "regional cultural center". In more concrete terms, it is a collection of innovative, political, social, cultural and counter-cultural grassroots organizations. It is a fairground, classroom, dance studio and performance center. Its organizations and exhibits range from the Mexican Museum, to Greenpeace, to Friends of the River, to The Young Performers Theater. There are many offbeat, unusual exhibits, activities and tours for the tourist who wants to get beneath the Chinatown gloss of this city.

Do not miss out on a visit to the **S.S. Jeremiah O'Brian**, last of the World War II Liberty Ships, a national monument that still sails. (Open to the public. Tel. 441-3101.)

The famous **Tassajara Bakery**, run by the San Francisco Zen Center is worth visiting just for its graceful decor. For a recording of Fort Mason events, call Tel. 441-5705.

Exploratorium

The Exploratorium, located in San Francisco's Palace of Fine Arts opposite the Marina, is a unique institution for the teaching of science.

The dome of the grandiose Palace of Fine Arts is easily visible. (3601 Lyon st. Open Wed. 1-9:30 pm, Thurs.-Fri. 1-5pm, Sat.-Sun. 10am-5pm. Opens earlier on summer weekdays. $4 adults (good for six months), $2 seniors, 17 and under free. Free on Wednesday after 6, and free the first Wednesday of each month. Tel. 563-7337.)

Whether creating magnetic sculptures, unleashing waves, or gazing half-hypnotized at a "sun-painting", the visitor is thrust directly into the world of science and becomes an eager, curious child facing the natural world. This scientific funhouse grew out of the experience, philosophy, values, initiative and never-ending awe of an amazing man.

Frank Oppenheimer, brother of J. Robert Oppenheimer, the "father of the atom bomb", was an eminent scientist in his own right. Before and during World War II, Oppenheimer was deeply immersed, like his brother, in the development of atomic energy. He was involved in the early atomic tests and the application of nuclear energy toward aircraft propulsion and land research on cosmic rays. Then, like his celebrated brother, and many others, he suffered from harassment by the House Un-American Activities Committee during the McCarthy purges of the 1950s. The eminent research scientist suddenly became an outcast, and took up cattle ranching in a small Colorado town. Even in this enterprise, he remained the creative experimenter who made his own tools and tried new solutions.

Oppenheimer began teaching science at the local high school and urged his students to explore the wonders and reality of the scientific and natural

CALIFORNIA

Palace of Fine Arts.

worlds with their own hands, through direct experience and experimentation, whether it meant designing their own lab experiments or examining car parts in the local dump. Students from that obscure Colorado town garnered state and national science prizes.

Oppenheimer eventually returned to the world of university teaching. He studied science museums in Europe, and in 1968 opened the Exploratorium, which, in his words, is not really a museum, but rather "the woods of natural phenomena through which to wander".

The one-time scientific pariah and his staff created a "woods" of 450 exhibits, centered around the myriad phenomena available to the human senses. Artists are much involved in planning exhibits. A harp sings in the wind. Sunbeams shoot through prisms and mirrors to create a mural. The wave organ, jutting in public display over the water at the Marina itself, creates music from the motion of the waves.

The workshop in which exhibits are created is out in the open and becomes part of the exhibits itself. In this enclave of educational chaos, there are no guards, no rules, and no lists of restrictions.

CALIFORNIA

The Mission

The predominantly Mexican **Mission District**, south of Market and between 16th and 24th sts., had a reputation for being run-down and dangerous. It is actually a very exciting, lively place to walk, but it's best to dress casually and not to carry flashy photo equipment.

There was a time when it was solidly Mexican, and filled with cheap *taqueras*. The *taqueras* are still here, the food cheap, delicious and filling, but they are being complemented now by Peruvian, Bolivian, El Salvadoran and Nicaraguan restaurants, in addition to the Arab and Asian restaurants on the fringe, and McDonald's and Pioneer Chicken. The Mission is filling up with immigrants, many of them unofficial and uncounted, but illegal or not, culturally they are enriching this neighborhood. Meanwhile there is also an influx of little espresso joints, and crowded cafes with a bohemian clientele. Walk around this area, take in some of the bright and powerful political murals that pop up in unexpected places (the public mural is a well-developed Mexican art form), and watch the people. Some of the best Latin world beat music in the city can be found in little joints in the Mission.

The Mission is the place to buy a meal-in-a-burrito. It is impossible to eat a burrito elegantly as it is likely to explode on first bite and run down your chin and hands. When you are finished and your temples throb from the hot sauce, cool down with a *paletta*, a fresh fruit bar which is refreshing and cheap and available in exotic flavors like mango.

On Capp and 16th, one small block east of Mission, is the old, ornate **Victoria Theater**. A little way down, at 65 Capp, is the **Capp Street Project**, a unique art program in which an artist lives on the premises for a specific time, working on a large art project which will be open to the public.

Mission Dolores, the oldest building in the city, dates back to 1782. It was originally established at another site in 1776, as the sixth in Junipero Serra's chain of missions. (Dolores st. and 16th st. Open 10am-4pm.)

Castro Street

The strutting street-wise youths of the Mission make a sharp contrast to the men along Castro street, the next neighborhood up the hill to the west. Castro street is the center of a proud, strong and organized gay community. Strolling along and taking in all the color can be enjoyable, though the card stores are not for the easily embarrassed. The chic "fern bars" each seem to have their own particular type of gay clientele. The development is now extending to upper Market street as well. The neighborhhod is easily reached by MUNI Metro.

The gays of Castro have recently helped shape the city physically, culturally and politically. Gay entrepreneurs have transformed some of the pre-earthquake Victorian buildings into boutiques, book stores and bars.

CALIFORNIA

They have elected a number of gay representatives. The **Gay Games** and **Gay Pride Day** attract spectators and participants of all ages and preferences.

The local gay community was recently shocked by the murder of gay supervisor Harvey Milk and Mayor George Moscone. More recently the appearance of AIDS has devastated the community. With the first shock over, local gay organizations have taken assertive action in mobilizing public action to fight AIDS.

West and south of this area are **Twin Peaks** and **Mt. Davidson**, both of which offer expansive views of the city. Mt. Davidson is the highest point in the city, nearly 1000 feet high.

Civic Center

In one of those classic ironies of municipal layout, the beautiful, expansive complex that makes up the **Civic Center** is located on the western edge of the decrepit Tenderloin district and the wide, open plaza is a favorite hangout for vagrants. The plazas are also the site for large public arts exhibits. Stretching for five blocks, from McAllister and Market west to Franklin, the Civic Center network includes the UN Plaza, the public library, City Hall, Civic Auditorium, the opera house, the Museum of Modern Art and various administrative buildings.

The **City Hall** has a dome higher than the national Capitol's, and a long pool reflecting the lights at night. Contrasted to this, the glass and white concrete **Davies Symphony Hall** is designed in very modern style. This hall is part of the **San Francisco War Memorial** and **Performing Arts Center**. (Tours are offered every Monday, 10am-2:30pm every half hour. Tel. 552-8338.)

The **Veteran's Building**, adjacent to the opera house on Van Ness, houses the **Herbst Theatre**, which was the site of the signing of the United Nations Charter in 1945 and which houses large murals from the 1915 Panama-Pacific Exposition. Next door, the **San Francisco Museum of Modern Art** houses rotating collections of works by Matisse, Klee and other 20th century masters. The museum also has a cafe and bookstore. (Van Ness at McAllister. Open Tues., Wed. and Fri. 10am-6pm, Thurs. 10am-10pm, Sat.-Sun. 10am-5pm. Admission $3.50, under 12 $1.50. Admission free on Thurs. after 6pm. Tel. 863-8800.) The nearby area of Hayes st., behind Davies Hall, has cafes, restaurants and some interesting galleries and bookstores.

SOMA

South-of-market (SOMA for short) was an area of run-down apartments, flophouses, greasy chili joints, parking lots, warehouses and factories, but this area has been going through a renaissance of sorts. In the last few years, artists have taken over some of the warehouses, and punk and rock clubs and trendy resturants are opening, as are new theaters.

CALIFORNIA

Cow Hollow
Photograph from San Francisco Convention & Visitors Bureau

Union Street

Cow Hollow, once a dairyland area curving around the marina from Van Ness to the Presidio, might today be renamed Yuppie Hollow, and the only milk found here today is used in the coffeehouses along **Union Street's** 1600 to 2200 blocks. The old Victorian buildings here have been refurbished and transformed into miniature shopping malls. Passages between the buildings lead to courtyards lined with boutiques, and to barns filled with antiques. There are restaurants, bars, and cafes in the nooks and crannies of the Victorian row. One can choose from the variety of international cuisine which is offered here, such as Chinese, Indian, Italian, Japanese, Mexican and Russian. Several of the restaurants feature national entertainment. On Sunday the patios are filled with brunchers. In the evenings, the singles bars are patronized by trim and healthy looking pleasure seekers.

Around Union almost everything is slightly overpriced, just to stay in harmony with the atmosphere. Up Fillmore toward California and Sacramento are pockets of the same type of bar, but these are a little more reasonably priced.

CALIFORNIA

Clement Street

Many San Franciscans who want good Chinese food prefer the area of Clement Street to Chinatown. This new "restaurant row" of San Francisco is located not in one of the old, quaint, downtown established neighborhoods, but rather in the Richmond district, an everyday neighborhood set apart from the more bustling downtown area. It was once an area of Russian-Jewish immigrants, but now has a large Chinese population. The neighborhood would be basically nondescript if not for the strip of great restaurants running through it. On Geary, the main street parallel to the south, there is also an abundance of good new restaurants. A Saturday afternoon on Clement st. will find local neighborhood residents milling around the street, shopping or just window shopping in small shops, or hanging out at the local watering holes. There is hardly a tourist in sight. It has the atmosphere of a small-town main street. Clement st. is easily accessible by public transportation. Check with MUNI for exact routes.

Japantown

Japantown, also known as Nihonmachi, is a new center and not very big. The Japanese population of San Francisco is about 12,000. Japantown is located on the edge of the Western Addition, a neighborhood of low-income housing units, not known as a particularly safe area.

Japantown basically consists of a five-acre complex of modern shops and restaurants, centered around the **Peace Plaza**. The adjoining **Buchanan Street Mall**, between Post and Sutter is a small walking area lined with cherry trees. Beyond this, there is a sprinkling of Japanese restaurants and shops on the surrounding streets.

In the center of Peace Plaza is the five-tiered **Peace Pagoda**, donated by the children of Japan in memory of the victims of the atomic bombings of Hiroshima and Nagasaki.

Japantown loyalists claim that the sushi rage on the Pacific coast started right here, but then Little Tokyo in Los Angeles makes the same claim. In any case, there are numerous sushi bars, some very well-reputed, as well as several places specializing in Japanese noodles.

If you want to extend your knowledge of Japanese culture beyond *Shogun*, Japantown is the place to search for books. The book store here carries an enormous variety of books (both in English and Japanese) on every aspect of Japanese history and culture. On the bottom floor of the shopping complex at the east end of Peach Plaza there is a display of amazing wooden sculptures. They are so finely and realistically detailed that the huge sea serpents seem about to breathe fire. Such sculptures sell for about $5000.

Japantown, normally quiet and sedate, explodes with life during its several annual festivals. **The Cherry Blossom Festival**, held during two consecutive weekends towards the end of April, is an extravaganza. Some shows and exhibits charge admission, while many others are free. Thousands of people of all racial and ethnic groups gather for the parades, the performances, the incessant taiko drumming and the endless rain of cherry blossoms, a symbol in Japan of transient beauty. In August, the **summer festival** is held and shortly after that is the **Nihonmachi Street Fair**.

Haight-Ashbury

Twenty years ago, **Haight st.** and the surrounding Victorian neighborhood (of Haight-Ashbury) was filled with the electrifying excitement, the color, the vibes and the drugs of the "new age" – the hippie era. Some of rock's greatest and most drug-pumped musicians lived and played in the area. When George Harrison walked down the street, it might as well have been the second coming. The Panhandle and Golden Gate park filled with youth for impromptu concerts, frisbee games and LSD sharing. The smell of pot was everywhere. The Victorian houses became crash pads, the stores took on new, garish fronts and sold the latest in drug paraphernalia. Underground newspapers heralded the new revolution. Psychedelic posters covered the walls. Streets were jammed with long-haired, blue-jeaned, beaded, broke and bloodshot youth.

Inevitably the crash came. Those who had turned on, burnt out. The pushers and exploiters moved in. Heroin made the rounds. Jimi Hendrix, Janis Joplin and Jim Morrison were only the better-known of the many who pushed and drugged themselves to death. With the start of robberies, rapes, muggings and sordid premature deaths, the "new age" proved as tarnished as the old. Later the punks moved in with their dyed hair and shaved heads, their chain and leather fashions and fashionable rage.

Now the Haight is on an upswing, while still keeping its funky and alternative character and a feel for its past. The street has a strip of reasonable and tasty eateries. It's a good place to stoke up on a solid breakfast before a day of walking through Golden Gate Park, or to warm up with a cappuccino and a stuffed burrito. Along the Haight are small unusual art galleries displaying everything from primeval African masks to post-modern grotesquery.

Within a compact area are various stores which, in different ways, express some echo of the explosions of the sixties: a good old-fashioned "head shop", a radical book store, a fantasy book store, a record store of great oldies, several vintage clothing stores, a few organic veggie cafes, ethnic art and pop-art posters, and a boutique of sexual gadgetry. To keep the spirit authentic, there are still groups of bizarre-looking people floating up and down the street, some with hair below their shoulders, some with

CALIFORNIA

Think he stocks Steinway?

hairdos like peacock plumage. Some look incredibly young and others sadly old.

In the middle of the Haight is the *Red Victorian Moviehouse* (1659 Haight. Tel. 863-3994). Next door is the bed and breakfast inn of the same name. This theater offers great old movies, including daily matinees, in a setting as pretty and entertaining as anything on screen, and the popcorn is free.

At *Haight Books* (1682 Haight) the books are piled high and there are places to sit. A bright arched store front with gargoyles and other creatures marks *Play With It* (1660 Haight). Inside there is every kind of toy that your nephew, kid or you could want. There's a play table for children, and an artificial waterfall plunges from the gallery into the miniature boat pond.

The *Anarchist Collective Bookstore* (1369 Haight) includes a library and reading area. Don't request Ayn Rand. Despite the heavy name, *Bones of Our Ancestors* (622 Shrader, off Haight) sells fine silver work, gems and cut stones, crafted by a couple who could win mellow-of-the-year award.

Bicycle rentals are available at *Avenue Cyclery* on Haight just up from Stanyon, for $2 or $3 per hour.

CALIFORNIA

Duck pond – Golden Gate Park

Golden Gate Park

The long, narrow, green strip that is Golden Gate Park, is criss-crossed with cycling paths and foot paths, and has small secluded spots for reading, relaxing or courting. There are wide fields, ponds with ducks and swans, several museums, bright gardens, and an open-air stage for weekend concerts. One could easily spend a day in the park, especially on a weekend when it is closed to traffic and all sorts of people gather and stroll through. Some of the weekend roller-skating here is almost ballet.

The area was covered with shifting sand dunes when acquired by San Francisco in 1852. Squatters claimed it as their own and backed that claim with armed guards. When the city proposed plans for a large municipal park, the idea was ridiculed. Yet the city administration – with tremendous foresight – persisted with the plan, battling shifting sands and shifting politicians. In 1887, John McLaren, a Scottish gardener, was appointed Park superintendent at the age of 40, and until his death at age 96 he dedicated himself to shaping a beautiful, variegated landscape with thousands of species of plants from all around the world.

Ironically, the park which was once ridiculed, helped shape the city. The trolley lines that were laid down from the east to make the park accessible defined areas for rows of houses and new neighborhoods. The park also became a refugee center after the 1906 earthquake, and was home to some families for almost a year.

The park is bordered by Stanyon st. on the east and the ocean on the west, Lincoln on the south and Fulton on the north.

CALIFORNIA

Several bike and skate rental outlets can be found along Fulton. The narrow Panhandle extends east from Stanyon, skirting Haight-Ashbury.

Park headquarters, at Fell and Stanyon sts. can provide maps and information. (Open daily 9am-6pm. Tel. 558-3706.)

The **Conservatory of Flowers** just west of headquarters, resembles an old Victorian palace which some wizard, with a sweep of his hand has turned into glass. Among the 7000 plants are rare orchids that normally grow at elevations up to 5000 feet in dense fog. The conservatory's mark of distinction is its ability to grow plants from high-altitude subtropical and cloud forests.

Centered around the music concourse, which hosts free Sunday concerts at 1pm, are the park's main museums: The California Academy of Science, with the Steinhart Aquarium and Morrison Planetarium, and on the opposite side of the concourse, the de Young Art Museum and the Asian Art Museum.

The **Academy of Science** is the oldest scientific museum in the west. (Open from 10am-5pm, 10am-7pm in summers. $3 for adults, $1.50 for seniors and ages 12-17, 75 cents for children 6-11, and free for under six. The first Wednesday of every month is free.) It presents a varied array of exhibits, depicting natural history, the physical sciences, the evolution of man and the diversity of primitive cultures.

The **planetarium** offers special shows on such subjects as Halley's Comet and extraterrestrials. (Separate tickets. $2 for adults, $1 for youth and seniors. Tel. 750-7141 for recorded schedules and sky information.) The planetarium also presents the colorful, wild Laserium show. ($5 regular, $4 matinee, $3 seniors and youth. Tel. 750-7127 for schedules.)

The **de Young Museum** has a well-rounded selection spanning the history of western art from its Egyptian and classic origins, through to modern European art. The American Galleries span the history of America as depicted through its art. (Open Wed.-Sun. 10am-5pm. $3 admission valid for the Asian Art Museum and Palace of the Legion of Honor on the same day. Saturday morning and the first Wednesday of each month is free. Tel. 558-2887. During the summer, both the de Young and the Asian Art Museum are open late each Wednesday to 8:45pm, with free entrance after 5pm, free tours, and free special events such as concerts or lectures.) There is also a cafe in the museum, which makes a summer Wednesday evening an ideal time to absorb yourself in art.

The **Asian Art Museum** in a wing of the de Young, is internationally known for the scope of its collection of eastern art, which includes the famous Avery Brundager collection. The library is open from 1-4:45pm Tues.-Fri. Entry to this museum is free the first Wednesday of each month.

Near the two art museums is the **Japanese Tea Garden**, constructed in 1894. (Open from 8am-6pm, $1 adults, 50 cents seniors and youth, and under age six admitted free. Free to all before 9am and after 5pm. A brochure with a map and history of the garden is available at the ticket

Victorian grandeur of the Conservatory of Flowers

booth for 25 cents.) The tea house is a pretty spot to relax. (Open 10:30am-5:30pm.)

The distinctive Japanese landscape was created by a wealthy Japanese gardener who had worked with nobility in Japan. He and his family lived in a house in the garden and sculptured the landscape around them, with the help of immigrant gardeners from Japan who worked on the grounds in exchange for room and board. However, ugly political reality penetrated even this delicately sculpted Japanese garden and the family was expelled and interned, along with many thousands of American Japanese during World War II. The "Japanese Tea Garden" became "The Oriental Tea Garden". Only several years after the war was the original name restored but the original gardening family never regained its position.

The garden today is an exotic little island of pagodas, fish ponds, curved wooden bridges and carved Japanese gates. Exotic plants flourish in the **Strybing Arboretum and Botanical Gardens**, which contain a huge variety of plants from Chile, Australia, Southeast Asia, the Mediterranean

CALIFORNIA

and California. (Open daily, 8am-4:30pm weekdays, and 10am-5pm weekends and holidays. Admission free.) The **Garden of Fragrance**, designed for the visually impaired, displays plants chosen for their color, texture and fragrance.

Scattered throughout the park are 11 lakes, each with its own character. Rent a boat to row to Strawberry Hill in the middle of Stow Lake, where you'll find Rainbow Falls. For something completely American, there is the buffalo paddock. The park has riding stables toward the western end. For those who want to experience the Victorian atmosphere of the park, there are buggy rides, ranging from 10 to 90 minutes, and $5 to $60, accordingly.

South of Golden Gate Park, near the corner of 19th Ave. and Sloat, is the **Stern Grove**, a beautiful natural amphitheatre surrounded by fir, eucalyptus and redwood trees, where a great series of free concerts is held every Sunday during the summer. Tel. 558-4728 for programs.

The City's Coast

Although San Francisco is a crowded city, the entire western edge of the city's peninsula is fringed with parks and recreational areas, from Fort Fenston in the south to the tip of the peninsula beneath the Golden Gate Bridge, and continuing east along Crissy Field and the Marina to Fort Mason. Most of these areas are joined, and together they comprise the **Golden Gate National Recreation Area** (GGNRA) administered by the National Park Service. Following the paths that link these areas together – either in their entirety or in sections – is an excellent way of getting to know this unique city. This urban-natural area extends across the bridge into Marin County up to Point Reyes. At Fort Ferston it is possible to see the concrete remains of the bunkers and gun emplacements designed to protect the Pacific Coast from Japanese invasion during World War II. It is a great place to watch or photograph hang gliders as they leap off the cliffs or soar above the beach and water. Opposite Ocean Beach on Sloat st. near the Great Highway, is the **San Francisco Zoo**, which includes a children's zoo. (Open daily 10am-5pm. Tel. 661-4844.)

Ocean Beach extends north to the rocky headland on which the *Cliff House* is built. Since 1863 this restaurant has offered refreshment and gorgeous views. It is an extremely relaxing place to sit and sip some Irish coffee. Downstairs below the Cliff House is a platform affording a closer view of **Seal Rock**, covered with seals which are easily seen and heard. Located here is a National Park Service Visitor Center (Tel. 556-8642), with a small exhibit on the history of the area. Information is available on the trails which lead from here to the Golden Gate Bridge and beyond. Across from the visitor center is the **Musee Mechanique**, displaying old arcade games which test your strength and tell your fortune. The **Camera Obscura** gallery/museum takes the visitor inside a camera and allows a close view of Seal Rock.

CALIFORNIA

Sculpture at Palace of the Legion of Honor

Above the Cliff House is **Sutro Heights Park**, offering a view of Seal Rock and the coast. Down the slope to the north are the ruins of the gigantic Sutro Baths which served as a quiet country resort for many years but which finally burned down.

Just north of Sutro Heights, a trail leads down the tree-covered slopes to **Land's End**, a small protected cove in which you might think you're in another world, especially on a moody, foggy day. There is no vehicle access and no swimming allowed, due to rough waves. Above these slopes in **Lincoln Park**, off California st. is the **California Palace of the Legion of Honor**, modeled after a French palace, and housing an art museum. The emphasis is largely on French art. Greeting visitors is Rodin's famous sculpture *The Thinker*, and inside the museum there are more of his sculptures. (Open Wed.-Sun. 10am-5pm. A single admission fee of $3 allows entrance to the **de Young Museum** and the **Asian Art Museum** as well. Free the first Wednesday of each month. Tel. 588-2881.)

From the museum, **El Camino Del Mar** follows the coast through shady groves, and offers beautiful views of the Golden Gate with ships sailing under the bridge. Nearby **China Beach** is one of the few swimming beaches in the city. (Open 7am to dusk with changing rooms, showers, restrooms and a lifeguard.) A little beyond it is **Baker's Beach**, offering nice views but no swimming. The coastal road here runs between parkland

CALIFORNIA

The Thinker – Palace of the Legion of Honor

and the **Presidio**, the large military base that looks more like a country club.

Hiking trails through the western edge of the city lead to the Golden Gate Bridge. There is a parking area for cars, and buses 28, 29 and 76 stop here. The 76 continues into the national recreation area in the western part of the Marin Peninsula. One of the nicest things you can do with a free day is to take a bus to the bridge, walk across and hike on to Sausalito via the side road to the east, past Fort Baker. After refreshment and browsing in Sausalito, return by ferry to the city.

Fort Point, now a preserved historical site, is situated near the water directly beneath the Golden Gate Bridge, at the narrowest point of the strait between ocean and bay. Built before the Civil War, it was modeled after the many fortresses in the east which were in use during the war. Fort Point, however, never had occasion to test its invulnerability. The view of the bridge is unique. There is a museum, and guided tours are available. (Open daily from 10am-5pm. Admission free. Tel. 556-1693.)

To the east of Fort Point is **Crissy Field**, with a foot path and open beach. This brings a walker to the marina, and the long green with its guided exercise path. Beyond that lies Fort Mason, which houses the GGNRA headquarters (see "Fort Mason").

*C*ALIFORNIA

Accommodations

As might be expected, San Francisco offers a wide range of accommodation, something to suit the taste, needs and budget of almost any traveler.

There are, of course, the classic old San Francisco hotels, which include the *St. Francis*, the *Sir Francis Drake*, the *Fairmont* and the *Mark Hopkins*. All these are in the area of Powell st. or the adjacent Nob Hill. Some afford fantastic views, as well as tasteful luxury. They are, as one might guess, quite expensive.

There are other, newer luxury hotels that have sprouted in the central areas of the city. There is the *Hyatt*, at the Embarcadero, and there are several in the area of Fisherman's Wharf.

On Geary st., near the Marina neighborhood, there are more standard motels at various prices. At the lower end of the spectrum, there is a concentration of cheap, but still decent and safe hotels and hostels in the Tenderloin area and the area south of Mission st. The neighborhood may be questionable at a late hour, but the facilities themselves are generally secure. The best bet, in this price range, is the excellent and pleasant *AYH Youth Hostel* in Fort Mason. However, in case of heavy booking, it is good to know about other hostel-type options. Other AYH youth hostels are found in the area surrounding the city.

In recent years, the number of Bed & Breakfast Inns in the city has increased. Some of these are located in beautifully restored Victorian buildings.

For information, referrals, and brochures on local B&Bs, contact the Association of Bed & Breakfast Innkeepers of San Francisco: 737 Buena Vista West, San Francisco, 94117. Tel. 861-3008.

Deluxe Hotels

Each of these is opulent in its own way. Rooms are distinctive, often individually designed. Services border on pampering. Most have a turn-of-the-century atmosphere, and most start at well over $100 per night for a single.

The Fairmont: 950 Mason. Tel. 772-5000, or Tel. 800-527-4727.

Mark Hopkins Inter-Continental: 1 Nob Hill. Tel. 392-3434, or Tel. 800-327-0200.

St. Francis: 335 Powell st. Tel. 397-7000, or Tel. 800-228-3000. Still housed in the original stone building. A beautiful lobby and attached bar.

Sir Francis Drake Hotel: 450 Powell st. Tel. 392-7755.

Hyatt Regency: 5 Embarcadero Center. Tel. 788-1234. Different from the traditional hotels, this modern luxury hotel has a lobby like an immense greenhouse and a famous revolving bar high above the streets.

Moderate Hotels

Cartwright Hotel: 524 Sutter st. Tel. 421-2865, or Tel. 800-227-3844. Cozy

CALIFORNIA

and central, with individually designed rooms. Single $62-$65, double $72-$75.

Hotel Beresford: 635 Sutter st., near Mason. Tel. 673-9900. A very warm, friendly Victorian-style hotel, with gaslight lamps. Attached is the *White Horse Tavern*, a replica of the 18th-century original pub in Edinburgh. Extremely reasonable, around $50.

Hotel Cecil: 545 Post st. Tel. 673-3733, or Tel. 800-227-3818. Rooms are bright and large, with tiled baths. Sun-deck and cabanas. $52-$62.

Budget Hotels

Temple Hotel: 469 Pine st. Tel. 781-2565. situated in the Financial District, clean, quiet and inexpensive. Rooms available with or without bath. Single without bath $18, with bath $23. Excellent weekly rates, about $80 per single with bath.

Adelaide Inn: 5 Adelaide Place. Tel. 441-2261. Clean, no private baths. Small, *pension*-like establishment, with kitchenette for guests. Continental breakfast. Singles $20, Doubles $24.

Obrero Hotel: 1208 Stockton ave. Tel. 986-9850. A small, simple hotel in Chinatown, serving huge breakfasts that will keep you satisfied all day. Singles about $30, doubles $35.

The Red Victorian Bed and Breakfast Inn: 1665 Haight st. Tel. 864-1906. In the heart of the Haight right next to the funky movie house of the same name. If there was ever such a thing as a hip B&B, this is it. Beautiful Victorian decor, individually decorated rooms. A little expensive, but definitely unique. Singles with shared bath $45, doubles with shared bath $50.

YMCAs, YWCAs

YMCA: 166 Embarcadero. Tel. 392-2191. $18-$30. Use of athletic facilities included.

YMCA Chinatown: 855 Sacramento st. Tel. 982-4412. $14-$20. Some rooms with bath, some without. Athletic facilities included.

YWCA: 620 Sutter. Tel. 775-6500. For women, and men accompanying women.

Youth Hostels

There are five youth hostels in the Bay area which are located right on the bay or the ocean:

San Francisco International Hostel: Building 240, Fort Mason, San Francisco. Tel. 771-7277. Located in a Civil-War era building, with easy bus or walking access to all major areas of the city.

Golden Gate Hostel: Building 941, Fort Barry, Sausalito. Tel. 331-2777. The building is a historical landmark, set within miles of hiking trails in the gorgeous Marin Headlands, accessible to hills, lagoons, beaches and Muir Redwoods, as well as to Sausalito itself.

Point Reyes Hostel: Point Reyes Station. Tel. 663-8811. An old ranch house

CALIFORNIA

set near the quiet beaches, estuaries and sand dunes of beautiful Point Reyes National Seashore. Reservations recommended, especially on weekends.

Montara Lighthouse Hostel: 16th., Cabrillo Highway 1, Montara. Tel. 728-7177. Set in the old light station itself, 25 miles south of San Francisco, near trails, boating facilities and tide pools of the marine reserve.

Pigeon Point Lighthouse Hostel: Pigeon Pt. Rd., Highway 1, Pescadero. Tel. 879-0633. 50 miles south of San Francisco, in a series of old Coast Guard bungalows, near tidepools, trails and redwoods.

All these hostels are easily accessible by public bus, BART or commuter train. Call the hostel itself for exact transportation.

Food

Just walking through a crowded San Francisco street will whet your appetite. Everywhere you turn you see restaurants. Good intentions to diet will crumble. You will be a slave to your taste buds, and a sweeter slavery there never was.

The classic old San Francisco restaurants combine sparse decor with an emphasis on grilling. Fresh fish grilled on intensely hot mesquite charcoal is a local favorite. It is, however, extremely difficult to pinpoint a local cuisine, because there is so much of everything here. There are excellent Chinese, Mexican and Italian restaurants throughout the city.

Chinese restaurants often have an informal lunch-counter atmosphere which in other places you'd find only in greasy diners. The plethora of Chinese restaurants has been supplemented in recent years by other Asian restaurants: Cambodian, Laotian, Thai, Filipino, and of course Japanese. One need only sample a few of the Asian ethnic restaurants in San Francisco to realize that each has its distinctive native cuisine. Similarly, Latin American restaurants are springing up, exposing the city to foods from El Salvador, Nicaragua and Peru. There are also the French, Russian, Persian, Basque and Greek Restaurants.

Not surprisingly, San Francisco has been in the forefront of developing vegetarian restaurants beyond the sprout sandwich stage into gourmet restaurants featuring vegetables you've probably never heard of.

But for those with basic cravings, diners, and fast-food stands can also be found here, as can lots of great ice cream stands – although in San Francisco you don't eat ordinary ice cream, you head for North Beach for the famous Italian gelato. Some restaurants are described below grouped according to area.

Financial District/Downtown
The downtown and Montgomery st. environs have no shortage of old, polished San Francisco bars and restaurants. Some of the best seafood, especially grilled fish, can be found here.

CALIFORNIA

Tadich Grill: 240 California, in the Financial District. Tel. 391-2373. The lines can be long here, and most people are waiting for the superb seafood.

Jack's Grill: 615 Sacramento st. The bare, simple surroundings belie the quality that has made this a San Francisco by-word. Rumor has it that the 3rd floor was once a brothel (seems like everyplace in the city was).

Scott's Seafood: Embarcadero 3. A branch of the original on Lombard st., serving the same menu of seafood that is reputedly among the best in the city.

Sam's Grill: 374 Bush st. Tel. 421-0594. Yet another classic standby, with curtained booths for a special rendezvous. Delicious grilled fish and sourdough. Reasonably priced.

John's Grill: 63 Ellis st. Tel. 986-0069. Dashiell Hammet brought Sam Spade into this dark bar. Lunches about $6.

Chinatown

Many of Chinatown's restaurants serve lunch specials from $2.50 and up, consisting of rice, a noodle dish, and vegetable-meat topping. They are tasty, filling, and reliable. Many restaurants in the area also have their own specialties. Everyone seems to have a different favorite place in Chinatown. This is the place to try something completely new. Filling and delicious dinners can easily be found here for $5 or less.

Dim Sum: Very popular. Waiters wheel wagons of various dishes between tables and customers choose what they want. The bill is tabulated by the number of plates, usually at about $1.50 per plate.

Sam Wo's: 813 Washington, up from Grant. Walk upstairs past the kitchen (in which you can snoop if you want). Excellent lunches.

Hunan Restaurant: 853 Kearny. A remarkable little hole-in-the wall. One of the first to popularize the hot, spicy, northern Chinese cooking. Don't come here for atmosphere. Often there's a line, but there's usually space at the counter, from which you can watch the performance of the cooks.

Ocean Garden: 735 Jackson. Excellent seafood, from about $5.

Caledon: 881 Clay. A few notches above the cheap chow mein joints. Dinners start from $9.

Fong Hang: 761 Jackson. A tiny bakery selling delicious fresh pastries.

Chuck's: Powell and Clay: The lunch counter in the back is as uninspiring as the name. However, in this strange combination of an American diner and Chinese restaurant, you can find your basic Chinese soups and chow mein dishes. It is extremely inexpensive, and you can finish off the meal with a thick-shake for $1.30.

Louie's: 1014 Grant ave. Large and always busy. Delicious and fresh food, dim sum specialties pushed through aisles. Very reasonably priced.

North Beach

Eating out and hanging out in North Beach is a local sport which is

CALIFORNIA

extremely easy and inviting to take up. Many restaurants run lunch specials, which often consist of a heavy meat-and-pasta meal and start at about $6.

Washington Square Bar & Grill: 1707 Powell st. Tel. 982-8123. This is a known hangout for local newspaper writers and other literati. The food leans toward the Italian, the atmosphere towards well-dressed informal, and the piano player is fantastic.

The US Restaurant: 431 Columbus. Tel. 362-6251. Another veritable local institution. In the old days, customers would cram into the little wedge-shaped restaurant (immediately next to the open kitchen) wherever a free space could be found. Now, the restaurant has expanded next door, and customers still cram in wherever space can be found. Large portions of meat and pasta. The crowded tables and friendliness of the local regulars make it easy to strike up a conversation. Dinners start at about $6.

Little Joe's: 525 Broadway. The sign says "Rain or shine, there's always a line" and it's true. Noisy, bustling, smoke-filled, with a happy atmosphere which will help you digest the hefty Italian meals that start at about $6.50.

Il Pollaio: 555 Columbus. Tel. 362-7727. Compared to the surrounding establishments it looks like a small fast-food joint, and the name, which means chicken coop, doesn't add to the character, but the chickens, marinated and grilled until they glisten, make delicious meals starting at about $4.25.

Des Alpes: 732 Broadway. This Basque restaurant is tucked away from the bustle of Broadway. There are specials every night. It's easy to order the set meal, which will take you all the way to coffee and dessert for about $8.50.

Maykadeh: 470 Green st. Tel. 362-8286. The Persian haute cuisine served here is exotic to the American palate. Even the Middle Eastern Basmati rice stands out. The *ghorme sabzee*, roughly translated as braised and spiced lamb, is worth trying. Then again, just about everything is. Portions are large, and most main courses cost about $6.50.

Capp's Corner: Powell and Green. A small and very well-known North Beach joint, with celebrity pics all over the walls, and the large Italian lunch specials scribbled daily on the board. $6.95.

Dixie Cafe: 532 Columbus. Seafood from Creole-Cajun New Orleans country. Come here for your Gumbo Smoky Shrimp and Redfish My-O-My. Moderate.

Iacopi Deli: Union and Grant. One of the last of the small local delis, with plentiful offerings for a picnic in Washington Square down the block, and some home-made cheeses in the selection. Diagonally across the corner is a bakery.

The Bohemian Cigar Store: At Union and Columbus. Shaped like the prow of a ship where the two streets meet across from Washington Square, this tiny, homey place draws a regular crowd of young locals. At peak hours you might have to stand at the counter.

Cafe Trieste: Vallejo and Grant. An old North Beach standby with pictures all over the walls of patrons singing Italian opera. Bring your leather jacket and leather bag here, and your sketchbook so you can sketch as you are sketched by others. At the large central table eavesdrop on discussions on art education and some great dirty jokes.

Vesuvio's: 255 Columbus. Stained glass, poetry on the outer wall and poets in the dark interior. A beat survivor.

The Mission District

Taqueria San Jose: 2830 and 2282 Mission. There are those who claim that these are the state-of-the-art burritos.

La Olla: 2417 Mission. Latin American spicy meat dishes in a pleasant atmosphere in surroundings of beautiful crafts. $4.50 up.

La Boheme Cafe: 3318 24th st. Old tables, books, a community bulletin board, and good coffee are found here.

El Faro: 2813 Mission. Very popular for its stuffed burritos.

Tenderloin/Civic Center

Kimball's: 300 Grove st. Tel. 861-5555. A light and airy decor. Opposite the Performing Arts Center, it is crowded and popular after performances.

Hayes Street Grill: 320 Hayes. The grilled fish and the sourdough bread have made this place a big hit. Fish starts at about $12.

The Billboard: 678 Post. Reasonable and delicious Indonesian food.

Padang: Post and Jones. Another excellent Indonesian surprise deep in the Tenderloin area.

Athens Greek Restaurant: 51 Mason. Looks almost like a small lunch counter. Authentic and filling, heavy on meats, $5 and up.

The Hippopotamus: Van Ness and Pacific. Actually north of the Civic Center area on Van Ness, this is a famous local burger place.

SOMA

The latest in trendiness includes restored old 1950s diners. The decor looks authentic, but misses the unpretentiousness that made the old places what they were. Several are found around Church and Market. Try *Sparky's Diner*, 242 Church st., for one that strikes true with its decor, food and prices.

Union Street

Perry's: 1944 Union st. A popular and busy place. The grilled food is excellent, but a bit overpriced.

Cheshire Cheese and Mad Hatter Tea: 2213 Fillmore. Cheese, muffins and coffee served in a cozy setting.

*C*ALIFORNIA

Clement Street
Just a stroll down this aisle of restaurants, cafes, diners and pubs will make you hungry even if you have just eaten a prime steak and eggs.

Taiwan Restaurant: 445 Clement. A diverse menu, and a $3.25 lunch special. Often very crowded.

The New Ocean: 239 Clement. Often hailed as the top Cantonese restaurant in the city. Starts at $4.50. Open until 3am on weekends.

Hong Kong Cafe: 651 Clement. By picking from the small stuffed dishes in the counter window, you can build yourself a sizeable and inexpensive meal to be enjoyed while strolling along.

The Mandalay: 4348 California st., one block off Clement near 6th ave. This is something rare even in San Francisco: a Burmese restaurant, most of the menu is Chinese. The distinctive cuisine includes dried shrimp and a salad made of green tea.

Churchill's: Clement and 6th ave. A comfortable, relaxing neighborhood bar.

Haig's Delicacies: 642 Clement. The place for chutneys, nuts, coffees, exotic canned fruit, olives with the long-handled coffee pots of the Mideast.

Hamburger Haven: 9th and Clement. A simple unpretentious diner with $1.79 breakfast specials.

Japantown
Isobune: 1737 Ost st., Japan Center. Tel. 563-1030. A sushi restaurant, in which platters of sushi come around by boat on a small stream. Besides the novelty, the morsels are so delicious you'll be tempted to reach for more and more (the bill is figured by the plate).

San Wan Restaurant: 1682 Post st. Tel. 921-1453. A fantastic Chinese restaurant, located in Japantown, across from the Japan Center. Enormous portions, many Chinese customers, endlessly running waiters who somehow manage to get you everything you need, and scorching hot-and-sour combinations.

Mifune: 1737 Post st. Tel. 922-0337. Delicious and reasonably priced Japanese noodles.

Haight-Ashbury
La Pyramide: corner of Haight and Cole. A delicious giant burrito costs $2.00.

Seventh Heaven: 1448 Haight. A French-Russian bakery. Try the piroskies.

Chabela: 1803 Haight. A great take-out Mexican place for a hot picnic in the park. The long lines for lunch give good testimony.

Cha Cha Cha: Next door to Chabela. Very small, tastefully done, serving Spanish food that is several cuts above the standard burrito-and-bean fare.

CALIFORNIA

Haight Victorian Spirits: 1621 Haight. Gourmet deli, cheeses and wines, whatever one needs for a park picnic. There are also tables near the window.

Blue Front Deli: 1430 Haight. They serve a mean felafel.

Crescent City Cafe: 1418 Haight. Cosy, simple and reasonably priced for breakfast.

The Ganges: 775 Frederick. This small and friendly Indian restaurant is not in the core of the Haight itself, but around the southeast corner of Golden Gate Park. A delight, with delicious vegetarian dinners costing about $5.

Clubs

The music scene in San Francisco changes constantly. The city is rooted in traditions of jazz, but picks up and helps shape the latest trends as well. New wave and punk rock have reached raucous prominence in recent years, and many new clubs have opened in SOMA. Stand-up comedy has gained popularity in small clubs and cabarets. The listings here are, of course, only partial. Check the local newspapers and entertainment weeklies to catch the latest in music.

Full Moon Saloon: 1725 Haight. Tel. 668-6190. Hanging in with good old rock, blues and reggae.

I-Beam: 1748 Haight. Tel. 668-6006. Started out predominantly gay, and still is on Sunday afternoon, but patronage is mixed during the rest of the week. One of the early new wave and rock discos.

The Mabuhay Lounge: 433 Broadway in North Beach. Tel. 956-3315. The Filipino restaurant has been transformed into punk paradise. The action warms up toward midnight. One-drink minimum.

The Oasis: 11th st. and Folsom. A clear dance floor over the pool.

The Stud: 11th and Folsom.

Bajone's: 1062 Valencia. Tel. 282-2522. Part of the Mission's Latino music scene, filled with locals, featuring jazz, blues and world beat.

The Great American Music Hall: 859 O'Farrel st. Tel. 885-0750. The best of the best in everything from jazz to folk.

Keystone Korner: 750 Vallejo st. Tel. 781-0697. Played by local and visiting artists, great jazz bursts the seams of this club. $3 minimum.

Milestones: 5th and Harrison. A fine club for jazz.

Finocchio's: 506 Broadway. 982-9388. The granddaddy/mama of drag shows, what was once outrageous and shocking is now a tourist attraction.

The Holy City Zoo: 408 Clement st. Tel. 752-2846. A small club featuring aspiring comics.

The Boarding House: 901 Columbus ave. Tel. 441-4333. Folk, country-rock and some comedy. Often features big names.

CALIFORNIA

Pier 23: At the Embarcadero, two blocks north of the Ferry building. Tel. 362-5125. It's Dixieland jazz in an old longshoreman's bar.

Useful Addresses And Phone Numbers
Area Code: 415.
Visitor Information Center: Hallidie Plaza. Tel. 974-6900. At Powell and Market, below street level, near the entry to the BART station. 24-hour information recording: Tel. 391-2000.
International Hospitality Center: 312 Sutter st. Suite 402. Tel. 986-1388. Courtesies and services for foreign visitors.
Center for International Educational Exchange (CIEE): 317 Sutter St. Tel. 421-3473. Student travel information.
Teleguide: Recreation and entertainment information filed in computers that are available to the public in various BART stations. For details, call Tel. 957-2999.
San Francisco International Airport (SFO) information: Tel. 761-0800, or Tel. 876-2811. 24 hours daily.
Greyhound: 50 7th st. Tel. 433-1500. Downtown.
Trailways: 425 Mission st. Tel. 982-6400. At Transbay Terminal.
Green Tortoise: 1st and Natoma. Tel. 285-2441.
Amtrak: 425 Mission st. Tel. 556-8287. At Transbay Terminal. There are shuttlebuses which cross the bay to Oakland station where trains arrive and depart.
San Francisco Municipal Railway (MUNI): 673-MUNI. Info from 9am-5pm.
AC Transit: Tel. 839-2882. Buses to and within east bay area.
Samtrans: Tel. 761-7000. To San Mateo County, and south along peninsula.
Golden Gate Transit: Buses to and within Marin County.
Caltrain: Tel. 557-8661, or Tel. 800-558-8661. Regional trains.
Bay Area Rapid Transit (BART): Tel. 788-BART.
Travelers Aid Society: 38 Mason. Tel. 781-6738; also 50 7th. Tel. 868-1503. 24 hours.
Ambulance: Tel. 431-2800.
U.S. Customs: 555 Battery st. Tel. 556-4440.
National Park Service: Fort Mason. Tel. 556-4122. General information, and specific information on places within the Golden Gate National Recreation Area.
Heritage Walks: 2007 Franklin st. Tel. 441-3004, or Tel. 441-3000. Guided tours on various aspects of old San Francisco architecture, and the history of the waterfront.
California Road Conditions: Tel. 557-3755.
Suicide Prevention: Tel. 221-1424.
Rape Crisis Center: Tel. 647-7273. 24 hours.
Ticketron: 495-4089 for recording; Tel. 393-6914 for ticket info.

SEA GULL
Aquatic bird of the gull family. It has long wings and a short neck. Its legs are also relatively short with webbed feet. Gulls have white, grey or pale brown plumage. They are found near all oceans, but may also be sighted inland, in search of food.

CALIFORNIA

Around San Francisco

The Peninsula

South of San Francisco, the peninsula extends toward San Jose, the rich Santa Clara Valley and the Santa Cruz Mountains. The area is rapidly developing into one suburban mass.

Stanford University is the large and verdant centerpiece of Palo Alto. One of the finest and most prestigious universities in the country, it contrasts sharply with the active and sometimes stormy atmosphere of Berkeley. Around the university are some very good book stores, plus some interesting shops, cafes, restaurants and cinemas. At the student center in **Tressider Union,** campus information and free maps can be obtained. (Tel. 497-4719.)

A free shuttle runs through the huge campus. Bicycles can be rented on campus. Student-guided tours are conducted during the school year and summer. Swimming, windsurfing and boating are available on the artificial lake on campus. The two main sites to see on campus are the **Stanford Linear Accelerator** and the **Museum of Art.** The mile-long research facilities of the accelerator can be viewed by pre-arranged tour. (Tel. 854-3300, ext. 2004.) The Museum of Art includes ancient art as well as a Rodin collection.

The city of **San Jose** has grown without any apparent order. Gobbling the surrounding rich farmland and small towns, it has spread and sprawled into a city larger than San Francisco. San Jose is the unchallenged center of the high-tech **Silicon Valley**.

You might visit the **Winchester Mystery House.** (1525 S. Winchester blvd., by Route 17 and I-280. In summer, 9am-6pm. Call to check on shorter hours in fall and winter. Admission $8.25, age 12 and under $6. Tel. 247-2101.) Firearms heiress Sarah Winchester tried to outwit the ghosts she knew were pursuing her, by making her house into a huge maze, with 160 rooms, and doors and stairways leading nowhere. The kitschy, commercial tour also leads nowhere, but the story is bizarre enough to lure in the unsuspecting.

The string of small towns, state parks and reserves along the San Mateo coast, along Highway 1, have thus far been spared the suburban expansion climbing the eastern slopes of the hills. There are coves, beaches and tidepools to explore. South of Half Moon Bay, San Gregorio Beach with its shoreline caves is especially beautiful. South of Pigeon Point is the **Ano Nuevo State Reserve** for the big lumbering elephant seals. This is one of the few areas where these animals can be approached closely.

CALIFORNIA

Five miles inland at **Butano State Park** there are redwood forests, laced with trails.

Two pleasant youth hostels are found at Montara Lighthouse Point, and further south at Pigeon Point. There are several state park campgrounds along the coast as well, at Half Moon Bay and Butano State Park.

Berkeley

There's a time when the operation of the machine becomes so odious, makes you so sick at heart, that you can't take part, you can't even tacitly take part. And you've got to put your bodies upon the gears and upon the wheels, upon the levers, upon all the apparatus, and you've got to make it stop.

Mario Savio
Free Speech Movement Leader
Berkeley, 1964

Berkeley, a city of 100,000, east of the bay, has traditionally been a center of political and intellectual ferment. This was intensified during the 1960s and '70s when the city became one of the main centers of the Vietnam War protests. Citizen groups tackled rent control law, the police and the power utilities, as well as international issues. In the early 1970s, a radical coalition was elected to the city council, but somehow it never accomplished much and lost much of its momentum and original support.

Berkeley is located off I-80 north of the Oakland Bay Bridge. The University avenue exit is the main one and leads right to the university, but finding parking in the campus area is extremely difficult.

Berkeley is easily accessible from San Francisco by BART. A shuttle, named Humphrey Go-BART, runs from the main BART station at Shattuck to the university campus and university properties in the hills. The local bus system, AC Transit, also runs to San Francisco but is generally slower than BART. However it covers the Berkeley-Oakland region extensively. Bicycles are allowed on certain BART trains, and a bicycle affords an easy and excellent way to tour the campus. They are available for rental around the campus area.

One central number serves as a transportation clearing house. No further calls should be necessary, as this number can refer you to any other transportation office you might need. Tel. 644-POOL.

Although much of the culture of Berkeley emanates from the university, the city has a vibrant life of its own, with lots of music clubs and coffee houses, and with innumerable political, spiritual, alternative and therapeutic groups announcing themselves from every pole and billboard. In the hills to the east are the beautiful, ornate homes of the wealthy, the professionals, and the prestigious professors. The campus area is dominated by thousands of students. In the flatlands toward the bay, live minority groups, as well as

CALIFORNIA

artists and old-time radicals who stayed in Berkeley after finishing school years ago.

The **Berkeley Campus** is the oldest of the nine University of California campuses. It started with a class of 191 students in 1873, and now has 31,000 students. Berkeley is one of the most honored and prestigious universities in the world. Its graduate school has been rated the best in the country, even better than Harvard's, and it is a public institution in which students do not pay very high fees. Relations between the huge institution and its students and the surrounding community have, however, periodically been tense.

In the fall of 1964 the Free Speech Movement split the campus wide open when the university attempted to restrict political activity on campus, especially the dissemination of political information by former students and outsiders.

An escalating game of nerves was played out in Sproul Plaza. A former student was apprehended by the police for distributing pamphlets in the plaza, and by the time a police car was called the police were astounded to find themselves blocked in by thousands of students. For 36 hours the trapped police car, with the detainee inside, became a convenient soapbox for endless political speeches. As one confrontation sparked another, 3000 students finally engaged in a passive sit-in in Sproul Hall, the administration building, and were dragged out one by one by the police.

By the next summer, the growing discontent on campus focused on the Vietnam War. The tactics of civil disobedience used by students the previous fall were applied to military objectives in the bay area. Throughout the sixties, the Berkeley campus sustained the strongest local anti-war movement in the nation. With political activity once more flourishing on campus and various groups exchanging ideas at Sproul Plaza, a whole flurry of causes spinning off from the anti-war movement also appeared.

In 1969 the campus again exploded, over a university-linked issue, centering around a tiny plot of land to be used for a new sports facility. The move would have entailed removing some homeless "street people" who had adopted the lot as their own. Suddenly "Peoples' Park" became a symbol of a basic clash of values, and the university was viewed as the personification of an impassive and dangerous power structure. There were mass rallies, on campus and in the park, followed by a police sweep of the park. The days of passive sit-ins had gone. Violent clashes occured on Telegraph avenue and, finally, one spectator was killed and another was blinded by police gunfire.

By the spring of the following year, Berkeley was one of the leaders in the nation-wide anti-war movement that disrupted the nation's colleges, as American forces bombed Cambodia. Governor Ronald Reagan called out the National Guard, and residents faced the incredible spectacle of tanks rumbling down Berkeley streets. In Sproul Plaza, thousands of demonstrators were hemmed in by Guardsmen wearing gas masks, while tear gas was dropped on the helpless victims.

CALIFORNIA

Campus protests lost momentum after that but occasionally flared up over specific campus-oriented issues. In 1974 student Parry Hearst, of the Hearst newpaper dynasty, was kidnapped by a radical group called the Symbionese Liberation Army. In a bizarre twist of events, the abducted heiress became a gun-toting, bank-robbing gang member spouting revolutionary rhetoric, and it appeared that something had gone askew with the idealistic protests of a decade earlier.

The late 1970s saw a resurgence of fraternities, sports, and a concern with practical majors leading to immediate careers. Today, issues such as Nicaragua and South Africa still stir a certain portion of the students. In the summer of 1986, a long campaign by campus and local activists resulted in the university divesting itself of financial interests in South Africa.

The student political information tables still stand in Sproul Plaza, where they caused turmoil 20 years ago, but they do not attract the same crowds. Students rush past, pause to listen to a guitarist, buy a donut or felafel or laugh at the evangelist on the corner of Bancroft and Telegraph.

At the **Student Union**, at Bancroft and Telegraph, you will find the Visitor Center. (Open Mon.-Fri. 8am-5pm, Saturday 10am-6pm.) Self- guiding tour maps are available and guided tours are held on weekdays at 1pm. Upstairs, watch the chess games in the lounge, or mingle with the students downstairs in the *Bear's Lair Pub*. A book store, student art gallery, and box office with a schedule of all campus events are located here. The free paper, the *Daily Californian*, lists all events, concerts, etc., on and off campus.

Walk through Sproul Plaza to **Sather Gate**, which once marked the southern end of the campus, under which many protest marches flowed in the 1960s. The bas relief sculptures of nude figures, controversial and kept in storage for over 60 years, were finally installed in 1981.

The campus, while serving a huge urban university, has a quiet, verdant almost rural beauty to it. Near the northwest corner of campus is a peaceful eucalyptus grove. Toward the other end of campus is the quaint and shady **Faculty Glen**, with an old log cabin at the top and a stream running at the bottom.

The structure in the center of the campus resembling a set of gaping concrete jaws, is the **Moffitt Undergraduate Library**, and nearby, on the east is **Doe Library**, the main library, with its long, cathedral-like reference room. Entering Doe from the north side, to the immediate right is one of those gems little known even to Berkeley students: a plush and polished reading room, in which you half expect to see Ralph Waldo Emerson puffing on a pipe by the fire.

Rather Tower, the **Campanile**, offers a panoramic view of the Bay. Take the elevator to view the 61-bell carillon. The bells chime out a variety of melodies every weekday, in concerts at 8am, noon and 6pm.

At Euclid and Hearst, on the north side of campus, away from the hubbub of Telegraph, is a block of stores, restaurants, and cafes.

CALIFORNIA

The university houses a number of museums on or adjacent to campus. A list of them with phone numbers is available at the Visitor Center.

Bancroft Library is located in North Hall, one of the two original structures of the university. The library contains the university's collection of rare books and Western Americana, in addition to temporary rotating exhibitions. The library holds the first gold nugget found in the California gold rush, and the collected papers of Mark Twain.

The **Earth Sciences Building** houses the Museum of Paleontology, the **Museum of Geology**, and the **Seismographic Station**. The **Museum of Paleontology** has an extensive collection of artifacts made by Ishi, the last known survivor of the Yana Indians of California. Ishi was found near Oroville and brought to San Francisco in 1911 by Berkeley anthropologists. The displays of his handiwork are sad reminders of the Indian cultures which disappeared incredibly fast during the 19th century. (Open Mon., Tues., Thurs. and Fri. 10am-4:30pm. Weekends noon-4:30pm. $1.50 adults, 25 cents for children under 16 and seniors. Free on Thursday.)

Across Bancroft avenue, from Krober Hall, the **University Art Museum** includes 11 exhibition galleries, a sculpture garden, and permanent collections of Asian and Western art, video and film collections, and a collection of the paintings of Hans Hoffman. There is a book store and cafe-restaurant. ($2 adults, $1 non-U.C. students, seniors and children 6-17. Free admission Thursday 11am -noon.)

Also housed in the museum is the **Pacific Film Archives** (entrance from Durant ave. side), with continuous programs ranging from the classic to the obscure.

Up in the hills behind the campus are the **Botanical Gardens**, and the Lawrence Hall of Science, accessible by Humphrey Go-BART. The **Lawrence Hall of Science** is a great place to feel the sense of wonder that science is all about. Viewers participate in many activities covering a wide range of the sciences. There are planetarium programs, films and lectures. (Open weekdays 10am-4:30pm, till 9pm on Thursday. Weekends, 10am-5pm. $2.50 adults, $1.50 seniors, non-U.C. students, youth 7-18. Free on Thursday after 4pm.)

Up the hill from the Science Hall lies green and rolling **Tilden Park**. The 30-acre Botanical Garden in **Strawberry Canyon** holds a tremendous variety of plants from several terrains. (Open 9am-4:45pm daily. Admission free.) In a compact area you can walk from desert to lush rain forest, and then enter a greenhouse for the jungle.

The **Berkeley Rose Garden**, at Euclid Ave. and Eunice, shows unusual roses and has a beautiful view of the bay. The **Judas Magnes Museum** exhibits an extensive collection of Judaica. (2911 Russel st. Open Sun.-Fri., 10am-4pm. Tel. 849-2710.)

On **Telegraph Avenue** there has been a distinct rise in the level of style and fashion of the stores, with the appearance of little espresso places, new boutiques, and chain book stores.

However some things along this perennial Berkeley strip remain unchanged; the street vendors selling crafts, the panhandlers, the cult missionaries, the great used book stores, and a few old hippies.

There is an interesting selection of book stores on the stretch of **Bancroft Ave.**, bordering Telegraph and facing the campus. There is the *University Press Bookstore*, the huge *Campus Textbook Exchange*, a combination book store-cafe, a map center, and the *Wilderness Press*, an excellent source for books on the outdoors.

People are still gathering at **People's Park**, east of Telegraph between Haste and Dwight Way. Young people sleep under the trees or lounge on old discarded furniture with the stuffing popping out. Backpacks, sleeping bags and ragged bundles are piled up. Mohawk haircuts and dyed hair, are blended with long hippie hair and beads, worn by kids who could be the children of those who created the style.

On the block of Telegraph between Haste and Dwight Way, some of the classic Berkeley hangouts still exist. On Dwight and Telegraph is *Shakespeare's Used Books*, next to the veritable *Cafe Mediterranean* (the Med) where customers have been discussing Kafka and announcing God for decades. Three other book stores on the block are institutions: *Shambala Books*, where you can sit on wooden benches and browse through every kind of spiritual text you could hope to find in this incarnation; multi-leveled *Moe's Books*, and *Cody's*, a huge store with a wide selection in every major field and a cafe.

Shattuck avenue is the main shopping area of Berkeley. It adjoins with University to form the main corner. There is a sprinkling of good restaurants, but far more variety is packed into the lively area off Telegraph avenue.

Accommodations
Berkeley is not the ideal place to seek lodgings. There is very little middle ground here. Lodgings are either in the very high bracket of the hotel/motel chains, or dingy old hotels along Telegraph. Along University ave. there are a few standard motels, none of them especially scintillating. On the bayshore near Route 80 there are some motor inns, and near the marina is the modern *Marina Mariott*. Tel. 548-7920.

Food
There is considerably more choice in restaurants than there is in lodging in Berkeley. On Telegraph, restaurants rise and fall quickly, but there are a few standbys that have developed excellent reputations, for good reason, through many student generations. Shattuck ave., more staid as a shopping area, has seen a number of new restaurants open in the last few years. With competition tight for the student market, there are many good eating deals around.

CALIFORNIA

Mario's La Fiesta: On Telegraph and Haste. Tel. 540-9213. Mosaics around the entrance, tiles on the tables, large and delicious servings on the tiles, and lines out the door sometimes. Very reasonable.

The Soup Kitchen: Telegraph and Dwight Way: Serves healthy food in a rustic atmosphere.

Edy's: 2201 Shattuck ave., in the heart of downtown. Carved wooden booths, old-time feeling. You almost expect to see ponytails and bobby socks. Good old-fashioned ice cream concoctions.

The Blue Nile: 2525 Telegraph. Excelllent Ethopian food. If you really want to show your worldliness, scoop up some entree with injira bread and feed your companion.

Chez Panisse: 1517 Shattuck ave. Tel. 548-5525. A restaurant in a different class to most of the local places. Known for mesquite-grilled entrees. Expensive.

Spengers Fish Grotto: 1919 4th st. Tel. 845-7771. Near the highway. A grotto it is, and an established, popular seafood place.

Useful Addresses And Phone Numbers
Chamber of Commerce: 1834 University ave. Tel. 845-1212.
University of California Visitors Information Center: Student Union, in Sproul Plaza. Tel. 642-5215.
Council on International Educational Exchange (CIEE) Travel Center: 2511 Channing Way. Tel. 848-8604. A goldmine of information for member and student travelers.
Greyhound: Tel. 834-3070.
Amtrak: Tel. 982-2278. Station in Oakland.
AC Transit: Tel. 653-3535.
Bay Area Rapid Transit (BART: Tel. 465-2278.
Berkeley Switchboard: 1901 8th st. Tel.848-0800.
Rape Hotline: Tel. 845-RAPE.
Ticketron: Tower Posters, 2350 Telegraph ave. Tel. 548-5638.

Marin County
Marin County is located on the peninsula north of San Francisco, connected by the Golden Gate Bridge. It is a combination of small towns, affluent suburbs, beautiful hills, shady glens and rugged coast. The peninsula is served by both MUNI and Golden Gate Transit. The latter provides the only local transportation.

The Marin sector of the GGNRA is wild, rugged cliffside country that gives a totally different perspective to the city skyline.

You can sit at isolated **Point Bonita**, thrust out into the Pacific far beyond the bridge, in the midst of a cold ocean wind and churning waves, feeling

CALIFORNIA

totally alone in the world, and still have time after an exhilarating hike, to sip beer or coffee in a hip, fern-filled, polished and cozy Sausalito cafe.

MUNI bus 76 starts from downtown San Francisco, crosses the Golden Gate Bridge and heads west to **Rodeo Beach** on the edge of the Pacific and out of the city. From here you can choose from a network of trails that will take you in any direction, including north, to the extensive trail system of Mt. Tamalpais State Park. For a beautiful, not too difficult hike, follow the **Bobcat Trail** up into the ridges, to the **Morning Sun Trail**, and then across the freeway to Sausalito and a ferry ride home. There is no better place in the Bay area to watch the sunset than from a ferry, as the sun sinks behind the span and spires of the Golden Gate Bridge.

Tennessee Valley, accessible only by foot from the end of Tennessee Valley Road, is worth the hike of about two miles. It is a lush narrow valley ending in a small beach, completely isolated from the urbanized world.

The Marine Headlands Visitor Center (Open 8:30am-5pm, Tel. 331-1540) sponsors a wide range of guided hikes, history programs, and workshops. Included in these are guided hikes to the isolated lighthouse at Point Bonito. (Open 8:30am-5pm. Tel. 331-1540.) The *Golden Gate Hostel* is situated near the southern cliffs of the headlands (see San Francisco, "Accommodations").

Located in Fort Cronkite on the Marin headlands is the **California Marine Mammal Center**, a non-profit organization dedicated to rescuing and rehabilitating injured and ailing marine mammals, mainly seals and sea lions, but occasionally dolphins and whales as well. Open to visitors, but usually only to groups, so call first. (Open 10am-5pm. Tel. 331-0161.)

Sausalito, on the Bay side of the Marin peninsula, was once a small, isolated fishing village, connected to the city by ferry prior to the building of the Golden Gate Bridge. Backed by the Marin headlands and fronted by the wharves and bay, its rustic houses were dug into the steep hillsides. Jack London once lived and worked here.

Now it has been elaborately decked out for tourists, its old buildings filled with quaint and pricey tourist shops. Nevertheless, it is a pleasant place to stroll through, especially after a bracing walk across the Golden Gate Bridge or through the wild headlands. There are bars, restaurants and cafes, and visitor information is available at the Sausalito Chamber of Commerce, (333 Caledonia st. Tel. 332-0505).

The **San Francisco Bay and Delta Model**, built and operated by the U.S. Army Corps of Engineers, is a hydraulic scale model which reproduces the tides, flow, currents and other forces at work in the bay region. (2100 Bridgeway. Tues.-Sat. 9am-4pm. Tel. 332-3870.)

Beyond the main Sausalito docks floats a separate world of houseboats. The imagination – not to mention the material – that go into these creations is amazing. There have periodically been quarrels between the houseboat dwellers and development authorities, but they are still afloat.

CALIFORNIA

The Golden Gate Ferry makes the run to San Francisco's Embarcadero, and the Red and White Fleet ferry docks at Fisherman's Wharf.

East of Sausalito lies the peninsula of **Tiburon**, with the small port section at the southern end, across from Angel Island State Park. Less crowded than Sausalito, Tiburon is also a nice place to stroll and has what is reputedly the best selection of waterfront restaurants on the bay, with a wide range of cuisine and prices. They are lined up, literally, side by side, some with open decks. Tiny **Main Street** has the usual art shops, and you can enjoy some wine-tasting around the corner at Tiburon Vintners. Further on is **Ark Row**, consisting of turn-of-the-century boats which were beached and turned into a row of small shops.

The Red and White Fleet Ferry from San Francisco serves both Angel Island and Tiburon, and nearby is the Angel Island Ferry, traveling between the port and the island park. A fine day's excursion would be to explore Angel Island by foot or bike, then continue to Tiburon for a meal, and return to the city. From time to time, the ferry company makes a special arrangement whereby, if you eat at one of several specific Tiburon restaurants, you can receive $2 back from the price of the ferry ticket.

Angel Island is a natural and historical preserve in the mouth of the bay, just south of Tiburon. Serving at various times as an Indian hunting ground for sea otters and seals, a whaling supply station and a cattle ranch and military base, it finally became the arrival point for immigration from the west. A flood of European immigrants was expected after the opening of the Panama Canal. They never came, but waves of Asian immigrants arrived, and encountered the vagaries of American prejudice. Filipinos and Japanese were admitted, while Chinese were held in barracks, where their inscriptions of frustration can still be read today.

The island is closed to cars, but bicycles are allowed. There are paths for cycling, a beautiful five-mile loop trail, and a history and ecology museum. Campsites are available by reservation. Regular ferry service is available from both Tiburon and Fisherman's Wharf.

For ferry information from Tiburon, Tel. 435-2131; from Fisherman's Wharf, Tel. 546-2815; for campsite reservations, Tel. 800-952-5580, and for general information Tel. 435-1915.

Mt. Tamalpais State Park is a favorite with local hikers. It has dense forests and magnificient views, as well as access by foot and car to the popular Stinson Beach Park. Its summit is accessible only on foot. "Mount Tam" is also where the newest outdoor rage was born. People who formerly spent hundreds of dollars on fancy racing and touring bicycles can now spend hundreds of dollars on "mountain bikers": lower, sturdier, wider, knobby-wheeled bicycles that can zoom up and down dirt paths, slopes and trails. A map of trails is available at the Pantoll Ranger Station on Panoramic Way, Tel. 388-2070. The map indicates bike-in camping spots ($1 per night, first-come, first-serve). A trail following mountain ridges, creeks and redwood stands leads to the rustic *West Point Inn*, where coffee

CALIFORNIA

He's come a long way

and granola bars await. Rooms and cabins available from Tues.-Fri. $12 per person. Tel. 388-9955.

Mountain bike rentals:
Ken's Bike and Sport: 94 Main st. Tiburon, $20. Tel. 435-1683.
Point Reyes Bikes: 11431 State Highway 1, $16-$20. Tel. 663-1768.

In a cool, moist canyon beneath the slopes of Mt. Tamalpais is the **Muir Woods National Monument**, the natural redwood grove that is closest to the San Francisco metropolitan area. The grove, saved from felling by its inaccessibility but forever threatened, was finally placed under federal protection and named after John Muir, the inspiration behind the modern conservation movement. Reached by a loop road off Route 1, Muir Woods makes a beautiful short walk in itself or serves as a pleasant stop on a longer hike among the extensive trail network in the area. The entrance gate is open from 8am to sunset. It is hard to believe that this primeval forest, so close to the city, somehow managed to survive. On weekends parking can be a problem.

Point Reyes
The Point Reyes National Seashore is a blending and meeting of several

CALIFORNIA

beautiful landscapes: green rolling pasture land, scrubby chaparral ridges, lush meadows and forest, expansive sand dunes, large tidepools, sea-sculpted caves, and jutting cliffs exposed to the full force of the Pacific. All these terrains are covered by an extensive mesh of trails, suitable for both day hikes and overnight camping expeditions. Point Reyes is long enough and varied enough to give a sense of openness and space even during a crowded holiday. When you climb down to the lighthouse at Point Reyes itself or reach any of the other promontories exposed to the salty wind and smells of the tumultuous Pacific, the rest of the world just does not seem to exist.

Route 1, the coastal highway that reaches Point Reyes and continues north, runs right along the **San Andreas Fault** which continues into the Tomales Bay that separates Point Reyes from the mainland. Two major plates of the earth's crust meet along this fracture, causing a large rift containing large and small faults within it. Reflecting the pressures and stresses deeper in the earth's core, this fault zone is an area of comparatively rapid topographic change and motion, including the floating of the large plates, commonly referred to as "continental drift." This explains, for example, why rocks in this craggy coast match those of the Tehachapi mountains 300 miles to the south. From fold to fold and ridge to ridge the climate and vegetation change rapidly. Even the weather changes rapidly, not only from day to day but hour to hour. These sharply contrasting ecological zones support a great variety of wildlife which feeds upon the myriad riches of this interzonal area.

Shifting winds, nutrient-rich cold water, and other climatic factors combine to create a marine ecosystem as varied and abundant as the one it meets on land. Whales and porpoises may pass south along the coast a few hundred yards away from grazing elk. The protected marine sanctuary, which encompasses the **Farallon Islands** as well as the Point Reyes beach, contains the largest breeding rookery for seabirds on the American Pacific coast. Hundreds of thousands of birds live and breed here.

The strong undertows at Point Reyes make swimming too dangerous and it is forbidden. The Bear Valley Visitor Center (Tel. 663-1092) posts a schedule of programs. Camping sites are spread out in the southern half of the park and are all primitive. The *Point Reyes Hostel* is on Limantour Road, off Route 1. During the summer a free shuttle bus runs from the seashore headquarters to **Limantour Beach**.

Educational boat trips sail for the Farallon Islands or follow whale migrations. The Oceanic Society Expeditions (Tel. 474-3385) and the Whale Center (Tel. 654-6621) both offer trips.

Marine World/Africa U.S.A.

South of the Napa Valley, the I-80 brings you to the town of Vallejo, at the very western edge of the agricultural Central Valley. The wild-animal extravaganza, Marine World/Africa U.S.A., opened here in 1986 after

CALIFORNIA

moving from Redwood City. It is part circus, part zoo, part reserve, part research facility and part open and innovative classroom. It is bright and exciting, and has been planned with care. The theme park has an amazing variety of cats, snakes, exotic birds, elephants and primates, as well as whales, dolphins and sharks. Rare habitats have been creatively reproduced. There is always something going on, always a show, in addition to the displays that invite children and adults to learn while playing, or play while learning.

Exit off I-80 to Marine World Parkway and follow the signs. Special Red and White Fleet high-speed ferries now follow the San Pablo Bay to Marine World, from Pier 41 at Fisherman's Wharf in San Francisco. For details, Tel. 415-546-2800. Greyhound also reaches Marine World.

Marine World/Africa U.S.A. is open daily 9:30am-6pm (check for extended hours in summer). $13.95 for adults, $9.95 for seniors and ages 4-12, no admission age 3 and under. Tel. 707-643-ORCA for recording, Tel. 707-644-4000 for administration.

CALIFORNIA

Wine Country

Napa Valley

California produces 90% of all the wines in the United States. The Napa Valley is the finest wine-making region in California, and the lush valley produces wines of international fame. The great climatic range enables the nurturing of a surprising variety of wine grapes. The days are hot, the nights cool, and the air is filled with the smell of grapes during the harvest season.

The first grapevines were brought to the Napa Valley in the 1820s by Spanish missionaries, for sacramental purposes. By the 1850s, vineyards had spread throughout the valley, and some decades afterwards they and their reputation spread to the east coast. Disease and prohibition, from 1919-1930, crippled the industry. When wine production revived, during the 60s and 70s, it propelled the Napa Valley into the forefront of the wine-producing regions of the world. Wine is the major theme of this valley and the main reason the highways on a summer weekend are lined with cars.

About 100 wineries grace this valley, most scattered along Route 29 between Napa in the south and Calistoga in the north. The renowned ones provide a good starting point, but there are other smaller, more obscure wineries which are also worth exploring. Poking around the small farms and wine cellars in the countryside, and meeting the vintners is part of the fun.

It is difficult to negotiate the Napa Valley without a car, especially if you wish to visit some of the less accessible wineries. Greyhound service connects the towns along Route 29. Within the town of Napa itself there is a good bus system known as the VINE.

Cycling is an excellent way to see this valley. Bicycles can be hired in Napa or Calistoga. The flat country backroads make for easy riding. The Napa Chamber of Commerce has maps with route suggestions.

St. Helena is the center of the valley's wine making industry. Some of the best known California labels can be recognized on the visitor's map and roadside signs. Christian Bros., Beringer Bros. and Charles Krug (the oldest operating valley winery) are located north of town. The architecture of these wineries can be as interesting as the wines. Some have the atmosphere of medieval castles or monasteries. The Beringer winery ages its wine in huge vats in a network of tunnels carved out of the adjacent hillside by Chinese workers. Near the town there are other smaller wineries.

The **Beaulieu Vineyards** at Rutherford have a beautiful tasting and display room. The well known **Inglenook Vineyards**, just north of Rutherford, runs

CALIFORNIA

a popular tour. The **Sterling Vineyard** has a beautiful view of the valley, and the tram for carrying visitors up costs $3.50.

Many events and festivals revolve around wine; the **Grape Festival** and the **Harvest Festival** are held in August, and some of the hotels sponsor weekly wine-tastings.

Driving around the valley, with stops for tasting, is one of the most pleasant things to do here. If you drive north to Calistoga along Route 29, the return drive by Route 128, skirting the slopes of the eastern hills, makes a pleasant return route to Napa. This route leads past Lake Berryessa. Public land is interspersed with private resorts. Along the western shore are restaurants, boat ramps, campsites and picnic spots.

Wine Tasting Tips

It is easy to feel overwhelmed by the volume and variety of wines in the fertile northern valleys of California. It seems that every other wine is a prize-winner. How is the novice to distinguish between them?

There are a few general guidelines for evaluating wine. Move from white, to reds, to dessert wines, because the reds leave more tannins on the tongue and dull the taste. Check the wine for cleanness or cloudiness, and a pleasing color. Swirl the wine to release its "nose": a combination of aroma (from the grape) and bouquet (from the wine-making process). When tasting, check for fruitiness, tartness, smoothness or hardness.

The Davis 20-point system, based on such qualities as clarity, color, scent, sweetness, acidity, body and flavor, can give you some standards for judgement. Literature is available from the various wine organizations listed, and the winery tour guides can advise you.

There are also guidelines for proper wine-tasting behavior. It is crucial to know how to raise the glass to the light and squint critically; how to sniff delicately; how to sip, purse the lips, roll the tongue, pause meaningfully and frown. Then come the vital first words – spoken with a slow nod – such as: "A marvelous spicy rush, but a fading finish... a lovely late afternoon wine with a tickly center." After the fourth or fifth glass, more expansive poesy is allowed: "As light as a sparrow's song... as rosy as a young girl's cheeks".

It is possible to visit local farms and taste and purchase apples, peaches, strawberries, walnuts, etc. The county publishes a guide to farms that welcome and encourage visitors. Write: Napa County Farm Trails, 4075 Solano ave., Napa 94558, or inquire at the Napa visitors center. An open-air farmer's market is held on Fridays at the Dansk Square parking lot, south of downtown St. Helena.

Calistoga, at the northern end of the valley, has retained the atmosphere of an old western farmtown. The commercial section is really just one street, with old covered sidewalks. The old railroad station at the east end of town has been refurbished, as a small mall, and the old railcars are the attractions. The local Chamber of Commerce is located here. In the middle

CALIFORNIA

of the block across the street is the old **Calistoga Inn,** a renovated original that served travelers in the last century.

Calistoga attracted tourists with the region's mineral springs. One of California's major early figures, the flamboyant Sam Brennan, creator of San Francisco's first newspaper (which announced the gold rush to the world) first bought up the springs and pushed through a major plan to make the area a resort for city-dwellers. The springs have been tapped, channeled and sealed off by elaborate spas and inns. The luxury of wallowing in thick black mud, plus whirlpool, steam room and blanket wrap, costs from $20-$30.

Calistoga's **Old Faithful Geyser** shoots a plume of steam and water up to 60 feet high about every 40 minutes. (Located about two miles north of Calistoga at 1299 Tubbs lane. Open everyday, including holidays, 9am-5pm in winters, 9am-6pm in summers. Tel. 942-6463.)

Just north of town, keep an eye open for the **Treasure-House of Worldly Wares.** (1401 Tubbs lane. Open 10am-5pm daily except Thursday. Tel. 942-9976.) Hopi boots, Eskimo carvings, African lyres, Persian pendants and an Egyptian mummy mask all find a place in this crammed and colorful shop. Most interesting of all is the owner, a Ponca Indian named Stevie Whitefeather.

Robert Louis Stevenson State Park is located on Mount St. Helena, five miles north of Calistoga on Route 29. The famous Scottish writer lived there in 1880 with his new bride, in a old mining shack. Here he wrote *Silverado Squatters*, relating his experiences in the area. The forested mountain sides inspired the setting for *Treasure Island*. Open during daylight hours, the park has a hiking trail leading to the mountain summit, with vistas of the distant high peaks of the eastern ranges. The **Silverado Museum** in St. Helena features a collection of Stevenson memorabilia and manuscripts. (1490 Library Lane, St. Helena. Tues.-Sun. noon-4pm. Admission free. Tel. 963-3757.)

Accommodations

The emphasis in Napa Valley is on elegant country-style old hotels, or B&Bs. In Calistoga there is a concentration of spa hotels. These places are very relaxing, and some are stunning. They also tend to be a little over-priced, but have much more atmosphere than the standard motel or hotel.

Wine Country B&B Reservations: Tel. 257-7757.

Hideaway Cottages: 1412 Fairway, Calistoga 94515. Tel. 942-4108. Cottages ranging from small to two-roomed. Nicely furnished. Mineral pools. $35-$75. Weekly rates.

Calistoga Inn: 1250 Lincoln ave., Calistoga 94515. Tel. 942-4104. Comfortable rooms in a landmark building. Shared baths. Continental breakfast, and wine in each room. $35 single, $40 double.

CALIFORNIA

Silverado Motel: 500 Silverado Trail, Napa. Tel. 225-9848. Simple, adequate. $26-$45.

Camping
Bothe-Napa Valley State Park: 3601 St. Helena Highway. Tel. 942-4575. Located 20 miles north of Napa, between St. Helena and Calistoga. About 50 sites, hiking trails. Can get crowded in summer. Between April and Oct., reservations through Ticketron.

Additional camping is available at the Fairgrounds in Calistoga (Tel. 942-5111) and the Fairgrounds in Napa (Tel. 226-2164). Private campgrounds by Lake Berryessa.

Some Napa Valley Wineries
Full lists of valley wineries, with their specialties, tasting and tour hours, available from the local Visitor Centers and Chambers of Commerce.

Charles Krug Winery: 2800 Main st. (Route 29), St. Helena. Tel. 963-2761. The oldest in the valley, owned by the Mondavi family. Frequent tours, historical displays. Open 10am-4pm daily.

Robert Mondavi Winery: 7801 St. Helena, Rte 29. Tel. 963-9611. Tours and tasting.

De Moor Winery: 7481 Route 29, Oakville. Tel. 944-2565. Tasting room, self-guided tours. A small but renowned winery.

V. Sattui Winery: Corner Route 29 at White ln, 2 miles south of St. Helena east of highway. Tel. 963-7774. Tasting room, gourmet deli, picnic grounds. Consistent winner in major competitions. Wines sold exclusively from here.

Beringer Vineyards: 2000 Main st. St. Helena. Tel. 963-7115. Tours and tasting. A very commercial tour, but the carved caves and vaults are worth seeing.

Inglenook Napa Valley: 1991 Route 29, Rutherford. Tours, tasting. Known for Cabernet Sauvignon.

Important Addresses And Phone Numbers
Area Code: 707.
Emergency: 911.
Napa Chamber of Commerce: 1900 Jefferson st. Tel. 257-1112.
Napa Valley Visitor Information Center: 4076 Byway East. Tel. 257-1102. Near a big wooden tower on the east side of Route 29.
Calistoga Chamber of Commerce: Calistoga Depot, 1458 Lincoln ave. Tel. 942-6333.
General Transportation Info: Tel. 252-6222.
Napa City Bus: 1130 1st st. Tel. 255-7631.
Evans Airport Service: Tel. 255-1559. Daily service between Napa City and SFO, $11. Reservations.

CALIFORNIA

Greyhound: Napa, 226-1856; Yountville, Tel. 944-8377; Calistoga, Tel. 942-6021.
Napa Charter Lines: Tel. 224-2351.
Highway Conditions: Tel. 643-8421.
Wine Country Tours: Tel. 963-5760.

Sonoma Valley

The crescent-shaped Sonoma Valley stretches north from the San Pablo Bay to Santa Rosa. The mountains to the east keep out the dry intense heat that hits the Napa Valley, and the western mountains block the heaviest fogs, and only light fogs and cool moist breezes penetrate.

In the early 19th century, Spanish, Russian and American interests collided in this fertile valley. Local expressions of larger diplomatic struggles were played out here, and Sonoma became the flashpoint for the rebellion of local American settlers against Mexican rule.

Sonoma was settled comparatively late. The **Mission San Francisco Solano**, the northernmost and last in the mission system, was founded here in 1823. By 1830 it was the dominant influence in the valley, with 1000 local Indians under its authority, but that dominance was short-lived.

In 1833 Captain Mariano Vallejo was sent by the Mexican government to contact the Russian outposts and establish Mexican settlements, but the Franciscan mission thwarted his efforts. Returning four years later, he reduced the mission to the status of a parish church, freed the Indian workers and redistributed mission lands. Vallejo himself received a huge land grant and set up a productive agricultural empire. His far-reaching civil and military power shaped Sonoma's development. His adobe home on the plaza, La Casa Grande, drew visitors from around the world.

Amid increasing American desires for the rich lands of California, a group of 30-40 American frontiersmen captured the Sonoma settlement in June, 1846 without resistance. They arrested Vallejo and imprisoned him. They raised a home-made flag of a bear, and the famous "Bear Flag Rebellion" made California an independent republic, until the United States took over a month later. But the uprising was far from the heroic enterprise lauded in California history. The Americans had been seeking a pretext to make their move. General Vallejo returned home to find his ranch stripped of livestock and other commodities by the self-proclaimed patriots.

Vallejo had the dignity to take an active role in American politics in California even after the regime he had been part of was deposed. He was a delegate to the state's constitutional convention and was elected to the State Senate. He even offered a tract of land for the building of a permanent capitol. Although his great holdings were steadily whittled away, he never became embittered but remained dignified, and immersed himself in composing a five-volume history of Mexican California. When he died in 1890 at age 82, hundreds of people filled the little central plaza of Sonoma, then carried the body to the small cemetery above town.

CALIFORNIA

Old Sonoma – shady, quiet and compact – is still centered around the original small **plaza**, and one can pass a couple of hours here strolling and exploring. The verdant plaza holds the Visitor Center, where you can pick up a self-guiding tour explaining the old adobe buildings that stand scattered around you. There are several good and reasonably priced restaurants and delis around the plaza.

Many of the historical landmarks, and the **Sonoma State Historical Park**, are on Spain st. just north of the plaza. Here stands Vallejo's first home, with a small Indian exhibit in the rangers' building right next to the *Toscano Hotel*. In the *Toscano* itself, built in 1858 and meticulously restored, you'd expect to find Jack London or Mark Twain lounging in the lobby with their feet up drinking a glass of brandy.

The park includes the **mission complex** near the corner of E. Spain and 1st st. The missionaries' quarters is the oldest building remaining in the complex. Exhibits depict the various stages of history in Sonoma. In the courtyard, craft demonstrations from earlier periods are held. Part of the original Bear Flag (most was destroyed by fire) is still found in the mission.

Nearby is the *Blue Wing Inn*, reportedly built by Vallejo, which may have housed John Fremont, the explorer and officer who was instrumental in consolidating American rule in California.

The **Vasquez House**, set back on 1st st. east of the plaza, was transported by ship from the east at a cost of $64,000, by Joseph Hooker, army officer who later achieved fame in the civil war. It now houses a library and tiny coffee shop where the proprieter is friendly and proud of the town, and the coffee costs 25 cents.

The **Depot Museum**, Behind Sapin st., recreates an old railroad station, with all details authentic down to the brakeman's lantern and ticket counter. Only the "all aboard!" is missing. In Depot Park between 1st st. East and 1st st. West. (Open Wed.-Sun. 1-4:30pm. Adults 50 cents, children 25 cents. Tel. 938-9765.)

One of the most interesting spots in the plaza area is the **Stained Glass Works**, which displays and sells stained glass pieces crafted on the premises by handicapped adults. The detailed and variegated pieces, beautiful in their own right, become more interesting when the production process is seen. (115 East Napa st. Tel. 996-5180.)

The Sonoma Valley witnessed the earliest experiments in the state with vine cultivation and wine production, and there are wineries throughout the valley as well as in the town.

The **Sebastiani Winery**, an easy stroll from the plaza along E. Spain st. (there is ample parking near the winery), is the largest and one of the best-known valley wineries. (389 E. 4th st. Regular tours. Open 10am-5pm. Admission free. Tel. 938-5532.) Some of its vineyards are 100 years old. The 20-minute tour is entertaining, well organized and not full of the usual drinking jokes. The oak casks and redwood tanks here emit intoxicating smells and are decorated with beautiful wood-carvings. There is also a museum of Indian artifacts.

The **Buena Vista Winery**, about a mile east of the town center, was founded in 1857, the first in California with stone cellars. (18000 Old Winery rd. Open daily 10am-3pm. Tel. 938-8504.) Now a historical landmark, it is worth a visit for the limestone catacombs alone. There are picnic grounds and playground equipment made of barrels and casks. The winery also hosts performances, including Shakespearean plays.

The **Gundlach Bundschu Winery** is also one of the old-timers. The personnel are pleasant, the grounds pretty. There are regular tastings and self-guided tours. (2000 Denmark st. Open daily 11am-4:30pm. Tel. 938-5277.)

The foundation of the **Glen Ellen** winery can be traced back to General Vallejo's time when he owned the property, and it is one of the better-known wineries in the area. (1883 London Ranch rd, Glen Ellen. Tasting from 10am-4pm. Tours by appointment. Tel. 996-1066.)

Wine Seminars International offers tours, seminars and video presentations for those wishing to learn the subtleties of wine-tasting. Write or call: PO Box 1287, Sonoma, 95476. Tel. 938-9060, or Tel. 800-328-3029 ext. 208.

Accommodations
The greatest concentration of hotels and motels is found in the Santa Rosa area, and at various points along Highway 101. There are, however, a number of small inns scattered through the Sonoma countryside. For suggestions and information, contact: Wine Country Inns of Sonoma County, P.O. Box 51. Geyserville, 95441. Tel. 433-INNS.

Food
Sonoma Cheese Factory: 2 West Spain st. Tel. 996-1931. Watch how the cheese is produced by hand and sample the results. A deli as well, and a garden patio.

La Casa: Spain st. at 1st st. East. Tel. 996-3406. In a historic building, Mexican food reasonably priced.

Depot Hotel 1870: 241 1st st. West. Tel. 938-2980. The atmosphere is rural, the cuisine hearty.

Useful Addresses And Phone Numbers
Area Code: 707.
Valley Visitors Bureau: 453 1st st. Tel. 996-1090.
Sonoma County Transit: Tel. 527-7665.
Sonoma Airporter: Tel. 938-4246. Transportation to San Francisco Airport.

CALIFORNIA

RUSSIAN RIVER

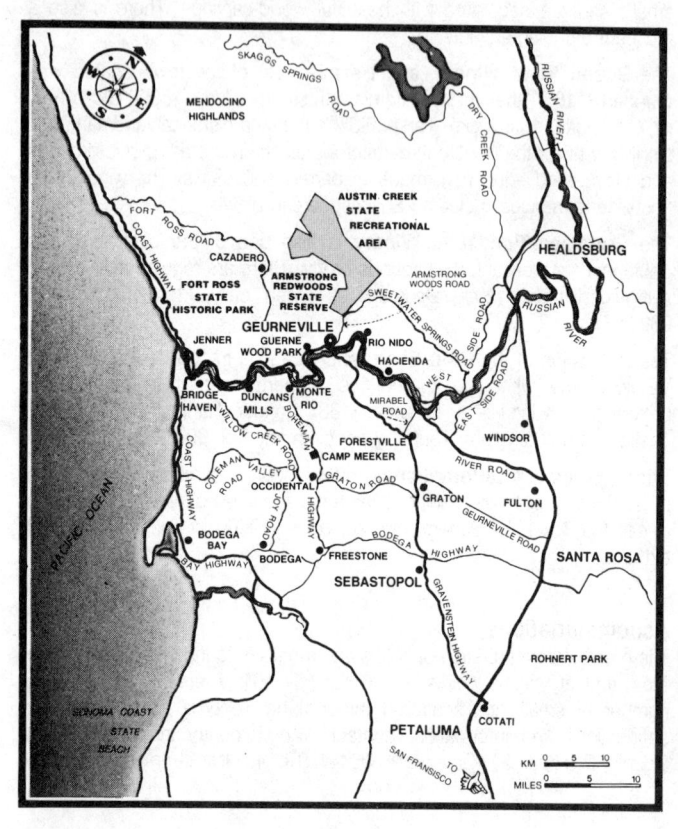

Russian River and Sonoma Coast

The Sonoma Valley connects with the **Russian River Valley** region, which leads out to the Pacific. The hillsides and the valleys which are carved by the Russian River and its tributaries are exceptionally fertile, covered by deposits of loam and shady soil. The warm summers, the cool winters and the fog drifting in from the Pacific along the Russian River Valley create an environment distinct from Napa's, yet still excellent for vine-growing. In autumn, the low hills gleam an unbelievable gold and the aromas of fermenting fruit fill the air. Towering stands of redwoods grow here. The coastline is rocky, and backed by cliffs.

The Russian River Valley has attracted various populations, with small-time farmers, suburbanite developers and commuters, vintners, fishermen,

CALIFORNIA

hippie back-to-the-land types, and recently an influx of urban gays who have set up resorts in some of the small towns.

How to get there

The best way to travel through this area is by car, but if limited to the bus system, it is still possible to get around Sonoma county, with a little planning. A number of municipal and regional bus companies connect all parts of the county, but it is important to check schedules and coordinate times, to avoid long waits.

Golden Gate Transit (GGT) provides a daily service between Santa Rosa, Marin County cities and towns, and San Francisco, with stops at cities and towns in Sonoma County along Highway 101. One route serves Sebastopol and Forestville. During the weekday rush hours, you can ride along with business-attired commuters on the express buses. The main transfer point between GGT and the other bus services in the county is at the transit mall in downtown Santa Rosa.

Sonoma County transit reaches all areas of the county. It connects with the City Bus in Santa Rosa, the GGT system, and the local systems of the small towns along the Russian River. Transfers within the same bus system are free. A transfer to another bus system allows a reduction in fare. You can pick up the various bus schedules at city halls, libraries, Chambers of Commerce and some major businesses throughout the towns of Sonoma County. Greyhound also serves Sonoma County, with direct buses from San Francisco, eliminating the need to transfer.

Guerneville is the center of the Russian River resort area. During the summer it is crowded, and the cafes and restaurants tend to be a little more expensive than in some of the other towns. From near the main junction of the town, there is an easy walk down to the sandy bank of the river itself. The houses, which are a considerable distance from the shore, were flooded and some were washed away during the great floods of 1985 which ravaged the entire valley. Guerneville has become a popular resort for the gay community of San Francisco.

Just 2.5 miles north of Guerneville off route 116 are the cool primeval redwood forests of the **Armstrong Redwoods State Reserve**, which adjoins the **Austin Creek State Recreation Area**. About twenty miles of hiking trails run through them, from the deep cool redwood-filled valleys to the scrubby peaks. Easy trails loop through the redwood grove which includes some of the tallest trees left in this region of California. Check local papers to see whether a play or concert is being presented at the reserve's 1200-seat amphitheatre.

There is a drive-in campground at **Bullfrog Pond**, as well as primitive walk-in campgrounds further to the west. For information, contact the park's head office at 17000 Armstrong Woods Road, Guerneville, 95446. Tel. 869-2015 or Tel. 865-2391.

CALIFORNIA

The **canoeing** is fantastic along the wide and gently meandering Russian River. Numerous rental companies will arrange to launch your canoe at one point and pick you up further downstream. The river is gentle most of the way and there are numerous landing beaches with road access. There are a number of companies promoting canoe trips. The information office at Guerneville will have some addresses. Rates vary from between $25 and $30 per canoe for a full day's paddling. Discount coupons are available from local Chamber of Commerce offices.

The winery of **F. Korbel and Bros.**, open since 1862, is located in an old, beautifully landscaped complex, and is famous for its sparkling wines. (13250 River Road, Guerneville. Open daily, May-September. Tasting 9am-5pm, wineshop 9am-5:30pm. Call for winter hours. Tel. 887-2294.) In addition to its tasting room and winery tours every 45 minutes, there are free tours of its beautifully cultivated gardens.

For the annual jazz festival in August, **Russian River Jazz**, the audience gathers near the river to hear a wide variety of jazz, including some big names. For a predominantly rural county, there is a surprisingly active theater scene, with over 15 small community theaters, of varying styles, approaches and degrees of professionalism. The **Odyssey Stage Company of Sonoma** (Tel. 545-7708) has received good reviews for its innovative and sometimes daring productions. For general information on local and other artistic events and resources, peruse the free local weeklies, or contact the Cultural Arts Council of Sonoma County (Tel. 579-ARTS).

A loop drive into Russian River country makes a beautiful one or two-day excursion from San Francisco. From San Francisco, take route 101 north to Santa Rosa, the main population center of the Sonoma region. Take the 116 exit for Guerneville, which passes through **Sebastopol** and other small towns up to the Russian River. The highway follows the river to the sea, at **Jenner**. North of Jenner, the winding coastal road leads through increasingly rugged land with high overlooks over the ocean. To the south, the beautiful ocean-side cliffs continue. The coastal return route to the city, passes pretty **Bodega Bay** with its small fishing town and peaceful bayside seafood restaurants. Further south it passes Point Reyes and the seaside parklands of Marin County. North of Santa Rosa on route 101, at **Healdsburg**, the wineries begin.

After driving up to Healdsburg, as you head north on 101, you'll pass the town of **Cloverdale**, which sponsors a knee-slapping, foot-stomping fiddle festival every year. Last year it was held in January. Check the date if you plan to drive through the area, by calling the Cloverdale Historical Society (Tel. 894-2067). Follow the river course from Healdsburg or Cloverdale. The small roads parallel to the highway and Russian River are lined with wineries. The road follows the river which flows west past the wineries, all the way to the ocean. Some of the old wineries still age their wines in the one hundred year old stone cellars, while others are more modern.

For a map pinpointing and describing the various wineries, as well as

CALIFORNIA

events and general information, contact: Russian River Wine Road, P.O. Box 127, Geyserville, 95441. Tel. 433-6935.

Although route 116 is the main road from route 101 to the ocean, if you wander along some of the smaller roads south of the river, you'll find some incredibly green, rolling countryside. Try to direct your wandering to the town of **Occidental**. It is hardly two blocks long, but firmly established on a foundation of pasta. Facing each other like feuding castles, are two excellent Italian restaurants, the *Union Hotel* and the *Negri*. Both pile on the pasta, salads, fresh sourdough bread, sauces, meats and cheeses. The *Union Hotel* shakes up the forest on Friday and Saturday nights with foot stompin' music, and the bar has a lumberjack atmosphere like a macho beer commercial. From route 116 take the Bohemian Highway south from Monte Rio to Occidental.

Just east of Jenner on route 116 is **Duncan Mills**, with a population officially listed at 20. An old resort, railroad depot and lumbertown, much of the original architecture has been restored, and Duncan Mills today is basically a walk-through museum of restored Victorian buildings, a railroad museum, manicured gardens and cultivated quaintness.

Route 116 meets the Pacific Coast Highway and the ocean near the small Jenner Visitor's Center, a small semi-open shelter with self guided exhibits and explanations of the animal life along this stretch of coast. The coastal highway is like a winding roller coaster here. Bluffs and promontories divide the shoreline into a series of small, crescent-shaped disconnected beaches and coves. The climate here is much cooler than even a few miles inland. In the winter, the whales migrating south, pass by just off the coast where the ocean floor drops suddenly away. North of the Jenner junction, the Russian River meets the sea, meandering around sandbars that are covered in spring with seals mating and giving birth. Sharks occasionally drift into the inlet. The largest, caught last year, weighed over a ton. For information, call State Park headquarters at Bodega Bay, Tel. 875-3483.

North of Jenner on route 1, stands **Fort Ross State Historical Park**, the reconstruction of Russia's 19th century fort. (Park and museum open daily, except holidays, 10am-4:30pm. Parking $2. Tel. 847-3286.) It is easy to feel the isolation the soldiers must have felt in this southernmost exposed and remote outpost.

During the nineteenth century the Russians were reaching south to hunt for sea otter and to grow wheat and crops for their Alaskan settlements, and to establish a foothold for further inland expansion. The Spanish were meanwhile reaching up from the south, trying to solidify their hold on the colony which had technically already been in their possession for hundreds of years. The Americans, meanwhile, had been exploring overland as far as to the Pacific, and as far north as the mouth of the Columbia River. The local Indians had used the site seasonally to collect abalone. All this made for a clash of cultures and nationalities in microcosmic isolation. The museum depicts the story clearly and vividly. In the replicated cabins, the fur hats and leggings, and the embroidered leather bags, are remarkably similar to the relics of an American frontier memorial. The architecture, however, has clearly Russian characteristics.

Bodega, south of Jenner, is the home of the county's fishing fleet, docked in Bodega Harbor. It is a small fishing village of less than 4500 people. Small shacks and stands sell fresh seafood, clam chowder, smoked fish and deli items. From the restaurants at the harbor, one can watch the small fishing boats dock with their fishing passengers and full loads of fish. The fish are hauled up in crates, swung over and dumped into the huge basins on the scales. The fishermen shovel ice over the silvery mounds of fish. No tourist props here. They gut the fish which their passengers have caught and toss the guts over the railing, while circling gulls swoop down and restaurant customers try to enjoy their seafood.

Accommodations

The Russian River Valley is the perfect region to indulge yourself with a stay in a cosy and rustic B&B. They are scattered throughout the valley and in the small towns, both inland and along the coast. Standard hotels and motels are found mostly along Route 101 in the Santa Rosa vicinity. For information on local B&B inns, contact Wine Country Inns of Sonoma County: P.O. Box R51, Geyserville, 95441. Tel. 433-INNS.

State park camping is available at **Bodega Dunes** and **Wright's Beach**, in addition to **Anderson Creek State Park**. For reservations contact Ticketron, not the park. The County also operates several campgrounds. The **Doran Park** campgounds is located at the southern end of Bodega Harbor, at the very tip of the narrow jetty separating the harbor from the ocean. For information and reservations for the county campgrounds, call Tel. 722-5602, toll-free in-state Tel. 800-822-CAMP, toll-free out-of-state Tel. 800-824-CAMP.

Useful Addresses And Phone Numbers

Area Code: 707.
Sonoma County Convention & Visitors Bureau: 637 First st., Santa Rosa, Tel. 545-1420.
Russian River Chamber of Commerce: P.O. Box 331, Guerneville 95446, Tel. 823-3032.
Sonoma County Transit: Tel. 1-800-345-RIDE (toll-free in county), or Tel. 576-RIDE.
Golden Gate Transit: Tel. 544-1323.
Greyhound: Tel. 542-6400.
Mendocino Transit Authority: Tel. 576-RIDE. MTA runs a van down the coast into Sonoma County.
Santa Rosa Transit: Tel. 576-5306, or Tel. 576-5238.

CALIFORNIA

The North Coast: Mendocino and the Redwood Country

Mendocino Coast

Occasionally the suggestion arises, even in the state legislature, that the northern section of California secede from the state. The barbed joke hints that this is a different world up here, more attuned in geography, resources, climate, society and mentality to Oregon and the Pacific Northwest. Spanish influence barely reached here: no missions, no Spanish names, no red-tile roofs and white-washed adobe. The tiny coastal villages seem to have been transplanted from New England, where many of the early settlements' founders originated.

This is the land of lumber. The acreage of towering trees – redwoods especially, but Douglas fir and others as well – seems endless. Since the days of the earliest White settlements, the lumber industry dominated the region's economy, followed by fishing, ranching and other activities. The lumbermen cleared the slopes rapidly and the two thousand year old redwoods were suddenly threatened with extinction. But the lumber industry itself has fallen on hard times, and is no longer the king it once was. The vast network of lumber operations and milltowns has shrunken over the years. The coast is dotted with the debris of that earlier age; barren stump-studded slopes, abandoned and rotting installations and abandoned milltowns.

Except for the quaint village of Mendocino, and the line of redwood parks to the north, there are few well known tourist sites in this neck of the woods. However, if you are a beach-stroller, bluff-climber, tide pool prober or lighthouse-lover, a hunter of driftwood, taster of wine, and fanatic for New England you will find this area fascinating. The pace up here is slow, easy and deeply relaxing.

Fog blankets the Mendocino coastline in summer, and storms pound it in winter. During the tourist season, from Memorial Day to Labor Day, the nights can be cool and damp. The fog is not constant, but when it drifts in, it can drip down your neck and moisten your clothes. You can almost bottle it.

In June, you'll witness the colorful explosion of azaleas and rhododendrons. October may surprise you with balmy days. But winter, stretching to April or even May, creates a world of grey sea along grey cliffs, and foghorns bleating through grey fogs under grey clouds.

CALIFORNIA

Redwood tree

How to get there
By car, head north from San Francisco, inland along Highway 101 or on Route 1 on the coast. Highway 101 is faster but misses the coastal rollercoaster road of Route 1. Several roads connect the two parallel highways, offering the chance to see the beautiful diversity of this countryside, and still make good time.

CALIFORNIA

Greyhound runs along Route 101, serving Ukiah and Willits. Greyhound operates out of Eureka as well, north toward Arcata and south toward Fort Bragg. A regular run between Fort Brag and Santa Rosa stops at Mendocino. The **Mendocino Transit Authority** (MTA) operates a coast van between Eureka and Sonoma, which stops at junctions with links to the transportation systems of Sonoma County.

Heading up 101 brings you to Mendocino's well known wine country. The many valleys, ridges and mountains divide the region into a patchwork of "microclimates", creating individuality and variety between the valleys and great diversity among the grapes and wines produced here.

The wineries are clustered in several areas. The southern inland valley around Hopland, on Route 101, is fringed by vineyards. There are wineries at either end of town, with tasting rooms. For those with a more proletarian palate there is also the **Mendocino Brewing Company.**

Further north, in the deep valley surrounding Ukiah, are more wineries, as well as restaurants and motels. For an especially lovely drive off 101, turn northwest on route 128 just north of Cloverdale. This two-lane country road glides through the gently folded, green and golden hills of the Anderson Valley, toward the coast. Between Booneville and Navarro the wineries are scattered, some with picnic areas, and there are stores along the way to pick up picnic fixings.

Driving north up the coastal road, the first town along the Mendocino coast is Gualala, an old lumbertown transformed to a more tourist oriented center. The non-profit **Gualala Arts** organization presents the "Art in the Redwoods" festival in August. Store fronts in **The Gallery** center proffer some fine craftwork, paintings and sculpture. North of Gualala, the coast road undulates past jutting cliffs, headland, coves, islands, slivers of beach, salt marshes and rare giant dunes. Take your time here to relax and take in the scenery.

Four miles north of Gualala is **Anchor Bay,** which offers restaurants and Bed & Breakfast nooks. Protected on the north and south by jutting land masses, the coast here is sunny when the rest of the earth disappears in fog. Ten miles further north is **Point Arena**, with its lighthouse dominating the nearby bluff. It is accessible and can be climbed. (Open 11am-2:30pm daily, admission $1.00).

Mendocino, the muted jewel of this coast, began with the inauspicious name of Meiggsville. In the 19th century Harry Meiggs came seeking a wrecked cargo of Chinese silk. He ended up founding the area's first sawmill. Although Meiggs headed on to build a rail system through the Andes, the logging industry remained and prospered. Meiggsville became Mendocino, a logger's town of saloons, hotels and brothels all built in the gabled and turreted style of an old New England village. Today it appears much the same, minus the brothels.

CALIFORNIA

It is a quiet isolated village of artists, artisans, fishermen and small tourist oriented shops, but it keeps its dignity and charm.

The stark headland cliffs, just beyond town, which form Mendocino Headlands State Park are breathtaking. A walk along the cliffs on a foggy day, followed by a soak in one of the local hot tub establishments, and a drink in a wood-paneled bar, makes for a beautiful day.

The **Visitor Center for Mendocino Headlands State Park**, at the Ford House on Main st., provides maps and information. (Open Thurs.-Fri. noon-5:30pm, Sat.-Sun. 10am-5:30pm. Tel. 937-5397.)

The **Mendocino Art Center** is the town's cultural and artistic center. (45200 Little Lake st. Open daily 10am-5pm. Tel. 937-5818.) The influx of artists and the educational programs give the town a cosmopolitan touch. The center's gallery is open all week, and there is a Sunday afternoon concert series.

For the kind of tiny town resort it is, Mendocino's food and lodging are reasonably priced, and most things here are done with care and quality.

Russian Gulch State Park lies just north of Mendocino, with its carved and pockmarked headland. It is a pleasant hike up Russian Gulch Creek to the waterfall. Further to the north, **Van Damme State Park** is known for its pygmy forest of waist high conifers. The trees are stunted by poor soil but manage to hang on. (Admission $2 per day.)

Fort Bragg is a lumbertown of about 5000, and a dirty industrial smudge it is, contrasted with the immense greenery around it, but it has reliable, reasonably priced standard motels, as well as a few nice B&B lodges. Fort Bragg and Eureka have plenty of cheap down-home eateries, as do some of the smaller mill towns along the coastal route. On North Harbor dr. several seafood restaurants offer reasonably priced delicious meals, serving the morning's catch hauled to Noyo Harbor by the local fleet.

South of Fort Bragg, the **Mendocino Coast Botanical Garden** encompasses 14 acres of shady glades in dazzling color. (18220 Route 1 by Route 20. Open daily 8am-5:30pm. Tel. 964-4352.) Route 20 itself provides a scenic and direct connection between the coast road and 101, Fort Bragg and Willits. There's hardly a town to be seen, only endlessly stretching forests, with some camping spots. Here, the logging trucks on the road may determine your speed on the narrow winding road.

An interesting option is to take the Skunk Train (so named for the smell of the early engines), along a 100-year old rail route, hewn through the mountains to haul lumber. An open-air car allows you to take in the wind and scenery. The 7-hour round trip from Fort Bragg includes an hour stop in Willits. A shorter ride chugs to the old logging town of Northspur. (Fare for the full trip is $12, and $6 for ages 5-11. The depot is on Laurel, south of Main st. Tel. 964-6371.)

CALIFORNIA

Redwood Country

I see that you're a logger, and not just a common bum, 'cause nobody but a logger stirs his coffee with his thumb.

American Folk Song

North of Fort Bragg, Route 1 veers inland at Rockport and joins Route 101 at Legget. North of Legget along the highway begin the parks of towering redwoods.

Today's redwood stands comprise less than 10% of the vast acreage of these trees that once thrived on the California coast. Of those surviving, slightly more than 50% are protected, and the greatest concentration of these trees, including some of the tallest, grow along this section of the coast. They are of tremendous girth, towering well over 300 feet (the length of an American football field), and sometimes grow so closely together that their hefty trunks appear to form a solid wall. Here the world is immersed in shade, fog, and lush luminous greenery. In some areas the line between the protected forest and the shorn earth is stark and clear, and the scarred, denuded land extends literally to the edge of protected groves.

Coming from the south, **Richardson Grove State Park**, (Tel. 247-3318), is the first redwood park, about eight miles south of Garberville. One of the smaller redwood parks, it nevertheless has some stunning groves. It is very popular, and its three campgrounds are often full in the summer. The interpretive center has regular ranger programs and guided hikes.

North of Garberville is the **Humboldt Redwoods State Park**. The largest redwood park in the region, it links together several separate groves, and contains the famous **Avenue of the Giants**, along which most of the park's visitors pass. From the south, the route begins about six miles north of Garberville. This 33-mile stretch of road parallels Route 101 and the south fork of the Eel River. It passes through lush and misty pockets carpeted with ferns and moss, while the endless walls of redwoods on either side cast everything in deep, cool shadow. **Rockefeller** and **Founder's Grove** are the best known groves. They encompass some of the tallest of the redwoods, and there is a pleasant nature trail at Founder's Grove. The Visitor Center explains the natural history of these groves, and schedules campfire programs and guided hikes from July to Labor Day. For information on park activities, call Tel. 946-2311.

Garberville itself is home to a string of bars, standard motels and the elegant and expensive *Benbow Inn*, which in its heyday gave shelter to such luminaries as Herbert Hoover and Spencer Tracy.

Garberville is also the reputed center for the local marijuana industry. This is no small honor, for marijuana has become one of California's biggest cash crops, though the travel brochures don't boast of this. These coastal hills and valleys form the center of the high country.

In the 60s and 70s, when thousands of young emigrants from the urban mainstream headed for the hills seeking a simpler, home-spun way of life,

Awed by nature

they brought their smoking habits with them. Garden plots of home-grown crops turned into a cottage industry, and sophisticated techniques and experimentation improved the quality and potency. Markets developed in the cities, especially as the American government squeezed or threatened to squeeze the Mexican sources. In the isolated hills and valleys marijuana fields proliferated. Local authorities even distributed instructions for the hiker who stumbled upon a marijuana plot during a stroll. They launched raids and employed helicopters and advanced infrared spotting techniques. Some of the local growers, who have been transformed from rebels into hip entrepreneurs, guard their investments with armed sentries and guard dogs.

Parallel to the stretch of redwood parks, the coast extends toward **Cape Mendocino**. No roads run along the length of this rough coastline, but various inland roads reach the coast. The towns in this region, which is known as **"The Lost Coast"**, were once thriving fishing, lumber and mining communities, but were bypassed by the port at Eureka and the layout of the highways.

CALIFORNIA

From South Fork on Route 101, take Mattele rd. west toward **Petrolia**, for a worthwhile excursion. The area is not frequented by crowds, and the beauty is pristine and primitive. The road skirts the **Kings Range National Conservation Area** (primitive campgrounds are available, with no registration needed), then passes through Petrolia, and later hugs the headlands. There are stretches of black beaches here, where one can enjoy the silence and solitude. Further along is the little doll-house town of **Ferndale**. The restaurants here are reasonably priced, the shops unusual, and the home-made candies delicious. The **Ferndale Museum** at Shaw and 3rd gives a vivid glimpse of north coast history. (Open May-Oct., Wed.-Sat. noon-4pm; Oct-May, same hours, but closed Tues. Tel. 786-4466.)

Eureka, on Humboldt Bay, is a typical lumbertown: from its trucks to its smokestacks to the lumberjack breakfast specials. The industrial rumbling and dirt contrasts sharply with the rambling and intricate old Victorian buildings which bear witness to the old lumber kingdoms.

The prime example of this style from an opulent past is the **Carson Mansion** at 2nd and M st., near the refurbished business district. Nearby is the **Clarke Museum** with its collections from local Indian and pioneer culture, and an exquisite marble exterior. (240 East st. Open Tues.-Sat. 10am-4pm. Tel. 443-1947.)

Fort Humbold sits on a hill, facing over the bay. The museum and logging exhibits give some feel for the rough and simple lifestyle of a typical 'jack. (3431 Fort ave. off Route 101. Open daily 9am-6pm, Admission free. Tel. 433-4588, or Tel. 433-7952.)

Arcata, 10 miles to the north, houses **Humboldt State University**, and has a few fancy cafes and restaurants. The university's **marine laboratory**, at Land's End, in the fishing village of **Trinity**, hosts self-guided tours among the aquariums which display local and rare anemones, mollusks, crustaceans and fish. (Open Mon.-Fri. 8am-5pm, Sat.-Sun. noon-5pm during the school year. Admission free. Tel. 677-3671.)

If you are planning to enter the Arcata-to-Ferndale annual Kinetic Sculpture Race in April, remember that all entries must be amphibious and human-powered.

The **Redwood National Park** merges with three state parks – Jedediah Smith, Prairie Creek and Del Norte – to form a contiguous 30-mile strip of protected redwood land, between Crick and Crescent City. In most areas the park parallels Route 101 on both sides of the road, and the drive through is beautiful in itself. The parks include a shoreline of beautiful duned beaches, rocky coves and bluffs. There are pull-offs and parking areas which afford access to easy strolls and various groves. The **Tall-Tree** grove can be reached by an 8-mile hike or by shuttlebus in the summer. Sections of the park clearly show how real and immediate the threat to the redwoods is; the earth has been stripped right up to the park border.

CALIFORNIA

The trails in the park make good day trips or single overnighters, but are not so suitable for extensive backpacking. There are nature trails at the Lady Bird Johnson Grove and Lagoon Creek, and one near the Prairie Creek Headquarters for both sighted and blind people. Prairie Creek, closer to the ocean than some of the other parks, is especially luxuriant in ferns, lichens, moss and other plant cover. In **Jedediah Smith**, canoes and organized kayak trips glide along the Smith River in summer.

The **National Park Headquarters** in Crescent City provides information for the state parks as well as the national park. (2nd and K sts. Open weekdays 8am-5pm, and until 7pm in the summer. Tel. 464-6101.) The **Prairie Creek Headquarters** on Route 101 in Crick has exhibits and information. (Open daily 8am-5pm, until 8pm in summer. Tel. 488-2171.)

Accommodations
The Mendocino area contains many B&Bs, some built in a distinctly New England style. Prices range from moderate to expensive, and facilities from rustic to luxurious. This is really the land of B&Bs. They fit in perfectly with the tone of the countryside, whereas regular motels spoil the country atmosphere.

There are some motels around, however. They can be found in Fort Bragg and in Eureka as well. In the Eureka area, the average motel price is lower than in more southern parts, starting from $16-$20.

Mendocino Inns: Tel. 961-0140. Central referral service for several Mendocino inns.

Mendocino Hotel & Garden Cottages: 45080 Main st., Mendocino, Tel. 937-0511, or Tel. 800-352-6686. A well-known hotel in a beautiful setting, with rooms and cottages ranging from $38 to $200, singles and doubles.

Benbow Inn: 2675 Benbow rd., just south of Garberville. Tel. 923-2124. Has remained a pocket of rustic elegance for many years. Expensive, but it may be just right for a special occasion.

Camping
From the Mendocino area north to the Oregon border, state parks with camping facilities are plentiful along the beaches and in the region of the major redwood groves. Many have drive-in campgrounds, while others have more primitive walk-in campgrounds, and campgrounds primarily for hikers and cyclists.

In the Mendocino area, Russian Gulch State Park (Tel. 937-5804) is particularly beautiful. MacKerricher State Park, three miles north of Fort Bragg, is popular. (Tel. 964-9112 or .Tel. 937-5804). State parks in the vicinity of Avenue of the Giants tend to fill quickly.

For State park information in the Mendocino/Fort Bragg region, call Tel. 937-5804. For state park camping information in the Redwood National Park area, call the office in Orick: Tel. 488-2171.

CALIFORNIA

A youth hostel run by the AYH is located in Arcata: *The Arcata Crew House Hostel*, 1390 I st. Tel. 822-9995.

Food

Brannon's Whale Watch: 45040 Main st. Entered through an old whale-watching tower, this spot is popular for lunch and breakfast. The upstairs view will encourage you to linger over another cup of coffee.

The Cheese Shop: Little Lake and Lansing, Mendocino. The atmosphere many be rural but the selection is fit for a gourmet, with everything needed for a picnic on the headlands.

Seagull Inn Cellar Bar: Lansing and Ukiah st., Mendocino. The beautiful bar is actually upstairs. Locals and visitors drink and listen to the live music.

Cap'n Flint's: 32250 North Harbor dr., Noyo Harbor (Fort Bragg). A popular local seafood resturant. Reasonably priced.

Samoa Cookhouse: 445 West Washington st., Eureka. This was a genuine lumbercamp cookhouse. The dinners would fill even Paul Bunyan.

Useful Addresses And Phone Numbers:

Chambers of Commerce:
Fort Bragg: 332 N. Main st., Tel. 964-3153.
Ukiah: (serving Mendocino as well) 495 E. Perkins st., Tel. 462-4705.
Eureka Visitor Bureau: 121 F st., Tel. 443-5097.

Mendocino Transit Authority: 241 Plant rd., Ukiah. Tel. 462-1422.
Greyhound:
Ukiah: 7370 S. State st., Tel. 462-3682.
Fort Bragg: 140 E. Laurel, Tel. 964-0877.
Eureka: 1603 4th st., Tel. 442-0370.

State Parks:
Mendocino/Fort Bragg area: Tel. 937-5804.
Redwood National Park area: Tel. 488-2171.

Redwood National Park Headquarters: 2nd & K st., Crescent City. Tel. 464-6101.

CALIFORNIA

San Joaquin Valley

California is a Garden of Eden,
It's a Paradise to live in or see,
But believe it or not, you won't find it so hot
If you ain't got the Do Re Mi

Woody Guthrie

The San Joaquin Valley is a great, elongated, flat expanse of farmland and prairie running north-south through the center of the state. It merges with the Sacramento Valley in the north to form one long strip of fertile farmland. Far more compact than the sprawling grainfields of the American Midwest, and fed by the waters of the Sierras, this rich valley produces one-sixth of America's agricultural produce.

This is the state's heartland, but it is the place that everyone passes through and no one lingers in. Motorists between San Francisco and Los Angeles race along Interstate 5 at the western rim to avoid the slower coastal routes.

I-80 leads through the valley towards the ski slopes, resorts and casinos of Tahoe and Reno. Government workers enter and leave Sacramento through it, and hikers use its eastern roads to penetrate the Sierras.

This seemingly pastoral valley has witnessed some of California's most dramatic social struggles. In this valley the railroads, with their vast land holdings, were pitted against the farmers and ranchers at the turn of the century. Through the writings of John Steinbeck, notably in *The Grapes of Wrath*, the entire American nation learned of the plight of the "Oakies", the Dust Bowl refugees from the great plains who, during the 1930s, crossed the desert and over the California hills by the thousands, seeking work, sustenance and land, only to be held back by the controlling interests and their hired gangs.

The racial biases of many Californians against Chinese, Japanese, Mexican and Philippino farmworkers were highlighted in the central valley. They were exploited, paid sub-standard wages and lived in appalling living conditions. They were also accused of stealing American jobs and introducing strange foreign customs.

Even today, farm labor imported from Mexico – cheap, exploited and often illegal – has become a highly-charged issue. Immigrants from more distant places, such as Portugal and Southeast Asia, have also settled here. Some 40-50,000 Laotian Hmong are gaining a foothold in both farming and town occupations. These immigrants will eventually bring major changes to the tight traditional social fabric here.

CALIFORNIA

The agricultural nature of the land itself is facing great challenges. High-tech industries are moving in, attracted by the research centers at Davis and the expanding urban centers of Sacramento, Fresno and Bakersfield. Sacramento, once viewed as an absurd site for the State Capital, is developing its own urban outskirts towards the Sierra foothills, and toward the west, where suburban development is already spilling over from the Bay Area, as housing costs skyrocket there. An increasing number of farm towns face the question of whether to retain their rural character, or to become amorphous commuter towns.

Urban expansion would sacrifice thousands of acres of prime farmland, at a time when California agriculture is already feeling the recession that has hit American agriculture in general. The valley holds a sixth of all the irrigated cropland in the U.S., but in the last 5 years the state's agricultural exports have shrunk by a third, and smaller countries are taking over the leadership from California in the marketing of certain crops. Not since the Great Depression have there been so many farm sales and mortgage foreclosures. When the banks (the Bank of America recently foreclosed on a huge amount of central valley farm acreage) resell the land, the speculators, developers, huge combines and foreign investors have a chance to move in and remove it from farm production.

The casual traveler, however, who finds the time to leave the freeways to follow the flat grid of backroads, will find that this is still the traditional countryside. Even a short detour may bring some pleasant surprises. Here you'll find old brick railroad stations (not Disneyland props), and diners where you'll discover some home-fried bargains (you might also end up with plain grease, but that's part of the game). Here you'll pass farm boys in their trucker caps driving tractors on the road, waitresses with bee-hive hairdos and country drawls, and billboards advertising cattle feed or urging repentance. This is the land of county fairs and barbecues, 4-H clubs and local rodeos. Bullfights are held at Escalon, on Route 120, south of Stockton (along one route to Yosemite).

The valley is steeped in the sounds and smells of farm production, every season with its particular signs. During winter, it's the fermenting residue of beet processing, and the gins and ragged white debris of cotton-picking; in spring there is the successive blossoming of almond, cherry, peach and plum trees; and the autumn air fills with the pungent sweetness of the grape harvest. Then there is the thick odor of the peat land, the smell of onions and fertilizer, the gold of endless fields of grain and the dairy cattle grazing in the low eastern hills.

How to get there

Bakersfield, Fresno, Merced, Modesto, Stockton and Sacramento (the main towns and cities of the valley) are connected by the 99 Freeway, which runs north-south along the eastern fringe. I-5 parallels Route 99, but along the western rim. It continues north beyond Sacramento, into the narrowing Sacramento Valley and climbs into the Shasta range. The valley cities

CALIFORNIA

Felled giant

often serve as stopovers en route to the Sierras. Greyhound, Trailways and Amtrak link the main cities.

Bakersfield

Near the southern point of the valley, **Bakersfield** is separated from the L.A. metropolis by the bare and rocky Tehachapi range and its winding Grapevine pass. Bakersfield has its own countrified sprawl, with gas stations and fast-food stands spreading towards the flat horizon. Recreation opportunities lie to the east, along Route 178. **Sequoia National Forest** covers the southern extremity of the Sierras, south of Sequoia National Park. Through this area the churning, twisting Kern River offers whitewater rafting. Lake Isabella, on the Kern, is the recreation center in the area. There is abundant free camping in the National Forest.

Route 178 continues east past Lake Isabella and provides a magnificent, if leisurely, route for crossing the Sierras. It climbs to well over 5000 feet at Walker Pass, and then drops along the steep eastern slope to the Owens valley beyond.

Along Highway 99 there are numerous motels, done in contemporary egg-carton, and ranging from cheap (under $25) to overpriced. Unless you can be lulled to sleep by the roar of trucks at midnight, check the room's noise level first if you are pulling off the highway for a snooze.

CALIFORNIA

Visalia

North of Bakersfield, **Visalia** is the starting or finishing point for trips into Sequoia National Park, especially the southern part which includes the backpacking paradise of Mineral King. The park lies about an hour away. The road heading east from town has a few cheap motels. You will find camping spots in the vicinity of Lake Kaweah, before you get to the national park itself. Groceries are cheaper here than in the park. Visalia is on the main chain of train and bus stops (though the Amtrak station is in adjacent Hanford), but transit to Sequoia is abysmal to non-existent.

If, after a week of eating powdered eggs and oatmeal in the back country, you crave a taste of decadence, head for *Mearle's Drive-in*, on Route 63 between Vesalia and Tulare. The huge blinking milkshake on the roof will be your beacon. On Friday night cars and pick-ups surround the place, which is filled with old couples out on the town, farm families, and young bucks with squeaky-clean dates. In the age of designer ice cream cones, this throwback sells delicious old-fashioned cones for 50-85 cents. *Pita Mania*, at 225 Main at Eccina, serves huge lunches for $3.

Fresno

Fresno is the financial center of the San Joaquin Valley, as well as the junction for several routes into the Sierras. Route 41 heads to Yosemite, Route 180 goes south-east to Sequoia/Kings Canyon, and Route 168 winds east into the Sierra National Forest. Amtrak and the two major bus companies serve the city.

Fresno has a rich ethnic fabric. Its well-settled Armenian population produced the great writer William Saroyan. Chinese, Japanese, Basque and Chicano communities have moved in, and the city is now the center for the waves of Hmong Laotians who have moved into the valley.

The old Chinatown, along Kern st by G, F and E sts., is a good place for Mexican, Japanese and other ethnic food. The farmer's market, on Divisadero st. at Route 41 has some fine local produce, as does the outdoor market held at the corner of Merced and N sts. on Tuesday, Thursday and Saturday from 7am-3pm.

You'll probably only be passing through Fresno, but you might stop at the **Underground Gardens**. (5021 W. Shaw. Open June 15 Sept. 6, 10am-4pm. Off-season, during weekends and holidays. Admission $4. Tel. 275-3729.) This maze of 65 rooms, grottos and gardens was carved out of solid rock by an early resident.

The **Hmong Craft Shop**, a non-profit shop, displays some exquisite quilts, wall hangings and other pieces made by some 300 Laotian craftswomen. (842 N. Fulton. Open Tues-Fri. 10am-4pm, Sat. 10am-2pm. Tel. 237-7106.)

The **Discovery Center** is a hands-on science museum and outdoor center with a laser phone among its high-tech toys. (1944 N. Winery. Open Tues.-Fri. 9:30am-5pm. Tel. 251-5531. Admission.)

CALIFORNIA

Merced

Merced offers the most direct access to Yosemite Park, via Route 140. It is served by Amtrak and the major bus companies. The Yosemite Transportation System operates from the Greyhound station and runs a daily bus to Yosemite Valley for $13 each way. California Tours also offers tours to Yosemite. Tel. 383-1563.

Merced has a number of reasonable, standard motels on Motel Drive, parallel to Route 99. Stock up on groceries for the mountains at the plentiful roadside stands.

Important Addresses And Phone Numbers
Bakersfield
Chamber of Commerce: 1000 Truxtan, 8:30am-5pm. Tel.327-4421
Kern City Board of Trade: 2101 Oak st., 8am-5pm. Tel. 861-2367: Lots of information.
US Forest Service, Greenhorn District: 800 Truxtan, Rm 322, 8am-5pm. Tel. 861-4212. Details on camping and hiking in the Sierra National Forest.
Amtrak: 15th & Ist. Tel. 327-7863.
Greyhound: 1820 18th st. Tel. 327-7371. Service to L.A. and valley cities.
Trailways: 1821 18th st. Tel. 327-7961.
Golden Empire Transit: Tel. 324-9874: City-wide system.

Visalia
Area Code: 209.
Convention and Visitors Bureau: 720 W. Mineral King, Visalia 93291. Tel. 734-5876: This office will help you plan your visit to Sequoia and Kings Canyon National Parks, especially what it calls a "48 Hour Mini Vacation". Some discount coupons are included.
Greyhound: 211 S. Court st, Tel. 734-3507.
Amtrak (Hanford): Tel. 800-872-7245.

Fresno
Area Code: 200.
Chamber of Commerce: 2331 Fresno st. Mon.-Fri. 8:30am-5pm. Tel. 233-4651.
Greyhound: 1033 Broadway. Mon.-Fri. 6am-1pm, Sat.-Sun. 24 hours. Tel. 268-9461.
Trailways: 1333 Broadway. Tel. 237-7181.
Amtrak, Tulare & Q. Tel. 252-8253.

Merced
Merced County Chamber of Commerce: 732 W. 18th st. Mon.-Thurs. 9am-5pm, Fri. 9am-4pm. Tel. 722-3864.
City Chamber of Commerce: 3197 Main st. Mon.-Fri. 9am-5pm. Tel.384-3333.
Greyhound: 725 Main. Mon.-Fri. 7:30am-9:30pm. Tel. 722-2121.
Trailways: 147 W. 16th st. Tel. 722-0331 or Tel. 722-3409.
Amtrak: K&W, 24th st. Tel. 722-6862.

CALIFORNIA

Merced Transit System: 72 West Ave. 50 cent fare. Tel. 723-4237.
Merced Area Regional Transit System: 50 cent fares. Picks up and delivers passengers. Tel. 383-1111.

Sacramento

The city of Sacramento boomed during the gold rush and became the state capital. It became the terminus for wagon trains, stagecoaches, steam paddlers, the Pony Express, the telegraph lines and, finally, the country's first transcontinental railroad. It was in Sacramento that the scheme for the railroad was born, among a group of ambitious and imaginative businessmen, namely Leland Standford, Mark Hopkins, Collis P. Huntington and Charles Crocker, who were destined to play a major role in the shaping of the young state's growth and economy. Sacramento became a political center and the center for the state government's bureaucracy.

Sacramento is situated on a main route connecting San Francisco to points lying east, and is also in the middle of a fertile agricultural valley, thereby making it a center for produce distribution.

Although in the past the city was not exactly famous for its dynamism or culture, lately it has been stirring itself. The capitol was renovated, the surrounding commercial area is being overhauled. A new cultural life is developing. Sacramento now has lively music and art scenes. There are numerous art galleries, featuring some excellent local artists, and there are clubs and bars scattered around the downtown area playing jazz and other music.

Be aware that the heat and humidity in summer are often almost unbearable.

How to get there

Sacramento continues its role as a major intersection and distribution point. Two major interstate highways cross here. I-80 runs from San Francisco to the east coast, and I-5 runs from Mexico to Washington State. I-99, skirting the eastern edge of the San Joaquin Valley, also reaches here.

Sacramento's **Metro Airport** serves national as well as regional and state carriers. Sacramento is also a junction for major **Amtrak** lines, with trains running west to San Francisco, east over the Sierras, north to Seattle, and south through the length of the San Joaquin Valley. **Greyhound** and **Trailways** have regular and extensive service to Sacramento.

Transportation

It is easy to maneuver through the city by car, thanks to the logical grid of lettered and numbered streets. Several bus lines operate locally. Regional Transit buses serve most of the Sacramento area and its suburban satellites. The **Yolobus** line connects downtown, Old Sacramento and

CALIFORNIA

SACRAMENTO CITY CENTER

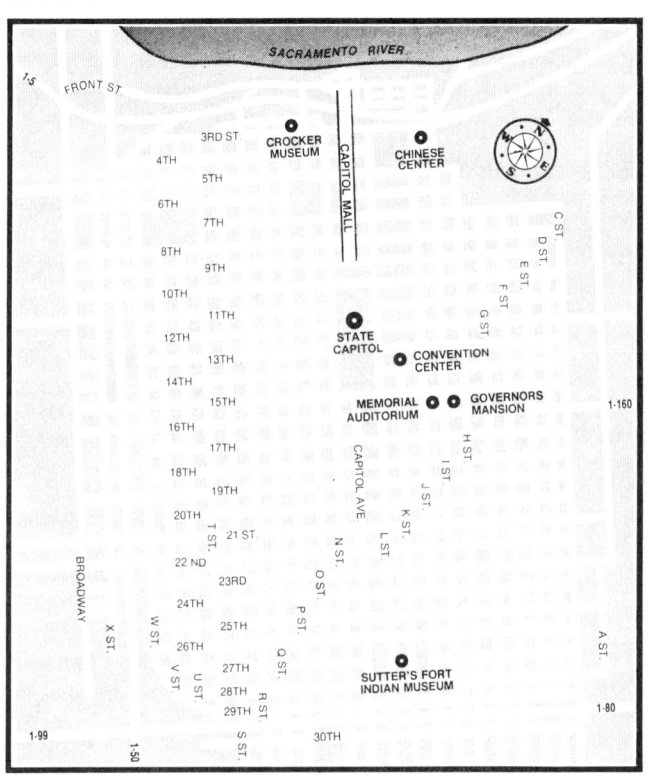

West Sacramento, as well as Davis and other surrounding towns. Commuter Bus Lines covers the city. A downtown tram line, using renovated trolley cars travels along the K Street Mall between the Convention Center and Old Sacramento. The schedule is slightly reduced on weekends. Sacramento is pleasant for cycling, with its many parks, bicycle paths and flat terrain.

The local **Convention and Visitors Bureau** distributes thick glossy magazines and directories listing everything you might want to do in Sacramento. A special Discover Sacramento Switchboard offers updates on art, entertainment and recreation activities. In addition, Sacramento is a fine place to dig out all sorts of unusual information, by virtue of its being the center of the state's considerable bureaucracy. The state offices offer a tremendous range of resources, libraries and public information offices. The **California Office of Tourism** is the best one-stop information source

CALIFORNIA

for the visitor. Every region in the state is covered. In addition to scanning the racks of tourist-oriented brochures, ask to see the office's publication list, for pamphlets and information sheets on a wide range of subjects concerning this multi-faceted state.

The main points of interest (with a couple of exceptions), cluster around two areas: the State Capitol, and Old Sacramento.

Old Sacramento

Old Sacramento's six blocks combine authentic historical reconstruction with predictable tourist shops. 120 years ago this booming new city on the bank of the Sacramento River was the western hub of the telegraph, stagecoach, Pony Express and the railroad. Old Sacramento is situated on Front st. near the river front, just west of the Capitol. The Visitor Information Center provides pamphlets for a self-guided walking tour that passes an array of old stores, warehouses, historical plaques, etc. Free walking tours are conducted on weekends, departing from the passenger depot near the California State Railroad Museum, at 10:30am and 1:30pm. The **California State Railroad Museum** is more than just a collection of locomotives. (I st. between Front and Second st. Open 10am-6pm. $3 admission, $1 children. Tel. 445-4209.) It illustrates how the railroads broke ground across the rugged countryside and revolutionized the country. Buster Keaton's brilliant and hilarious film *The General* is shown here. Museum admission includes the Central Pacific Passenger Depot, a reconstruction of the original depot that was once a bustling, thriving center. Steam train rides are available during the summer months from the depot to Miller Park.

Next to the Railroad Museum is the **Huntington-Hopkins Hardware Store**, where the dream of a transcontinental railroad was discussed and launched. The second floor is the recreation of the Central Pacific's boardroom and library. (Open 10am-5pm. Admission free. Tel. 445-4209.)

The Old Eagle Theater, constructed as a theater in 1849, screens a 15-minute film depicting the city's past. $2 for adults, $1.25 for children. Tel. 446-6761.

Old Sacramento has become the unofficial center for a variety of Sacramento celebrations, such as Admission Day festivities in September, the Dixieland Jazz Festival on Memorial Day, and the Blues Festival in September. On these occasions, the streets and clubs spill over with crowds and music.

The Capitol Park is green and beautiful and the **Capitol** itself has been renovated. The adjacent downtown area is also in the midst of a facelift. The Capitol renovations include beautiful marble mosaic floors and crystal chandeliers, a touch of turn-of-the-century grandeur. The museum has exhibits on past governors, and a film details the restoration. (Open daily at 9am, guided tours available. Tel. 324-0333.) Near the Capitol is the majestic **Crocker Museum**. (216 O st. Open Tues. 2-10pm, Wed.-Sun. 10am-5pm. Admission $1. Tel. 446-4677.) The first art museum in the west, the building is a beautiful work in itself. The museum was founded by the railroad

CALIFORNIA

tycoon Edwin Bryant Crocker. He went on an art-buying spree to Europe with his wife and picked up some 18th and 19th century masterpieces that form the basis of the museum collection. He also commissioned works by American artists. The collection today includes contemporary pieces and the work of California artists.

An annual festival of the arts is held in May in Crocker Park, across from the museum (Tel. 443-3395).

California's governors no longer hang their hats in the **Governor's Mansion**, among the oriental carpets, Italian marble fireplaces and French mirrors. The 15-room Victorian mansion is open to the public. (16th and H sts. Open daily 10am-5pm. Adults $1, children 50 cents. Tel. 445-4209.) Further north on 16th st., is the **California Almond Growers Visitor Center**. (1701 C st. Tel. 446-8439.) Almonds are a major California food export, and here you will learn everything you've ever wanted to know about them. Films, exhibits, and guided tours at specific times.

Sutters' Fort, the original settlement of Sacramento, was established in 1839, near the Sacramento River. Its history is presented through a self-guided audio tour. Behind the fort is the **State Indian Museum**. (Open daily, 10am-5pm. Adults $1, children 50 cents. Tel. 445-4209.)

As if being the state capital wasn't enough, Sacramento claims the title of **"Camellia Capital of the World"**, and salutes the flowering shrub in March with two weeks of parades, exhibits, bicycle races, a beauty queen contest and the Camellia Ball.

Accommodations

The two major freeways that pass through Sacramento are lined with hotels and motels. Most major chains are represented.

In the heart of downtown, are some old, rather run-down and sleazy hotels. Along 16th st., in the area of the Governor's Mansion, a number of motels are clustered, ranging widely in price and facilities. In West Sacramento there are more motels, slightly lower in price, about half a mile from Old Sacramento. For a listing of West Sacramento lodgings, call the West Sacramento Hotel/Motel Association. Tel. 372-5378, or toll-free in-state, Tel. 1-800-962-9800.

The most basic, standard motels here start at about $22. The hotel tax is quite steep here, about 10%.

There are few camping facilities in the immediate area. On Route 50 to the east, towards Placerville, is the Folsom Lake State Park with campgrounds, as well as recreational activities centered around the lake (Tel. 371-6771).

Food

Annabelle's: On J st. just east of 2nd st., in Old Sacramento. The great lunch buffet here includes all you can eat of spaghetti, lasagna and a salad bar, for $2.97, 11am-4pm.

CALIFORNIA

Los Padres : J st. near Front. A bit gaudy and a bit crowded, but the decor is unusual and the portions large, and not too overpriced for a tourist haunt.

Whistle Stop: On Front st. near L st. A place in Old Sacramento where the breakfasts are reasonable.

Zelda's Original Gourmet Pizza: 1415 21st st. Original or not, it is justifiably popular for its deep-dish pizza.

El Charro: 2019 Q st. Delicious Mexican food.

Useful Addresses And Phone Numbers
Sacramento Convention & Visitors Bureau: 1311 I st. Weekdays 8am-5pm. Tel. 442-5542.
Old Sacramento Visitors Center: 130 J st. Mon.-Sat. 10am-5pm. Tel. 443-7815.
California Office of Tourism: 1121 L st., Suite 103. Tel. 322-1396.
Discover Sacramento Hotline: Tel. 449-5566. 24 hours.
Sacramento Metro Airport: Tel. 929-5411.
Airported Van Lines: Tel. 444-2222. Transportation between the airport and downtown.
Capitol City Coop: Tel. 371-8151. Buses to San Francisco Airport.
Amtrak: 4th and I st. Tel. 444-9131.
Greyhound: 1107 L st. Tel. 444-6800. At Capitol Park.
Trailways: 1129 I st. Tel. 443-2044.
Commuter Bus Lines: Tel. 321-BUSS.
Yolo Bus-Commuter Lines: Tel. 756-BUSS.
Regional Transit: Tel. 444-2877.
Davis Medical Center Operator: Tel. 453-2011; Emergency Dept. Tel. 453-3790.
Psychiatric Emergency: Tel. 454-5646.
Suicide Prevention: Tel. 441-1135.

Davis

Just west of Sacramento on Route 80 is the **Davis Campus of the University of California**. Established as an agricultural school, it became a general campus in 1959, but is one of the leading agricultural research centers in the world, in such disciplines as agronomy, nutrition, plant pathology, wine-making and veterinary medicine.

The campus has about 20,000 students and it seems as if each one has at least three bicycles. The campus and adjacent student-oriented community form a separate entity, a sort of pastoral college town.

Along Putah Creek at the southern edge of campus there is a lush, shady arboretum with a bicycle path, a redwood grove and picnic grounds. A visit to the campus could include the **Gorman Museum of Native American**

CALIFORNIA

Art in the Tecumseh Center. The **Silo**, a "modern" dairy barn in 1914, which now houses offices and a snack bar, is the student crafts center. If you're into weeds, the botany department in Robbins Hall has one of the largest weed collections in the world. If you prefer golf, the department of horticulture (near the faculty club) has a putting-green area for studying grass, on which visitors are welcome to try their skill. The **Memorial Union Building**, center of student life, has a coffee house, pub, book store and other facilities.

Across from the Union is the terminal for UNITRANS, a student-owned and operated bus system, featuring a fleet of authentic London double-decker buses, which runs through most of the Davis area during the school year, and connects with the regional transit system running to Sacramento.

Important Addresses And Phone Numbers
Memorial Union Information Desk: Tel. 752-2222.
Information Services: 129 Mark Hall. Tel. 752-0539. For maps for self-guided tours.
Campus Events and Information Office: 4th floor, Memorial Union. Tel. 752-1920.

GOLD PROSPECTOR
"Forty-niner" hoping for a flash in the pan.

CALIFORNIA

Gold Country

Steamers and sailing-vessels came for some time as overcrowded with passengers as the passengers' brains were overcrowded with illusions.

Josiah Royce, California historian

In 1848, there were about 14,000 people in California. By 1852, the population reached about 200,000. Behind those seemingly dry numbers lay the convolutions and upheavals of the **California Gold Rush**.

When James Marshall discovered gold at Sutter's Mill, he and Sutter tried to keep the news quiet at first, but by late spring everybody in California was heading for the Sierra foothills. Other settlements were neglected, and soldiers and sailors deserted to work in the mines.

Fantastic stories spread, about fist-sized nuggets in the stream beds, and gold dust on the pathways. "Authentic journals" reported walking through the foothills for three weeks and picking up lumps of gold worth $50,000.

It is true that some of the first searchers had tremendous strokes of luck. The richest sources were tapped first, and fortunes were made that first wild summer of 1848. Some "enterprising" miners used Indians to work the mines while they worked the profits.

By autumn, the news of quick and easy fortunes reached the east. Dreams of a wild, free life in a faraway world lured men from their routines and families. Eager, unskilled youths made easy prey for the swindlers who sniffed fortunes in the pockets of men rather than in pockets of earth.

To reach the "golden land" was no easy venture. Travelers crossed the western frontier by foot, horse or wagon – others circled Cape Horn by steamer, or disembarked at the Isthmus of Panama, and from there went by foot or horse across to the Pacific coast and boarded steamers heading north. Travelers by sea were exposed to tropical humidity, disease and corruption. The Pacific voyage was marked by storms, and the chill fogs of the California coast. Often the navigation charts used were unreliable. Beyond that, however, lay the Golden Gate. The incredible beauty of the land must have been a most welcome sight after the arduous journey: the narrow, hilly peninsula, the immense bay opening up, the city of San Francisco a collection of tents clinging to the hillsides, and ships crowding the wharves.

The miners expected to make their fortunes and then return home. Most never made that fortune. Some left, some stayed and found other jobs. Some wandered from camp to camp. They had no interest in sinking roots and in creating a community. They were concerned only with surviving from

CALIFORNIA

day to day, waiting until they struck their lode. The wages they made were spent on exorbitantly priced goods. A loaf of bread could cost as much as a dollar, a blanket $100. There are many stories of farm boys dragged down into miserable lives of roaming around the drinking and gambling camps.

Enterprising newcomers made greater fortunes supplying the needs of the miners than they could have made mining. Mines required lumber and miners demanded meat. Huge areas of pine forests were felled, and vast numbers of deer, elk, bear and other game were slaughtered. Loads of jerkey and hides were exported from San Francisco. An immigrant tailor made a pair of strong canvas pants for a miner, using metal rivets for the pockets to hold heavy tools. The new style caught on, and today Levis are as universal as Coca Cola.

Foreigners, especially the Chinese, were distrusted as miners, but were exploited as cheap labor. Local Indian tribes were exposed to disease and cruel treatment at the hands of the miners, and many tribes were decimated.

The early miners sifted through stream beds with small pans resembling strainers. It was a lonely and exhausting job. With the advent of sluicing, mining became a major operation, often involving the diversion of rivers and combing of the sediments. The towns, originally ragged clusters of tents which sprang up wherever gold was found, became lines of wooden shacks and cloth houses along muddy streets. Councils were appointed to keep order. Justice for wrong-doers was swiftly decided by makeshift courts; flogging and banishment for some crimes, lynching for more serious ones.

About five hundred of these flimsy, transient mining camps sprang up between 1848 and 1860, first in the deep ravines where the first findings were made, then on the gentler slopes as the search widened. More than half the towns disappeared completely and only a handful became permanent towns. The places still seen in the gold country today give one a glimpse of a world bursting with courage, determination and greed, which transformed California irrevocably.

Gold country runs north and south along the Sierra foothills, from Nevada City in the north to the area of Oakhurst in the south. It is beautiful countryside, with rounded hills and deep gorges with high cliffs. Route 49 is the main route through the towns and sites of the gold country. Gold country is roughly divided into three sections: From Oakhurst to the Sonora-Columbia area in the south; from Columbia to Auburn in the central region; and from Auburn north, encompassing Grass Valley, Nevada City, then Oroville to the northwest and Downieville to the northeast.

Each town is lined with the same remodeled hotels, reconstructed plank sidewalks, and old brick storefronts displaying postcards and chocolate chip cookies rather than dry goods and shovels. Despite the similarity of the towns, the region invites diversion. Following the backroads and small

CALIFORNIA

highways of the gold country affords one an interesting and beautiful, if time consuming, approach to the parks of the Sierras.

Traveling through the gold country is difficult without a car. Travel by Greyhound is possible, but may be time-consuming. Some towns have local bus systems.

I-80 slices through the hills towards Lake Tahoe and Reno, and passes Auburn close to the center of gold country. Route 50, heading east from Sacramento, reaches Placerville, the main center of gold country during the region's hedyday. The road climbs east toward the southern end of Lake Tahoe.

Nevada City

Nevada City has preserved its Victorian architecture and the atmosphere of a real town, with more than one street to stroll through. Somehow, Nevada City has established itself as the hip center of the Mother Lode. Its preserved western appearance provides the setting for movies or ads. San Francisco artists often retreat here. The annual **Music of the Mountains Festival** at the end of June draws big name musicians. Restaurants are diverse, elegant, organic, trendy and expensive. A lively music scene offers everything from folk to blues to classical guitar.

The Chamber of Commerce can provide a self-guided walking tour. Although none of the buildings are particularly interesting in themselves, together they paint a general picture of how a thriving gold rush town must have appeared.

The *National Hotel*, on Broad st., is the oldest continuously-running hotel in the country, as well as a historical landmark. Mark Twain stayed here. The hand painted wallpaper, the old overstuffed furniture, and the polished bannisters give the hotel an authentic feel.

The *Nevada Theater*, just up the street, is the oldest in the U.S., and the place where famous 19th century entertainer Lotta Crabtree made her debut. She grew up in Grass Valley and was taken under the wing of Lola Montez, an early European dance sensation already past her prime. At the age of eight, Lotta was dancing for small local functions. After her debut in Nevada City, she toured the mining towns for years, often in grueling one-night stands, until she finally moved on to San Francisco, then to New York where she earned international fame and made a tremendous fortune.

On Spring street, the **American Victorian Museum**, houses Victorian memorabilia and knickknacks, as well as an excellent radio station (KVMR, 89.5 FM) and a lively bar. The museum also holds events during the famous, turn-of-the-century style 4th of July celebrations.

Food and Accommodation
Nevada City has a number of quaint B&B inns, but you pay for the charm,

CALIFORNIA

with prices ranging from $55 and up. The funky old *National Hotel* is more moderate ($25 and up). There is a saloon with live music downstairs. (Tel. 265-4551.) Motels are found in Grass Valley, and near the highway.

Useful Addresses And Phone Numbers
Area Code: Tel. 916.
Chamber of Commerce: 132 Main St. Tel. 265-2692.
Greyhound: Spring and S. Pine sts. Tel. 272-9091.
Gold Country Stage: Tel. 265-1411.

Around Nevada City
Grass Valley is located on Route 49 just a few miles south of Nevada City. Its **Empire Mine State Historic Park** gives a clear picture of the workings of a major mine. (One and a half miles north of Highway 20, on Empire st. Open daily 9am-6pm until Labor Day, the 9am-5pm until March 31st. Nominal admission. Tel. 273-8522.) This was one of the largest and richest hard rock mines in the Mother Lode, and the first electrified mine. The museum has beautiful gardens and mine buildings and interesting equipment. There are daily tours and audio-visual programs.

Heading north toward Yuba Pass, Route 49 cuts through some rugged country. The town of **Downieville**, hugging both shores of the Yuba River, still preserves the old architecture and narrow winding streets of the early town. This town was once jammed with miners, and holds the dubious distinction of being the only gold rush town where a woman was hanged. Juanita, a Mexican dance hall girl, stabbed a miner, and although she claimed that she had acted in self-defence and was with child, she was hanged from hastily-built gallows.

A turn east at Tyler-Foote Crossing Road will lead to **Malakoff Diggins State Historic Park**. Here, the world's largest hydraulic mine blasted away half a mountain and left behind a huge ugly pit, a monument to human disregard for nature. Nature, however, smoothed over the scars and shaped and polished the jagged cliffs into beautiful formations. Hiking trails abound, and there is a state campground at North Bloomfield, the deserted boom town that is now part of the park. (Tel. 265-2740.)

Auburn

Auburn, on I-80, is the most easily accessible gold town. The town has an upper and lower part. The lower part has been historically preserved as **Old Town**, with restaurants and antique shops. The whole town can be walked in 10 minutes, but a mini-bus, with stops along **Lincoln Avenue**, the main street, connects the two sections. Buses leave every 45 minutes. The Chamber of Commerce provides a free guide to historic buildings.

In Old Town there is a square surrounded by sandwich bars, shops, bars and pizzerias under the gaze of a statue of a giant "forty niner". The smell of Mexican food wafts from two restaurants. *Tio Pepe*, at the end of the

CALIFORNIA

square behind the red fire station, is spacious, with Mexican decor, and is moderately priced. A few doors down from the fire station is the *Cafe Delicais*, which is smaller, simpler, cheaper, and usually packed. The *Hong Kong Restaurant*, 958 Lincoln Way, up the hill from Old Town, is the best deal in town and maybe in all the hills; $3.19 for a Chinese lunch buffet.

Useful Addresses And Phone Numbers
Chamber of Commerce: 1101 High St. Tel. 885-5616.
Placer County Transit: Tel. 885-BUSS.

Georgetown

Off the section of Route 49 between Auburn and Coloma, Highway 193 heads for Georgetown and makes a loop back to the main road. This route is off the beaten track. Some of the scenery is stupendous, along a winding road that dips into deep sharp-cliffed gorges.

Georgetown itself extends for only about two blocks, along one wide street. There are no special sites here. The town, however, in its unadorned simplicity, is authentic and peaceful. The area has many cycling routes and hiking trails, and the nearby American River offers white water rafting. Founded by a group of sailors, Georgetown was situated near one of the richest lodes. By 1853, about $2 million worth of gold was found in the area. When the gold diminished, the town managed to remain stable and even boasted an opera house.

In this tiny place there are two hotels worth mentioning. *The Georgetown Hotel* on Main Street dates back to 1896. Rates range from $35-$55, and each room has a different decor, often with beautiful antique furniture. There are no private baths, but the claw-footed bathtub traveled around Cape Horn, if that's any solace! Downstairs, the bar is a local hangout, with live music at night. (Tel. 916-333-4373.)

Across Main Street and up a block or so is the *American River Inn*, a restored 1853 inn (the original one burnt down and was reconstructed at the turn of the century). The price, $45-$67, includes full breakfast and use of the pool, sauna, and cycles. (Tel. 333-4499.)

Coloma

Coloma, on Route 49 north of Placerville, is the place where James Marshall first found gold. The area was called *Sutter's Mill* then, on the south fork of the American River. By the summer of 1848, 2000 miners were camped on the river banks, and a year later 10,000 were mining here. Coloma was the natural hub of the gold country until the digging center finally shifted away and the town declined.

Today, most of the small town lies within the **Marshall Gold Discovery State Historical Park**. The park includes some old stone buildings, a Chinese store, and a cabin where Marshall lived after he discovered gold. At the river bank is a plaque marking the spot where he supposedly made his first discovery, and nearby stands an exact replica of Sutter's Mill.

CALIFORNIA

Across the road is the small and excellent park museum outlining the history before and after the discovery. (Open daily 10am-5pm. $2 admission. Tel. 622-3470.)

On the hill behind the old town is a tall bronze statue of James Marshall, in a heroic pose. From the museum, you can drive your car to the monument or take a one-mile round-trip hike by way of the Marshall cabin. The town swells with visitors around January 24th, the anniversary of the discovery of gold, when the event is re-enacted.

Placerville

Placerville, at the junction of Routes 45 and 50, replaced Coloma as the center of gold country. It became a stop for covered wagons after the Sierra crossing, a supply center for the mining camps, a staging point for expeditions to the Nevada silver mines, and a station on the Pony Express line. It also became known as Hangtown, after proving to be an efficient lynching center. Those days are vividly recalled by the dummy hanging from the second-floor of a building on Main Street.

Placerville also seems to have inspired early Californian capitalism. Railroad magnates Leland Stanford and Mark Hopkins both started here as small-time merchants. John Studebaker, the auto industrialist, once worked here as a wheelwright, and meat packer Philip Armour worked as a butcher.

Today, Highway 50 runs along a scenic, rugged route to the Sierras, South Lake Tahoe and Nevada, and Placerville provides a pleasant resting spot. There are reasonable and varied restaurants in the small old town center.

The **Gold Bug Park and Mine**, located on Bedford street, just east of Route 49, is a pretty city park with miles of hiking trails and a real mine. There is a beautiful white-water rafting stretch on the South Fork of the American River from Chili Bar near Placerville, west of Folsom Reservoir. One and two-day trips are offered on this stretch of river, by various rafting outlets. A list is available from the Chamber of Commerce.

The Placerville area is fruit growing and wine country. Visitors can stop in on any number of farms along a route mapped out by the local growers' cooperative. It is a nice way to get a look at the countryside outside the towns and tourist services, and to fill yourself with apple pie, apple butter and apple wine. Maps of the apple farms and wineries which are open for visits and tasting are available from the local Chamber of Commerce. In June, there is a professional rodeo and the arrival of the annual Highway 50 wagon train following the route of the old wagon trains from Carson City, over the Sierra Nevada to Placerville.

There are many B&B inns in the area, combining history and old-time Victorian luxury. The Chamber of Commerce has a complete list. There are also reasonable – if nondescript – motels on the outskirts of town. Most campgrounds in the immediate area are private. About seven miles to the

CALIFORNIA

east on Route 50 is the Eldorado National Forest Information Center which can provide a list of nearby campgrounds, some primitive, some more fully equipped, ranging in price from free to $6. Information on camping in the wilderness areas near South Lake Tahoe is also available.

From far and wide, travelers come to *Poor Red's* in El Dorado, famous for its ribs. Several miles south of Placerville, on Main st.

Useful Addresses And Phone Numbers
Area Code: Tel. 916.
Chamber of Commerce: 542 Main st. Tel. 626-2344.
Greyhound: 1750 Broadway. Tel. 626-1010.
El Dorado National Forest Visitor Center: Highway 50, 7 miles east of Placerville.

Calaveras County

Calaveras County, toward the southern end of the gold country, had two tremendous strokes of fortune: it was situated on one of the richest areas of gold deposits, and it was named in Mark Twain's famous story, "The Celebrated Jumping Frog of Calaveras County". The gold has long since diminished, but the second resource is still being mined.

Twain spent some time at the main hotel in **Angel's Camp** listening to the tales of the miners. His name has become associated with almost everything in the town, and frogs have become the town's symbol. They are painted on the sidewalks, and every year a jumping frog contest is held on the 3rd weekend in May, in which the human owners end up hopping around more than the amphibious contestants. (Frogs are available for rent for those who don't bring their own).

At the north end of town is the local historical museum, which is not really worth visiting, but the counter of the museum serves as a Visitor Center where you can obtain a map with a self-guided walking or driving tour of the Angel's Camp area.

Head northeast up Route 4 for some nice surprises. First there is **Moaning Cavern**, near Vallecito. Although it has been hyped up, it is interesting and it really does moan. If stairways bore you, try rappelling down 180 feet by rope (extra fee). Be aware, however, that 13,000 years ago some didn't make it and human bones have been found at the bottom. Continue along Route 4 to **Murphys**, a cute, tree lined, one-street town. At the *Murphys Hotel* you can see the Ulysses S. Grant Presidential Suite, and the room where Mark Twain stayed.

About 16 miles further is **Calaveras Big Trees State Park**, the only spot outside Yosemite or Sequoia National Park where you'll find sequoias. There is a North Grove and a South Grove, the North Grove at the park entrance and the southern about nine miles away. A mile-long trail loops through the northern grove, and a self-guided trail map is available. This

CALIFORNIA

park is very family oriented. The Visitor Center (10am-5pm daily) offers slide shows, nature exhibits, and schedules of guided walks and campfire programs. The campground ($6) comes complete with bears. Reservations needed for most weekends. (P.O. Box 120, Arnold, CA., 95223, or through Ticketron. A $3 advanced reservation fee is attached to camping fee. Tel. 795-2334.)

The town of **San Andreas** was established by Mexicans in 1849, but they were elbowed out by the Americans, and then the Chinese came, reworking the diggings abandoned by their less patient predecessors.

Only a few of the gold rush buildings remain today. There is a beautiful old courthouse, which houses the Chamber of Commerce, a museum with an interesting collection of artifacts, and the local historical society. It is worth walking around here and showing some curiosity about the region; the staff will reward you with warmth and some unusual local legends.

The cemetery on the western outskirts of town has stones bearing some chilling and pithy epitaphs. Black Bart, the notorious stagecoach robber, was caught, tried and convicted in San Andreas, and purportedly slept in the jail behind the courthouse. Black Bart was quite a character. Failing to find gold legally, he worked as a clerk for a stagecoach company and studied the schedules, routes and drivers until the stagelines became easy prey. Meanwhile, he moved to San Francisco with his newly acquired wealth and became a prominent businessman who hobnobbed with the powerful. When his finances declined, he changed outfits and hit another stagecoach, always polite and gentle and leaving behind a few lines of poetry.

Important Addresses And Phone Numbers
Area Code: Tel. 209.
Chamber of Commerce: Old Courthouse Building, 30 N. Main st., San Andreas. Tel. 754-3391.

Southern Mother Lode
Columbia State Historic Park has a strange existence. It is a tourist attraction, a state park, and a replica town of days gone by when people sold sarsaparilla and penny candy, but at the same time a real lived in town complete with courthouse. Even though you know that the guy in the old-fashioned costume does not usually dress like that, and that the blacksmith plys his trade largely for the benefit of tourist, the town is lived in and so well-preserved, that it gives an unmatched feeling for the past. Maps and guides can be obtained at the Visitor Center. (Tel. 532-4301.)

If you want gas, drugstores, cheap stucco motels and other symbols of modernity, then go to Sonora. Further west, off Route 49, is **Jamestown**, an attractive antique looking town with brightly painted two-story frame buildings. Ride the steam-powered trains at the **Railtown 1897 State Historic Park**. (Fifth Ave., off Route 49/108. Tel. 984-3953.)

Useful Addresses And Phone Numbers
Area Code: Tel. 209.
Chamber of Commerce: 158 W. Bradford st., Sonora. Tel. 532-4212.
Tuolumnue County Visitors Bureau: 16 W. Stockton st., Sonora. Tel. 948-INFO.
Greyhound: 260 E. Nonoway, Sonora. Tel. 532-1356.

SALMON
Fish of the family Salmonidae. It has a shiny, scaly skin which is a uniform silver color. Because of its tasty flesh, it is much in demand by man, and by predators such as bears and wolves. The salmon spawns in fresh water, but once it reaches adulthood, it swims to the sea, where it remains for 18–24 months. It completes the cycle by returning to the river from which it came.

CALIFORNIA

Sierra Nevada

Then it seemed to me the Sierra Nevada should be called not the Nevada or the Snowy Range, but the Range of Light. And after ten years spent in the heart of it ...it still seems to me above all others the Range of Light is the most divinely beautiful of all the mountain chains I have ever seen.

John Muir.

The Sierra Nevada, east of the great San Joaquin and Sacramento Valleys, forms a solid granite mass running some four hundred miles from the area of Plumas county in the north to the Tahachapis and the Mojave Desert in the south. So sharply do the eastern and western slopes differ, that it is hard to picture them forming the same system. The range of vegetation, wildlife and landscape in the Sierras is almost incomprehensible. From the east, the hills rise gently from the central valley, through the chaparral and grass covered foothills, the legendary gold country. Along a 60 mile stretch, these gentle slopes rise toward the high country. The high country, the jagged north-south spine of the mountains etched with canyons and meadows, with peaks ranging from 7000 to 15,000 feet high, can be crossed only through a few passes, and has a winter season with up to 20-30 feet of snow and which lasts from November to July. On the east, these peaks drop precipitously. Moist winds from the Pacific bring rain to the western slopes, but the eastern escarpment gets very little rain, and the vegetation is semi desert, blending into the desert itself. The view which faced pioneers more than a century ago, was one of a solid, impenetrable granite wall. Many settlers lost their lives trying to haul their wagons and cattle up these almost impassable inclines. Even today, with super-highways blasted through the granite, and powerful autos, maneuvering along these ridges and passes can be hazardous.

These mountains, with their sharply contrasting environments support a tremendous variety of plant and animal life. Their western slopes provide the only habitat for the largest living organisms on earth, the giant sequoia trees. The ranges just east of the Sierras contain another unique ecological habitat containing the oldest trees on earth, the bristlecone pines, some of which are over 4000 years old.

Both the eastern and western slopes of this massive range contain gold, as well as other minerals. The forests have provided huge amounts of lumber, game and pelts. The western foothills, in addition to gold, provided grazing land and orchards. Along the entire length of the range, rains and melted snows have made the central valley the richest agricultural basin in the country and have supplied San Fransisco Bay with fresh water.

The fantastic recreation opportunities comprise an equally precious resource. The fishing, camping, hiking, boating, downhill and cross-country skiing are

Landscape in the Sierras

all superb. Whether your taste is for gambling in the carnival-like casinos on the Nevada border, or for hiking on the unsurpassed Pacific Crest Trail (which runs from Mexico to Canada), there is something for everyone in these mountains, and sometimes it seems that everyone rushes up together on one weekend. The resorts are crowded, the traffic can get tangled and the campgrounds resemble suburban blocks excised from L.A. and dropped down here in the wilderness. There is steady pressure for more development and more resorts, as well as more tree-cutting, dam-building, and the continued channeling of river courses. As recently as ten years ago, there was an almost successful proposal to blast a freeway through the supposedly inviolate borders of Sequoia National Park in order to develop a ski resort.

Despite the crowds and pressures to develop the area, the Sierras can still provide the kind of majesty, inspiration and peace that John Muir described a century ago – you just have to look a bit harder these days.

The Amazing Sequoia Tree

Bordered by desert, high plateaus and the ocean, California has developed some unique ecological features. Ways of life that disappeared from other regions of the world found small pockets of protection here. Conspicuous among these is the giant sequoia.

CALIFORNIA

These trees stand alone as the largest living things on earth. Though tall, they are not the tallest, and though old, they are not the oldest. But for sheer overall bulk, nothing is larger. They can approach or exceed 300 feet in height, the length of an American football field, and their circumference can reach 100 feet. These massive trees are supported by roots that are only several feet deep, but, like long sinewy fingers, they grip the surface in every direction for up to 100 feet. High and mighty as they are, these trees live delicately balanced lives. Some have reached an age of 3200 years, and when the Greek and Hebrew civilizations were just beginning to develop, some of these trees were saplings in the same forests we can visit today. The Sequoia, the coastal redwoods, and a single tree in China are all that remain of a family of trees that once covered the earth.

When the Giant Sequoias were first discovered, efforts immediately began to both exploit and protect them. Early lumbermen fashioned special saws and techniques to down the thick trees, some of which have girths approaching 30 feet. A branch alone may be six feet thick. But the brittleness of the wood, and the height from which the trees fell, made efforts to harvest them impractical. Its cousin, the coastal redwood, was not so lucky.

Though the huge trees were protected, their delicately balanced ecology was little understood. For years, anxious rangers snuffed out forest fires to protect the trees, only to realize at last that fire played an essential role in the growth process of the sequoias. Fire prepares the soil for optimal sprouting, and clears the debris so that the tiny seed can reach the soil. Fire pops the seed from a closed cone, and also burns off young fir trees that grow in the shade and crowd out the sequoia seedlings. The mature trees have a thick, soft, fibrous bark up to two feet thick, that acts as a natural asbestos and insulates the tree from fire when other trees are destroyed. Even when, over many years, successive fires caused by accumulated debris burn through and perhaps hollow out a sequoia, the tree can continue to grow.

The sequoia tree was named by an Austrian botanist to honor an obscure intellectual giant, the great Cherokee Indian, Sequoya. A crippled mechanic and an artist, Sequoya invested 12 years of intellectual labor developing a system of English notation for Cherokee syllables, thus opening a whole world of literacy and literature for the Cherokee, who had already successfully adopted the White civilization. This did not prevent their removal to the west in a grueling march at bayonet point that killed thousands. Sequoya joined his people in their exile and devoted himself to the search for a common Indian grammar.

Kings Canyon/Sequoia National Parks
Some of the most magnificent scenery in all the Sierras is found in the southern reaches of the range, in **Kings Canyon and Sequoia National Parks.** The largest of the giant sequoias, are found here in dense groves with hundreds of trees. Here the peaks of the high country reach 12,000-14,000 feet, and Mt. Whitney reaches almost 15,000 feet. So rugged are the mountains here that no road traverses the entire park, and access is from the

CALIFORNIA

Giant sequioa tree

CALIFORNIA

west only. Kings Canyon and Sequoia form one continuous strip along the Sierra range, but no road joins them directly.

There is no direct route between the Yosemite and Sequoia parks. Motorists must drive to Fresno, and then back into the Sierras in a long wide V, and this discourages many visitors from going to Sequoia after Yosemite. Besides, they've already seen the big trees in Yosemite, and the spectacular Yosemite Valley. Sequoia, then, is not nearly as crowded as Yosemite. There is no built-up area as there is in Yosemite Valley. The tourist services blend in much more subtly with the setting, and the beauty is spectacular. Kings Canyon was praised by John Muir as even more beautiful than Yosemite.

Sequoia became a national park in 1890, the same year as Yosemite. General Grant National Park, also established that year, protected the Grant Grove of sequoias and the surrounding area. In 1940, Kings Canyon was established, incorporating the General Grant Park.

From Route 99 in the San Joaquin Valley, the main routes entering the parks are Route 198 from Visalia in the southwest, and 180 from Fresno in the northwest. Fresno and Visalia can be reached easily enough without a car, but transportation to and within the national parks is difficult without a car. Major airlines serve Fresno, bus companies serve Fresno and Visalia. Amtrak serves Fresno and Hanford near Visalia. Rent-a-car service is available to the parks from Fresno or Visalia. Guest Services, the concessionaire with a monopoly on Sequoia food and lodging, operates a mini-bus between Fresno and various visitor centers (and their own lodges) in both parks, for a rather high price of around $15.

Kings Canyon National Park

Route 180 from Fresno enters **Kings Canyon National Park** at **Grant Grove**, which is separate from and west of the main body of the park. From here, a road leads east into Kings Canyon. The 46-mile General's Highway leads south to Sequoia, past the park's most renowned sights.

Grant Grove contains a visitor center, a small commercial center, and the grove itself. The visitor center offers films and very good displays about the evolution and life-cycle of the Sequoia, as well as the attempts to cut them and to save them. Grant Grove contains four of the world's five largest trees. The **Grant Tree**, a national shrine, is between 2000 and 2500 years old. There are several famous trees here, in addition to stumps left where trees were cut down by early loggers. There are pleasant short hikes within and around the grove. A longer 10-mile loop goes to **Redwood Grove** to the south, a beautiful and less crowded grove.

The main and only highway winding into the heart of Kings Canyon Park ends in **Cedar Grove**. The canyon is stunning and overpowering as your car weaves at the base of its massive, granite walls. The canyon is 8000 feet deep, the deepest in the U.S. Just outside the park border is **Boyden Cavern**, a commercially developed cave with beautiful stalagmite and

CALIFORNIA

stalactite formations. It is more expensive ($3) and commercial than Crystal Cave, which is in Sequoia Park towards the southern end.

Cedar Grove has some visitor facilities, including campgrounds and several stores. Trails to **Zumwalt Meadows** and **Roaring River Falls** make easy and pretty hikes. Cedar Grove is a hub for trails penetrating the high country to the east and north. One beautiful all-day hike leads to **Mist Falls**. The **John Muir Trail**, which starts at Mt. Whiney, passes through Cedar Grove and extends as far as the large wilderness in the northern park of Kings Canyon Park. This trail runs along the crest of the Sierra to Tuolumne Meadows in Yosemite. It is for experienced hikers and needs some advance planning. Nevertheless, those willing to put in the planning, time and effort will get an incomparable feel for these mountains.

Cedar Grove's four campgrounds are generally open from late April to late October, as weather permits. Food service, laundry, showers and horseback riding are available. Reservations are recommended for the lodge.

Sequoia National Park

From Grant Grove, the **General's Highway** leads into Sequoia National Park. You can follow this past the main sequoia groves, all the way to the southern end of the park.

Redwood Canyon, along General's Highway about four-and-a-half miles southwest of Grant Grove, can be reached by foot. (The trailhead is by **Quail's Flat**.) Located in a small valley, it contains one of the more pristine sequoia groves and is one of the few places where you can camp out under the huge trees. The highway continues south, past the **Lodgepole Visitors' Center** which is an excellent source of information about the park, before heading to **Giant Forest**. Between Lodgepole and Giant Forest, along the General's Highway, are some of the finest groups of sequoia, as well as the largest concentration of visitor facilities and crowds. Also found here, between the two points, is a fine network of trails for pleasant day hikes. Some of the most popular are the **Lakes Trail** from Lodgepole, the **Congress Trail** from the General Sherman tree, and the hike to **Morro Rock** offering an expansive view of the western peaks and the San Joaquin Valley. The various trails allow the casual visitor and hiker to take routes as easy and short, or long and strenuous, as he wants.

Horseback riding is available at the **Wolverton Pack Station**, south of Lodgepole. (Tel. 565-3445.) Downhill ski and snow play areas are also found at Wolverton. The ski season runs from about December through April. Cross-country ski touring centers around **Grant Forest Village**.

The Giant Forest contains the General Sherman tree, which is the largest of the sequoias, making it the largest living thing on earth. In the same grove are other sequoias, slightly smaller but still huge and impressive.

The drive to **Crescent Meadow** includes the auto log and tunnel. John Muir called this meadow "the gem of the Sierras."

CALIFORNIA

KINGS CANYON AND SEQUOIA NATIONAL PARKS

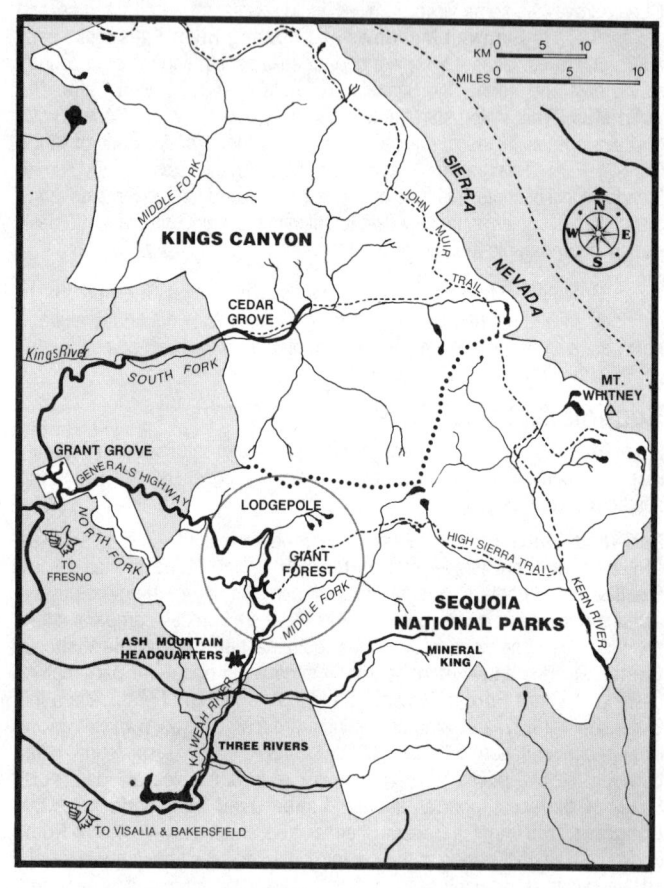

South of the Giant Forest, just past the **Guardsman Trees**, is the turnoff for **Crystal Cave**, a cavern featuring stalactites, stalagmites and an underground stream. Guided tours leave every hour from 10am-3pm, through to about mid-September. Arrive at the parking lot at least 15 minutes before the tour as it is a half-mile strenuous walk to the cave entrance from the parking lot. The cave is a breezy 48 degrees Fahrenheit (9 degrees Centigrade) so bring a jacket or sweater. (Admission: $1.50 adults, 75c seniors, 50 cents ages 6-12.)

South of Crystal Cave is the **Eleven Range Overlook**, which really does seem to overlook layer upon layer of shaded mountainous horizon toward the

CALIFORNIA

west. From this point the road winds precipitously downwards from the glades of giant trees to sparse chaparral country, still within the park. At the southern end are the park headquarters at **Ash Mountain**, and several campgrounds. Just outside the park, at the hamlet of Hammond, is the road leading back into the park, specifically to the wilderness at Mineral King.

Mineral King

Mineral King is a pristine alpine meadow toward the southern end of Sequoia, reached by an extremely winding road that should only be attempted in cars in good condition. Allow one-and-a-half hours to negotiate the 25-mile route. The effort is worthwhile. Here, you stand in high alpine meadows, isolated from the rest of the park, with trails climbing steeply from the valley floor to the high lake basins around you. At **Silver City**, a private community along the road within the park, there are limited facilities including cabins, food, gas and groceries. A park station near the Mineral King ranger station arranges day rides and pack trips.

Mineral King was little-known and little used until 1965 when the forest service awarded a bid to the Walt Disney Corporation for the construction of a gigantic ski resort. Of course, such a center needed a high-speed, modern highway blasted through the mountains to shuttle the 10,000 skiers a day who were anticipated. The plan sparked heated opposition by conservationists. Cartoons appeared of a giant Mickey Mouse stomping through the woods with a shovel, chasing away Bambi and her friends. The battle lasted 13 years and finally reached Congress. The pocket of Mineral King was at last attached to Sequoia National Park, but had become a well-known spot. Mineral King is slated to remain relatively isolated, accessible to those who really want to get there. One drive-in campground is available at Cold Springs.

Just south of the park on Route 198 is the town of **Three Rivers**, with the usual array of rustic motels, private campgrounds and restaurants. For down-home belly-filling meals starting at $4.50, try the *Noisy Water Cafe*, 41775 Sierra Drive, on the north side of the road.

Mount Whitney

Access to **Mt. Whitney**, the highest point in the contiguous United States at about 15,000 feet, is accessible for hiking and viewing from the east side of the park. The turn-off for Mt. Whitney is at **Lone Pine**, on Route 395 (also serving as the juction for the approach to Death Valley, the lowest point in the U.S., 90 miles to the east). Mt. Whitney is the most frequently climbed peak in the Sierra Nevada, if not in the U.S. The 10.7 mile trail begins at the **Whitney Portal** trailhead, which is 13 miles west of Lone Pine. The road is usually open from May to early November.

This trail can be strenuous, especially to those not acclimated to high altitude, and altitude sickness can be a problem. Patches of snow can remain on the upper section of the trail all year long.

CALIFORNIA

Summer days can be quite warm at the lower elevations, but temperatures at the summit are cool, and even on summer nights, temperatures often drop to freezing or below. Afternoon thunderstorms are common. Prepare for a bit of winter and summer: sunglasses, sunscreen, a brimmed hat and mosquito repellent, as well as raingear and warm clothes.

If you have some hiking experience, give it a try for some spectacular views. A woman 89-years old did it (although when she tried at age 90, she had to stop just two-and-a-half miles short of the summit). Commercial shuttle service to the Whitney trailhead is available at Lone Pine from **Eastern Sierra Shuttle**: Tel. 619-876-4435. For more information on climbing Whitney, call or write the Mt. Whitney Ranger District, P.O. Box 8, Lone Pine, 93545. Tel. 619-876-5542.

Lake Tahoe

Lake Tahoe straddles two states and two worlds. Nevada lies along the eastern shore, and California on the western. Also to the west and southwest there are high rugged mountains, snow covered even in the summer. Among these mountains is **Desolation Wilderness** a beautiful area set aside for hikers, where no vehicles are allowed. This is a real wilderness, a hiker's challenge and paradise. Yet within viewing distance of these peaks are the ski lifts, and the strip of motels and restaurants, and the flashing lights of the casinos of Stateline, the tiny resort on the Nevada border, literally across the street from California.

Tahoe itself is truly a jewel in the wilderness, pristine and immense, 22 miles long and 12 across. The lake was formed by the faulting and uplifting of the Sierra Nevada block, as well as by later damming by the lava, and sculpting and gouging by glaciers. The waters are incredibly blue, due to the great depth (averaging 1000 feet), the purity of the water, and the clarity of the atmosphere. The water is clear enough to see down to 120 feet.

In 1859, with the discovery of silver at Comstock Lode in northern Nevada, loggers clear-cut the surrounding forests, hauled them over the eastern crests, and floated them by flume to the mining communities. Vast areas of woodland were slashed and razed, but, amazingly, the forests regenerated themselves.

However, about a century later came another onslaught against the ecologically delicate lake. The natural beauty of the predominantly private shoreline was spoilt by the building of resorts. Waste was dumped into the lake, and the mountain gem was being seriously damaged. Steps were taken rapidly to save the land that remained, and to limit and control continuing development.

Today, the area abounds with reserves to explore. Tahoe is a point upon which everyone converges: hikers, boaters, canoeists, revelers, skiers or gamblers. It is one of the prime vacation spots in the country. Recently, it has turned into a year-round resort, with extensive skiing facilities drawing the crowds in the winter.

CALIFORNIA

The quietest period is early fall, when it is too cold and rainy for boating, swimming and most hiking, and too early for the fresh snows. Prices fluctuate not only between seasons, but during the week as well. Even during the off-season, the resort fills up on weekends, because it is so accessible and convenient to major urban centers. The endless row of hotels at South Lake Tahoe is packed over weekends, even in autumn, but during the week in the off-season, Tahoe is a vacationer's market. Visitors can choose among the motels, with rooms ranging from as little as $16 per night to luxury resort facilities. As for eating, the casinos on the Nevada border offer great bargains similar to those in Reno and Las Vegas, though more limited. Great buffets are served for a few dollars and up.

How to get there

The two main approaches to Lake Tahoe from the California side both stem from Sacramento. Route 50 heads east through Placerville, and up through the Sierra foothills along an old covered-wagon trail, toward the lower end of Tahoe. The road is wide, but not a super highway. It is mind boggling to imagine covered wagons crossing this serpentine pass. I-80 climbs up to Truckee, north of Lake Tahoe, and over Donner Pass.

The **Lake Tahoe Airport**, located near South Lake Tahoe, is served by AirCal and Pacific Coast. PSA periodically offers special packages including airfare, lodging, car rental and ski tickets, and PSA Great Escape Vacations. Shuttles run from Reno's airport, with its national carriers to Tahoe's resorts.

The **Amtrak** station at Truckee is on the California Zephyr line between San Francisco and Chicago. No tickets are sold at that station; make reservations, board the train, and pay the conductor. **Greyhound** also serves Truckee.

Tahoe Area Regional Transit runs buses between Incline Village in Nevada at the northest end of the lake, to Tahoma about halfway down the western shore. Buses also run between Tahoma and South Lake Tahoe.

At the south end of the lake, a bus serves key recreation sites between the town of South Lake Tahoe and the Forest Service Visitor Center at the southwest tip.

Although the western shore of Lake Tahoe can be quite hilly, the area around South Lake Tahoe is a beautiful area for bicycle riding. It is a popular means of local transportation and rentals are readily available.

Several companies operate commercial boat cruises, combining travel and pleasure. They sail between the north and south shores of the lake, stop at the casinos, and also dock near the ski resorts. The Chamber of Commerce can provide company names and addresses.

Additional sites and activities

Emerald Bay, towards the southern end of Route 89, is a stunning sight

Unspoilt nature – Lake Tahoe

when first glimpsed from the road. It is a popular spot for overlooks and walks down the cliffside to the shore. Trails lead along the beautiful rock shoreline, down from the **Emerald Bay Overlook** (closed when icy) to **Vikingsholm**, a reproduction of a Norse fortress, which is open for guided tours during the summer. Both parks have camping facilities, but campgrounds are continually crowded during the summer.

Across the road from Emerald Bay is a parking area for the short, steep hike to the footbridge above the cataracts of **Eagle Falls**. If the snow has cleared, you can continue on the same trail about one mile to **Eagle Lake.**

South of Emerald Bay, the **Lake Tahoe Visitor Center**, operated by the USFS, offers nature talks by ranger and self-guided tours on the flora and fauna of Lake Tahoe. "The Trail of the Washoe" exhibit shows how the lake's local Indians lived off the land for thousands of years with little impact on the environment. (Tel. 541-0209.)

The Forest Service and State Parks operate tours throughout the baronial estates that graced the southern lakeshore at the turn of the century. For information: Tel. 544-6420. The **Valhalia Estate** and **Baldwin Log Cabin** host concerts ranging from chamber music to bluegrass in the summer. Check with the Forest Service Visitor Center for schedules.

CALIFORNIA

Lake Tahoe has a tremendous concentration of ski resorts, including the famous **Squaw Valley**, site of the 1960 winter Olympics. Between them, the resorts provide a variety of runs, as well as several hundred miles of cross country trails. Most of the ski resorts are clustered along the western shore of the lake. Several of them offer shuttle connections to hotels and resort areas. In February, the annual winter carnival of **Snowfest** fills the lakeshore resorts with concerts, dances, theater, parades and skiing exhibitions. (Tel. 583-7625.)

The aerial tram ride at the **Heavenly Ski Resort**, south of Stateline, off Route 50, climbs to an elevation exceeding 8000 feet, offering a breathtaking view of Lake Tahoe and the Sierra Nevada. There is also a restaurant at the top with great views, which serves Sunday brunch for $3.95, when purchased with a tram ticket. (Tram tickets cost $9 for adults, $5 for children age 12 and under. Tel. 541-7544.)

A little further south of the lake is the **Grover Hot Springs State Park**, surrounded by hiking trails and abruptly rising peaks, and containing two deliciously hot pools. Camping is available. Located 3 miles west of Markleeville, which is on Route E1. From Lake Tahoe, take Route 89 south to Route 88, skirt east to Woodford, and then south on E1 for the turnoff to the park at Markleeville. (During summer season, open daily 9am-9pm. $1 adults, 50 cents age 17 and younger. Tel. 694-2248.)

The **Desolation Wilderness**, looming west of the South Lake Tahoe region spans both slopes of the Sierra Nevada. It embraces 10,000 foot high peaks, glacial valleys and over 100 lakes, and it draws enough hikers and campers to necessitate the rationing of camping permits. The adjacent **Mokelumne Wilderness** is smaller, less crowded, and still rugged. Check with the Forest Service Visitor Center for maps, details and weather conditions in both areas.

Truckee is a small mountain town right off I-80, spruced up for tourists but not overdone. With its original buildings and wooden sidewalks, it maintains the ambience of an old frontier town. There are a few nice restaurants and cafes. The information center is located in the train station, on the south side of the main street just beyond the traffic light. (Tel. 587-2757.) Just north of I-80, off the Truckee exit, is a **Forest Service Information Center**, with details on camping and hiking throughout the immense **El Dorado National Forest**. It covers all the territory along the western shore of Tahoe and further west into the Sierra peaks, including the stunning Desolation Wilderness, and stretches down into the foothills.

At **Donner Lake**, just west of Truckee, the famous Donner party encamped during a terrible Sierra winter in 1846. Their story is one of poor judgement, misfortune, heroic struggle and grim survival. A group of almost 90 people headed west in the summer of 1846 in wagons, under the leadership of two brothers, George and Jacob Donner. By the time they reached the vicinity of Reno, in October, the party was already fraught with tension and bickering due to a serious mistake in routing. They had lost wagons and much cattle. After receiving some relief from one of their

CALIFORNIA

members who had crossed the pass earlier to Sacramento, they rested for a week and began the climb over the Sierras. The delay was a fatal mistake, for the snows fell early and heavily. The party was trapped near the lake, huddled in makeshift cabins and brush tepees, while the land lay buried under 22 feet of snow. On improvised snowshoes, a party of 15 hiked west to seek help. Only seven lived, reduced to cannibalism to survive. A relief party reached the others at the lake only in February. The survivors were eating oxhide and bones, and there were more signs of cannibalism. The last survivors were saved only in April. 42 of the 89 members died before reaching their destination.

The cannibalism caused much controversy, and in one case there were even accusations of murder. A museum at **Donner Memorial State Park**, at the southeast corner of Donner Lake, presents the tragic story. (Open 10am-6pm daily. Nominal admission.)

Donner Lake can provide a pleasant alternative to lodging around Lake Tahoe, especially during the summer. The accommodations at Donner Lake tend to be less expensive than at Tahoe, and the facilities of the lake itself less crowded. Cabins are available with weekly as well as nightly rates.

Accommodations

The hotels and motels are lined up almost side by side all along Highway 50 through South Lake Tahoe. At Stateline on the Nevada side are the casino-hotels. During the week visitors have their choice, but during weekends, even during the off-season of early fall, all these lodgings may be jammed, and prices are higher too.

Generally, the lodgings tend to be cheaper further away from the border casinos. The various casinos offer free shuttle service to the motels on the California side.

One interesting lodge, far away from the hubbub of South Lake Tahoe, is the *Strawberry Lodge*, a refurbished pine and rock structure. The area is surrounded by thick pine forest, the atmoshpere is warm and friendly. The lodge is adjacent to hiking areas in Desolation Wilderness. There is a restaurant on the premises. (Rates begin at $33 per night for a double. P.O. Box 1075, South Lake Tahoe 95705. Tel. 659-7200.)

Also at South Lake Tahoe, there is a thriving rental business in condominium time sharing. These arrangements sometimes work out more economically than resorts. Most units have some sort of kitchen facilities, and can often be divided among two or more parties. For information, call Security Timeshare Marketing: Tel. 544-5611.

There are about seven state parks in the Tahoe region. The ones on the rim of the lake can be crowded through the summer. Parks further away, such as **Donner Memorial State Park** (Tel. 525-7277) or **Grover Hot Springs** (Tel. 831-0494) are usually less crowded. Both are set in beautiful scenery. State parks range in price from $3 to $6. The central state park office for the area has details on the parks.

CALIFORNIA

The huge **El Dorado National Forest**, bordering Lake Tahoe on the west, has numerous campsites, ranging in price from free to $9 per night. On Route 89 north of Truckee, there are less crowded campgrounds along the road.

Food
The best eating in South Lake Tahoe is found in the casinos of Stateline. Although the choice is more limited than at the major resorts, there are excellent buffets here. All-you-can-eat breakfasts begin at 99 cents, lunches cost only a few dollars, and sumptuous prime-rib buffets go for as little as $5.95, but there are lines during peak hours.

Useful Addresses And Phone Numbers
Area Code: 916.
South Lake Tahoe Chamber of Commerce: About 2 miles west of the stateline on Route 50. Tel. 541-5255.
North Lake Tahoe Chamber of Commerce: Lighthouse Center, Tahoe City. Tel. 583-2371.
Truckee-Donner Chamber of Commerce: Tel. 587-2757.
National Weather Service: Tel. 447-6941.
U.S. Forest Service: Tel. 544-6420, 541-0209 (south shore); Tel. 583-3642 (north shore).
California State Parks: Tel. 525-7232.
Nevada State Parks: Tel. 702-831-0494.
Coast Guard: Tel. 583-4433.
Greyhound: 1099 Park ave. Tel. 544-2241 (South Lake Tahoe); Tel. 587-3882 (Truckee).
Tahoe Area Rapid Transit: Tel. 583-2371.
South Tahoe Area Ground Express (STAGE): Tel. 573-2080.

Toward Reno
California shares much of its long eastern border with Nevada. In the north, the border runs right through the Sierra Nevada and splits lake Tahoe down the middle. There are ski resorts on both sides, protected wilderness tracts on the California side, and casinos on the Nevada side, literally a few steps across the stateline in some cases. If driving to California along I-80, the main cross-country route, Reno is a convenient and popular stop. It is often used as an entertaining stopover point heading to or from California. Reno is the commercial and cultural center of northern Nevada's vast territory. At the eastern base of the Sierras, it is at the starting point of one of the main passes over the crests, in pioneer days as well as today. In addition to its casinos, Reno has cheap food and lodging which make it a tempting rest point before crossing the mountains, or a base for trips into the Sierras.

The casinos are the big attraction. At night, sitting on its high, open plateau beneath the shadowy mountains, Reno resembles an electric Emerald City, but in downtown itself, the waves of lights lose their dazzle. Reno, which calls itself "The Biggest Little City in the World" has neither the glamour and overwhelming excitement of Las Vegas, nor the rustic charm of one of the small mountain casino resorts.

Reno is served by Greyhound and Trailways. The Chicago-San Francisco Amtrak line runs right through the city. Regional and national carriers use Reno's airport.

The intersection at Virginia and 2nd st. forms the center of the casino area. Many of the casinos are housed in the large and blazing downtown hotels, as in Las Vegas. These include *Harrah's*, *MGM Grand Hotel*, *The Sahara Reno*, *Circus Circus*, *Mapes* and others. There are restaurants, coffee shops, bars and casinos open all night.

Reno, like Las Vegas has an abundance of inexpensive accommodation and fantastic dining deals. As long as the gambling impulse is under control, this is a penny-pincher's paradise. Even during the summer season, good rooms can often be found for $16-$20. There are plenty of blazing motel signs along the central strip, and spread out along the roads connecting to I-80. Many of the motels offer coupons, distributed by the casinos and redeemable for cash, free cocktails, slot machine plays, etc.

Breakfast buffets start at about $2, lunch buffets slightly higher. The various dinner buffets, offering immense spreads, start at about $4 (lunch buffets often have almost the same selection, at a lower price).

Useful Addresses And Phone Numbers
Area Code: 702.
Commission on Tourism: Capitol Complex, Carson City, 89710. Brochures and information on the entire state available upon request by mail.
Reno/Tahoe Gaming Academy: An initiation into the mysteries of the gambling games, and tours of the casinos. Tel. 348-7403.
Reno International Jazz Festival: Held in April and often featuring big names in jazz. Tel. 786-5409.

Yosemite
In 1851, Indians used to raid the White settlements in the central valley and then disappear into the Sierra Mountains. A force led by Major James Savage followed their trail through the foothills and into the high mountains and suddenly came upon an immense valley carved from rock that stunned them with its beauty and grandeur. Amazingly, Yosemite had remained undiscovered by White explorers until then. It was clear that the valley would never be the same again. The almost magical valley, with its sheer granite cliffs, its high falls and its sculpted domes, immediately attracted those who were overwhelmed by its beauty, and those who wanted to use,

CALIFORNIA

YOSEMITE NATIONAL PARK

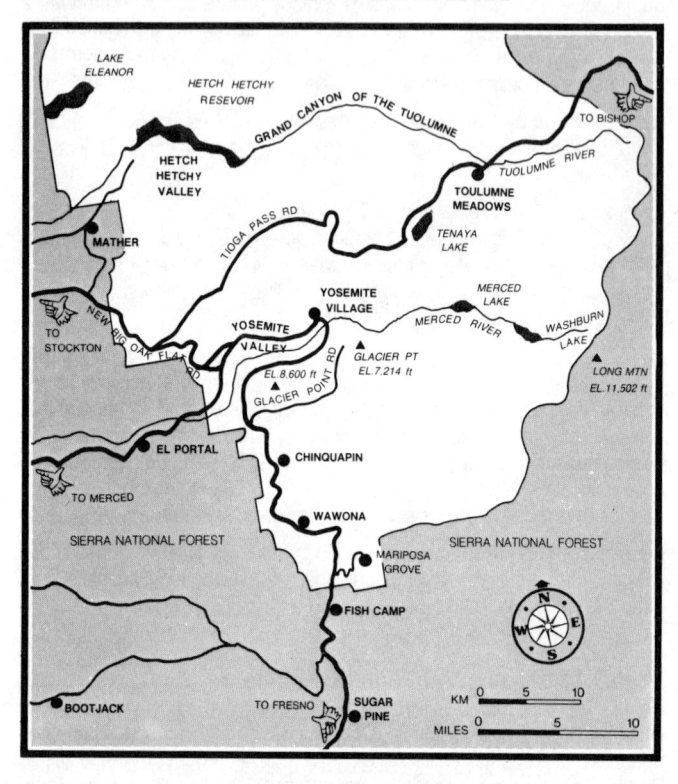

exploit and "improve" it. Although the boundaries of the park are secure today, the debate over its future continues, as the valley fills up every summer with campers and trailers, and resembles an L.A. suburb that has been transplanted into the wilderness.

Just a decade after its discovery, the need to preserve the wonders of this ice-carved valley was recognized, and in 1864 Yosemite became the nation's first state park, and initiated California's direct involvement with the protection of its natural areas. However, the protection was far from inviolate, and in 1890 the area was placed under federal jurisdiction, and guarded by the U.S. army. The army dealt with law-breakers forcefully. When stockmen allowed their sheep to continually strip the hillsides of vegetation, with the excuse that they could not control their flocks, the army drove the sheep across the mountainous area and released them, and the stockmen suddenly discovered new ways of controlling their sheep.

It was John Muir, a Scottish immigrant, who spearheaded the fledgling

CALIFORNIA

conservation movement. He also founded and headed the Sierra Club, and most especially fought for the protection of Yosemite. As a young man, he wandered through America on foot and stopped when he reached the Sierras. He knew the Yosemite Park intimately, and collected an enormous amount of data about the area. Geologists doubted that glaciers had formed Yosemite Valley, but Muir set out and discovered glaciers in the area, and also the scars of ancient glaciers. He was known to explore the rim of the valley overnight carrying no more than a notebook, a tin cup and some tea.

Muir began to write of the Sierras, with great eloquence and literary style that captured the public's attention. He purposefully and incessantly used his pen to prod the public into political action to protect Yosemite and other wilderness areas in the Sierras. He became a powerful force, with contacts in high places, and personally led President Theodore Roosevelt through the back country of Yosemite, the two men camping out in four-foot snow drifts. Muir convinced Roosevelt that large tracts of forest land should be protected from foresters. The fledgling **Sierra Club**, under Muir's leadership, became a forceful voice for preservation, and is now one of the most powerful groups in the entire American conservation movement.

Muir's greatest political defeat also involved Yosemite. North of Yosemite Valley, and clearly within the park boundaries, was the **Hetch Hetchy Valley**, second only to Yosemite itself in the unique beauty of its sculpted canyon. The city of San Francisco decided to build a dam here, although for a slightly greater investment a site elsewhere could have been chosen. The battle reached the Roosevelt Administration and the Congress. (The President supported the plan to build the dam within the boundaries of the park, despite Muir's objections.) The hard-fought battle tore a gap within the conservation movement, between those who wanted to manage resources with planned and multiple uses, and those who wanted to preserve the area exactly as it was (a rift that continues today within California and across the country). The battle dragged on for twelve years, until Congress finally approved the dam's construction, and building commenced in 1913. Muir was crushed by the defeat and the loss of the canyon, and died a year later. But the battle over Hetch Hetchy made a powerful impact and contributed directly to the creation of the National Park Service in 1916, which solidified the parks' existence and helped to formalize their boundaries.

How to get there

Yosemite National Park is located in the Sierras almost due east of the Monterey Bay area, across the San Joaquin Valley and beyond the foothills. No major freeway leads to its gate. Route 99, running north-south along the eastern edge of the valley, is the closest freeway to the west, and the point from which several local highways split off for Yosemite. There is no easy way to travel the length of the Sierras without leaving them and following the foothills or even returning to the flat central valley itself. Even in the foothills, only small winding roads zigzag along the length of the hills.

Majestic heights – Yosemite National Park

Route 120 leads from Manteca in the northwest to the northern entrance to the park. Route 41 comes from Fresno in the southwest, skirting the region of the Mariposa Grove on Sequoias, and Route 140 goes directly east from Merced to the Yosemite Valley. This is the main entrance to the park. Route 120, to the north of the Yosemite Valley continues east into the high country of the Sierras, where the peaks are the most rugged. This beautiful road passes through Tuolumne Meadows, which is the junction and center for backpackers tackling some of the lovely high country trails, and continues to the steep Tioga Pass and down to I-395. Route 120 is closed in the winter. As can be seen on the map, from Yosemite southwards to Sequoia, this is the only highway that traverses the sharply ridged spine of the Sierras.

Public transportation to Yosemite is non-existent. The closest is the private bus line, the Yosemite Transportation System (YTS),(Tel. 373-4171) which makes connections with commercial bus terminals in Lee Vining, Fresno and Merced, and with the Amtrak stations in Merced and Fresno. To Fresno and Merced a one-way fare hovers around $15. To Lee Vining it's over $30. Fast one-day tours are also available from San Francisco, but don't blink or you'll miss something.

CALIFORNIA

Hitchhiking within the park is quite acceptable. People who might not normally assist hitchers are willing to do so here, as it is clear that many hikers are making their way back to trailheads at the beginning or end of a hike.

When Yosemite Valley is congested, a car can be as much of a liability as in an urban downtown, but you can take advantage of the Valley Shuttle. Leave your car at the campground, or in the Curry Village parking lot. Some of the buses are double-deckers, which are a novelty if you haven't been to England. Some areas are open only to shuttles or to bicycles. Bicycles can be rented for about $10 per day. There are some beautiful rides on the valley floor; the path to Mirror Lake is particularly recommended. .

Accommodations

With very few exceptions, all eating and lodging concessions are run by the Yosemite Park and Curry Company. Reservations for private accommodations are made through one central office: Yosemite Park and Curry Co., Yosemite National Park, 95389. Tel. 209-252-4848 or Tel. 255-8345.

The greatest number and variety of lodgings are concentrated in the valley, but each of the regional centers of the park also provides private lodging. Tuolumne Meadows has tent-top cabins, a central dining lodge and drive-in and walk-in campgrounds. White Wolf, on the same road, has cabins and tents. Both facilities are open only in the summer. Wawona has lodges and the old *Wawona Hotel*.

Reservations for all Curry accommodations are essential in summer and are recommended all year round. A deposit of one day's rent must be paid in advance.

The *Ahwahnee Hotel* in the valley is a massive edifice of stone and timber, the kind of place where you want to sit by a roaring fire with a glass of sherry while recounting your tale of survival in a blizzard. Rooms start at over $100 per night, and there are also two-story cottages. *Yosemite Lodge* is a more standard hotel with moderate to high-moderate prices. *Curry Village* is a sub-division with canvas roofs. The concrete-and-canvas *Housekeeping Camp* units have double beds and wood burning stoves and cost slightly more than the Curry Village tents. They are open in the summer only.

The *Upper River*, *Lower River*, *North Pines*, *Lower Pines*, and *Upper Pines* campgrounds are all drive-in areas, costing $7 per night, at the east end of the valley, and comprise one giant trailer city. Reservations are required in advance for summer spots, but occasionally you can find someone willing to share a space, for partial fee payment. These sites are like parking lots covered in pine needles.

Do not, however, consider the option of snoozing in your car near a dirt road or putting your sleeping bag down somewhere in the valley, because you will probably be caught and fined.

CALIFORNIA

Two walk-in campgrounds in the valley often have space until late in the day, but don't rely on it during high summer season. *Backpacker's Camp* is located just behind the North Pines Campground, near Mirror Lake. Toward the western end of the valley is *Sunnyside*, used primarily by climbers, who tend to keep themselves apart. A few nights spent listening to them and you'll either be determined to scale El Capitan or equally determined never to climb a ladder again. Both campgrounds cost $2.

Motels, lodges and private campgrounds are also found in the small towns on the fringe of the park: in Lee Vining east of Tioga Pass, El Portal along Route 140, and Oakhurst along Route 41. Backcountry camping is free along the numerous mountain trails, but a wilderness permit is required. Even for backcountry hiking, reservations are recommended because the trails have quotas, and certain quotas fill up fast. Apply for a permit at the Yosemite Valley Visitor Center or at a ranger station. You may be asked for a rough itinerary. Some campgrounds have bear-proof lockers.

There are drive-in campgrounds, heavily frequented by trailers, along the main highways throughout the park. Some on the outer periphery may have available spots early in the day as people leave. During the summer, it is wise to make reservations for these spots too. Two campgrounds in Yosemite Valley and one in Wawona remain open the year round.

Activities, Services, General Information

The *Yosemite Guide*, a free newspaper, is your key to current park information. It contains a current listing of all interpretive programs, facilities and services, general information, and feature articles. The guide is available at entrance stations, ranger stations, and visitor centers. Current road, weather and camping information is available by telephone. Consult the Yosemite Guide for numbers.

Special information for disabled visitors, and wheelchair-emblem placards for vehicles for special driving privileges – are available on request at entrance and information stations.

Printed information in Spanish, Japanese, German, and French is also available on request.

The *Yosemite Road Guide* is a descriptive booklet keyed to numbered posts along park roads. It can be purchased at most information stations and gift shops in the park.

Numerous publications about the park are available at outlets throughout the park or by writing to Yosemite Natural History Association, Box 545, Yosemite National Park, 95389.

Every Visitor Center and some of the ranger stations conduct local programs of campfire evenings, general and specialized walks such as early morning bird-watching, and late night star gazing.

The park can be divided into three basic parts: the gently sloping west, with its groves of sequoia trees; Yosemite Valley, which is both the most

CALIFORNIA

beautiful and the most overcrowded; and the spectacular, jagged peaks of the high country, with Tuolomne Meadows as the central base. Within these areas is a remarkable range of terrain and animal life.

Western Area

There are three groves of sequoia in Yosemite. **Tuolumne** and **Merced Groves** are located just inside the entrance along route 120. Near the southeast entrance off route 41, is the **Mariposa Grove**, which is the largest, and the one with major interpretive services. Visitors park their cars and board free trams, which are accompanied by guides and circle through the grove. Included among the trees here is the Grizzly Giant, about 2700 years old. A tunnel cut through one of the trees, as a novelty, destroyed the shallow root network over the years, and a heavy snowfall finally toppled the tree. There are gentle trails, a small museum in a cabin, and plenty of opportunities to approach the trees directly.

Along Route 41 on the way to the Yosemite Valley, **Wawona** is a business and service center, as well as a restored historical village where frontier crafts are practiced and demonstrated. Stagecoach rides are available here. There are interpretive programs in the evening. Gasoline is also available. The old, rambling building just south of the junction is *Wawona Hotel*, built in 1875 and still operating today. Food and lodging are available at Wawona.

The one and only turnoff for the **Glacier Point Overlook** is also on Route 41, at Chiquapin Junction, and it's a detour well worth taking. On the way to Glacier Point is the **Badger Pass Ski Area** (the road beyond this point is closed during the winter). From the edge of a sheer rock cliff dropping 3200 feet to the valley floor, the view from Glacier Point is vast and fantastic. All the major features along the valley walls are clearly visible, and form an unusual perspective. Backing it all are the snow-covered peaks of the high Sierra. Bus tours from the valley floor reach this point. The Panoramic Trail is a beautiful trail of several miles from this point to the Yosemite Valley floor. The eight-mile trail offers a pleasant and not very strenuous hike.

The best way to do this hike is to leave your car in the valley, hitch up to Glacier Point, and then start hiking downhill. This will bring you to the top of Nevada Falls, and then past Vernal Falls. The descent past misty and verdant Vernal Falls leads to the valley floor, where a shuttle bus can take you back to your car.

The Valley

From naturalist John Muir to photographer Ansel Adams, artists, writers, and nature-lovers have been enchanted by Yosemite Valley. This glacier-carved canyon along the Merced River, with its sheer granite walls and bulging outcroppings, its sculpted domes and waterfalls plunging from hanging valleys, is one of the great natural wonders of the world. Over two million visitors a year visit Yosemite, and many of them never realize that the seven-mile valley is but a small sliver of the 1200-square mile park.

CALIFORNIA

Half Dome and **El Capitan** are probably the two best-known monoliths along the valley floor. Master mountain climbers try their skills on the sheer cliff of El Capitan. Half Dome can be reached by good hikers via the easier rear route, the last section with the aid of cables embedded in the rock. The top is wider than its seems from below, and offers incredible views. The waterfalls yield their greatest flow around May when swollen with melted snow. The greatest of the waterfalls is **Yosemite Falls**, plunging through two falls over 2400 feet. The other major falls are **Ribbon**, **Bridalveil**, **Nevada** and **Vernal Falls**. Vernal Falls and Nevada Falls are accessible from the Happy Isles Nature Center at the far eastern end of the valley, along the steep, slippery Mist Trail. At the top, trails head towards Half Dome, Tuolumne Meadows and Glacier Point.

The valley can be a depressing place. It became so overdeveloped by the 1970s that the Park Service began to impose certain restrictions. The rows of trailers in the campgrounds, with two antennas and blasting radios, seem incongruous with the surrounding beauty, and many of the stores and tourist facilities seem inappropriate to the character of the park. In recent years, the Park Service has closed some tennis courts, re-directed traffic, and introduced a campground reservation system for the valley, but with two million visitors a year, the valley can be awfully crowded, and make you want a vacation from your vacation.

Nevertheless, you should not miss the opportunity to explore and enjoy the valley, as there is an enormous amount to discover, but do not forget to explore further in the huge park area beyond the lip of the valley.

The valley is the center of everything in the park. Here you can hire horses, take climbing lessons or sit on the porch of the luxurious but rustic *Ahawanee Hotel*. In the mosaic of meadow and woodlands in the west, immerse yourself in spring's wildflowers.

Yosemite Valley has a comprehensive system of interpretive programs, and every Visitor Center in the park conducts local programs too.

The **Valley Visitor Center**, located just west of Yosemite Village, provides an interesting introduction to the natural and human history of the valley and park. The **Indian Cultural Museum**, and the **Indian Village**, behind the Visitor Center, commemorate the local Indians who dwelled in this valley for thousands of years, living by hunting game and collecting acorns. At the east end of the valley, accessible by shuttle, is the **Happy Isles Nature Center**, named for the tiny islands formed by the confluence of the Merced River and Illouette Creek. Several heavily-wooded acres provide exhibits and information on the park's features, and a ranger can answer questions. This is also the starting point (or end point) for the trail to Vernal Falls, Half-Dome and Glacier Point.

Tuolumne Meadows
Tuolumne Meadows is the center for Yosemite's high country, and a base for motorists, day-hikers and overnight trekkers. The alpine meadows, the lakes and granite slopes in this area form some of the most stunning

scenery in the High Sierra, and it is easily accessible from Tuolumne by even a short hike.

Tuolumne Meadows, the largest sub-alpine meadow in the Sierras, teems with wildflowers and wildlife in early summer. To the east, on Route 120 is the eastern entrance to the park, beyond Tioga Pass, which is about 10,000 feet high. Tuolumne Meadows is a hub for a network of short and long trails following the High Sierra watershed and penetrating into some of the wildest sections of Yosemite. The famous **Pacific Crest Trail** (called the John Muir Trail at this section) passes through here. Many hikers use this as a starting or endpoint for hiking one section of this trail. Ambitious and experienced hikers can follow this trail south all the way into Sequoia National Park. There is a beautiful but well-trodden overnight hike from here to Yosemite Valley. Another beautiful route for good hikers follows the Tuolumne River into the appropriately named Grand Canyon of the Tuolumne. Horses can be hired here.

One of the best times to visit Tuolumne, as with the whole park, is early fall, before the November snowstorms. At these heights, the aspens, willows, pines and other deciduous trees create a stunning autumnal collage. There are fewer guided activities after Labor Day, but enough to keep the eager visitor busy, and without the bother of crowds. Lodging, camping and motels in Lee Vining are more easily available.

Eastern Slope

East of the high bulwark of the Sierras is a vast area of arid plateaus, twisted volcanic formations, and islands of forest and greenery. The main route along the eastern slope is I-395. South of the Tioga Pass in Yosemite, no road crosses the spine of the Sierras to the separate, other-worldy eastern terrain. About 30 miles north of the Tioga Pass, off 395 to the east, is **Bodie**, one of the few remnants of the little-known gold rush on the eastern slope of the Sierras. Once boasting a population of 12,000, some 65 saloons, and an average of one murder a day, Bodie is now a genuine ghost town, preserved by the state park system in its state of natural decay. At the ranger's house on Green st., pick up a visitors brochure.

Due east of Lee Vining is **Mono Lake**, haunting and moon-like. The lava-strewn islands are the remaining signs of ancient volcanic explosions from the depths of the lake. The tufa spires add to the strange appearance. It is possible to canoe among them, and to take ranger-guided walks through this unusual landscape. The remnant of an ancient inland sea, Lake Mono has no outlet. The beaches around the lake are eroded pumice. The lava-strewn islands constitute the state's largest rookery for California's gulls.

For years, statewide environmental and local interests have battled L.A., which since 1941 has diverted water from four of the five streams that feed the lake, using the water for its own municipal supply. That water,

CALIFORNIA

combined with water from the Owens Valley, south of the lake, is diverted to Los Angeles by aqueduct and constitutes the bulk of the city's water supply. The stream diversions lowered the level of the lake over the years, threatening brine shrimp in the lake and the California gulls that feed on them, although the recent rainy years have helped to raise the water level somewhat.

Mono Lake is managed by the Bureau of Land Management. Information on the lake and on tours can be obtained from the Lee Vining Information Center on I-395, as well as at the Bakersfield District Headquarters of the Bureau of Land Management: 800 Truxton, Room 302, Bakersfield, 93301. Tel. 805-861-4191.

Half-an-hour's drive south of this unearthly feature are the very earthly pleasures of **Mammouth Mountain**, a popular ski resort in alpine woods style, which is one of the largest in the country. In addition to the downhill ski slopes there is an extensive network of cross-country trails, and hiking trails leading into the high country's **John Muir Wilderness**. The ski season is unusually long, lasting occasionally to the Fourth of July.

For information on Mammouth's ski conditions, call the 24-hour Snowline: Tel. 619-934-6166. Mammouth has a wide range of accommodation and restaurants. For the Chamber of Commerce, call Tel. 619-934-2712. The ranger station's visitor center (Tel. 714-934-2505) can give details on the many camping grounds in the area.

Mammouth is located on Route 203, the gateway to some of the **Inyo National Forests**, scenic forested backcountry. Campgrounds open in late April or early May and stay open after Labor Day, until the first snows close them. Most cost from $4-$6. As in most popular resorts, the prices here are a bit higher than surrounding areas, with motel rooms starting at about $30.

Devil's Postpile National Monument also lies on Route 203. The 60-foot columns, resembling a giant pipe organ, were created 900,000 years ago as molten lava poured from the earth's crust. At Rainbow Falls, the San Joaquin River plunges 140 feet over lava ledges. **Oh! Ridge** (no, that's no typo) provides a spectacular view of June Lake, as well as something just as rare in these parts: a campground that is not always full. In the summer, a shuttlebus operates from Minaret Summit to the monument. The monument is administered by the Sequoia/Kings Canyon office, at Three Rivers, 93271. Tel. 565-3342.

The scrubby bristlecone pines, oldest organisms in the world, grow in the bare, exposed terrain of the White Mountains. The sequoias are mere babes in the woods compared to the gnarled and grizzled bristlecones, which are more than 4000 years old. The oldest, the Methuselah Tree, is 4700 years old, and was already ancient at the beginning of the common era. Some of the fallen trees date back an incredible 9000 years. The bristlecone pine forest is reached by taking Route 395 to Bigpine, about 15 miles south of Independence. Head east on Route 168 for 13 miles, to

CALIFORNIA

Westgard Pass, then 10 miles north on White Mountain rd. Contact the Inyo County Park Department for information: Tel. 619-878-2411. No gas, water, or commercial services are available in the forest itself. Evening ranger programs are held. There is an information station in the forest.

CALIFORNIA

Shasta and Lassen

The northern border region of California is rugged, isolated and stunning. It is a different world up here. The mountain scenery is as gorgeous and overwhelming as in the Sierras, though geomorphologically quite different, and here there are no crowds. Enormous amounts of snow fall on the foothills of Cascade Range, which extends all the way up to Washington. Valleys of fertile volcanic soil are filled with flowers in spring. There are high, semi-arid plateaus, black twisted volcanic formations, and bubbling sulfuric pools. The long Central Valley, which extends southwards as far as Bakersfield, reaches its northern limit around Red Bluff and Redding at the southernmost peaks of the Cascades.

To the north and west of Lake Tahoe, the Sierra Nevada seem to merge with the Cascades, but in fact they are two distinct ranges. The peaks of the Cascades in California – Mt. Shasta, Mt. Lassen and the others – were shaped by volcanic action, and the formation of this mountain landscape is by no means complete. Some frozen lava flows in the north are only 500 years old, and in the Lassen area, there was volcanic activity as recently as 1915.

There are some quaint old mining and logging towns which have been spruced up a bit for tourists. The 1849 gold rush reached this far, and in fact there were several major finds here. The main attractions in California's far north are the wonderful natural formations, and the recreational opportunities which they afford. The main recreation areas are Whiskeytown-Shasta-Trinity National Recreation Area, Mt. Lassen Volcanic National Park, and Lava Beds National Monument. Surrounding each of these protected areas are huge tracts of national forest land.

I-5 is the main traffic artery penetrating the northern mountains, coming from the Central Valley and continuing into the central valley of Oregon. In the Lassen-Shasta area, along the I-5 route are the two main towns in the region; **Red Bluff** and **Redding**. Red Bluff is indeed located on a red bluff above the Sacramento River. Between these two towns, a visitor can find most of the basic amenities necessary. There are good reasonably priced restaurants as well as the usual fast-food stands, and several basic reasonably priced motels. For forays into the backwoods, stock up here on neccessities – the range is broader and prices lower than in the national parks or small mountain towns.

A popular circular route passes through both the Mt. Lassen and Mt. Shasta regions. Follow I-5 north beyond Redding and through the national recreation area, to the town of **Mt. Shasta**, which is situated on the foothills of the massive mountain of the same name. The town is small, with some

Lake in Lassen Volcanic

motels, restaurants and grocery stores, and serves as a re-entry point for serious climbers and backpackers who roam the national forest which includes Mt. Shasta (the mountain, not the town) or try to scale the peak itself (this is only for serious climbers). From this point, Route 89 heads east, and then curves south toward Mt. Lassen. Several small towns are connected by this highway. South of Lassen's national park, Route 36 turns west toward Red Bluff and I-5. A glance at the map will show that, in addition to this basic loop, there are numerous other options for trips in the region.

The **Whiskeytown-Shasta-Trinity National Recreation Area**, north and west of Redding, is made up of three separate, unconnected units (thus the three-part name). Each area has a lake which is the centerpiece of its recreation activities, and each lake is artificial, created by the damming and channeling of waters for the benefit of Central Valley agriculture. Although the natural water courses were modified, and reservoirs were created in dry valleys, the surrounding areas were protected and reserved for public use. The lakes created by the Central Valley Water Project (launched as a federal work project during the Depression), filled the various dips and folds

CALIFORNIA

of the valleys and formed long, winding shorelines filled with coves and peaceful backwaters.

The lakes, especially in the Whiskeytown and Shasta sections, draw armadas of sailboats, powerboats, windsurfers and waterskiers. On **Shasta Lake**, huge houseboats can be rented and navigated at slow speeds along the various byways of the long lake. The **Shasta Dam** itself, at the confluence of the Sacramento, Pit and McLoud rivers, is one of the world's largest, and the centerpin of the Central Valley project. Free tours are given from 9am-6pm daily in the summer.

In the northwestern area of the Trinity section of the recreation area, is the **Salmon-Trinity Alps Wild Area**, an uncrowded and beautiful hiking region.

The Trinity Alps embrace mountain ridges, deep canyons between the Trinity River and Salmon River, and more than 55 lakes. Permits are required for backcountry campers. Be sure to check conditions before hiking in this isolated wilderness, by calling Forest Service Headquarters in Weaverville (Tel. 916-623-2131).

The volcanic forces over the ages have given the Lassen terrain an appearance and feel all its own. The park is dominated by **Mt. Lassen**, a plugged volcanic peak. From 1914, eruptions occured intermittently for seven years. The park encompasses a variety of volcanic formations. Its extensive trails wander among hot pools, volcanic peaks and lush valleys enriched by volcanic soil.

Many of the main attractions near the main road are accessible by car or by taking a short walk from the main road. The park's two Visitor Information Centers are located near the northwest entrance, at **Manzanita Lake**, and at the southwest entrance near **Sulphur Works**. The main park road, **Route 89**, arcs around the base of Mt. Lassen itself. The central portion of this highway is closed in winter due to the heavy snows, which can fall as early as October and last into late spring.

The main route to the park follows I-5 north to Red Bluff, and then Route 36 heading east. This road passes park headquarters at **Mineral**. Train service is available to Red Bluff. Greyhound runs to Mineral. It is advisable to stock up on groceries in Red Bluff or Redding rather than in the park.

Sulphur Works is not a factory but a thermal area of steam vents, irridescent hot pools and bubbling mudpots. It can be reached by a two-mile self-guided trail. The **Bumpass Hell** self-guiding trail leads to the largest concentration of hot springs in the park. The round trip is about 2.5 miles. The trail to the summit of Mt. Lassen is about 2.5 miles in one direction, but do not be misled by the short length of the trail. It is a tough climb along switchbacks to the 10,457-foot peak. Take your time, and bring a sweater and hiking shoes appropriate for snow, even in summer. The view from the top is breathtaking.

Many trails head to the east of the park, which has almost no regular roads.

CALIFORNIA

There is a variety of loop-hikes which go past strings of alpine lakes. A segment of the Pacific Crest Trail crosses the park.

There are several main camping areas in the Lassen park. Those near the road are, of course, the most crowded. The walk-in campground at Sulphur Works is near the hot pools and away from the crowds. Back country camping is bountiful and beautiful. Outside the park to the north is a vast expanse of forest service territory, with developed sites as well as plenty of dirt roads and places where people can camp. The towns of Red Bluff and Redding, on I-5, both have a wide array of accommodation, at reasonable prices. Basic, simple motel rooms are available for $20 per night and sometimes less.

Lava Beds National Monument, located just below the Oregon border in the northeastern portion of California, is known for its strange lava formations, and for the short but dramatic Modoc Indian War of 1872-73.

The sharp craggy landscape is the result of 5 million years of volcanic activity which has continued right up to very recent times. The youngest cinder cones are only 1000 years old.

The rich volcanic soil supports a complex plant and animal community. For centuries the Modoc Indians hunted in the valleys and mountains, and used the reeds in Tule Lake to fashion their homes and boats.

The Modocs were connected with other Indian bands that lived in the Klamath Basin, which extends into Oregon. As settlers moved into the region, the American government attempted to relocate the various bands to a reservation, including tribes that had been age-old enemies. The Modocs wanted a reservation on their own land, and over a period of years began deserting their assigned reservation, until an army expedition was dispatched in 1872. Under the leadership of a chief named Captain Jack, 52 Indian rebels dug into the natural fortress of the lava beds and caves, and held off over 1000 soldiers for five months. Gradually the Indian force was whittled down or captured, until finally Captain Jack surrendered. With three other leaders he was hanged, and the surviving remnant of his band was taken to a reservation in Oklahoma.

The main approach to the park is from Route 39 to the east. The monument is about 30 miles south of the town of Tulelake, and 58 miles from Klamath Falls in Oregon. Public transportation reaches Klamath Falls, where cars can be rented.

A single road runs the length of the park, in a crescent from the northeast to the southeast corner. There is an information kiosk near the northeast entrance, but the main information center is near the southeast entrance.

Black lava flows and various formations can be seen throughout the park. Much of the monument is inaccessible by auto, and more than half is designated wilderness area. Ranging in elevation from 4000 to 5700 feet, the monument is exposed to cold weather and snow during any season.

The park's sites divide roughly into two parts. In the north are historical reminders of the heroic but futile Modoc War, including **Captain Jack's Stronghold** with a self-guiding trail through it. The monument's best known features, the innumerable lava tubes and caves, are concentrated mainly in the south, near the Visitor Center.

The Visitor Center presents exhibits on the Modoc Indians. Adjacent **Mushpot Cave** – the only one which is lighted – offers explanations of the geology. A film is featured here four times daily. The other caves can be explored by flashlight. Flashlights can be borrowed from the Visitor Center. Guidebooks to the caves are on sale, and plastic helmets can be rented. The **Cave Loop Road**, dotted with caves, begins at the Visitor Center and is the most accessible and popular area for some easy amateur spelunking.

Daily guided walks, cave trips and campfire programs are available in the summer. During the winter, deer wander into the area in large numbers, and observing them is a popular activity. Situated on the Pacific Flyway, the monument is a fantastic place to observe the migrations of ducks and geese during the spring and fall. They fly by the millions over this territory and often stop here to rest.

The main campground is located at **Indian Well**, near the Visitor Center. Off-the-road camping is allowed in the **Modoc National Forest**. Free sites are found at the forest service campground of Howard's Gulch, 30 miles south on Route 139. Reasonably priced standard motels are found in Tulelake.

INDEX

A
Anacapa Island 155
Angel's Camp 303
Anza-Borrego Desert State Park 82
Arcata 282
Auburn 300

B
Bakersfield 287
Balboa Park, San Diego 52
Balboa Peninsula 68
Berkeley 252
Beverly Hills 121
Big Bear Lake 145
Big Sur 167
Bodega 274
Bodega Bay 272
Bodie 332
Borrego Springs 82

C
Calaveras County 303
California Desert 73
Cambria 163
Cannery Row, Monterey 180
Carmel 176
Carmel Bay Ecological Reserve 177
Carmel Mission 176
Castro Street, San Francisco 228
Channel Islands National Park 153
Chinatown, Los Angeles 107
Chinatown, San Francisco 214
City's Coast, San Francisco 238
Civic Center, San Francisco 229
Clement Street, San Francisco 231
Cloverdale 272
Coloma 301
Coronado 55

D
Davis 294
Death Valley 76
Death Valley National Park 76
Desolation Wilderness 316
Disneyland 68
Donner Lake 320
Downieville 300
Downtown, Los Angeles 104

INDEX

Downtown, San Diego 49
Downtown, San Francisco 212
Duncan Mills 273

E
Eastern Slope, Yosemite 332
Embarcadero, San Diego 51
Eureka 282
Exploratorium, San Francisco 226
Exposition Park 110

F
Ferndale 282
Financial District, San Francisco 211
Fisherman's Wharf, Monterey 180
Fisherman's Wharf, San Francisco 219
Fort Bragg 278
Fort Humboldt 282
Fort Mason 225
Fresno 288

G
Garberville 279
Gaslamp Quarter, San Diego 49
Georgetown301
Glen Ivy Hot Springs 90
Gold Bug Park and Mine 302
Gold Country 297
Golden Gate National Recreation Area 238
Golden Gate Park 234
Griffith Park 117
Guerneville 271

H
Haight-Ashbury, San Francisco 232
Hancock Park 118
Harmony 163
Healdsburg 272
Hetch Hetchy Valley 325
Hollywood 111

I
Indian Canyons 87

J
Jamestown 304
Japantown, San Francisco 231
Jenner 272
John Muir Wilderness 333
Joshua Trees National Monument 80
Julia Pfeiffer Burns State Park 172

*I*NDEX

K
Kings Canyon National Park 312
Knott's Berry Farm 71

L
La Brea Tar Pits 118
Laguna Beach 65
La Jolla 56
Lake Arrowhead 145
Lake Havasu City 75
Lake Tahoe 316
Lassen 335
Lava Beds National Monument 339
Las Vegas 79
Little Tokyo, Los Angeles 106
Long Beach 139
Los Angeles 95

M
Malibu 124
Mammouth Mountain 333
Manzanita Lake 338
Marin County 257
Marine World/Africa U.S.A. 261
Mendocino 277
Mendocino Coast 275
Merced 289
Mexico 60
Mineral King 315
Mission Bay 56
Mission District, San Francisco 228
Mission on Santa Ines 153
Mission San Juan Capistrano 64
Mission San Luis Rey 63
Mission San Miguel 161
Mojave Desert 73
Mono Lake 332
Monterey 178
Morro Bay 161
Mountain Rim 145
Movie and Television Land 103
Mt. Lassen 338
Mt. Shasta 335
Mt. Whitney 315

N
Napa Valley 263
Nevada City 299
North Beach, San Francisco 216

O
Occidental 273
Old Monterey 179

INDEX

Old Sacramento	292
Old Town, San Diego	54
Orange County	68

P
Palm Springs	83
Palos Verdes	139
Paraiso Hot Springs	183
Pasadena	110
Peninsula, San Francisco	251
Petrolia	282
Pfeiffer Big Sur State Park	171
Placerville	302
Point Loma	55
Point Reyes	260

R
Red Bluff	335
Redding	335
Redwood Country	279
Redwood National Park	282
Reno	322
Russian River	270

S
Sacramento	290
Salinas	183
San Andreas	304
San Antonio de Pala Mission	63
San Bernadino Mountains	145
San Diego	47
San Francisco	195
San Francisco Bay	210
San Gabriel Mountains	145
San Jacintos	145
San Joaquin Valley	285
San Jose	251
San Luis Obispo	175
San Rafael Wilderness	153
Santa Barbara	147
Santa Barbara Island	155
Santa Barbara Mission	151
Santa Cruz	187
Santa Cruz Island	155
Santa Monica	127
Sebastopol	272
Sequoia National Forest	287
Sequoia National Park	313
Shasta	335
Shasta Lake and Dam	338
Sierra Nevada	307
SOMA	229
Sonoma Coast	270

INDEX

Sonoma Valley 267
Sonoran Desert 73
South Coast 63
Southern Mother Lode 304
Stanford University 251
State Street, Santa Barbara 149
Sunset Strip 115

T
Tijuana 60
Trinity 282
Truckee 320
Tuolumne Meadows 331

U
Union Street, San Francisco 230

V
Venice 129
Visalia 288

W
Western Area, Yosemite 330
Westwood Village, UCLA 123
Whiskeytown-Shasta-Trinity National Recreation Area 337
Wilshire 118
Wine Country 263

Y
Yosemite 323
Yosemite Valley 330

Notes

Notes

Notes

NOTES

Notes

QUESTIONNAIRE

In our efforts to keep up with the pace and pulse of California, we kindly ask your cooperation in sharing with us any information which you may have as well as your comments. We would greatly appreciate your completing and returning the following questionnaire. Feel free to add additional pages. A complimentary copy of the next edition will be sent to you should any of your suggestions be included..
Our many thanks!

To: Inbal Travel Information (1983) Ltd.
2 Chen Blvd.
Tel Aviv 64071
Israel

Name: _____

Address: _____

Occupation: _____

Date of visit: _____

Purpose of trip (vacation, business, etc.): _____

Comments / Information: _____

C / 8 / A

INBAL Travel Information Ltd.
P.O.B. 39090 Tel-Aviv
ISRAEL 61390